Fine WoodWorking TECHNIQUES 5

Fine WoodWorking TECHNIQUES 5

Selected by the Editors
of Fine Woodworking magazine

The Taunton Press
Newtown, Connecticut

Typeface: Garamond and Univers
Paper: Mead Offset Enamel, 70 lb., Neutral pH

The Taunton Press, Inc.
52 Church Hill Road
Box 355
Newtown, Connecticut 06470

A FINE WOODWORKING Book

FINE WOODWORKING® is a trademark of The Taunton Press,
Inc., registered in the U.S. Patent and Trademark Office.

International Standard Book Number 0-918804-17-5
Library of Congress Catalog Card Number 78-58221
Printed in the United States of America.

CONTENTS

INTRODUCTION

Welcome to *Fine Woodworking Techniques 5*. This series of reprints brings together the technical information from back issues of *Fine Woodworking* magazine and preserves it in durable, easy-to-use volumes. *Techniques 5*, the latest in the series, is based upon the technical articles from 1981, issues No. 26 through 31. As in past *Techniques* volumes, the main articles are paced by selections from the magazine's reader-written *Methods of Work* department. In addition, in this volume, for the first time, you'll find a number of interesting selections from the magazine's *Questions & Answers* column, as well as pertinent follow-up information taken from Letters-to-the-editor.

Each article, method and question in *Techniques 5* is reprinted in its entirety. Changes have been made only where corrections or cross-references were needed. The articles are arranged according to subject matter for easy reading, and indexed for ready reference.

Whether you work wood as a hobby, a trade or a profession, we hope you will find this book a handy and useful tool.

MACHINES

Mechanical Advantage

About woodworking machines, and a visit to Rockwell and Powermatic

by John Lively

"It's a shame," he said, "that they don't make machinery like they used to." But there wasn't much sorrow in his voice, for Bob Johnson is one of the few men in the country who can claim to be a Victorian millwright. He and his wife, Mary Ellen, make their living selling exotic woods and restoring vintage machinery for such clients as the Smithsonian Institution. For the last 20 years the Johnsons' special passion has been putting together their own collection of classical machines, which are housed in several timber-frame buildings on their wooded farm in Rossville, Ga. To complete the grand scheme, they are building a railroad into the neighboring woods to fetch timber to feed a steam-powered sawmill. "This is our museum," he said as he pulled open the huge door, "but we have to work in here too. Once we've restored one of these old machines, we use it as hard and as often as we would a new one."

As my eyes got used to the dim light, I made out a hulking presence just beyond the doorway, but it took me a moment to recognize the thing—a leviathan jointer. Its beds were 30 in. wide and 8 ft. long, and its cutterhead so massive that three Babbitt bearings held the shaft on its axis. Built by Oliver Machinery Co. in 1905, this monster could joint an entire tabletop or door face in a single pass, or straighten structural timbers of any size. Yet its pinstriped base and thoughtful proportions made it appear lighter and friendlier than you'd expect a ton of cast iron to look.

"Everything's a mess right now," Johnson lamented, pointing to a dismantled steam engine in the next room. "I traded a 180-year-old engine for that one, and until I get it going, I'll have to run my overhead line shafts with this awful electric motor." He threw a wall switch and the whole place came to life. It was like being inside a giant wind-up toy, with big wheels turning little ones and leather drive belts slapping from one end of the shop to the other. "Look at this," he beckoned, while prodding a wide belt from its idler onto the drive pulley of his bandsaw, made in 1886 by Connell & Dengler and standing a full 8 ft. tall. It ran with a ghostly silence, without the slightest whisper of mechanical noise or vibration—just a gentle, low-pitched whoosh as its wheels fanned the air.

Johnson killed the power. All the wheels coasted to a stop, while I continued to stare at this marvelous bandsaw. With its spiral-spoked wheels, its gracefully curved main frame, fluted column and contoured base, it looked more like sculpture than like a machine for cutting wood. There could be no doubt that its makers were as much concerned with the aesthetics of its form as with the smoothness of its operation.

A few steps behind the bandsaw squatted the ugly member of the family, an 1895 American No. 1 variety saw, every bit of it, except for the arbor and worm gears, a thick and formidable piece of cast iron. Its external rack gear and obtrusive adjustment wheels made it gawky, a grim triumph of func-

This bandsaw epitomizes 19th-century woodworking-machine design and manufacture. Made in 1886 by Connell & Dengler, its graceful form and imposing stature combine with rugged mass and close-tolerance millwork to make for smooth and powerful operation.

tion over form. But it had a businesslike quality you had to admire, an unabashed utilitarian aspect.

As I proceeded to poke around, Johnson spoke affectionately about the machines, explaining that 19th-century millwrights designed these tools like works of art, often blending practicality and fair shapes into a harmony that hasn't been equaled since. Their foundrymen, he told me, were generous with cast iron, believing that a heavy machine was a good one. You won't find any fabricated steel bases on this old machinery, or any pot-metal castings or any die-stamped parts. They are all grey iron and alloy steel, with working parts precisely turned or milled and mating surfaces hand-scraped and often honed.

We walked out of the shop into the bright spring sunshine. In the yard, beneath the dogwoods and lying among the weeds, was a myriad of rusting machine parts—cogged wheels, flywheels, bushings, connecting rods and boilers, which when put back together again would become the logging train and the sawmill at the end of the line. Trying to imagine Johnson's finished fantasy, the fully operational mill and shop, the brightly painted steam engine puffing off into the North Georgia hills, pulling its train of log cars behind, I had to wonder how far we've really come from those halcyon days of big and beautiful machines. Has modern metallurgy and industrial technology made them obsolete? Has OSHA banned them from the marketplace? Or have they just become economic impossibilities, impractical in a world of mass production and costly transportation?

The truth is, such machines are obsolete. Bandsaw wheels must be enclosed, so it doesn't matter much how they look. Cast iron is expensive stuff that must be used sparingly now if a profit is to be made; cast parts are heavy, increasing the cost of transportation and handling. So today's manufacturers of trade tools use cast iron only where they must, and fabricate the remaining parts from weldments of sheet steel or die stampings. Ornament has been lost almost altogether, replaced by design notions of clean, functional shapes.

The old mechanical wonders have given way to lighter, sleeker machines, and 19th-century millwrights have been supplanted by industrial engineers and behemoth corporations, whose assembly lines turn out more machinery for more woodworkers than were ever dreamt of in the 19th century. And what every woodworker wants to know is how much quality has been sacrificed along the way. Did the good machines go out with the old ones?

Shop machinery hasn't lost its ability to do hard work. Indeed, without it most contemporary woodshops couldn't exist, and the phrase "amateur woodworker" would be a contradiction in terms. Regardless of the romantic attachment we have for our jack planes, spokeshaves and chisels, despite our skill in using these tools, the heavy gut-work in our shops gets done by the machines. Our table saws, jointers and thickness planers leave us free to hand-cut dovetails, smooth-plane tabletops and experiment with various finishes for our chests and cabinets. When we're rushed to get that job out the door, the machines do everything but prepare the surfaces for finishing, and sometimes they do even that.

Even so, woodworking machinery has frequently been an embarrassment to those who consider themselves true craftsmen. The very nature of machine production has been conceived to be at odds with the spirit of craftwork, and some heavy philosophizing has been aimed at making the crafts-

man rest easy with his machines. Gustav Stickley, whose writings early in this century popularized the Arts and Crafts Movement in America, argued persuasively that every woodworker should make full use of machinery, for it alone could relieve him of mindless toil, giving him the leisure to perfect his designs and to add those finer decorative touches that only the hand can create. Yet, Stickley believed that machine work should be limited to preparing materials for use—for sawing, planing, boring, mortising and sanding. He warned against using machines to achieve ornamental effects, as this made impossible the craftsman's only real means of self-expression, and rendered his works sterile and anonymous. Stickley's injunctions are still valid. The best of contemporary woodworking combines the sensitive and skilled use of hand tools with the intelligent and efficient use of machinery.

Such an ideal situation depends, of course, on machines behaving like good servants, and not like cantankerous flunkies. It's a satisfying experience to operate properly working, well-tuned equipment, while a malfunctioning machine is often worse than no machine at all. The bandsaw that vibrates to excess and takes a ragged cut, the cumbersome table-saw fence that's warped and won't align, the jointer whose tables droop and cut concave edges, and the thickness planer that is forever jamming up and sniping boards are just a few of the problems that bedevil woodworkers every day. Machine down-time is costly in terms of production lost and repair expense, and the frayed nerves of the woodworker are an inevitable part of the bad bargain.

*   *   *

The term "trade-tools" refers to medium-priced woodworking machines that are commonly used by tradesmen—carpenters, cabinetmakers and patternmakers—and in school shops. They are also designed to hold up under production-line operations in furniture factories and millworks, though often you will find heavier, more expensive machines in these situations. In the broad spectrum of machinery on the market, from the hobby-craft tools for the weekend handyman to the extra heavy-duty machine tools designed for industrial applications, trade tools occupy the middle ground in quality, performance and cost. For the average woodworker, whether a professional or a serious amateur, trade tools are the best bet.

Although there are quite a few smaller manufacturers of trade tools—Vega, General, Boice-Crane, Davis & Wells and Poitras—Rockwell and Powermatic are the largest in North America. Because these two companies are the Chevrolet and Ford of the woodworking-machinery industry, we decided to visit them to get some general impressions about their manufacturing processes, and also to ask some specific questions about their machine quality and customer service. The people at Rockwell said they would arrange for me to tour one of their plants and to interview several executives. The people at Powermatic suggested that I spend five days at one of their workshops on machinery maintenance. I accepted both offers, expecting that the experiences would be entirely different. And so they were.

The majority of Rockwell's woodworking tools are made at their factory in Tupelo, Miss. This is where the venerable Unisaw is made, along with their complete line of radial saws, the 14-in. bandsaw, the several models of shapers, the 4-in., 6-in. and 8-in. jointers, the 6-in./12-in. belt/disc sander and the 24-in. scroll saw. All of their other woodworking machines are manufactured at their plant in Bellefontaine, Ohio.

My visit to the Tupelo factory began in Bill Ramsey's office. He's plant manager and is directly responsible to Rockwell Power Tool management. Also there were Lou Brickner, marketing manager for woodworking machines, and Bernie Cox, product manager for Rockwell's Power Tool Division. "How do you know how many machines you need to make in a given month?" I asked. Ramsey explained that this is a complex calculation; output varies and is based on marketing data compiled in the home office, taking into consideration orders from distributors, sales promotions and the availability of certain parts and raw materials. "What about the person who buys one of your Unisaws and finds it's got a bad bearing or warped extension wing?" I asked. "Can he expect to get the faults corrected or the defective parts replaced?" Ramsey replied that all new machines are guaranteed against defects and that Rockwell's service system is advanced and efficient. "All the parts in all the distribution centers throughout the country are carried on a computer file," Ramsey said. "If one distributor doesn't have a particular part, he can call the home office and learn the location of the nearest service center that has it in stock, and can order it for his customer."

I listened to this with keen interest, and then recounted how several years ago I had bought a Rockwell lathe duplicator and had discovered upon opening the box that what should have been an angle-iron tool rest was just an unformed flat bar. I had taken it back to the dealer and asked for a replacement part. The dealer told me to go to an iron yard and buy a length of the stuff because ordering parts from Rockwell was like trying to get sympathy from the IRS. He said it would take months to get the piece, if I got it at all. Ramsey gave me a hard, sober look and there was a moment of quiet. "Well," he said, "That was several years ago, and mistakes do happen, and sometimes communications with distributors are not as good as they should be." He went on to say that the Rockwell people are quite aware of the fact that product quality suffered during the 1970s, but now they've made a renewed commitment to quality control.

I told Ramsey that a number of woodworkers have written to us saying that the old Delta machines were well built and reliable but that since Rockwell has been manufacturing the Delta line, there's been a decline in quality, that some parts have become tinnier and flimsier. "There's some truth to that," he replied, "but we're now reversing that trend." He offered an example. The platen for the Delta belt/disc sander was originally a cast part. Then someone decided to cut costs by making the part from a die-stamped piece of sheet metal. But they then discovered that during prolonged use the sheet-metal platen would deform from the heat of heavy sanding. So now they've gone back to using the cast-iron platen. Lou Brickner cited another example: The Unisaw rip fence, which used to be made from stamped steel, is now a hefty, ribbed-aluminum extrusion, two extrusions actually, one nested inside the other. By loosening a couple of lock screws, the lower half of the fence can be brought into contact with the table surface, a handy feature for ripping veneers and other thin materials.

I had one more question: "Suppose a customer needs a part badly or has just bought a defective machine and wants it corrected. Suppose the distributor he bought it from won't or can't get the part or fix the machine within a reasonable time. What recourse does the customer have? Is dealing with Rock-

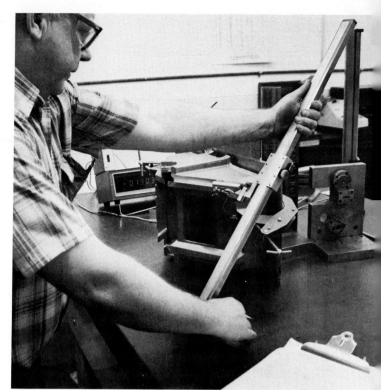

A quality-control engineer uses mechanical and electronic gauges to see whether the milled dovetailed ways in this base for a Rockwell 8-in. jointer fall within the prescribed tolerances. The engineers select bases off the line at random during the day. A test failure stops the run until the error is corrected. Rejected parts are re-machined or scrapped.

well really a bureaucratic hassle?" Ramsey smiled. "Of course not. I've got letters right here in my desk from customers I've dealt with directly. I spent several hours on the phone just the other day trying to run down a part for a fellow, only to find out that he'd been using the wrong part number all along." He said that most customer-service problems are communication problems. In the first place a customer should get good service from his distributor; but if he can't he should write or call the nearest Rockwell service branch. If that fails to produce results, he can call or write the home office (Power Tool Division, Rockwell International, 400 Lexington Ave., Pittsburgh, Pa. 15208) or the plant in Tupelo (PO Box 1508, Tupelo, Miss. 38801). "We're serious about customer service," he said, "and will do whatever we have to, within reason, to see that problems get ironed out. The president of the Power Tool Division sits on our service committee. That's how serious we are about it."

I spent the balance of the day touring the plant, and saw how the most important shop tools are manufactured. The plant doesn't have an in-house foundry, so cast parts are jobbed out and must be inspected on arrival. Some castings, I was told, are annealed—heated to 1400°F for 30 minutes—to relieve stress. This makes the iron easier to mill and to grind, and also makes for more stable, warp-free cast parts.

Such stability is particularly important for jointers. Their tables must be perfectly flat and parallel to one another, or they won't cut a true edge on a board. If built imprecisely, they're useless. For this reason, and because jointers are made almost wholly from grey iron castings, I was especially interested in seeing how Rockwell made theirs. The 8-in. jointer begins as several castings—a trapezoidal base, infeed and outfeed tables, a fence and a number of smaller castings that make up the fence-support assembly. Dovetailed ways are

Above, at the end of a long assembly line, these workers in Rockwell's Tupelo, Miss., plant make the final checks on 14-in. bandsaws. One adjusts the blade-guide system, while the other sets the 45° positive stop on the tilting table. From here the machines go to be packaged and to await shipping.

machined into the sloping sides of the base and into corresponding inclines on the tables. The ways allow both tables to travel up and down (chiefly to adjust the depth of cut) and still remain parallel to one another. Cutting these ways precisely is so important that the operation gets checked several times during the day by a quality-control engineer, who selects a base at random and takes it to his lab. There, he clamps the base to a surface plate, and using a vernier height gauge and other measuring devices, he finds out whether the component falls within the prescribed tolerances. If it doesn't, all the pieces in the run—since the last test—are checked. If the defective components cannot be corrected by re-milling, they're scrapped.

When the base, with the cutterhead installed, and the two tables meet at a sub-assembly station, they are wedded, the gibs installed and the tables aligned and locked into place. Now the entire machine is mounted on a jig and passed several times beneath an overhead grinding wheel, which surfaces both tables at once, ensuring parallel alignment end to end. This is a sensitive operation, and the person doing it must be careful, as excessive head pressure on the grinding wheel can burn and discolor the iron or produce an uneven surface. Such errors can be eliminated by further grinding, but too much of this will yield thin table surfaces, and the jointer beds will end up as expensive pieces of scrap iron.

All the machines I saw being built were fairly old designs, most of them haven't been altered in 30 years. I asked Brickner if Rockwell was planning to bring out new machines to compete with trade tools made by such overseas companies as Makita and Injecta/Inca. He answered yes, that this summer Rockwell plans to introduce a new medium-priced thickness planer which will be made in Brazil and sold under the name Rockwell/Invicta. Then I asked whether Rockwell plans to

bring out anything else in the way of new machinery. His answer was a cagey "yes and no." Yes, they do have several things in the development stage presently; no, they don't intend to redesign any of their basic Delta machines. He said there wasn't any point in tampering with successful products that had been industry standards for so many years.

Before I left, I made a point of asking Brickner what he though about Powermatic machinery. "They make good stuff," he admitted without hesitation. Then he added, "It's good to have good competitors."

*   *   *

Along with 22 others, mostly salesmen who'd been sent to Powermatic's plant in McMinnville, Tenn., by their bosses to learn about operating and maintaining woodworking machinery, I sat in a large classroom sipping coffee and waiting for the instructor to arrive. About 14 times each year, Powermatic holds these five-day workshops. The fall and winter sessions are attended by dealer salesmen and servicemen, while the six summer sessions are conducted for university industrial-arts students and teachers, who usually earn college credit for their participation.

Around 8:30 A.M. Jim Ramsey, Powermatic's product manager (no relation to Rockwell's Ramsey), walked into the room. After giving a brief history of the company, he got to the real reason we were listening. Most service problems, he told us, could be avoided if the machine operator understood his equipment thoroughly, and knew how to adjust it and how to keep it in tune. "I can't be emphatic enough," he said, clutching the podium. "You'd be surprised at how many people start turning knobs and screws without having the slightest idea what they're doing."

Before beginning the lesson on jointers, Ramsey talked at some length about the advantages of having an in-house pattern shop and foundry. Powermatic is licensed, he said, to use the Meehanite process, a patented technology for making a high-grade, close-grained grey iron that is superior for use in machinery castings. The process ensures that the molecular constitution of the cast iron is consistent from day to day and from year to year, a condition that makes milling and grinding more efficient and that contributes to product uniformity. "We can control," Ramsey added, "the aging time for our castings." He explained that the traditional method of letting cast parts sit for months uncovered in the open air is still the best means of relieving internal stresses created by the casting process. Aging gives these stresses time to resolve themselves before the part is milled and ground. "By having our own foundry," he said, "we don't have to machine green castings, and consequently we wind up with fewer warped saw tables and jointer fences."

But regardless of aging and other means of relieving stress, he continued, some castings do warp after they leave the plant. Jointer fences, he said, are the worst offenders. He walked to the rear of the classroom, where all the machines were set up for demonstration, and pointed to the fence on the 6-in. jointer. "Now, no one will want to believe this, and I've had a hard time convincing a lot of smart people, but cast iron *will* bend; you can straighten a warped fence." (See Box, on next page, to learn how.)

Over lunch I got a chance to ask Ramsey about Powermatic's customer service. The upshot of it all was that their machinery should hold up for decades of hard use, given the usual amount of maintenance and care; bearings might need eventual replacement, but the basic cast parts should last indefinitely. They are guaranteed to be free of defects, or they'll be replaced. "We train our distributors to be able to tell whether a machine is really defective or whether it only needs adjustment or re-alignment; these guys will go into someone's shop, inspect the tool and try to fix it there." It's a rare thing, he said, when a machine has to be returned to the factory for repair or regrinding. "Since we've been conducting these workshops," he concluded, "we've minimized customer service problems." However, a customer who can't get satisfaction from his local dealer should write Customer Service, Powermatic Houdaille, McMinnville, Tenn. 37110.

The afternoon session on motors and electrical controls was conducted by Roy Baker. Though his chief function is customer service, he's intimately acquainted with the machines themselves, and serves along with Jim Ramsey as the other instructor in the maintenance workshops. After class he took me on a two-hour tour of the plant. Baker and I walked up and down the labryinthine aisles, and I was a little surprised at how similar the whole operation was to Rockwell's, with the exception that Powermatic doesn't make a line of radial-arm saws, whose manufacture takes up considerable space in Rockwell's Tupelo plant. At one station along the way I reached down into a parts box and picked up a handwheel for a Model 66 table saw. "This is a pretty nice casting," I said, "but why go to all the trouble to cast such a good handwheel and then make the little center locking knob out of a plastic that can crack when the setscrews are tightened?" I once owned a Model 66 table saw and had cracked both its locking knobs while trying to tighten their setscrews. "Geez," Baker answered, "we've got to save money somewhere." (Two months later, I was told in a phone conversation with Jim

On jointer maintenance

"The most common complaint about jointers," says Jim Ramsey, chief instructor at Powermatic's machinery workshops, "is that the tables droop, or that jointed edges aren't true." To correct these problems several checks are required. First see how the operator is jointing his stock. If he concentrates his feed pressure on the infeed table, he'll probably wind up with a concave edge (a spring joint). Proper jointing calls for applying feed pressure over the infeed table only long enough to establish a straight edge about 18 in. long at the front of the board; then the feed pressure should be shifted to the outfeed table and be concentrated over the stock about 6 in. beyond the cutterhead.

Drooping tables can result from insufficient pressure on the gibs, the flat, steel bars that fit in the dovetailed ways between the bearing surfaces of the tables and the base. Their job is to compensate for wear. Ramsey demonstrated by loosening all the gib screws on the in-

feed table of the jointer in the classroom. Then he laid a straightedge across both tables, and as he had predicted, the infeed table was close to $\frac{1}{16}$ in. lower on its outboard end than at the cutterhead. As he tightened the gib screws, the table was gradually raised and finally made uniform contact with the straightedge along its full length. The gib screws must be tight enough to hold the tables parallel, but no tighter.

Another thing to check for is the proper alignment of the countersinks in the gibs with the tapped holes along the ways in the base (see drawing, lower left). The cone-head screws must fit into these countersinks or the beds can't be properly snugged up in their ways and the tables will sag. If a gib has to be re-aligned, loosen all the screws, position the gib (you'll need a flashlight to peer into the hole), and then lock the handle down. Next tighten the gib screws firmly and back off each a quarter turn. Finally tighten the jam nuts. Now the two tables should be perfectly parallel.

Ramsey maintains that the way you change and set the knives is critical to a jointer's performance. Never remove all the knives at once and then re-install them or replace them with a new set. Rather, remove a single knife and then replace it with a fresh one (or with the same one resharpened) and then set it. Taking out the knives all at once and replacing them one at a time can subject the cutterhead to harmful stresses and cause it to distort. If you must replace all the knives at one time, you should gradually torque the chipbreaker bolts down, going from one knife to the next, keeping the pressure equal all around the cutterhead. When tightening chip-

breaker bolts, begin in the middle and work out to the ends. Otherwise the knife can creep up or down as you apply more pressure, and you'll have an awful time trying to keep the knife at its proper height during installation.

If a jointer fence is twisted or warped or not perpendicular to the surface of the tables, your jointed edge will not be a consistent 90° to the face of the board, and you'll find you're gluing up big barrels instead of tabletops. So check the right-angularity of the fence often, and should you discover that the fence is perpendicular to the table at one point and not at another, you probably have a twisted fence. If you hold a straightedge lengthwise along the fence and detect any deviation, your fence is bowed. Ramsey says you can correct both of these problems.

If the fence is bowed, detach it from the fence-support assembly, and set it (crown up) astride two blocks on the floor. Slowly apply weight to it, usually by standing on it in the middle. At a critical point, you will feel the metal give slightly, which signals that it has returned to its original shape. It will not bend beyond this point, but will break if further pressure is applied. And, Ramsey says, it will not warp a second time, as all the wicked stresses have been exorcised by bending it again. If the fence is twisted, clamp one end in a woodworking vise and tighten a pipe clamp or bar clamp on the other end. Using the leverage from the bar, slowly apply gradually increasing pressure in the required direction. When you feel the metal give, stop. Don't try to muscle out the warp with a quick jerk, or you will break the fence.   —J.L.

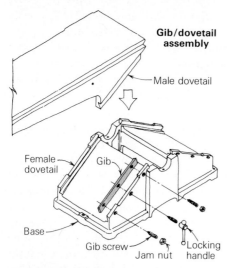

Gib/dovetail assembly

Male dovetail

Female dovetail

Gib

Base

Gib screw

Jam nut

Locking handle

To reduce the chance of warping and to help relieve internal stresses, castings are seasoned. These jointer tables (above) in Powermatic's "boneyard" will lie rusting in the open air from three to six months. At left, Jim Ramsey, Powermatic's product manager and instructor for the company's oft-held maintenance workshops, tells how jointer tables will droop if the gib screws aren't properly snugged up. Loose gib screws, along with gunk and build-up along the ways are, according to Ramsey, the chief causes of sagging jointer tables.

Ramsey that Powermatic's engineers had redesigned this part. The new knobs will be cast from solid, not ribbed, plastic and will have threaded brass inserts to hold the setscrews. He assured me that the prototypes have been tested and that they will not crack.)

Then Baker took me outside for a walk through the "boneyard," the several fenced-in acres of cast-iron parts—everything from planer bases and bandsaw main frames to tablesaw fences and trunnion boxes. All the castings were stacked in neat piles, some small, others mountainous. Some parts were painted green, some yellow, some blue. "Why all the colors?" I asked. He explained that each month of the year was assigned a color, that when castings came from the foundry to age in the boneyard they were painted so that their age would be apparent at a glance. "This keeps us from bringing a casting into the plant and milling it before it's had time to age for at least three months," he said.

I had been promised a tour of the foundry, so late in the afternoon on my last day there, Baker and I drove the short distance to the place. On the way I asked him what he thought about Rockwell machinery. "I used to work for Rockwell," he replied with a little grin, "and I know their line pretty well, and really can't knock it. But I think Powermatic has the best 14-in. bandsaw in the business."

At the foundry, the patternmaker and his apprentices had locked up and gone home for the day, so I didn't get a chance to talk with them or look around the patternshop. But Baker explained that all of Powermatic's machine parts begin as wooden patterns which are sent out to have aluminum working patterns made from them. The original wooden patterns are returned and stay in the patternshop. We walked about, winding past long banks of patterns hanging from the wall, past molding and coring operations, past hot, unflasked molds, with their castings cooling inside. On we went by the quaking conveyor that shakes the sand off cold castings, until at last we arrived at the heart of the place—the twin furnaces. I mounted the steel gangway to the little booth where the operator was getting ready to charge the furnace. He was maneuvering an overhead electromagnet that clutched a load of scrap iron, including some rejected machine parts, and he stopped it just above the far furnace, whose thick, iron lid slid slowly back. Red and white light shot from the opening with palpable force. The operator lowered the magnet into the fiery pot and released its load. There was a burst of light, with sparklers flying high into the air and flames leaping up as though to consume the magnet. This is how all machines die and are born again, in the white-hot soup that turns into cold, grey iron.

*   *   *

Foundry practices have come a long way from the time when Bob Johnson's huge machines were made, when strength depended largely on the sectional thickness of a casting and when getting a good batch of molten iron was literally pot luck. With the introduction of the Meehanite technology in the 1950s (and subsequent, more advanced procedures), the entire casting process, from mixing the sand to pouring the metal, came under scientific control. The improved quality of the cast iron meant that sheer mass was no longer needed to achieve strength, and it also meant that the grain structure of the metal could be manipulated to suit the kind of part being cast. Scientific control has almost eliminated hard spots in cast metal, irregularities that make a casting brittle and that can dull and sometimes break metalworking bits and cutters. So now the machining of cast-iron parts can flow at a production pace and the quality of the finished tools can remain fairly consistent.

Nineteenth-century machines were big because they had to be, and ornament could be incorporated into their structure because sectional thicknesses were so great and weight so negligible a consideration that a given part could take almost any shape the millwright fancied, so long as it did its job. The pretty S-curved spokes of Johnson's giant bandsaw wheels were not engineered for getting maximum strength from minimum metal. Rather, they were designed for appearance and to cope with the problem of shrinkage as the castings cooled. But these days the need for lighter, more portable trade tools, along with high-speed spindle requirements, makes stress engineering preeminent. Thus woodworking machines and their functional parts have to look like what they have to do. So what we have lost in mass and stature, we have gained in better machine performance and improved metal quality. Too bad we can't have both. ☐

On choosing machinery

If someone were to ask me whether I'd buy a Rockwell or Powermatic spindle shaper or whether I'd choose a Powermatic Model 66 10-in. table saw over a Rockwell Unisaw, I couldn't give a simple answer. But here are some general observations. Even though Rockwell jobs-out its castings, they appear a little cleaner and crisper inside and out than Powermatic's castings; on the other hand, Powermatic's castings are a little heavier and thicker in section than Rockwell's; and on the average, a Powermatic machine weighs a little more than the equivalent Rockwell model. The Powermatic 8-in. jointer, for example, is about 50 lb. heavier than the Rockwell 8-in. jointer. As far as I could tell, both manufacturers paid equally close attention to machine-finish tolerances, spindle run-out tolerances and general machine performance. Equally close in every case but one: Rockwell's tolerance for its 8-in. jointer is 0.01 in. end to end; Powermatic's tolerance for its 8-in. jointer is 0.0015 in. end to end—a significant difference. Powermatic's ground table surfaces look a little nicer than Rockwell's, but this has no effect on stock feeding or mechanical performance.

Rudolf Bass Co., in New York, sells more woodworking machines than any other distributor in the country. They handle and service both Powermatic and Rockwell lines. I phoned Richard Bass and asked him which of the two firms made the better machine, and he answered that to choose intelligently one had to check out the machines model for model, compare the features where they are different, and decide on that basis. And, he said, there's a good deal of personal preference involved. For some applications a Powermatic machine would be the right choice, for others a Rockwell model would get the job done better. "It's just not something you can generalize about," Bass said. He then added that to make a good choice one should also take into account the kind of service the dealer can provide for each. "But when you get right down to it," Bass quipped, "Powermatic's machines are green, Rockwell's are grey."

Most distributors I spoke with agree that woodworkers would have less trouble with their machines if they would read their owner's manuals, set the machines up properly and adjust them correctly to begin with. Another mistake a lot of woodworkers make is trying to save a few bucks by skimping on the motor and electrical controls. Too often a person will spend $1,400 on a good table saw and then get the cheapest motor he can and a simple manual switch with no overload protection. A 10-in. table saw should have at least a 3-HP motor; a 5-HP one would be even better. Motors that are underpowered for the work they do can overheat, and they consume more current as well. Having more HP than you need is best, because power consumption is reduced, along with the danger of burning out the motor or causing an electrical fire.

Several years back, when copper got scarce because of political goings-on in Chile and other places, electric-motor manufacturers introduced the T-frame motor, which is now generally sold in place of the old U-frame motors. T-frame motors have formed-steel bodies and steel end bells, whereas the U-frame motors have cast-iron bodies and bells. T-frame motors are smaller and have fewer field windings, and use 30% to 50% less copper than U-frame motors rated at the same HP. This means that T-frame motors can burn out faster and will produce less starting torque than the equivalent U-frame motors. You can still buy U-frame motors, but they're very expensive. This is another good reason for getting a motor whose HP rating is as close as you can possibly afford to the highest rated for the particular machine.

Having said all this about buying new equipment, I'd prefer to own old machines, and if I were getting ready to outfit another shop, I'd beat the bushes to see what bargains I could scare up. Some woodworkers I know seem favored by good fortune, as they always manage to stumble on good pieces of used machinery without really looking for them. The rest of us have to haunt the auctions and pester the used-machinery dealers until at last we find what we're looking for in some dark corner of a warehouse or barn. Though the demand for used equipment is increasing as more woodworkers discover its worth, there are still plenty of old machines sitting around gathering dust all over the country. The trick is to find them, and to be able to tell how much work is needed to restore them to operating condition, something we'll be writing about in future issues.

The best table saw I ever owned was a 20-year-old Davis & Wells. Its arbor-raising mechanism was a rack-and-scroll gear, and the arbor assembly rode in gibbed dovetailed ways. When I gave the dealer my $450, the inside of the saw was filled with gobs of pine rosin and several thick layers of compacted sawdust. He told me it had been worked hard for years in a factory that made prefabricated buildings and that for the price he couldn't guarantee anything. I loaded the monster in my pickup, took it home and then took it completely apart, cleaned off all the hardened gook, honed and polished the ways and put it back together again. I was surprised at how smoothly the arbor tilted, how easily I could crank it up and down, how accurately it did its work. Davis & Wells (now owned by Rankin Industries, 11090 S. Alameda St., Los Angeles, Calif. 90262) still makes this saw, but a new one costs $2,250, without the motor and electrical controls. —*J.L.*

Fixing the Shopsmith's wobbly spindle

Here is a tip Shopsmith Mark V owners will find helpful. I purchased a new Mark V about a year ago, and was pleased to find it a highly versatile and a generally well-built machine. However, the amount of side-to-side play in the spindle was, in my opinion, somewhat excessive. This play was particularly noticeable when drilling and turning. It appeared to be due to the fact that the spindle is supported by a single ball bearing at the front of the quill. Replacement of this bearing yielded no noticeable improvement. I took the quill and spindle to a local machine shop run by an experienced tool-and-die maker. He examined the parts and confirmed the feasibility of adding a bearing to the rear of the quill. The modification is shown in the sketch.

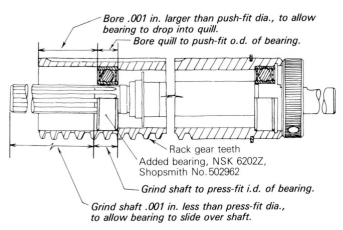

Bore .001 in. larger than push-fit dia., to allow bearing to drop into quill.

Bore quill to push-fit o.d. of bearing.

Rack gear teeth

Added bearing, NSK 6202Z, Shopsmith No. 502962

Grind shaft to press-fit i.d. of bearing.

Grind shaft .001 in. less than press-fit dia., to allow bearing to slide over shaft.

The splined outside diameter of the shaft was ground to permit press-fitting the new bearing onto the shaft (the amount of grinding required is minimal; thus the depth of the spline teeth is not significantly altered). The quill was then chucked in the lathe and bored to accept the outside diameter of the bearing as a push-fit. Note that this bore must be deep enough to permit full retraction of the quill into the machine without interference between the bearing and the face of the splined drive inside the machine. The bore and the outside diameter of the shaft were then slightly relieved to facilitate assembly of the components. This modification has eliminated the spindle's side-to-side play, resulting in increased accuracy in both the drill press and horizontal boring modes of operation. It has also greatly reduced the amount of chatter encountered in faceplate lathe work. Total cost of this modification was less than $20, including the machining and the purchase of a new bearing.

—*James E. Harriss, Dubuque, Iowa*

My six-year-old Shopsmith Mark V has experienced the same side-to-side play in the quill since I purchased it. I did the same basic bearing addition, although instead of using an

Shopsmith quill modification

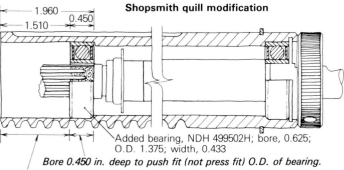

1.960

1.510   0.450

Added bearing, NDH 499502H; bore, 0.625; O.D. 1.375; width, 0.433

Bore 0.450 in. deep to push fit (not press fit) O.D. of bearing.

Bore 1.510 in. deep to 0.001 in. larger than push fit, so bearing will drop into quill.

NSK 6202Z bearing (0.5906-in. bore), I used an NDH 499502H (0.6250-in. bore). The drawing shows the specs. Using the NDH bearing there is no need to do any grinding of the splines. But to get a press fit of the bearing, the shaft must be either lightly and evenly dimpled or else knurled-and-turned to press-fit diameter between the end of the splines and the shoulder. The stock bearing used in front of the quill (SKF 466041) will also work but it is 0.003 in. larger in the outside diameter than the NDH bearing. I was extremely impressed with the results of the modification.

I was misled, though, by the estimate of less than $20 for the modification. I had to try a few shops before I found a machinist willing to do the work, and I neglected to get an estimate. I believe I was in a state of shock when the bill was handed to me. Anyone who is considering the quill modification should check around and above all get an estimate because prices will vary extremely. My after-the-fact investigations provided estimates from reasonable to astronomical...

—*Steve Aga, Glendale, Ariz.*

Safe jointer hold-down

A few years ago, after nipping a finger in a jointer, I became preoccupied with the safe operation of this machine. I pored through textbooks and catalogs searching for a hold-down/guard device that would be safe, easy to construct and inex-

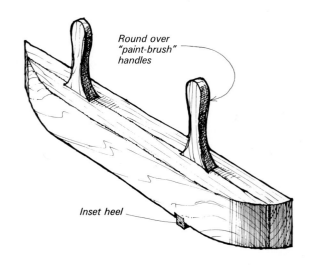

Round over "paint-brush" handles

Inset heel

pensive. I looked for a design that would protect both hands, be rigid, provide firm, steady pressure and allow good control of the workpiece. Finding nothing meeting my requirements, I eventually came up with the design shown above.

I keep three different lengths of hold-downs (24-in., 48-in., and 78-in.) to accommodate various lengths of lumber. Dimensions, however, are not critical and you should adapt them to your needs. Start with two lengths of 2x4. Dress the inner faces and cut dadoes into them to accept the "paint-brush" handles. Mate the dadoes and glue up. After the glue has set, square up the piece and cut the dado into the base to accept the ¾-in. heel so it protrudes about ½ in. Now bandsaw the curves in the leading and trailing ends of the unit and sand smooth. These curves allow the jointer's blade guard to open and close with a minimum of blade exposure.

Next set the heel and the handles. If possible wedge the ¾-in. square heel in place rather than gluing it. It may have to be replaced from time to time. Cut the heel and the handle bases a trifle short so they won't protrude and snag on the jointer fence or the workpiece. The hold-down is now ready for very safe surfacing work.

—*Bernard Maas, Cambridge Springs, Pa.*

The Basics of the Bandsaw
Setting up and using this versatile machine

by Tage Frid

The bandsaw is one of the most versatile machines in the shop. It can cut curves, it can rip, crosscut, resaw, and it can cut joints. It can also cut sides of beef with ease, so if you see bits of meat clinging to the wheels in these photographs, it's because that's what I've been doing lately. However, the bandsaw cannot make as smooth a cut as a table saw, because a table saw has a stiffer, thicker blade that stays straighter in the cut. A bandsaw blade must bend around its wheels, so it can also bend in the cut. It is a welded ribbon of steel. Because the two ends are difficult to weld exactly in line and the weld itself produces a raised surface on the blade, the blade pulses, both forward and back and sideways, when moving at high speed. This pulsing makes the cut uneven. Still, because the depth of cut is greater and the blade is narrower, a bandsaw can do things a table saw can't. It's best for cutting curves and for resawing wide stock with minimal waste.

To get the best possible cut on your bandsaw, you first have to choose the right blade and then install it properly. I had a 14-in. bandsaw for many years before getting the 20-in. saw (with a 2-HP motor) I have now. Besides its larger blade-to-column distance (throat) and its greater depth of cut, this larger saw can use a wider blade and run it under greater tension, two important factors in determining how smooth and straight the cut will be. You should always use the widest blade possible for the job. For straight cuts, as in resawing, I use a 1-in. wide blade. For most curve cutting, I use a ⅜-in. wide blade, which will cut to a radius of 1⁷⁄₁₆ in. For tighter curves a narrower blade is necessary; probably three blades (1-in., ⅜-in. and ⅛-in.) will cover most uses.

Another important factor in blade choice is the number and kind of teeth. Bandsaw-blade technology is most developed for metal cutting. There are all sorts of tooth styles and arrangements of tooth set, each one best suited for cutting a particular kind of metal, of a particular thickness, at a particular speed. The choices for wood cutting are not so numerous. For one thing, all wood-cutting bandsaw blades have every tooth set alternately; raker (or unset) teeth do not have an advantage in wood cutting. For a long time wood-cutting bandsaw blades had regular teeth, that is, like a handsaw, they had 0° rake and they were the same size as the gullets between them. This kind of tooth style is fine for cutting in thin stock, but by eliminating every other tooth and increasing the gullet size, chips clear better and the cutting is faster. This is called a skip-tooth blade. With the increased chip clearance, it's possible to put a rake on the teeth, usually 10°, which makes feeding easier, sawing faster. Depending on the

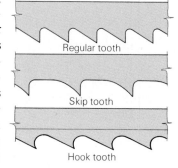

Regular tooth

Skip tooth

Hook tooth

manufacturer, this is called a hook-tooth, claw-tooth, saber-tooth or gore-tooth blade, and it's what most people use now.

The number of teeth per inch is also important for getting the best cut. The thicker the stock, the fewer teeth per inch you should use. Two or three teeth per inch is considered a coarse blade and is best for resawing. Ten or more teeth per inch will cut the best in thin stock. Most of my blades have around five teeth per inch, good for general work; all are high-carbon steel with hardened teeth and flexible backs.

Installing the blade—Some people spend a lot of time installing a blade, going back and forth over the adjustments, really making it more trouble than it has to be. The trick is in doing things in the right order. First unplug the saw, loosen the tension on the upper wheel and back off all the blade guides; this way you can slip the blade easily around the wheels (make sure the teeth are going in the right direction) and concentrate on tensioning and tracking without the guides getting in the way. Tension the blade by turning the tensioning knob that spreads the two bandsaw wheels apart. Most bandsaws have a tensioning gauge that shows the proper tension for each blade width (the wider the blade, the greater the tension). If your saw doesn't have a tensioning gauge, you'll have to develop a feel; some people pluck the blade like a guitar string and seem to know by the sound when the tension is right. Too much tension and the blade can break, too little and it will wander in the cut. When you've tensioned the blade enough to keep it on the wheels, track it. Tracking is done by turning a knob that tilts the axis of the upper wheel, which makes the blade move back and forth on the rubber rim. Rotate the upper wheel with one hand and as the blade coasts, adjust the tracking knob with the other hand until the blade rides in the middle of the rim. Finish tensioning the blade and test-track it again by hand. Now close the doors, plug in the saw, and test at higher speeds by bumping the motor on and off before letting it run continuously. If the blade runs true, you can proceed; if not you have to stop the blade (here's where a foot brake is a time-saver) or let the blade coast to a stop before opening the doors and retracking by hand. Never track the blade or open the door with the blade running at high speed. If the blade slips off or breaks, you want those doors between you and it.

With the blade tensioned and tracked, square the table to the blade; then you can adjust the blade guides. Bandsaws have two sets of blade guides, one below the table and one above. The top set adjusts up and down for different depths of cut. Each set of blade guides consists of a rear thrust bearing and two side supports, which may be ball bearings, hardened-steel blocks or pivoting plates. Ball bearings are best because then can be brought right up in touch with the blade, but they are expensive and clog easily with sawdust. Blocks and plates have to have some clearance, and blocks

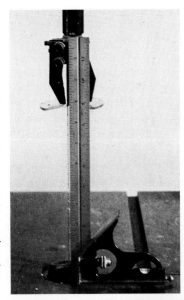

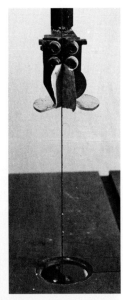

Installing a new blade on the bandsaw is easier if you do things in the right order. With all the blade guides backed off, the blade is slipped around the wheels and tensioned. Next the blade is tracked, left, by turning the upper wheel of the bandsaw with one hand while adjusting the tilt of the wheel's axis with the other. Never track the blade with the motor running and the door open. Next adjust the blade guides, first the thrust bearings, upper and lower, then the left-hand side guides. Use a square, right, to make sure you're not pushing the blade out of line, and a piece of paper between the blade guide and the blade for clearance. Then use the same piece of paper, far right, to set the right-hand side guide with the proper clearance.

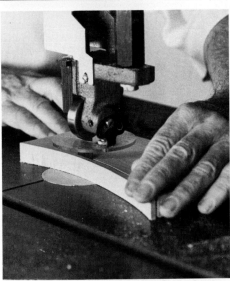

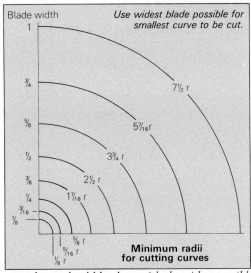

Blade width

Use widest blade possible for smallest curve to be cut.

Minimum radii for cutting curves

Two basic operations on the bandsaw: Cutting curves, above, should be done with the widest possible blade for the curve; the chart gives the limits of various blade widths. Using too wide a blade will result in heat and stress on the blade as its back rubs in the kerf; this can break or damage the blade. When sawing curves, be sure to keep your hands behind or to the sides of the blade. Resawing, right, is done with the widest blade the saw will handle and an L-shaped fence at the blade. The fence is rounded over where it rides against the planed surface of the board. This way the board can be fed on an angle to compensate for the tendency of most bandsaw blades to lead to one side or the other.

tend to wear at the front and to lose their setting from vibration. I'm happy with the plate side guides that came with my saw because once the plates are mounted, the support from the teeth to the back of the blade is fixed and their sideways position locks down good and tight.

The thrust bearings should be adjusted first. It doesn't matter if you do the upper or lower one first, but both should be set before adjusting any of the side guides. Bring the bearing up so it just touches the back of the blade. As mentioned earlier, a running bandsaw blade tends to pulse, so you'll have to check the adjustment as you turn the wheel by hand. As it runs, the back of the blade should just kiss the thrust bearing. Too close and it can wear the surface of the bearing; too far away and the blade will wander in the cut.

Set the upper and lower left-hand guides next, rather than both upper or both lower. I use a piece of paper (the thickness of a brown grocery bag) between the guide and the blade to gauge the clearance; with ball-bearing guides clearance is not necessary. It's important here that you use a square on the table to make sure you're not bending the blade to the right

with too much pressure from the guides. Besides proper sideways adjustment, you also have to set the guide properly in relation to the front of the blade. It should be just flush with the back of the gullets—too far forward and teeth will wear the guide; too far back and the guide won't provide adequate support. With both left-hand guides set, adjust the two right-hand guides, again using the piece of paper for clearance. Test the way the blade moves through the guides, turning by hand before switching on the machine. Be sure that the weld moves freely through the groove.

Basic bandsaw technique—Probably what you'll be doing most on the bandsaw is cutting curves. The important thing here is to keep your fingers to the side of the blade or behind it—never in front. And, of course, as with all bandsaw cuts, be sure to lower the blade guard to within ½ in. of the top of the stock you're cutting. This guides the blade better and lessens the risk of injury. The most common mistake most people make on the bandsaw is to cut a thick piece and then cut a thinner one without sliding down the guard. While leaning over, concentrating on the line you're cutting, not only are you liable to stick your head into the moving blade, but if the blade breaks, pieces can fly all over like shrapnel. Never use a blade too wide for the radius you are cutting. The stress of the back edge rubbing in the kerf can break the blade. Getting a smooth cut is a matter of evenly feeding and turning the work. Stopping in the middle of a cut can produce an uneven surface, as the blade's vibration widens the kerf. Plan your moves. If a shape will require tight curves or cutting in and backing out the blade, make relatively straight cuts in the waste to remove most of it; then you can concentrate on the contour line without the blade binding. Never force the work into the blade. If the blade doesn't want to follow the line you're cutting, head for the waste side and come back for a closer second cut.

The bandsaw is excellent for cutting circles. A jig similar to the one I use appears in the Methods column, *FWW #6*, Spring '77. This jig can also cut arcs of a circle, particularly useful when making forms for curved laminations (photos, facing page, top). The curved ribs of these forms must be identical; because of the bandsaw's depth of cut, you can stack and cut them all at once, thus ensuring uniformity.

The bandsaw is also most useful for resawing wide boards. Sometimes I will take a wide board and kerf it along either edge on the table saw, raising the blade between passes, before bringing it over to the bandsaw to complete the cut. Bandsawing thus goes faster and it's easy to keep the thin bandsaw blade in the wider table-saw kerf. But when I have a minimum of material to waste, as is often the case with figured wood I am bookmatching, I will resaw it on the bandsaw alone (last photo, previous page). I use a plywood L-shaped guide at the teeth of the blade, its vertical edge

---

Straight-line cutting and the bandsaw touch

by Arthur Reed

Although most shops reserve the bandsaw for curves, it's unequalled for cutting straight lines. We have two bandsaws in our shop, a 10¼-in. Inca and a 36-in. American, and together they do most of our sawing. We rip rough stock in thicknesses up to the blade-guide capacity, we resaw for veneer and for matched panels, and we size stock for furniture and cabinets. We even rely on the bandsaw for joinery.

Many woodworkers harbor prejudice against the bandsaw, probably from the frustration of having tried to saw a straight line without being familiar with the balance of forces that allows the machine to work. Perhaps more than any other machine, the bandsaw requires a delicate, learned touch.

One key to success is accurate and careful setting of the guides, so the blade can travel freely through the stock and yet be supported in its travel. Similar coordination is required between blade and rip fence. Bandsaw teeth form a narrow corridor in the stock, a corridor that must pass around the body of the blade without contacting it. Otherwise, the side pressure will twist the blade and make it cut unevenly. Thus the characteristic cutting path of the blade must be determined, and the rip fence must be aligned with it. Since this path is rarely parallel to the sides of the table, we assess the drift of our blades regularly.

True up one face and edge of a piece of 2x4 stock about a foot long. Mark a

pencil line on the face opposite the trued face, parallel to and about 2 in. from the trued edge. Slowly feed the stock, trued face down, into the blade with moderate force and feel for the drift by moving the cut away from and back onto the line. After about 8 in. of feed, you'll find the angle that keeps the saw cutting easily along the line. Turn off the saw, bring up the rip fence and adjust it to hold that angle. The Inca fence allows this adjustment; if yours doesn't, either mark the line on the table and clamp a board fence parallel to it, or make yourself an adjustable fence as shown in the drawing. Finally, take another piece of scrap and rip it along the fence. If the scrap seems either to pull away from the fence or to bind the blade, re-adjust. Otherwise, once set, the drift angle should be constant for the life of the blade, regardless of grain structure, hardness, softness or thickness of the stock cut.

It's also important to develop a technique for feeding the stock into the bandsaw. This determines to a great extent the quality of the cut. Feed should be constant and smooth, though the amount of pressure and sometimes its direction vary; they constitute the "touch," the operator's sense of how the cutting is going. On thicker, harder stock, be aware of the greater work the bandsaw teeth have to do, and feed at a rate the blade can handle. It takes time to develop the correct touch, to learn to back off when certain sounds are heard or when a familiar feeling is replaced by something not quite right. Developing touch is a matter of making mistakes and learning from them. □

Arthur Reed operates a custom woodworking shop in Elmira, N.Y.

Adjustable wooden bandsaw fence

Saw table, 24 x 24

To adjust fence for lead, loosen bolts, angle fence appropriately, then tighten bolts. Using ⁵⁄₁₆-in. bolts, the ³⁄₈-in. bores in fence will permit about 10° of play.

Side elevation

Clamping ear
T-square head
Fence, 1½ x 1½ x 18
⁵⁄₁₆ x 1½ bolt in ³⁄₈-in. hole, counterbored to ¾ in.
Hardwood guide bar, ¾ x 2 x 26
⁵⁄₁₆ x 2½ hex bolt and washer

3
Fence
Table
T-square head
⁵⁄₁₆-in. T-nuts in counterbores

rounded over, and follow by eye a scribed line. Because of variations in set or sharpness, sometimes through wear, sometimes on new blades, most bandsaw blades will lead to one side or the other. With this L-shaped guide you can shift the angle of feed to follow the lead of the blade. (One of my former students claims proficiency in using no guide at all; he prefers to resaw freehand and thus eliminates the possibility that blade-lead will bind the stock against the fence.)

To resaw with the L-shaped guide, first plane one face and joint one edge of the board. Draw a line on the unjointed edge, parallel to the planed face, and saw with the planed face against the guide and the jointed edge on the table. Push evenly and slowly; don't crowd the blade; let it cut. Keep the feed constant, and keep your hands away from the blade, especially toward the end of the cut; use a push-stick or reach around the blade and pull the board through. Whatever you do, don't push those last couple of inches through with your thumb on the end of the board.

Resawing satisfactorily requires using as wide a blade as possible with two or three teeth per inch for adequate chip clearance. A 1-HP motor is the minimum; 2-HP to 3-HP is best for green wood. Make sure your blade is sharp and properly tensioned, and that the blade guides are adjusted and close to the work. If the cut bellies, it's probably because of inadequate chip clearance. Slow down your feed and/or use a blade with fewer teeth per inch. If you are getting deep striations on the sawn surface, it means one or more of the teeth on that side of the blade are damaged or set wrong. Try holding a carborundum stone flat against that side of the blade while it's running. Keep in mind that even when you get a smooth, flat surface from the saw, there is a good chance the board will cup because moisture content is rarely consistent throughout a board, and resawing exposes new surfaces to the air. You must allow for this and saw your stock thicker than you need. It is also a good idea to put resawn boards aside for a few days before finish-planing and jointing, so they will reach equilibrium with the shop atmosphere. How much stock can you expect to lose in resawing? There's the waste to the kerf, the waste to the jointer (when resawing a number of thin boards from one thick one, it's best to joint the sawn surface of the thick stock after each sawing) and the waste to cupping—figure on losing at least ¼ in. for each sawing.

Bandsaw joinery—There are several joints it makes sense to cut on the bandsaw, especially if there are a large number of them to do. Through dovetails can be cut almost completely on the bandsaw, tilting the table to saw the pins and freehanding the tails after marking them from the pins. Some joints can be done on the bandsaw in conjunction with the table saw. In cutting tenons or lap joints, for instance, the bandsaw can waste the cheeks after the table saw has cut good, clean shoulders. I prefer to make the two cuts on the table saw, but if you don't have a table saw, both shoulders and cheeks can be cut on the bandsaw, as shown in the photos at right.

To saw cheeks on the bandsaw, first mark on the stock the lines for both cheeks and shoulders. Install the widest blade possible and set up a rip fence a distance from the blade equal to the thickness of the cheek waste. Because this is a relatively short cut, it usually isn't necessary to angle the fence to compensate for blade drift (lead). You can set up the fence parallel to the table edge. Next clamp a stop to the fence that will keep the stock from traveling farther into the blade than to

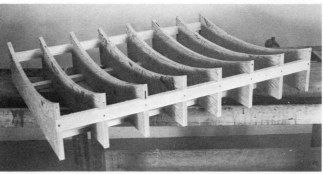

The bandsaw is ideal for cutting circles or arcs of circles when it's equipped with a plywood plate and pivoting trammel to which the stock is pinned. Top, plywood ribs are being cut to identical arcs for use in a bent-lamination form, above.

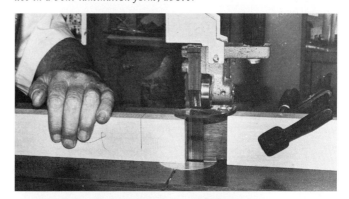

To saw tenon or half-lap cheeks, top, use a wide blade, a fence set to the thickness of the cheek waste and a block behind the blade to stop travel at the shoulder line. To saw the shoulder, above, use the miter gauge; clamp a block to the table for quick and accurate positioning of repetitive cuts.

the line of the shoulder. Hold the stock firmly against the fence and feed it into the blade up to the stop. Saw the cheeks for one side of all the stock you are joining. Don't flip the stock; reset the blade-to-fence distance before cutting the other cheeks to make sure variations in stock thickness do not produce variations in tenon thickness.

If you are also sawing the shoulders on the bandsaw, remove the fence and use the miter gauge. Place one of the pieces of stock against the miter gauge, positioning it so that the blade is in line with the shoulder to be cut. Without moving the stock on the miter-gauge fence, pull the stock and miter gauge back to the front of the table and mark the table where the stock ends. Clamp a stop block to the table at this mark, and you can use it for quick and accurate positioning of each piece to be cut. I don't find it necessary to put a stop block behind the blade to control the depth of the shoulder cut; with the cheeks already sawn it's a simple matter to stop feeding when the waste falls off. □

A bandsaw sawmill

by Lawrence Westlund

I have a 12-in Sears bandsaw and lots of large branches and small tree butts wanting to be sawn into small boards for boxes and the like. I built a free-standing table with a cutout into which my bandsaw table can be positioned and on which slides a carriage, complete with knees and dogs for holding round wood while the carriage is cranked past the blade. The mill for my saw, shown in the photo and drawing, can handle 7-in. diameter logs; dimensions, of course, can be varied for other saws. Most of the work is bolting the stock together to form the table. I did weld the iron for the knees and dogs, though these could be bolted as well. □

Lawrence Westlund is an amateur woodworker in Klamath Falls, Ore.

Bandsaw mill

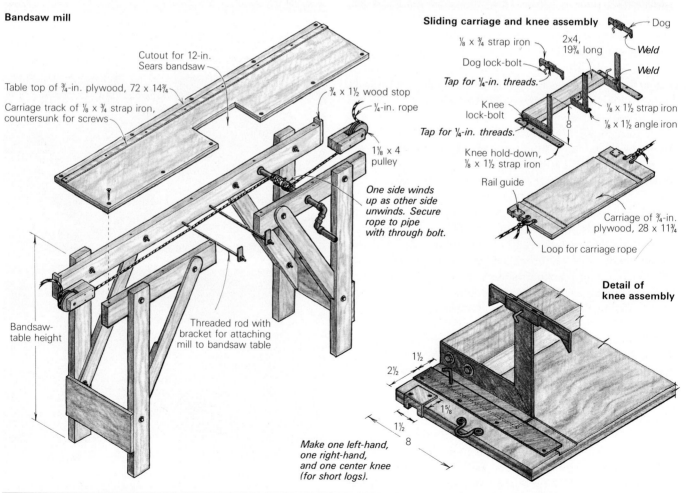

Cutout for 12-in. Sears bandsaw

Table top of ¾-in. plywood, 72 x 14¾

Carriage track of ⅛ x ¾ strap iron, countersunk for screws

¾ x 1½ wood stop

¼-in. rope

1⅛ x 4 pulley

One side winds up as other side unwinds. Secure rope to pipe with through bolt.

Bandsaw-table height

Threaded rod with bracket for attaching mill to bandsaw table

Sliding carriage and knee assembly

Dog

⅛ x ¾ strap iron

2x4, 19¾ long

Weld

Dog lock-bolt

Weld

Tap for ¼-in. threads.

Knee lock-bolt

⅛ x 1½ strap iron

⅛ x 1½ angle iron

Tap for ¼-in. threads.

Knee hold-down, ⅛ x 1½ strap iron

8

Rail guide

Carriage of ¾-in. plywood, 28 x 11¾

Loop for carriage rope

Detail of knee assembly

1½

2½

1⅝

1½

8

Make one left-hand, one right-hand, and one center knee (for short logs).

A Jigsaw for Cutting Delicate Stock

Treadle power and spring return are ideal for pearl inlay

by Ken Parker

Cutting mother-of-pearl and abalone is difficult at best. The material is abrasive, very hard, brittle and rife with natural faults. As I stubbornly tried to saw out my signature, it became apparent that I didn't have the right tool.

Usually, pearl is sawn by hand with a jeweler's saw, against a bird's mouth (see p. 184). Any skewing of the fragile blade may snap the pearl. Furthermore, a small piece is hard to hold flat with one hand against the lifting force of the return stroke. As you struggle to control the cut, hold the work and keep the stroke perpendicular, tension builds quickly and it's easy to apply forces that exceed the material's strength.

Sawing pearl in a power jigsaw presents different problems. Typically the slowest speed is much too fast and the stroke too short; instead of cutting efficiently, the sawteeth slide against the pearl, overheating and dulling quickly. Lubricating with light oils or beeswax to keep cutting temperatures lower and to ease the work obscures the cut with pearl-dust sludge and loosens the glue holding the paper pattern.

Industry uses small, template-controlled overhead pin routers to produce elaborate inlays in guitars, banjos and other stringed instruments. The single-flute, solid-carbide cutters are air/mist cooled and spin as fast as 100,000 RPM. But besides the prohibitive cost of such machines for the individual craftsman, these routers are still unable to make the finest cuts. A 4/0 jeweler's saw, for example, takes a 0.008-in. kerf, while router bits are usually 0.022 in. in diameter. Thus hand-cut pearl can have sharp inside corners that machine-cut pearl can't.

My solution is the foot-operated saw shown here. It is simple to build and has some important advantages for cutting pearl. It can be used as well for cutting veneer, especially for marquetry, though you would probably want to add a flywheel and rocker treadle for momentum. (An old Singer sewing machine has a design worth adapting, or see *FWW* #15, March '79, pp. 60-64). Foot power in my pearl-cutting saw is direct, and the return stroke is by way of a spring. The blade can thus be stopped instantly to prevent a strained piece from breaking. I clamp the upper part of the saw in my bench vise with the table at chin height. This provides good visibility and a relaxed posture; note that the teeth face the operator and the saw frame is behind the work. I rest my elbows on the bench and my chin on the table, blowing dust away with every stroke. There are two hands free to hold and maneuver the work, and the small table allows me to grip tightly, fingers on top and thumbs underneath.

Before describing the construction of the saw, some general remarks on cutting pearl: Use the largest blade possible for the contour you have to cut, and replace the blade before it gets dull, saving it for less critical work. As with all saw or file cuts in hard or tenacious material, the tool must move slowly enough to take a maximum cut per tooth. Excessive speed produces friction and dulls the saw while cutting very little, as

the teeth do not fully engage the work. Feel each tooth dig in and cut and the job will go surprisingly quickly.

It's best after pasting your paper pattern on the pearl (I use mucilage) to drill a hole at one end of the design and work from there instead of sawing in from the edge of the pearl. This provides support around the design. Try to cut exactly outside the pattern line. The only filing necessary should be on inside corners and at the ends of cuts. Jeweler's sawblades begin and end with graduated teeth. By using the top ¼-in. of the blade when turning tight corners, the "broaching" action aggressively chops out the waste and gives the blade room to turn. Furthermore, the extra rigidity at the blade end aids in accurate turning.

Construction—Begin with a rigid saw-frame. It is essential that there be no side play because racking strain can shatter

Foot-powered jigsaw designed especially for cutting delicate mother-of-pearl and abalone is mounted in the bench vise. A drawing of Parker's jigsaw appears on the following page.

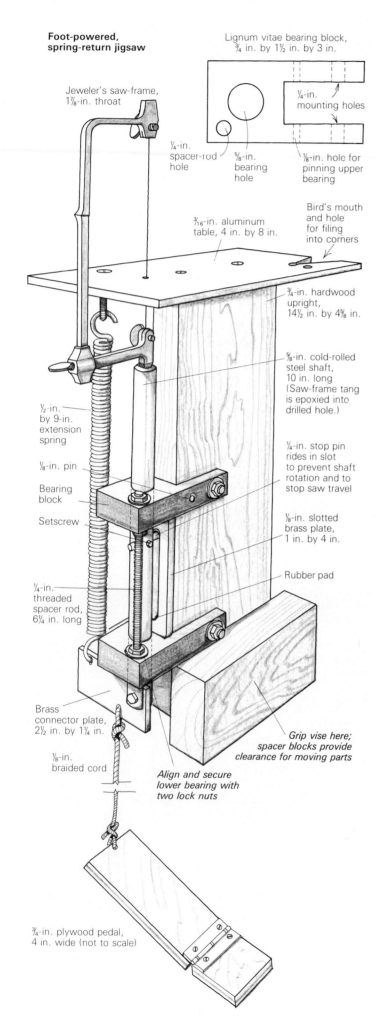

**Foot-powered,
spring-return jigsaw**

Jeweler's saw-frame,
1⅞-in. throat

Lignum vitae bearing block,
¾ in. by 1½ in. by 3 in.

¼-in.
mounting holes

¼-in.
spacer-rod
hole

⅝-in.
bearing
hole

⅛-in. hole for
pinning upper
bearing

³⁄₁₆-in. aluminum
table, 4 in. by 8 in.

Bird's mouth
and hole
for filing
into corners

¾-in. hardwood
upright,
14½ in. by 4⅝ in.

⅝-in. cold-rolled
steel shaft,
10 in. long
(Saw-frame tang
is epoxied into
drilled hole.)

½-in.
by 9-in.
extension
spring

¼-in. stop pin
rides in slot
to prevent shaft
rotation and to
stop saw travel

⅛-in. pin

Bearing
block

⅛-in. slotted
brass plate,
1 in. by 4 in.

Setscrew

¼-in.
threaded
spacer rod,
6¼ in. long

Rubber pad

Brass
connector plate,
2½ in. by 1¼ in.

⅛-in.
braided cord

Grip vise here;
spacer blocks provide
clearance for moving parts

Align and secure
lower bearing with
two lock nuts

¾-in. plywood pedal,
4 in. wide (not to scale)

the fragile pearl. The best style of saw-frame has a square shaft for a back member; its blade is tensioned by a thumb-screw. I used a jeweler's saw-frame with a 1⅞-in. throat, which can be had from a jeweler's supply house, as can an assortment of blades.

The tang of the saw-frame is mounted in a ⅝-in. cold-rolled steel shaft (more on that later) and the shaft slides up and down in a pair of bearings attached to a hardwood up-right. Lignum vitae works beautifully for these low-speed bearings. It is easily sawn and drilled, it is hard and resistant to abrasion, and it is naturally oily, though I keep the bear-ings moist with mineral oil when the saw is in use. Saw the outside dimensions carefully to minimize the need to true up the lignum by hand; it will dull all but the toughest edge tools. Seal freshly cut surfaces immediately with tung oil or wax to prevent checking that will ruin the part.

Spade bits are convenient for drilling the ⅝-in. bearing hole because they can be filed to size. Test-drill in a scrap of lignum, coat the inside of the hole with mineral oil and see if you still have enough clearance. The oil will cause the wood to swell and make the hole minutely smaller. To get a clean cut, clamp the work and use high speed and slow feed. Once you have a good fit in a test block, prepare the two bearing blocks for drilling by stacking and gluing them together with a dab of 5-minute (weak) epoxy or paper and white glue be-tween; assembly and alignment will go smoothly if the blocks have been squared, drilled and slotted precisely. Drill the ⅝-in. and ¼-in. vertical holes and saw the slots. Cross-holes for the mounting bolts may also be conveniently drilled before the blocks are split apart. Do not drill the ⅛-in. hole in the upper block at this time; it's more precise to drill and pin the block after it's mounted on the upright. Be sure to witness-mark the blocks to preserve alignment.

For the upright, use a piece of stable, straight-grained hardwood. Warping here can impede the saw's action. Thick-ness the stock, and square the edges and ends accurately. Spacer blocks are added later, as shown in the drawing, to provide clearance for moving parts when the saw is gripped in the bench vise.

This is the end of the woodworking part of this project. If you have never worked with metal before, you will benefit from the following primer. You'll be surprised to discover how nicely some of your woodworking tools will handle metal.
Sawing—At least two teeth in the work, as usual.
—*Steel*: Hacksaw; use heavy cutting oil; slow, even strokes.
—*Aluminum*: Bandsaws beautifully with standard woodcut-ting blades; light cutting oil or kerosene may be used for heavier cuts; wipe tires dry after cutting.
—*Brass*: Bandsaws well; use dull blade; do not lubricate.
Drilling—Smaller holes, higher speeds, lighter feeds. Use twist drills; center-punch the hole location; clamp the work or hold it in a vise.
—*Steel*: low speeds; heavy feed; lubricate with oil. For easy cutting and accurate hole size, drill with a succession of drills of increasing diameter; for example, for a ¼-in. hole, drill first with a ³⁄₃₂-in. drill, then a ³⁄₁₆-in., then a ¼-in.
—*Aluminum*: Fairly high speeds; light feed; lubricate with light oil or kerosene.
—*Brass*: Medium speeds; medium feed; do not lubricate. Best results come from honing the rake angle to 0°, thus pre-venting the drill from grabbing or screwing into the work.

To mount the saw-frame in the ⅝-in. cold-rolled steel shaft,

Parker's design allows a comfortable working posture, sensitive control of the stroke and a good view of the work. Thin, narrow sawtable, left, allows work to be held down securely between fingers and thumbs. Center, Parker cuts the mortise for his mother-of-pearl signature (0.030 in. wide) using a Foredom mounted in a simple, adjustable-leg tripod.

first remove the saw-frame handle and determine the diameter and depth of the hole that will accommodate the tang. If in doubt, drill oversize because the tang will be fixed with epoxy, which will fill any voids. Cross-drill the shaft for the stop pin that will slide in the brass track on the upright's back edge. The stop pin may be retained by a setscrew epoxied in place or, if a bolt is used, locked in place with nuts. Notch the bottom end of the steel shaft using a hacksaw, and file the notch to fit a brass or aluminum plate. The plate, bolted in place, serves to transmit the drive and spring-return forces to the shaft.

Now make the brass track, which keeps the shaft from rotating, limits travel and houses rubber pads for absorbing shock at the ends of travel. You can mill the track from solid stock or construct it from strips. Alternately, you can rout the slot in the edge of the upright, although a separate brass plate allows you to set up the saw with a blade and determine where the stops should be. Travel will be the slot length minus the stop-pin diameter and the thickness of the rubber pads. Travel on my saw is just under 3 in., the length of toothed area on a 5-in. jeweler's sawblade.

I made my table out of ³/₁₆-in. aluminum plate. You can vary the size to suit the work; a thin, narrow table is good for cutting inlay because you can fit your thumbs and fingers around to pinch the work to the table (photo, above left), decreasing the likelihood that it will lift and break on the return stroke. Drill holes in the table for mounting, for passing the blade through (this should be as small as possible) and for attaching the spring. Also drill a couple of holes or cut a bird's mouth to be used for filing at the end of the table opposite the blade.

Assembly—Hold the saw sideways during assembly. Mark positions for the bearing blocks, and clamp them to the up-

right, shimming the throat of the blocks out with thin cardboard so that as the bearings wear they can be angled to take up slop. Get the shaft to move smoothly and drill through the upright for the mounting bolts. Insert bolts, washers and nuts; tighten and make sure the shaft is still free. Drill the ⅛-in. hole through the upper bearing, pin it in place and remove the cardboard shims. Slide the threaded spacer rod, with washers and nuts, through the bearings, and lock it in place in the upper bearing. Adjust the lower nuts to bring the lower bearing into line, confirmed by easy movement of the shaft. Position the brass track on the edge of the upright and test the stroke to be sure the top teeth can be brought into the work. The track may be screwed, pinned or epoxied in place. Insert the stop pin in the shaft, and see that the shaft runs freely without rotation.

To mount the saw-frame in proper alignment on the shaft, install a blade on center in the saw-frame clamps, fill the hole in the top of the shaft with epoxy and slip the saw-frame tang in. Slide the shaft up and down and observe the blade travel using a try square on the table. Align the saw-frame accordingly and hold or support it in place while the epoxy hardens. If you need to reset the tang, heat the shaft end with a torch; most epoxies give up before 300°F.

Position the table so the blade passes through and mark and drill for shankless wood screws in the end grain of the upright. Screw the table into place, making sure it is perfectly square with the blade.

Bolt the connecting plate in place at the bottom of the shaft and attach the spring from it to the table. The cord from the pedal also attaches to the plate. With the heel of the pedal screwed to the floor and the upright clamped in your bench end-vise, you're ready to saw. □

Ken Parker makes arch-top guitars in New York City.

Mitering on the Table Saw
Scribe reference lines for accurate alignment

by Henry T. Kramer

Recommendations for cutting good miter joints rarely include using the table saw, although we commonly use this machine to crosscut 90° angles. While it is cheerfully conceded that the Lion Trimmer and other shearing cutters are best for many miter cuts when their fences are properly adjusted, these are expensive single-purpose tools and can't perform many of the operations a table saw can, such as blind or shoulder cuts, or dadoes at 45°. Because the only difference between setting up the table saw for miter cuts and for 90° crosscuts is a change in the angle on the miter gauge, logic tells us that there ought to be a way of setting the gauge to produce a true 45° cut.

The trouble usually lies in the degree markings, positive stops and pointer on the miter gauge, which are usually too far off to be of any use. Given the dynamics of angular measurement, they would still be hard to set accurately even if their calibrations were precise and true. Some manage by trial and error, and while trial is the ultimate check, there is a better way to get set. The answer is to establish a long reference line on the saw table at an accurate 45° to the gauge slots, and with the aid of a long fence and a 3-ft. straightedge, to use the line to set the miter gauge. The principle is straightforward: the longer the radii forming the angle, the less chance for error. In the case of an angle of five minutes of arc, radii 24 in. long define a chord of about 1/32 in., as shown in the sketch below. Now five minutes of arc is the finest reading on the best vernier bevel protractor available, so if you can work within a lineal error of 1/32 in., you can establish a very accurate reference line.

Before describing how to establish reference lines, I need to point out possible sources for error when crosscutting with a table saw and how I would correct them. First, the blade must run parallel to the miter-gauge slots; if it doesn't, loosen the trunnion bolts and carefully reposition the arbor assembly to true up the sawblade. Heel and toe (a condition when the blade is not parallel to the line of cut) can cause binding, which will burn the wood and produce a bad cut. Second, most miter-gauge guide bars don't fit snugly in their slots, and this play introduces error. You can fix this by holding the gauge firmly against the side of the groove nearest the blade when setting up and cutting, or you can eliminate the play by peening the guide bar or soldering a shim to it.

Third, since most miter gauges have short work-contacting surfaces, you should attach a longer fence to the gauge. You can make one from a carefully jointed strip of wood. In fact, it's a good idea to have on hand several of them of different heights and lengths for different jobs. The long fence provides for more accurate alignment and gives support directly behind the cut, which prevents thin or narrow stock from bowing and binding. A fourth possible source for inaccurate mitering is the tendency of the workpiece to creep into the blade, causing binding, burning and an uneven cut. You can remedy this by gluing a sandpaper strip to the wooden fence of the gauge and holding the workpiece tightly against it during the cut; or you can clamp the work to your auxiliary fence.

Having done away with these probable causes of error, you are ready to scribe three layout lines on your saw table (extension wings excluded) so you can accurately set your miter

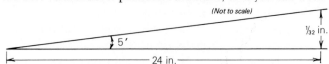

(Not to scale)

1/32 in.

5'

24 in.

Fig. 1: Layout of alignment marks

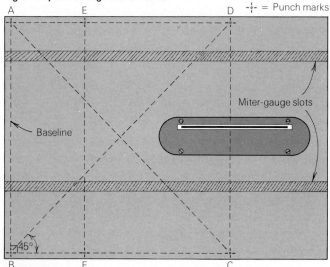

-¦- = Punch marks

A   E   D

Baseline

Miter-gauge slots

45°

B   F   C

Four points at corners (A,B,C,D) define square and diagonals. The two additional points about 7 in. up from baseline (E,F) are used to align gauge for 90° crosscuts.

Fig. 2: Aligning the miter gauge

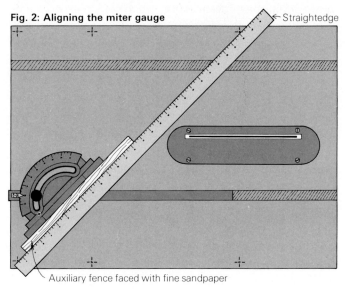

Straightedge

Auxiliary fence faced with fine sandpaper

Even a cheap table saw, at 20 in. by 27 in., can become an accurate mitering tool using this technique.

gauge at 90° and 45°. To begin, you'll need a 36-in. straight-edge, an accurate framing square (see *FWW* #17, p. 15 for a way to ensure its trueness) and a strip of wood sized to fit snugly into the miter-gauge slots and to sit proud of the saw table. Because the most reliable way to produce a 45° angle is by drawing a diagonal in a square, you should establish a square on the table. You don't need to scratch these lines into the table; locating the corners of the square with punch marks is sufficient.

The most difficult part of the square to construct is the base, running along the front of the table. The baseline must be perpendicular to the miter-gauge slots (if the slots are not parallel, get a new saw). Use as much of the table for this square as you conveniently can; its sides should be roughly ½ in. from the edges of the table, but don't use the edges for reference, only the miter-gauge grooves. Place the strip of wood in the right-hand groove and hold one leg of the square against it. Lay the straightedge against the other leg of the square, and draw the baseline using a very sharp pencil. Better yet, scribe this line with a machinist's scriber and layout dye. If you want to make a permanent line, use a machinist's scratch awl. Put the strip in the left-hand groove, flip the square, position the straightedge and complete the line so it runs the whole width of the table. Now you have a baseline that is exactly 90° to the miter-gauge grooves.

To establish the top line at the far end of the table, use the straightedge for a rough initial measurement of the height of the sides (precisely the length of the baseline). Then with a pair of dividers set to the exact distance from one groove (the one with the strip in it) to the end of the baseline, transfer this distance up to the top line, just above the expected height of the side. Now measure the length of the baseline carefully with trammels or by scribing the unmarked back of a 36-in. steel rule. With this and your dividers, locate one of the upper corners. Repeat this process to find the other corner, and the square is laid out. Now check all your measurements, beginning with the diagonals, which must be exactly the same length. When everything is right, locate each corner with a punch mark. If you haven't used a centerpunch much, practice first on some spare or scrap cast iron. The punch has to be held upright and hit dead on with a dead blow. A deliberate "rap-whap" will do it. When you're satisfied that you can strike the punch properly, punch-mark the four corners.

To align the miter gauge for 90° crosscutting, you'll need to mark out another line parallel to the baseline and about 7 in. up from the front edge of the table. Punch-mark the points where this line intersects the two vertical sides of the square. To get the most accurate setting you must hold a straightedge against the face of your miter gauge to set it for both 45° and 90° cuts. This straightedge must, of course, be long enough to be lined up on both punch marks at once. Keep in mind that the longer the auxiliary fence on your miter gauge, the more precise the alignment you'll get.

The approach of using long reference lines laid out on the surface of the table lends itself to other geometric constructions for other desired angle cuts. But if you scribe additional reference lines, you'll have to label them to avoid confusion. The key to this system is the length of the lines; the longer they are, the more accurate the results they'll give. In angular measurement, put not your trust in protractors. ☐

Amateur woodworker Henry Kramer lives in Somerville, N.J.

Aluminum Miter Jig

by Pope Lawrence

Here is a sliding miter jig for the table saw. Made from aluminum plate, with aluminum guide bars and a standard miter-gauge protractor head, it can be used to cut accurate miters, as well as 90° crosscuts. It is especially useful for mitering wide, thick stock and is adjustable so that other angles may be cut quickly, accurately and repeatedly. To make the base of the jig, get a piece of ¼-in. aluminum plate from a salvage yard or metal supply house and cut it about 18 in. long and 14 in. wide. The size will vary from saw to saw. An ordinary carbide-tipped blade in your table saw will do if you use prudence and care.

Using aluminum instead of plywood for the jig gives it greater rigidity, durability and accuracy, and makes a stable base for other table-saw jigs. Aluminum drills easily and cuts well enough with a carbide-tipped blade, but you must be cautious as it sometimes grabs the tool, especially a drill bit, as it penetrates the stock. Clamp the pieces down when drilling and wear safety glasses when cutting. You can also band-saw aluminum plate with an ordinary woodcutting blade.

Rip two strips from the plate for the guide bars and file their sawn edges for a snug but sliding fit in the miter-gauge slots. File a little chamfer on their two outer edges. Affixing the guide bars to the plate requires careful measuring and marking. Use ¼ x 20 flat-head machine screws, and tap the plate to receive them. Bore and counterbore the bottom of the guide bars so the holes are slightly oversized. This will allow you to make minor lateral adjustments to get the exact spacing between the bars. With the base complete, attach the protractor head and screw to it an auxiliary wooden fence, which you can equip with one or more toggle clamps (available from De-Sta-Co Division, Dover Corp., 350 Midland Ave., Detroit, Mich. 48302) to hold the workpiece against the base during the cut. Also you can clamp a stop block to the auxiliary fence for repetitive cuts of the same length.

When you've finished assembling the jig, mount a carbide-tipped blade on your saw arbor, set the jig in the slots and saw a kerf in the aluminum base plate so that it runs a short distance past the fence on the miter gauge when it's set for an acute 45° cut. This completes the jig and it's ready for use. ☐

Pope Lawrence, 32, is a cabinetmaker in Santa Fe, N. Mex.

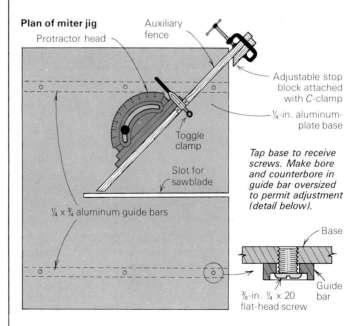

Plan of miter jig

Protractor head · Auxiliary fence · Adjustable stop block attached with *C*-clamp · ¼-in. aluminum-plate base · Toggle clamp · Slot for sawblade · ¼ x ¾ aluminum guide bars

Tap base to receive screws. Make bore and counterbore in guide bar oversized to permit adjustment (detail below).

Base · Guide bar · ⅜-in. ¼ x 20 flat-head screw

A Shop-Made Bowl Lathe
You can add ways for spindle turning

by Donald C. Bjorkman

After building my disc sander *(FWW #23, July '80)* and getting so much use out of it, I decided to build a lathe I've wanted for a long time but have been unable to afford. As most of my turnings are bowls and I do not have room in my shop to keep a full lathe, I designed a large bowl lathe that can be expanded into a bed lathe. It has a 17-in. swing inboard, a 74-in. swing outboard and a 48-in. span between centers. As with the disc sander, the motor is positioned low, contributing to the stability of the machine, and it is enclosed in a cabinet to protect it from shavings and dust. A door allows access for easy speed changes, and the cabinet can be used to store tools or hold sandbags for ballast. The motor platform slides back and forth on the shaft that supports it, so that by using two four-step pulleys, 16 speeds are possible. For this system to work, the machine must be level, or the motor will creep on the support shaft. With the size pulleys

chosen, the speeds range from approximately 500 RPM to 2,300 RPM. Although I have turned a piece containing 50 bd. ft. on a pattern lathe, I doubt that I will ever gamble with a 74-in. dia. item, as the outer edge at 500 RPM will be traveling at almost 10,000 FPM. Maybe I'll work up to it.

The frame is constructed of hard maple and all the joints are open mortise and tenon. The stress panels are ⅜-in. Baltic birch plywood, and the shaft and pulley cover is vacuum-formed plywood, the equipment and technique for which is discussed in *FWW #16, May '79, pp. 52-57.* The stress panels are glued into rabbets in the frame, except for the front panel which is screwed in place to allow complete access to the interior. The floor of the machine can also be removed so the corner braces can be bolted to the floor.

The sloping sides and perpendicular base of the machine require that the slot mortises in the base be cut on an angle. I

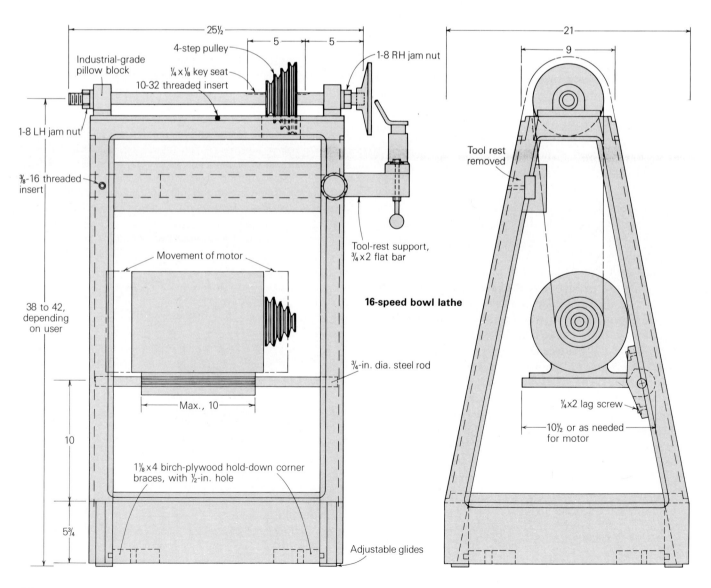

16-speed bowl lathe

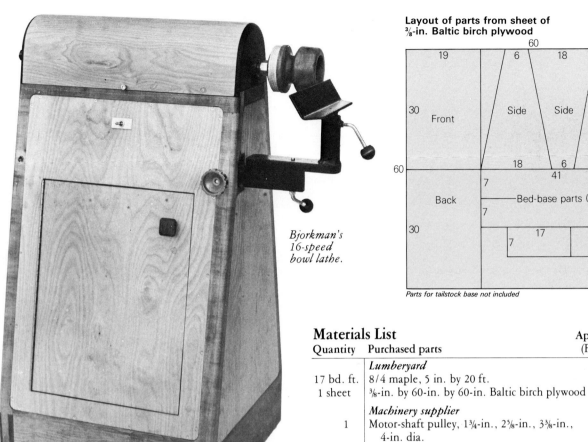

*Bjorkman's
16-speed
bowl lathe.*

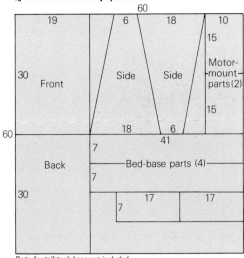

**Layout of parts from sheet of
³/₈-in. Baltic birch plywood**

		60		
19	6	18	10	
30 Front	Side	Side	15 / Motor-mount parts (2) / 15	
	18	6		
60		41		
Back	7	Bed-base parts (4)		
	7			
30		17	17	
	7			

Parts for tailstock base not included

Tool-rest assembly

Stock tool rest

10-32 x ³/₄ knurled hold-down bolt

4r

³/₄ x 2 x 8 flat bar

⁵/₁₆-in. nut, welded to steel tubing that fits tool-rest shaft

2¼-in. knob, force-fit to ³/₈-16 bolt

Tool-rest support

Machine ³/₈-in. slot. Rotate slotted bar 180° for larger bowls.

Three-legged tool-rest stand

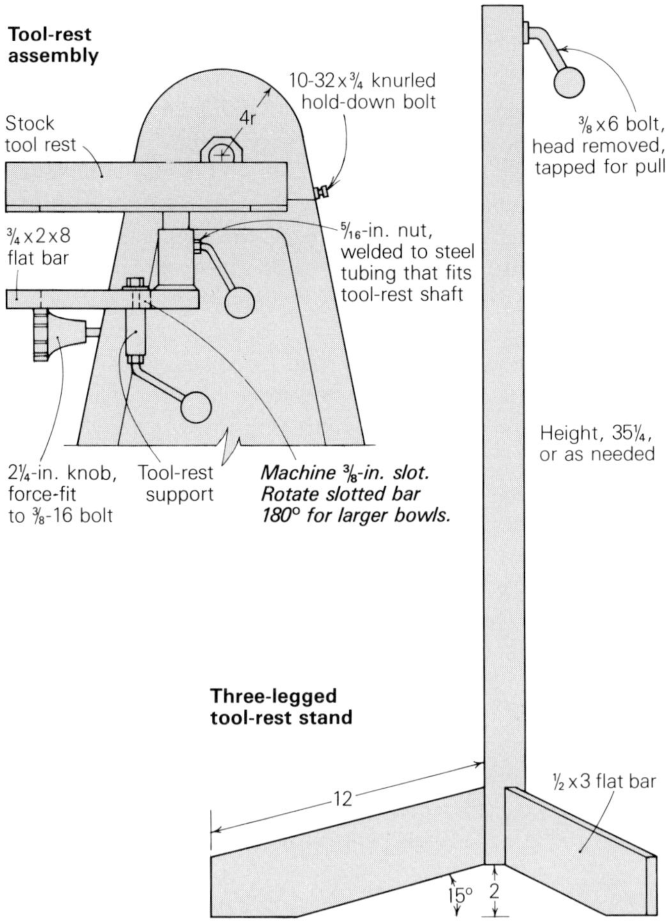

³/₈ x 6 bolt, head removed, tapped for pull

Height, 35¼, or as needed

½ x 3 flat bar

12

15° 2

Materials List

Quantity	Purchased parts	Approx. cost (Fall, 1980)
	Lumberyard	
17 bd. ft.	8/4 maple, 5 in. by 20 ft.	$ 35.00
1 sheet	³/₈-in. by 60-in. by 60-in. Baltic birch plywood	28.00
	Machinery supplier	
1	Motor-shaft pulley, 1³/₄-in., 2⁵/₈-in., 3³/₈-in., 4-in. dia.	9.50
1	1-in. shaft pulley, 3-in., 4-in., 5-in., 6-in. dia.	16.00
2	Medium-duty self-aligning pillow blocks	45.50
4	Heavy-duty adjustable nut glides	4.00
1	Motor switch	9.00
1	2¼-in. locking knob	1.50
	Tool rest and faceplates as needed	
	Steel supplier	
25½ in.	1-in. dia. cold-rolled rod	2.50
20½ in.	³/₄-in. dia. hot-rolled rod	1.00
2	³/₄-in. by 2-in. hot-rolled flat bar, 8 in. & 24 in.	4.00
4 in.	Tubing sized to tool rest	.50
1	1-8 RH jam nut	1.00
1	1-8 LH jam nut	1.50
	Welding of tool rest	5.00
	Machining of shaft	15.00
	Hardware store	
2	10-32 threaded inserts	
2	³/₈-16 threaded inserts	
8 ft.	14/3 SJ electric cord	
1	220 V electric plug	
1	⁵/₁₆-18 by 4-in. hex bolt	
1	³/₈-16 by 6-in. hex bolt	
4	⁵/₁₆-18 by 1¼-in. hex bolts	
4	⁵/₁₆-in. hex nuts	
4	⁵/₁₆-in. lock washers	
8	⁵/₁₆-in. flat washers	
4	¼-in. by 2-in. lag screws	
1	³/₈-16 by 3½-in. hex bolt	
4	½-13 by 3-in. hex bolt for pillow blocks	
4	½-13 hex nut	
4	½-in. flat washers	
3	Ball-shaped wooden drawer pulls	
1	1¹/₁₆-in. by 24-in. continuous hinge	
1	¼-in. by ¼-in. by 2-in. key for pulley	
1	½-in. by 50-in. V-belt	
2	10-32 by ³/₄-in. knurled finger bolts	
6	1¼ x 8 FH wood screws (Phillips)	
18	³/₄ x 6 FH wood screws (Phillips)	
1	Cabinet door catch	
	Total, miscellaneous hardware	24.50
	Total cost	$203.50

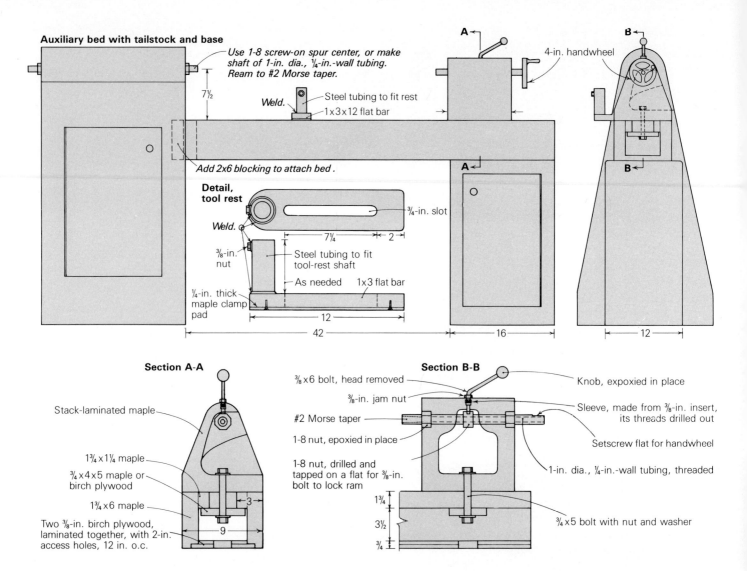

Auxiliary bed with tailstock and base

Use 1-8 screw-on spur center, or make shaft of 1-in. dia., ¼-in.-wall tubing. Ream to #2 Morse taper.

7½

Weld.

Steel tubing to fit rest

1x3x12 flat bar

Add 2x6 blocking to attach bed.

A

4-in. handwheel

B

Detail, tool rest

Weld.

¾-in. slot

7¼

2

⅜-in. nut

Steel tubing to fit tool-rest shaft

As needed   1x3 flat bar

¼-in. thick maple clamp pad

12

42

16

12

Section A-A

Stack-laminated maple

1¾ x 1¼ maple

¾ x 4 x 5 maple or birch plywood

1¾ x 6 maple

Two ⅜-in. birch plywood, laminated together, with 2-in. access holes, 12 in. o.c.

3

9

Section B-B

⅜ x 6 bolt, head removed

⅜-in. jam nut

#2 Morse taper

1-8 nut, epoxied in place

1-8 nut, drilled and tapped on a flat for ⅜-in. bolt to lock ram

Knob, expoxied in place

Sleeve, made from ⅜-in. insert, its threads drilled out

Setscrew flat for handwheel

1-in. dia., ¼-in.-wall tubing, threaded

¾ x 5 bolt with nut and washer

1¾

3½

¾

used the table saw and a simple tapered jig. When the frame is fully assembled, a ⅜-in. rabbeting bit and router cut the rabbets for the plywood panels to fit into.

The guide through which the tool-rest support slides consists of two 1½-in. by 4-in. pieces of maple that span the uprights of the frame. To form the ¾-in. by 2-in. channel in the guide, I grooved each piece and glued them together. To align the groove I wrapped the steel bar in wax paper and positioned it in the groove during glue-up. Then I cut the angle on the guide's face to match the slope of the sides of the machine. A 2¼-in. knob on a ⅜-in. bolt through a threaded insert in the machine frame locks the sliding section of the tool-rest support in place. The pivoting section of the support consists of an 8-in. length of flat bar steel welded to a 4-in. length of steel tubing. A ⅜-in. slot is machined in the flat bar for the ⅜-in. hold-down bolt to slide in.

You can make ways for spindle turning on this lathe from two pieces of 1¾-in. by 6-in. maple, 58 in. or however long you desire. Laminate a 1¾-in. by 1¼-in. piece of maple along the length of the top edge of each way to create the lip that the tailstock and tool rest clamp to. Reinforce the bed along its lower side with a double thickness of ⅜-in. birch plywood, rabbeted into the inside edge of each way. As you will not have plywood pieces long enough to extend the length of the ways, stagger the joints for strength. Drill 2-in. holes on 12-in. centers along the length of this plywood for access to the hold-down bolts on the tailstock and tool-rest support. By epoxying and/or flush-screwing a thin piece of maple to the bottom surface of the tool rest, you can prevent a metal-to-

wood sliding contact, thus forestalling damage to the wooden ways. Secure the tail end of the bed to the tailstock pedestal by bolting through the plywood along the bottom of the bed. The tailstock itself is stack-laminated maple. When the 1-8 nuts that hold the ram are epoxied into the tailstock, be sure to have the ram screwed in place so that the nuts are indexed to each other. The same is true when drilling the hole into the flat of the nut that locks the ram. With the tailstock in place bolt the ways to the headstock through two maple attaching blocks, one between the ways, the other between the frames under the spindle. It is important that both the longitudinal and horizontal planes of the bed are parallel to the centerline of the spindle; if not, you could end up with tapered turnings. Sight through the headstock spindle and move the tailstock until it is aligned. Shim where the headstock attaches to the bed as needed. You can also adjust the mounting of the pillow blocks.

The dimensions given are for my lathe and may be modified, but if the machine is built much larger, one piece of plywood will not be enough for all the stress panels. Also note that the spindle size and tool-rest holder were chosen to accept manufacturer's stock units. When buying steel, consider purchasing enough to build an outboard tool-rest stand. The materials list includes parts for the bowl lathe only. As motor prices vary considerably, I have not figured the price of one in the costs, but a ¾-HP to 1-HP motor is recommended. □

Donald Bjorkman is professor of interior design at Northern Arizona University in Flagstaff.

The Pin Router
Basic setups for this versatile machine

by Dennis R. Wilson

Typical industrial-capacity pin routers consist of a spindle chuck and motor, suspended from an adjustable column and arm or a cast-iron frame. Photo: Ekstrom Carlson.

The overarm router is basically a shaper with the cutting tool above the table. Not only can it shape and mold the outside edge of stock, but it can plunge-cut, groove, bore and excavate for inlay. The overarm router can also cut mortises, tenons and rabbets. It is especially valuable as a production machine for making identical parts, using jigs and templates.

The basic machine (right) consists of a C-shaped frame, a top-mounted spindle chuck and motor, and a movable table that can be raised and lowered by a treadle. Located directly beneath the centerline of the cutter spindle is a vertically adjustable guide pin. This is what gives the pin router its versatility as well as its name.

Modes of operation—There are six basic ways to operate the pin router. The first is freehand. This is similar to using a portable router freehand, except that you move the stock instead of the router, and there is the advantage of being able to see the work. Also, the table-elevating mechanism makes starting and stopping cuts within the perimeters of the stock easier.

The second mode uses a straight fence for straight-line shaping. Adjustable factory fences are satisfactory, or you can make your own from a dense hardwood or cabinet-grade plywood. If the fence is divided into two sections, the entire surface of the stock can be routed by offsetting the outfeed fence by the amount of stock being removed. This is similar to jointing. For shaping less than the whole edge, use a single fence and set it up as follows: Bring the table up so the cutter just touches the top of the fence, and align the fence with the deepest contour of the cutter. Then, with the router running, raise the table so the cutter plunges into the fence until you reach the depth of cut you desire. This will give the stock full

EDITOR'S NOTE: Manufacturers of pin routers include Ekstrom Carlson, 1400 Railroad Ave., Rockford, Ill. 61110; Rockwell, 400 N. Lexington Ave., Pittsburg, Pa. 15208; Porter, 522 Plymouth NE, Grand Rapids, Mich. 49505; Onsrud, 2100 S. Laramie Ave., Chicago, Ill. 60650, and Westflex, Box 5227, Westport, Conn. 06880. They are usually not difficult to find at used-machinery dealers or tool auctions for companies going out of business. Three ideas for fashioning your own pin router appear on page 25.

support as it is being routed. The fence should be cut open behind the cutter for chip clearance. Chips that are carried through to jam between the cutter and the work will dent the surface and show up as blotches in finishing. Evacuating the chips with a vacuum helps.

The third mode is shaping with the workpiece pressed against a pilot on the cutting tool. The workpiece can be straight or any irregular shape. This method works best with ball-bearing pilots, since solid pilots often score and burn the wood. In order to start the cut safely, a pivot block of hardwood with about a ¼-in. diameter tip can be clamped to the table about 1 in. from the cutter.

In mode four, the stock is pressed against the guide pin. This method, as method three, requires that a part of the stock edge is not cut, and the final shape of the piece must be finished smoothly before shaping the edge. The diameter of the guide pin and the height of the table determine the depth of cut. Stock can be routed straight or curved, and you can rout inside or outside edges, but use a starting block.

Mode five is basically the same as mode four, except the workpiece is set on top of a pattern or jig. The pattern is

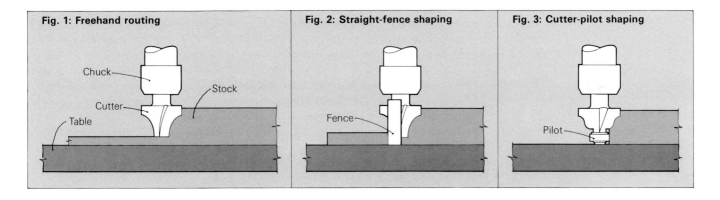

| Fig. 1: Freehand routing | Fig. 2: Straight-fence shaping | Fig. 3: Cutter-pilot shaping |

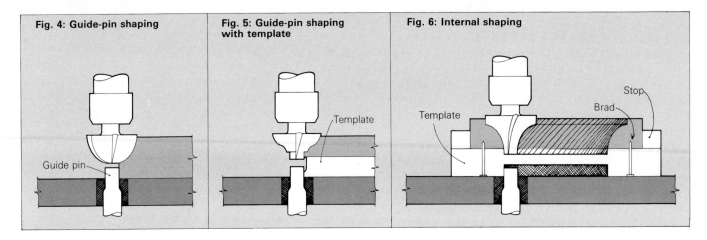

| Fig. 4: Guide-pin shaping | Fig. 5: Guide-pin shaping with template | Fig. 6: Internal shaping |

pushed against the guide pin, and thus the entire edge of the workpiece can be shaped. The workpiece can be held in place by screws, double-sided tape, brads or stop blocks. Normally the pattern is exactly the same size as the routed workpiece, but the pattern can sometimes be offset.

Mode six is for internal shaping, scroll cutting and flat-relief carving. The workpiece is fastened to a template whose underside has been routed out to follow the guide pin. The amount of stock removed is determined by the diameter of the pin, the diameter of the cutter, the size of the cutout and the height of the table. As in any shaping operation using guide pins or shaper collars, the precise shape of the cutout depends upon the pin radius and the cutter radius.

Mode six is good for routing multiple recesses for inlays. Place the inlay upside down on the template bottom and scribe a line around the inlay. Rout or cut this recess out precisely to the scribed line; the accuracy of the inlay fit depends on the accuracy of the recess in the template. Locate the workpiece on the top of the template. By using a ¼-in. diameter guide pin and a ¼-in. diameter straight end mill or router bit, the cutter will exactly duplicate the template recess.

Modes five and six are normally used where duplicates are being made or where the piece being routed would otherwise be difficult to handle safely. In production runs, quick-release clamps, such as the lever type made by De-Sta-Co (350 Midland Ave., Detroit, Mich. 48203), can be used to hold the workpiece down, and handles or grips can be added for better control when routing. Templates should be made of a material that is warp-free and hard enough to withstand pressure against the guide pin. Hard maple, plywood, tempered Masonite and aluminum work well. Any imperfection in the guide edge of the template will be duplicated in the work-

piece; wax the template and router table for smoother travel.

In all routing and shaping operations, safety and efficiency come first. Make sure no cutouts in the edge to be routed are smaller than the guide-pin diameter, and take care where abrupt changes in edge direction could catch and throw the workpiece. Either allow extra length for the workpiece or add a small starter block which can be cut off later. Shape profiles that require considerable stock removal with multiple passes, taking a light cut in each. Check the security of guides and clamps before turning on the router.

Cutters—Standard ¼-in. shank diameter router bits can be used as well as ¼-in. to ½-in. shank diameter end mills (two flutes provide the best chip removal and the cleanest cut). Special shaper arbors with collars can also be used. Some heavy-duty machines (including Ekstrom Carlson and Onsrud) can be fit with a rosette chuck which takes flat steel cutters (available from Woodworkers Tool Works, 222 S. Jefferson St., Chicago, Ill. 60606). The chuck has a ⅛-in. slot and an allen screw to lock in the cutter—a single knife made from an oil-hardening tool-steel blank with a cutting area 1½ in. to 3 in. wide and 1¼ in. high (photo below left). It is different from the cutter used on a standard shaper spindle though many of the grinding techniques and uses are the same (see "Shaper Cutter and Fences," *FWW* #20, January '80; "Furniture from Photographs," *FWW* #17, July '79; and "Making Shaper Knives," *FWW* #5, Winter '76). The important advantage of the rosette chuck is that the cutter is positioned only ⅟₁₆ in. off the diameter of the spindle, so the profile of the routed piece will differ little from that of the cutter. These cutters are ground to shape on both ends, but one end is relieved, so only the opposite end does the cutting.

The typical spindle speeds used in routing are 10,000 RPM or 20,000 RPM. My pin router is set up for 10,500 RPM because I use cutters up to 3 in. in diameter; I prefer the rosette chuck and blades that I have ground. With end mills or standard router bits less than 1¼ in. in diameter, 20,000 RPM could be used. Shaper collars used on the router should not run faster than 10,000 RPM and should be designed for overarm routers.

The methods illustrated here could be used on vertical milling machines, drill presses or on homemade rigs with a router. However, you should not use a rosette chuck here, since the router and drill press are not designed for the radial thrust loads these operations place on the equipment. □

Rosette chuck and T-blank, ground on both sides, but relieved so there is only one cutting edge.

Dennis Wilson, of Wynne, Ark., is a mechanical engineer who also operates his own woodworking business.

Homemade overhead and pin routers

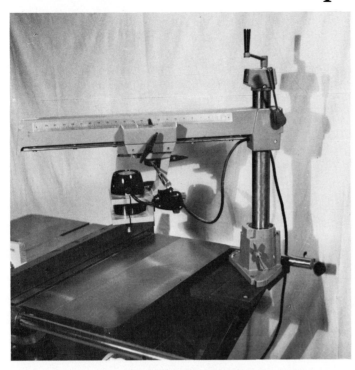

This home-brewed overhead router (left), made by Larry Churchill of Mayville, Wis., is not actually a pin router in that it doesn't have a guide pin, though it could. Instead, Churchill uses the fence and miter gauge of his table saw to guide the work. It was these features, the flat table and the need to save space that brought his table saw together with his router and the transport mechanism of a radial-arm saw. (HIT Distributors, 2867 Long Beach Rd., Oceanside, N.Y. 11572 has adapters that fit together most routers and radial-arm saws; Shopsmith, 750 Center Dr., Vandalia, Ohio 45377, has a router arm for converting a router into an overarm router.) Churchill's setup allows the router to be moved in relation to the work—for plunge cuts, straight-line routing, routing arcs and routing freehand without a router base to obscure the work. For this design, Churchill recommends a saw mechanism with the elevation crank overhead. Mount the base plate so the router moves parallel to the table. To rout arcs, remove the saw-arm miter stops. In designing the router bracket (Churchill used aluminum), make sure the bit will reach the table when the arm is lowered all the way. Photo: Larry Churchill.

When Laszlo Gigacz, of Jordan, N.Y., needed a pin router, he added to his router table an oak arm to position a steel shaft with stop collar directly over the router chuck (right). The upside-down pin router has advantages: The router is more rigid when mounted to a table rather than to an arm, and you can see the pin as it follows the template. If you have a router table already, this method couldn't be easier. The arm swings out of the way when you want your router table back. Photo: Staff.

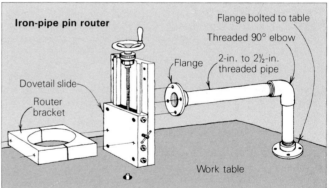

Iron-pipe pin router

Flange bolted to table

Threaded 90° elbow

Flange

2-in. to 2½-in. threaded pipe

Dovetail slide

Router bracket

Work table

Doug Wahl's pin router is basically 2½-in. black pipe and fittings. Wahl, of Washingtonville, N.Y., is a supervisor in a metal-working house. He machined the inside diameter of the T for a slip fit of the horizontal pipe, and welded the plate on top for tapping in the two bolts that secure the pipe. He machined the router bracket too, though Stanley sells brackets for their routers, and there's always the alternative of making a bracket from hardwood. The pin in the table is a socket-head cap screw with its head machined to the diameter of the router bit. It's secured through the top of the table by a nut and washer. The router can be elevated in fixed increments by substituting pipes of different lengths for the column. Fine adjustment is accomplished by means of the spiral groove in the router body (it's a Stanley R2-L, discontinued in 1951) and a key in the bracket, just like the adjusting arrangement between the router and its portable base. For routers that are not spirally grooved, Wahl suggests attaching the router bracket to a dovetail slide with crank screw (fashionable in hardwood or available in steel from Setco Industries, 5880 Hillside Ave., Cincinnati, Ohio 45233). The drawing above shows this alternative in a design simpler than the one in the photograph. It calls for standard pipe fittings and does not require welding. Photo: Doug Wahl.

Methods of Work

Enhanced table-saw miter gauge

For five years I have looked unsuccessfully for a 10-in. table saw with a "rolling table" facility for crosscuts and miters. The one I'm familiar with is a big, old Oliver. The new Rockwell and Powermatic sliding table attachments are similar in concept and are fine if you have $2,000 to spend on the saw and rig. They take up room on the left of the saw and are really designed for the large stock requirements of a cabinet shop. There are plywood jigs that sit atop the saw and serve the purpose, but I've found them to be inaccurate. My solution is simple, inexpensive and as effective as the expensive attachments if you are not cutting whole sheets of plywood.

Simply take your miter gauge apart and insert a piece of Formica between the miter-gauge bar and the protractor fence. Cut the Formica the same size as the left half of the table and fasten the smooth side down. When using the fixture you can press down on the piece of wood being crosscut without causing the wood to bind as it slides on the table. The Formica spreads the pressure over a wider area. The addition of a backboard faced with abrasive paper practically eliminates creep. —*Michael J. Hanley, Cedarburg, Wis.*

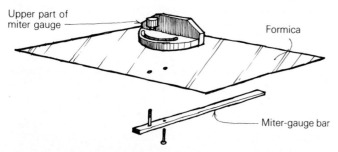

Crosscutting wide panels

Here is an accurate and simple way to crosscut plywood panels or boards that are too wide to cut using the saw's miter gauge. Start with a straight 1x2 longer than the panel is wide. Clamp the 1x2 underneath the panel so that it becomes a

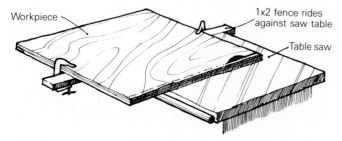

fence that runs against the saw table's edge. Carefully measure and position the fence using a framing square. Then clamp the new fence to the panel with C-clamps. The method can be adapted to ripping plywood and wall paneling by lengthening the fence. By clamping the fence to wide panels at an angle, you can make miter cuts that are virtually impossible any other way. —*Steve DeLay, Hollister, Calif.*

Rubber tire hold-in

The simple lawnmower-wheel fixture sketched at right has made featherboard hold-ins obsolete in my shop. I have two: one as shown and the other a mirror image of the first. I use them on both the table saw and the router table for ripping, cutting grooves, shaping, and other operations.

The advantages of this fixture over featherboards are significant: Feed friction is greatly reduced, hold-down pressure is adjustable and consistent (even when the stock is uneven)

and setup is quicker and easier. Since fore/aft friction is all but eliminated, there is little tendency for the fixture to squirm and turn under the clamp. Only one clamp will keep it in place, even on a waxed saw table. The disadvantage is that there is no kickback resistance as with featherboards. But kickback can be all but eliminated by using sharp, clean blades and carefully setting up for each cut.

The idea for rubber-tire pressure wheels is not mine—similar fixtures are used on large power-feed industrial woodworking machines. I suppose the wheel could be cut from plywood to save the extra few dollars for the ball-bearing lawnmower wheel and special axle bolt. But I find it comforting to see the rubber tire flatten a bit as it pushes the work against the saw fence. —*Bob DeFrances, Delray Beach, Fla.*

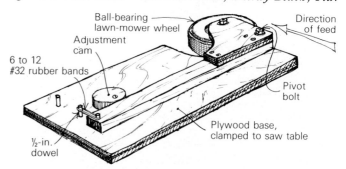

Jig indexing mechanism

This indexing mechanism can be incorporated into a variety of woodworking jigs for the table saw, drill press, overarm router, and other machines where accurately spaced cuts, dadoes or holes are required. The idea was originally given to me by Herman Kundera, a knowledgeable woodworker from San Bruno, Calif.

The mechanism consists of a spring catch mounted to the jig's fixed or base side and stops of finishing-nail heads set in the sliding side of the jig. The locations of the catch and the nails can be reversed if it's more convenient. For precise, accurate spacing, predrill holes for the finishing nails with a slightly undersized bit. Vary the nail spacing as required for the particular job at hand. Although I made my spring catch from a piece of hacksaw blade (anneal for bending and drilling, then reharden and temper), any thin piece of metal would be a serviceable catch. Fasten the catch to the jig with a roundhead screw.

In using the jig you will slide one part against the other. The spring will ride up and over the nail head and then click down. When you feel the spring click, move the jig back until the spring catch registers against the nail. Now you're ready to proceed with cutting, drilling or whatever.
—*Donald M. Steinert, Grants Pass, Oregon*

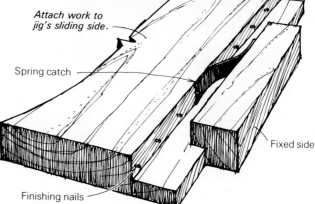

Eccentric router base

This router subbase allows me to rout an "in-between" size groove (for various stock thicknesses) without moving the guide fence or changing the setup. Because the subbase is eccentric to the router bit you can change the diameter of the base simply by changing the point of the base that rides against the guide fence.

To make the base, choose plywood, plastic or a 4-ply stack of plastic laminate for the material. You can cut the eccentric shape on a bandsaw or jigsaw, but for a smoother, more accurate base use a router table to machine the base. First drill a $\frac{1}{16}$-in. pivot hole at the center of the blank for the base and another $\frac{1}{16}$-in. pivot hole offset from the center. The offset determines the eccentricity of the base. I used an offset of $\frac{1}{8}$ in. which allows me to cut grooves up to $\frac{1}{2}$-in. with a $\frac{1}{4}$-in. bit. On a line through these holes drill a $\frac{1}{4}$-in. hole at a radius slightly larger than the radius of your router base. Before proceeding, it's a good idea to locate and drill the mounting holes in the subbase.

To cut the circumference of the base, mount the blank on the router table with the $\frac{1}{4}$-in. hole over a $\frac{1}{4}$-in. router bit.

Drill $\frac{1}{16}$-in. holes onto the router table through both the center pivot and offset pivot. Put a pin in the center hole, turn on the starting position, put the pin in the offset hole and rotate the base 180° in the other direction. You will have to finish the "step" area with a file. Before routing out the center of the subbase, you should pivot the base on the center hole and scribe measurement lines on the base for every $\frac{1}{32}$ in. of diameter change. Use a fine-tip waterproof pen.

To use the base to cut a $\frac{5}{16}$-in. groove, for example, clamp a guide fence in place on the work and rout a $\frac{1}{4}$-in. groove. Keep the zero-offset part of the subbase against the fence. Now rotate the base until the $\frac{1}{16}$-in. scribe line touches the fence. Keep the $\frac{1}{16}$-in. mark touching the fence and make another pass, taking care not to twist the router. The result is a $\frac{5}{16}$-in. groove. —*Mike Ramey, Seattle, Wash.*

Adjustable drill-press fence

This drill-press fence is quickly adjustable for boring holes the same distance from an edge or for routing with the drill press. The base is plywood; the fence is hardwood and adjusts using wing nuts and an arc-shaped slot in the base. The sketch shows the details. —*Pendleton Tompkins, San Mateo, Calif.*

1. Place blank on router table

2. Rout circular half of base

3. Move pin, rout eccentric half of base

$\frac{1}{4}$-in. router bit
Center pivot
Eccentric pivot
Mounting holes
Measurement marks
Completed base

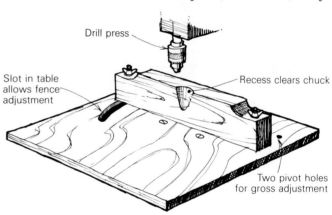

Drill press
Slot in table allows fence adjustment
Recess clears chuck
Two pivot holes for gross adjustment

Follow-up on bowl lathe, bandsaw basics

Regarding the headstock of Don Bjorkman's bowl-turning lathe (p. 20), I feel obliged to offer a suggestion that should improve the quality of work produced on it. The two bearings as shown are widely spaced, with a slender arbor of only an inch or so in diameter, inviting vibration problems...

The accompanying sketch shows a simple but effective

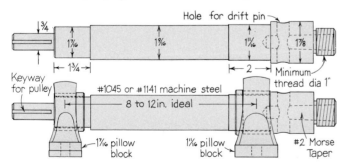

Hole for drift pin
$\frac{3}{4}$
$1\frac{7}{16}$
$1\frac{7}{16}$
$1\frac{11}{16}$
$1\frac{7}{8}$
$1\frac{3}{4}$
2
Minimum thread dia 1"
Keyway for pulley
#1045 or #1141 machine steel
8 to 12 in. ideal
$1\frac{7}{16}$ pillow block
$1\frac{7}{16}$ pillow block
#2 Morse Taper

spindle design. This design can be altered to suit many applications. The main points are that it offers a firm shoulder to seat against the front bearing, the spindle has plenty of beef to resist vibration, and the pulley location at the extreme left end allows easier belt management. This also removes the belt and pulley away from the left arm while turning the back of a bowl, but of course a guard should still be installed. I have shown a hole crossways the spindle to receive a tapered drift

pin with which to remove tooling having Morse tapers. A #2 MT should be the minimum size because of the vibration problem. Incidentally, Bjorkman's motor mount should have a locking device to eliminate belt and motor bounce.
—*R. Perry Mercurio, Kingfield, Me.*

To "The Basics of the Bandsaw" (p. 10), well done as usual by Tage Frid, I would add one piece of advice: When a bandsaw blade breaks; keep your cool, turn off the machine, stand back and wait two minutes. Only then, carefully open the top door.

In observing students' reactions to blade breakage, there is a very early tendency to open the door to see what is happening. They do not realize that the upper wheel can run on silently for several minutes after the motor has stopped. This wheel, especially if it is large and heavy, can quickly pick up the blade and project it at the operator.
—*Rob van Nieuwenhuizen, Barry's Bay, Ont.*

...Frid writes, adjust the tracking until the blade rides in the middle of the rim. This doesn't work for all bandsaws. In some, the blade will have to run on the front of the rim, else the blade will cause the wheel to tip over the center of balance, and the blade will come off at the back of the wheel.

The ideal position for the blade is with the teeth just outside the rubber. This will work perfectly for wide blades, but not for $\frac{1}{4}$ in. or smaller. —*John Kolkman, Thornhill, Ont.*

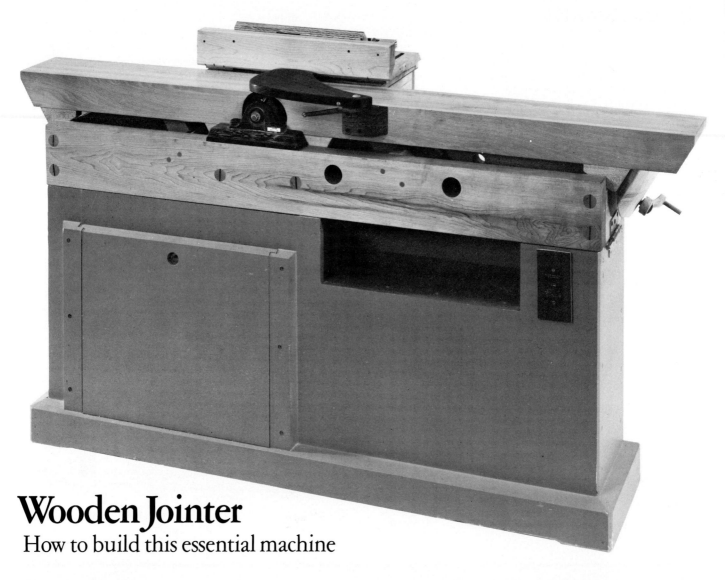

Wooden Jointer
How to build this essential machine

by Galen Winchip

Seven years ago I walked into a local hardware store to buy an odd assortment of stuff. "What are you going to make?" asked the quizzical gentleman waiting on me. "A wooden jointer," I replied, trying to sound confident. He was both astonished and skeptical, and did his best to persuade me to buy the jointer on display in the store. Despite his warning that a jointer is a precision tool and not the kind of thing you just throw together in your shop, I bought the items on my list and thus embarked on my first tool-building venture.

That first jointer worked, but it left several things to be desired. So I determined to make a jointer that would perform as well as a commercial model. I subsequently tested five designs, each one simpler, more reliable and more precise than the one before. Finally, I

arrived at the design for the jointer shown here. It requires no exotic, hard-to-find hardware or materials, and it doesn't call for any tricky methods of construction. Its performance rivals that of an industrially produced machine, though its price (about $350) is considerably less, and its feel and appearance are friendlier. I've been using this jointer for about 18 months, taking it from one job site to another, and I'm very happy with its design and with the results it produces.

Like certain of its industrial-duty,

cast-iron counterparts, my wooden jointer incorporates four sets of inclined ways or wedge-shaped bearing blocks. As shown below, these provide the means for raising and lowering the tables. The wedges on the bottom of each table (elevation blocks) ride up and down on the stationary ways (bearing blocks) attached to the frame assembly. This system is especially suitable for a wooden jointer because it supports each bed at four points, two at each end, eliminating the possibility of drooping tables and providing very

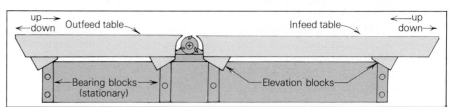

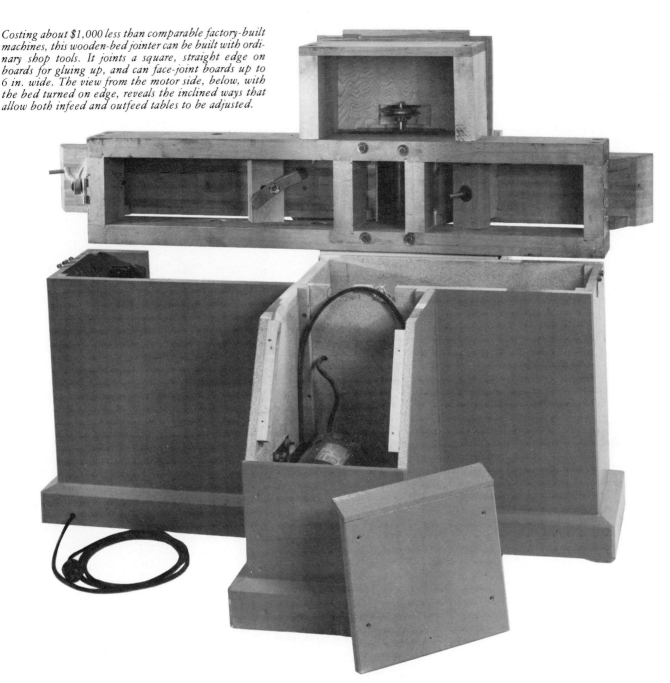

Costing about $1,000 less than comparable factory-built machines, this wooden-bed jointer can be built with ordinary shop tools. It joints a square, straight edge on boards for gluing up, and can face-joint boards up to 6 in. wide. The view from the motor side, below, with the bed turned on edge, reveals the inclined ways that allow both infeed and outfeed tables to be adjusted.

stable working surfaces. I've jointed a lot of long, heavy stock with this machine, and found it can easily cut a true edge on an 8/4 board, 8 ft. long and 10 in. wide.

The cutterhead is the heart of the machine, so you should get one that is well-balanced and perfectly round (square cutterheads are dangerous) and that has been turned and milled from a single piece of bar stock. It should have a cutting arc of about 3 in. and a hefty shaft, ¾ in. in diameter. Mine was turned and milled by a machinist friend, who got the shaft too small for my liking. I'll soon make a new one with a ¾-in. shaft, which will minimize vibration and increase durability. You can have a machinist do this work for you as I did, or you can buy a cutterhead as a replacement part from a woodworking-

machinery distributor. The cutterhead shaft runs in two self-aligning, ball-bearing pillow blocks, which you can get at any well-stocked industrial-supply or farm-supply store.

For driving the cutterhead, use a 1-HP or 1½-HP, 3,600-RPM motor. Select a pair of pulleys that will turn the cutterhead about 5,000 RPM (about 4,000 surface feet per minute).

The infeed and outfeed tables are laminated from quartersawn, face-glued boards. I used ¾-in. beech, but maple or another hard, heavy wood would do. Since the finished tables are 3 in. thick, you should rip the laminae to a rough width of around 3¼ in. to allow for a preliminary and a final surfacing of both sides. Use yellow (aliphatic resin) glue, and allow the tables to sit for several weeks before initial sur-

facing. The gluelines need time to cure thoroughly, and the laminated slabs need time to stabilize.

The tables shown here are proportioned to my own preferences: the infeed table is 10 in. longer than the outfeed because I find this easier for jointing long, heavy stock. But you can make them of equal length, as is common practice, or you can experiment to learn what suits you best. The same holds true for the dimensions of the fence. You can make one fence for the kind of work you do most, or you can make several of different sizes for different jobs. Since you're making your own, you aren't limited by what some manufacturer decides is the average size.

The jointer frame consists of two sides and three sets of blocks—two pairs of bearing blocks and a pair of clamping

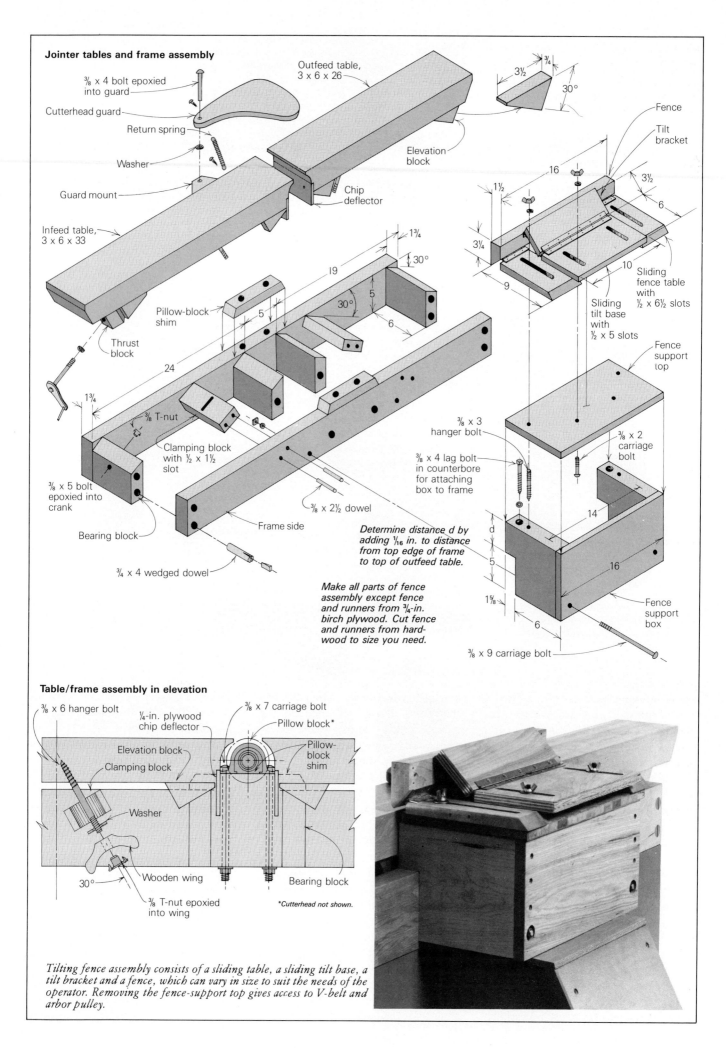

Jointer tables and frame assembly

Outfeed table, 3 x 6 x 26

3½
¾
30°

⅜ x 4 bolt epoxied into guard

Cutterhead guard

Return spring

Washer

Guard mount

Elevation block

Chip deflector

Infeed table, 3 x 6 x 33

Fence

Tilt bracket

3½

6

16

1½

3¼

9

10

Sliding fence table with ½ x 6½ slots

Sliding tilt base with ½ x 5 slots

1¾

30°

19

5

5

6

30°

Pillow-block shim

Thrust block

24

Fence support top

1¾

⅜ T-nut

Clamping block with ½ x 1½ slot

⅜ x 3 hanger bolt

⅜ x 4 lag bolt in counterbore for attaching box to frame

⅜ x 2 carriage bolt

⅜ x 5 bolt epoxied into crank

Bearing block

⅜ x 2½ dowel

Frame side

d

14

5

16

¾ x 4 wedged dowel

Determine distance d by adding ¹⁄₁₆ in. to distance from top edge of frame to top of outfeed table.

Make all parts of fence assembly except fence and runners from ¾-in. birch plywood. Cut fence and runners from hardwood to size you need.

1⅝

6

Fence support box

⅜ x 9 carriage bolt

Table/frame assembly in elevation

⅜ x 6 hanger bolt

¼-in. plywood chip deflector

⅜ x 7 carriage bolt

Pillow block*

Elevation block

Clamping block

Pillow-block shim

Washer

30°

Wooden wing

⅜ T-nut epoxied into wing

Bearing block

Cutterhead not shown.

Tilting fence assembly consists of a sliding table, a sliding tilt base, a tilt bracket and a fence, which can vary in size to suit the needs of the operator. Removing the fence-support top gives access to V-belt and arbor pulley.

30

blocks. The top edges of the bearing blocks are beveled at 30°, and the clamping blocks are slotted for clamping bolts. The clamping blocks, though not beveled, are set at a 30° angle to the top of the frame. The drawing (facing page) dimensions and locates these parts. Make sure when cutting duplicate parts that their dimensions and angles are precisely the same. This can be done by ripping and beveling a single board and then crosscutting identical parts to finished length. All the blocks must be oriented at a true 90° to the frame sides, and the clamping blocks ought to be positioned as close as possible to the center bearing blocks. The outer bearing blocks should be flush with the ends of the frame sides.

To add strength and to help position the parts during clamping, I cut narrow tenons on the bearing blocks and dadoes in the frame sides to house them. But you need not go to this trouble to get similar results—just clamp the frame sides together with the bearing and clamping blocks between, and then tap them into their exact positions with a mallet. This done, tighten the clamps, and bore for dowels through the frame sides into the blocks as shown in the drawing (¾-in. dia. holes for the bearing blocks, ⅜-in. dia. holes for the clamping blocks). The dowels will let you place the parts accurately when gluing up and will reinforce the frame assembly. The ¾-in. dowels are slotted and wedged. Since you're gluing end grain to long grain, epoxy is best; size the end grain before gluing and clamping. When the glue has set, sand the dowels flush with the frame sides.

The base, which you'll probably want to make while your table laminations are aging, is of ¾-in. high-density particleboard. Plywood will suffice, but it's more expensive and not as rigid or heavy. With a plan view that resembles a T, the stand is constructed using corner cleats, screws and yellow glue. This type of base has several advantages. One is that the motor is enclosed in a separate compartment, protected from dust and shavings. Another is that the shavings, being contained in a single bin, are easily removed. A third advantage of the T configuration is that the weight of the machine and the base rests on the three extreme points, and thus leveling is never required.

Surfacing the tables is easy if you have access to a thickness planer and a

Particleboard base contains separate compartments for the motor and for chips and shavings. Door to shavings bin slides up and down in rabbeted cleats. Opening in side under the infeed table gives quick access to the wing nut that must be loosened for making changes in depth of cut. The T configuration of the base concentrates the machine's weight on three points, eliminating the need to level it to the floor.

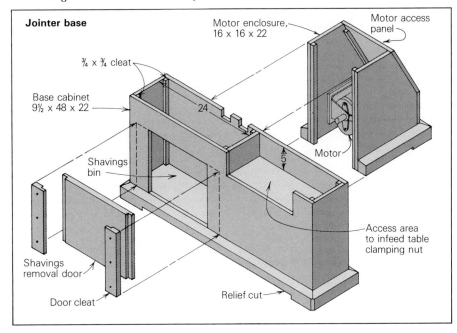

jointer wider than the one you're making. If you can't find a friend who'll let you use his, or a school shop where you can do this work, you'll probably have to pay to have it done at a local millwork or cabinet shop. You could even do it with hand planes, winding sticks and a straightedge, but you must be very patient to get the results required.

Begin by jointing one face of each table, being careful to take light cuts and to avoid sniping the ends. Then run both tables through the thickness planer for several light passes to bring them within ⅛ in. of their finished thickness. Again, be careful to set the planer's bedrolls properly to prevent snipe on the final pass.

Now place both tables upside down on a perfectly flat surface, butt them end to end, and separate them about 2 in. Get two small boards, each about 9 in. long, 2 in. wide and exactly ¾ in. thick, and put one across the outer edge of each table. Place the frame assembly upside down on the two boards, which will hold the frame ¾ in. above the bottoms of the tables. Position the frame and tables relative to one another, and check the spacing between the two tables to make sure there's room for the rotating cutterhead. Apply some yellow glue (or epoxy) to the top edges of the elevation blocks, and slide them into place between the inclined surfaces of the bearing blocks. Since the angles are complementary, the fit should be perfect. When installing the elevation blocks, don't wedge them too tightly under the bearing blocks; just bring the mating surfaces into light, uniform contact. If all eight elevation blocks are not exerting equal pressure against the bearing blocks, the tables will rock.

Securing the tables to the frame is accomplished by two ⅜-in. by 6-in. hanger bolts. The wood-thread ends are screwed at a 60° angle into the table bottoms. The machine-thread ends pass through the slots in the clamping blocks and are retained by homemade wing nuts (optional on the outfeed table). These have wood bodies with T-nuts epoxied into their centers. After the glue holding the elevation blocks in place has thoroughly dried, remove the frame assembly and bore angled pilot holes in the tables for the hanger bolts and screw them into place. Long hanger bolts are used in stairway handrailing; if you can't find any, buy a couple of long lag bolts, cut their heads off and die-cut National Coarse machine threads onto their unthreaded shoulders.

Now you can put the tables onto the wedged ways and clamp them in place with the wing nuts. Loosen each nut slightly and check to see that each table rides freely up and down the inclines and that there is no rock or play anywhere. If you detect any rocking, carefully remove a small amount of wood from the bearing surface of the opposite elevation block and check again.

When the tables fit and slide correctly, return the whole assembly (frame and tables) to your flat reference surface. With both tables resting flat on this surface, tighten the clamping nuts. Now take the whole thing back to wherever you did your initial jointing and surfacing, place your jointer upside down on the borrowed jointer and surface both tables in a single pass. Take a very light cut (1/32 in. or less) and check down the length of both tables at once

with an accurate straightedge. If they are truly straight and in the same plane, you can take your jointer back to your shop and continue construction. If not, find the source of the error (it could be in the iron machine), eliminate it and take another light cut the full length of both beds. Remove as little stock as possible, since you may want to surface the tables again in the future, should they warp out of true or their surfaces get badly gouged and pitted.

Surfacing complete, trim the tables to final width and cope an appropriately curved area where each table will extend over the cutterhead. The bandsaw is best for this. Don't cut the arcs so the blade exits on the top surface of the table, but rather so it exits on the end, about 3/16 in. below the top. This will produce a little land that makes the ends of the tables stronger, and leaves the straight lines across the tables intact. Keep the throat opening narrow.

The elevating mechanism for the infeed table consists of a ⅜-in. by 5-in. bolt epoxied into a wooden crank, a thrust block glued to the bottom of the infeed table and a T-nut countersunk into the end bearing block. The ⅜-in. National Coarse bolt has 16 threads per inch. Because the bolt moves the table up and down a 30° incline, and the sine of 30° equals 0.5, one revolution of the crank will move the table 1/32 in. vertically, a handy reference. You could mount a depth-of-cut indicator on one of the bearing blocks.

To change depth of cut, back off the clamping nut just enough to free the table, turn the crank to raise or lower it and retighten the nut. Excessive torque isn't necessary to hold the tables securely on their ways. For making the fine adjustments on the outfeed table, I keep the nut snug and smartly strike the end of the table with a wooden mallet to raise it slightly, or strike the end of the frame to lower it—similar to the way you tune a wooden handplane. Since the nut stays tight, you seldom need access to it. Mine doesn't even have wooden wings attached; I use a wrench when it needs adjusting.

To install the cutterhead, first dimension a pair of pillow-block support shims, which will hold the cutterhead at the proper height. Fiddle with the thickness of each shim to level the cutterhead with the tables. Screw the shims into place, replace the cutterhead and pillow blocks and mark the centers for

four holes to be drilled through the shims and frame sides. The diameter of the holes should be slightly larger than the ⅜-in. carriage bolts that will hold the pillow blocks in place. These bolts may have to be retightened from time to time, because seasonal shrinkage might loosen them. For safety, use self-locking nuts.

The fence assembly is mounted on a three-sided hardwood box. Its sides are notched to fit over the edge of the frame side, and it is held in place by two carriage bolts and two lag bolts. The plywood top of the fence-support box should sit about 1/16 in. higher than the level of the outfeed table. This clearance allows the fence table to slide freely across the jointer beds.

The fence itself can be made to any reasonable size, though its dimensions need not change those of the sliding fence table or the hinged tilting bracket and base. To make the table and tilting brackets, get some good ¾-in. birch plywood, and cut the three pieces to the sizes shown in the drawing on p. 30. Then cut two slots in the sliding table and two in the tilting bracket base. For hinging the parts together, you can cut a continuous hinge into three lengths or use three pairs of butt hinges. You may want to attach hardwood sled-type runners to the sides of the sliding table, as I have done. These will wear longer than plywood and will look better. Depending on the diameter of your arbor sheave, you might have to cove out an area on the underside of the fence support top to keep the belt from rubbing the wood. The fence table is locked in place by two wing nuts screwed onto ⅜-in. hanger bolts that extend through the table slots. The tilting bracket base is secured also by wing nuts screwed onto carriage bolts that extend through the fence table.

The cutterhead guard must be made of a sturdy hardwood (I used padauk). You may alter its standard shape as you please, so long as it moves easily away from the fence when stock is pushed against it and so long as it covers the unused portion of the rotating knives. The guard has a ⅜-in. bolt epoxied to it, and this bolt pivots in a hole in a mounting block that is screwed to the sides of the infeed table. A washer on the bolt between the mounting block and the bottom of the guard will ensure that the guard swings just clear of the jointer beds. A small tensioning spring holds

A look underneath the infeed table shows the positions of elevation blocks, clamping stud (hanger bolt) and thrust block, which contains elevation screw and crank. In the jointer frame underneath, you can see the inclined bearing blocks (ways), the slotted clamping block and the large wooden wing nut. The unfilled holes in the side of the frame remain from author's earlier experiment with a different means of securing the table to its ways. They have nothing to do with the existing arrangement.

Staff

Staff

Left, Winchip strikes end of jointer frame with a mallet to lower the outfeed table, just as in tuning a wooden handplane. Fore and index fingers on left hand detect the slight movement of elevation block as it travels minutely down the ways. Above, he joints the edge of an 8-ft., 5/4 red oak board.

33

the guard against the fence and against the stock being jointed.

I finished the machine with Watco oil and waxed the tops of the tables and the sliding surfaces on the wedged ways. The base I painted grey. No finish, however, makes wood completely impervious to moisture—I had to make slight adjustments in the outfeed table as its thickness changed minutely with the seasons. To correct any rocking or droop that might develop, insert paper shims between the bearing and elevation blocks. To spring-joint boards for gluing up panels, you could shim up the two inner elevation blocks on the outfeed table so that it slopes down from the cutterhead. A couple of pieces of notebook paper would be about right. Remember that the orientation of the outfeed table (both its angle and its height) determines whether the jointed edge will be slightly concave or slightly convex. If the table is high in relation to the knives, the jointed surface will be convex; if low, it will be concave. Also, it's a good idea to check the tables occasionally for proper alignment. Crank the infeed table up to the exact height of the outfeed table and then lay your straightedge across both beds. If there's any deviation from a true plane, remedy the error with paper shims between the bearing and elevation blocks.

Having spent quite a few years working in university wood shops, I'll be first to admit that industrial-duty machine tools offer greater built-in precision than shop-made machines. But the differences are small, and the advantages of being able to build your own machines are great. My first woodworking machines were home-workshop quality and were far inferior in terms of precision and stability to the shop-built ones I now use. Experience has taught me that good work depends as much on the skills of the craftsman and his sensitivity to factors that affect accuracy as on the built-in precision of his machinery. I have often observed students getting less than satisfactory results using good tools simply because they believed that machines should do accurate work in spite of the operator. The truth is, of course, that the operational skills and intuitive understanding of the craftsman are necessary to the precise work cabinetmaking demands. □

Galen Winchip, 29, is a professional woodworker and industrial-education instructor in Ames, Iowa.

Jointer safety

Some of the nastiest woodworking accidents result from careless or improper use of the jointer. A cutterhead rotating at 5,000 RPM looks seductively harmless; with its knives blurred into invisibility, all you see is a shimmering steel cylinder. Yet jointers regularly gobble up fingers, thumbs and sometimes hands. Surgical restoration is almost impossible—repairing tissue lost to a jointer is like trying to remake an original board from a pile of shavings. Such a nightmare can be avoided by being careful every time you use the jointer.

Before switching the machine on, make certain that the knives are firmly tightened in place. A loose knife can grab the work or come flying out of the cutterhead at high speed. Never use a jointer unless the cutterhead guard is in place. Even with the guard in place, large chips can be hurled from the machine with enough force to injure eyes. So always wear your safety goggles when jointing stock. Some jointers are equipped with a rabbeting table, and you must remove the guard to use this feature. But a jointer is not the best machine for rabbeting. It's better to use your table saw or spindle shaper or router. They do this job more safely and more efficiently. Though most jointers will cut as deeply as ¼ in. or more, you shouldn't take a cut any deeper than ⅛ in. in a single pass. You risk injury from kickback when taking too deep a cut, and you put unnecessary strain on the motor.

When jointing the edge of a board, keep your fingers well away from the table surface. When face-jointing stock, even thick stock, always use a push-block. Stock shorter than 12 in. should not be machine-jointed, so if your finished pieces will be less than a foot long, joint the longer board before you cut it up. For jointing stock thinner than ½ in., you should make a massive push-block, like the one shown below made by John Alcock-White for jointing one face of the ⅜-in. stock he laminates for bandsaw boxes. The block should be as wide and as long as the stock being jointed, and 4 in. to 6 in. thick.

Used over a long time for repetitive operations, the jointer's incessant drone can lull the operator into inattention. In such a semiconscious state, an accident is liable to happen. So be especially vigilant when your work is boring and perfunctory.

Posture and stance are also important. Learn to feed stock across the tables without overreaching and losing your balance. Adopt a posture that will allow you to exert consistent downward and horizontal pressure on the stock. This not only contributes to safety, but also affects the results of your work. When feeding, allow the machine to cut at its own pace. Don't force work into the cutterhead, or try to hurry the board across the tables. A slow to moderate feed rate is best, though pausing or creeping along during a cut can score the surface of the wood and overheat the knives.

The knives should be kept sharp, and should all be maintained at the exact height. You can touch up the edges periodically with the judicious use of a slipstone, but when knives are knicked or dulled beyond reason, you should have them reground. Instruct the person doing this to remove the same amount of steel from each knife. Improperly ground knives will put the cutterhead out of balance, which causes vibration and can lead to an accident, and will definitely bring about premature bearing failure. When sharpening, maintain the original bevel angle. If you try to hone or grind a secondary bevel on the edges, the result will be increased noise and vibration, and decreased cutting efficiency.

Constant alertness, common sense and a knowledge of cutterhead dynamics are the best safeguards against accidental injury. Used properly, a machine jointer makes a woodworker's task immeasurably lighter and introduces a high degree of precision into the work.

—*J.L.*

Wooden-Drum Stroke Sander
Shop-built machine saves space and money

by A.W. Marlow

Surely every woodworker, amateur as well as professional, needs a stroke sander to relieve him of the tedious, time-consuming hand-sanding of large flat surfaces. Everything about my contraption is crude and inexpensive. I built it when we were just crawling out of the Depression. Nothing was bought that could be homemade. After hand-sanding one or two tabletops, I discovered that if I wanted to eat regularly, a stroke sander was in order. So I had to match its design requirements with the money and space available.

A stroke sander is not a complicated machine. The upper part consists of an electric motor, two main drums, a tensioning/tracking idler drum and a metal framework to hold these components in the proper working relation to one another. The lower part of the machine is a table for holding the workpiece. This table is raised or lowered, depending on the thickness of the stock being sanded, and travels front to back beneath the moving sanding belt.

To operate the machine, the workpiece is laid on the table, which is elevated until the belt is about ¼ in. above the surface to be sanded. With the power on, one hand moves the table in and out below the moving belt, while the other hand presses down, moving forward and back, on the smooth side of the belt with a wooden platen. The amount of pressure on the platen and its movement must be coordinated with the in-and-out movement of the table. Sanding with this machine is like trying to pat your head and rub your belly at

the same time, but once you get the hang of it, work proceeds quickly, and all that's left prior to finishing is a light and easy hand-sanding with a finer grit.

I had to have a machine that would handle stock up to 7 ft. long, but one that would occupy minimal space in my shop. So I decided to place it in a corner, where I could suspend the upper parts of the machine from the wall and support the sanding table on the top of a storage cabinet. Instead of starting with a preconceived design and buying all the hardware initially, I let the thing evolve, meeting each technical problem as it showed its ugly face and buying metal materials as I learned what was needed. The bill of materials for the ma-

A stroke sander makes short work of smoothing large flat surfaces. Marlow built the machine below about 40 years ago, and used no factory-made drums or other hard-to-find materials. To make the most of shop space, he mounted the sanding table on top of a storage cabinet. End view of stroke sander, right, shows the relative positions of drive system and tensioning/tracking idler assembly. Arched block in foreground houses acme-thread screw that raises and lowers the sanding table. Photos, except where noted: Andy Marlow.

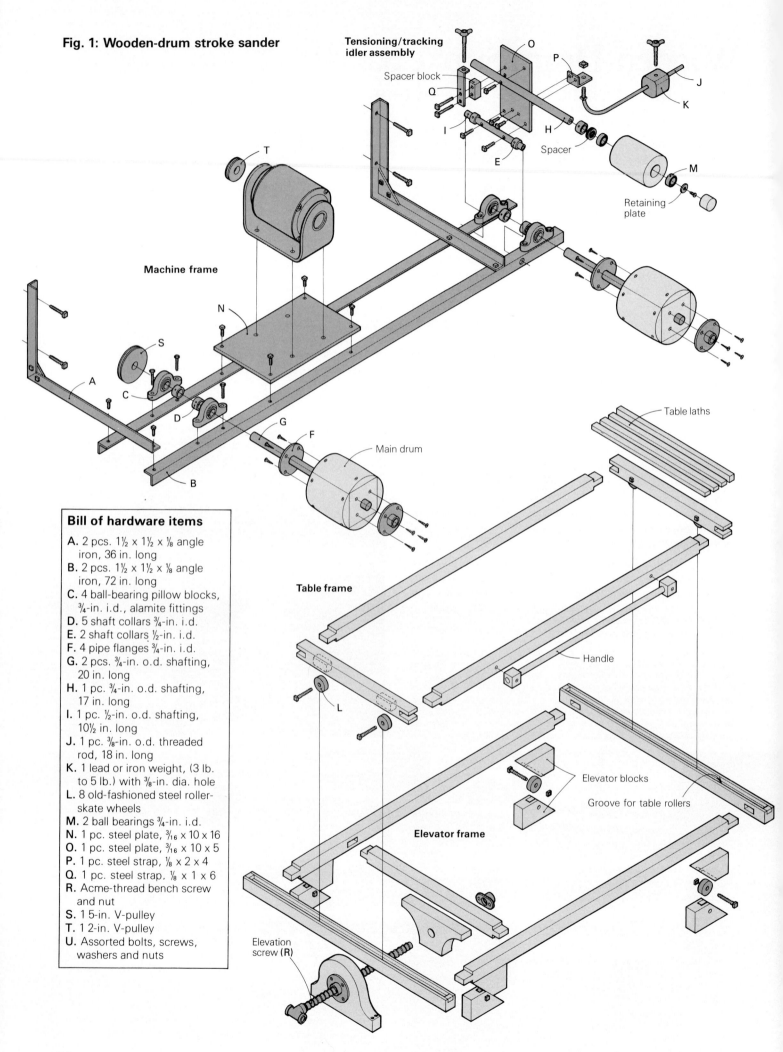

Fig. 1: Wooden-drum stroke sander

Tensioning/tracking idler assembly

Spacer block

O

P

Q

I

H

E

J

K

Spacer

M

Retaining plate

T

Machine frame

N

S

C

A

D

B

G

F

Main drum

Table laths

Table frame

Handle

L

Elevator blocks

Groove for table rollers

Elevator frame

Elevation screw (R)

Bill of hardware items

A. 2 pcs. 1½ x 1½ x ⅛ angle iron, 36 in. long
B. 2 pcs. 1½ x 1½ x ⅛ angle iron, 72 in. long
C. 4 ball-bearing pillow blocks, ¾-in. i.d., alamite fittings
D. 5 shaft collars ¾-in. i.d.
E. 2 shaft collars ½-in. i.d.
F. 4 pipe flanges ¾-in. i.d.
G. 2 pcs. ¾-in. o.d. shafting, 20 in. long
H. 1 pc. ¾-in. o.d. shafting, 17 in. long
I. 1 pc. ½-in. o.d. shafting, 10½ in. long
J. 1 pc. ⅜-in. o.d. threaded rod, 18 in. long
K. 1 lead or iron weight, (3 lb. to 5 lb.) with ⅜-in. dia. hole
L. 8 old-fashioned steel roller-skate wheels
M. 2 ball bearings ¾-in. i.d.
N. 1 pc. steel plate, ³⁄₁₆ x 10 x 16
O. 1 pc. steel plate, ³⁄₁₆ x 10 x 5
P. 1 pc. steel strap, ⅛ x 2 x 4
Q. 1 pc. steel strap, ⅛ x 1 x 6
R. Acme-thread bench screw and nut
S. 1 5-in. V-pulley
T. 1 2-in. V-pulley
U. Assorted bolts, screws, washers and nuts

chine (opposite page) includes only items that were truly needed and could be scavenged or purchased from local iron-mongers and hardware dealers.

The machine frame—Begin construction by fabricating the angle-iron machine frame (figure 1) for supporting the motor and drums. Use the two 36-in. lengths of angle iron for making the wall brackets. Cut in each a 90° notch 14 in. from the end, and bend the pieces to form a right angle (with flanges to the inside, you need a right-hand bracket and left-hand bracket). Strengthen the resulting miter joint with either a weld or a strap bolted across the angle. Drill two ¼-in. holes in each vertical (14-in.) arm; then two ¼-in. holes in each horizontal arm for attaching the 6-ft. rails. These holes should be drilled on 8¾-in. centers, with the first hole ¾ in. from the end of the bracket. Now you can mount the brackets to the wall. Position them 42 in. above the floor and about 62 in. apart. This distance can be exact on a masonry wall where you must bore for expanding lead inserts, but it will vary on a framed wall where you must screw the brackets directly to the studs.

After mounting the support brackets to the wall, temporarily clamp the 6-ft. rails in place and mark them for matching bolt holes. If all is correct, the right-hand ends of these rails should overshoot the right bracket about 10 in. to make room for the tracking/tensioning assembly and the pillow blocks for the right-hand drum. Also drill four ¼-in. holes in the 10-in. by 16-in. steel plate needed for mounting the motor. This mounting plate should be attached to the rails about 20 in. from the left end, so clamp it in place here and mark for holes in the rails. Now bore two ½-in. holes in the vertical flanges of the angle iron about 7 in. from the right-hand ends. These holes will accommodate the tension/tracking-plate pivot shaft.

The only holes remaining to be drilled in the long rails are those for mounting the pillow blocks. Alignment of these is crucial for belt tracking. So rather than mark for these holes when you first clamp the rails to the brackets, it is advisable to bolt the long rails to the brackets as for permanent attachment, even though you will have to remove them later to drill the holes. Using a carpenter's framing square, scribe a centerline across both front and back rail irons about 1 in. from the right end and 11 in. from the left end. Determine the distance between the two mounting holes in each pillow block and lay out matching holes on the irons. After drilling these, bolt the frame assembly together into one unit.

The main drums—The next step is to make the main drums. Figure 2 shows the number and dimensions of the parts required for each. Buy enough No. 2 white pine to make both drums. All pieces must measure exactly 1³⁄₁₆ in. thick. First, saw the four end pieces 4¾ in. by 4¾ in. Next, mark the exact center on two of these squares. Clamp one of the marked squares on top of an unmarked one, and with a drill press, accurately bore a ¾-in. hole through both at once. Repeat this operation with the other pair. Now cut the four narrow side pieces 4¾ in. by 6 in. (precisely the same width as the squares). Then cut the wide side pieces 7⅛ in. by 6 in. long. Draw centerlines down the length of all eight pieces, and measure out 1⅝ in. on both sides of the line and about ⅝ in. in from each end. This will give two bore centers on each end of all eight pieces. Counterbore on these centers ½-in. holes

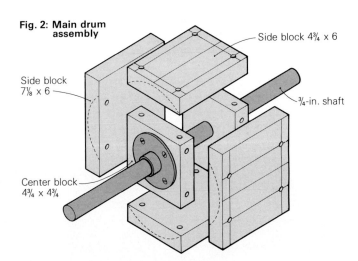

Fig. 2: Main drum assembly

Side block 4¾ x 6

¾-in. shaft

Side block 7⅛ x 6

Center block 4¾ x 4¾

Assemble the parts of the drum blank with the two end blocks held in alignment by the shaft. Remove finished blank from shaft and bandsaw it to a rough cylinder. Replace blank on shaft and mount it in machine frame, which becomes a makeshift lathe. Turn the drum true, leaving a ⅛-in. crown in the center.

to a depth of ⅝ in. Bore ¹¹⁄₆₄-in. clearance holes through the remaining wood thickness.

To keep the parts of the ends of the drum blank in alignment as you assemble them, take one of the 20-in. shafts and slide it through the holes in two of the squares. Spread the squares 6 in. apart, and be sure the grain runs from top to bottom on both blocks. Apply some yellow glue to the end grain of one of the squares, place one of the narrow side pieces flush with the end and even on both sides and screw it down tightly using 1¼-in. #8 woodscrews. Now shift the other square into proper alignment, and glue and screw it in place. If necessary, bore small pilot holes to start the screws. Turn the unit 180° and fasten the other narrow side piece. Next, attach the two wider side pieces in the same manner. You can at this point (if your bandsaw is big enough) mark out a 7-in. dia. circle on the end of each turning blank and rough-cut the circle. This will save time when turning the blanks into cylinders.

The drums are secured to the shafts with ¾-in. I.D. pipe flanges. Prepare the flanges by boring out the threads with a ¾-in. drill or by removing enough of the threads with a round file to allow the shaft to slide through. Next bore a ⁷⁄₃₂-in. hole in each hub, and thread each hole with a ¼-20 tap for receiving a setscrew. Now secure the drums, flanked by two flanges, on their shafts and slide one of the shafts into the left-hand pillow-block bearings. With the shaft collars in place, spread so they just touch the inside of the blocks, tighten all the setscrews. Bolt your motor (⅓ HP, 1,725 RPM) on its mounting plate and tighten a 2½-in. dia. V-pulley on the shaft. I recently installed another motor on my sander and its rotation is opposite from the original, so I installed the plywood outrigger shown in the photos. Slide a 4-in. V-pulley on the main shaft, position it in line with the motor pulley and tighten the setscrew. You now have a makeshift lathe for truing up the diameters of the drums.

A tool rest for turning must now be devised. The simplest is a steel bar or pipe supported at each end in some manner. Even with a good rest the RPM is so low that it would make a good turner cry, but the wood is soft and there are only two to do. Close to a 7-in. dia. is what to strive for, but more important is that there be about a ⅛-in. crown in the center. Do not allow the center to be flat or concave; that would mean

Tensioning/tracking idler assembly pivots on a ½-in. shaft in the frame to tension the belt. The idler drum rotates on a ¾-in. shaft that pivots on a bolt across the axis of the shaft. Photo: Staff.

Pivoted to its extreme left-hand position, the tension/tracking assembly can be seen in its entirety. The tensioning weight (here tied to a brick) fits onto a bent rod, which is attached to the pivoting plate by means of a flange. The thumbscrew adjustment at the top of the plate is used to control belt tracking. Photo: Staff.

trouble in tracking. Sand the turning with 60-grit paper, using calipers to be sure the ends are both the same diameter. Remove the drum and install the other to turn in like manner.

The tensioning/tracking assembly—First study the photos on this page and figure 1 (p. 36). Assuming that you've bored two ½-in. holes in the long rails to house the tensioning/tracking shaft, proceed to prepare the plate for bolting to the pivot shaft and for mounting the idler-drum shaft and tracking-adjustment screw. Drill two ¹³⁄₆₄-in. holes along the 5-in. edge of the plate as shown in figure 1. Lay this plate on top of the ½-in. shaft, which should extend equally on both sides. Mark the shaft for boring ¹¹⁄₆₄-in. holes, and drill and tap these for ³⁄₁₆-in. by ½-in. bolts. That will take care of the hinged bottom edge.

Along the top edge of the plate will be mounted the ¾-in. by 17-in. idler shaft. This shaft pivots on a ¼-in. by 1-in. hinge bolt to track the sanding belt. Bore a ⁷⁄₃₂-in. hole for the bolt 1 in. down from the top and 1 in. in from the right edge; then tap the hole for ¼-20 threads. Now bore a ¼-in. hole through the shaft 5 in. from one end.

Next prepare the ⅛-in. by 1-in. by 6-in. strap for installing on the plate. Before bending the strap, drill a ⁷⁄₃₂-in. hole ½ in. from one end, and tap this hole for insertion of the ½-in. dia. tracking-adjustment screw. At the other end, bore two ¹⁷⁄₆₄-in. holes for mounting the bracket to the plate. Now you can bend the strap 90° to produce a 1-in. flange on the threaded end. Provide a wooden spacer block (¹⁄₃₂ in. thicker than ¾ in. so the shaft can move freely) for mounting the strap. Bore this block for clearance holes and insert the bolts through the strap and the block. Then take the assembly over to the plate and position it in the upper left-hand corner, straddling the idler shaft. Pivot the idler shaft until it is precisely parallel with the top edge of the plate; then shift the strap and block up or down to equalize the space between the flange and the block. Mark and bore two ⁷⁄₃₂-in. holes and tap them for ¼-20 threads.

The photo above right shows a flanged 2-in. by 4-in. plate bolted to the bottom of the tensioning/tracking plate. This smaller plate is for mounting the tension bar and weight. The bar is best made from a ⅜-in. threaded rod about 18 in. long;

it is equipped with a 3-lb. to 5-lb. weight (more if necessary), which slides up and down the rod and is fixed at the proper place with a thumbscrew. Bore one end of the plate to receive the rod, and bore two ¼-in. holes in the other end for mounting bolts. Bend the plate 90° to produce a 1½-in. flange on the end with the two holes. Then center the small plate on the tensioning/tracking plate so the mounting holes are about 1 in. above the pivot shaft. Mark and bore two ⁷⁄₃₂-in. holes for attaching the weight plate; tap them and then bolt the small plate in place.

Now slide a shaft collar onto each end of the pivot shaft, and insert the shaft in the two ½-in. holes in the long rails, taking care to center the plate between the rails and to spread the collars so they just touch the inside edges of the angle iron. Tighten the setscrews to secure the collars.

Now turn to making the idler drum. Dimension two pieces of wood 7 in. by 4½ in. by 2 in. thick. Down the center of each piece, plow a groove ¾ in. wide by ⅜ in. deep. When the two halves are glued together, these channels should align to make a ¾-in. square hole through the drum blank for accommodating the shaft. Having glued up the halves and left them in the clamps overnight, cut the blank to a finished length of 6 in., making sure the ends are square. Now make a pair of tapered plugs, each ¾ in. long, ¹¹⁄₁₆ in. square at one end and ¹³⁄₁₆ in. square at the other. Seat them solidly in the ¾-in. square holes, and mark their centers for turning.

Mount the blank between centers in a lathe and turn as you did the belt drums, leaving a ⅛-in. crown in the middle. Measure accurately the O.D. of the ball-bearing race, and turn a snug-fitting recess for it ¼ in. deeper than the width of the bearing race, leaving enough wood to keep the center intact. Remove and flip the piece end for end, carefully find the centers and turn a recess in the other end. After turning, the remaining wood can be bored out on the drill press. Insert bearings, slide the pulley on the shaft and if (for any reason) it does not run true, it can be placed on the main left-hand shaft temporarily and turned true, using a flange for driving. This idler must run true to keep vibration at a minimum.

The front end of the shaft should have a tapped hole in its center for a ³⁄₁₆-in. R.H. machine screw to hold a retaining plate for the bearing. The plate can be a washer with an

Grooved track in the side member of the elevation frame accommodates skate wheels on the bottom of the traveling sanding table. Blocks glued in grooves stop the table travel. Anchor block beneath crossmember in frame holds nut for elevation screw.

O.D. larger than ¾ in. On the shaft at the rear bearing, a number of washers or a short sleeve will be needed to fill the space between bearing and collar. When a wing or thumb bolt is turned into the tapped ¼-in. hole for tracking adjustment, this unit should be operable.

The elevator frame and carriage track—To make the most efficient use of space beneath the machine, begin by constructing a storage cupboard; its top should be 29 in. high. This completed, start work on the elevator frame and carriage track (photo above). Made of softwood, the track bars are 1¾ in. square and 36 in. long. Plow grooves down their lengths, ¼ in. deep and 1⁄16 in. wider than the skate wheels. Stop the grooves front and rear by gluing in little blocks. The front and rear frame members, also 1¾ in. square, are 48 in. long. These are positioned 22 in. apart and tenoned into the track bars. A crossmember, to which you will later attach the elevator-screw anchor block, is tenoned into the frame members 8 in. in from the left-hand track.

The elevator frame is raised and lowered on four pairs of blocks, their mating surfaces inclined at 45°. The bottom ones (bearing blocks) are 1¾ in. thick, 2¾ in. high and 5½ in. long and are fitted with steel roller-skate wheels. The top angled corners must be mortised out sufficiently to allow the skate wheels to revolve freely when placed so the wheel's radius extends ⅜ in. above the wood. The upper blocks (elevation blocks) are grooved along their inclined surfaces 1⁄16 in. wider than the skate wheels and ¼ in. deep. All blocks are drilled and counterbored for attaching to frame and cabinet top with screws.

Fasten the elevation blocks to the frame, and place four shims under the frame at each corner, holding it off the cabinet top just enough to clear the bottom of the elevation blocks. Now center the frame front-to-back under the belt and position it end-to-end about 3 in. in from the extreme right of the long angle-iron rails. Apply glue to the bottoms of the bearing blocks and slide them into place under the elevation blocks. Allow the glue to set overnight; then lift off the frame and seat the necessary wood screws.

Shown in figure 1 is the elevation-screw anchor block. It's about 3 in. wide and 8 in. long and should be bored to receive the nut for the acme-thread bench screw. After the nut is installed, screw the block to the bottom of the crossmember. The position of the fixed block will depend on the length of the screw you use.

The traveling table—The sanding table consists of a carriage frame, which is fitted with skate wheels, and a slatted top for holding the workpiece. Using open mortise-and-tenon joints, make the carriage frame 22 in. wide and 48 in. long from 1¾-in. square stock. About 3 in. in from the front and rear, cut mortises for the skate wheels. Then bore the sides of the mortises for axle holes, which will allow the wheels to extend ⅜ in. below the frame. The carriage frame must travel back and forth freely in the tracks.

Now cut a bunch of laths about ⅝ in. thick, 1 in. wide and 22 in. long. The far right-hand strip should be ⅜ in. thicker than the rest, as it will act as a stop for the workpiece. Space them about ½ in. apart and fasten them to the carriage frame with glue and countersunk screws or nails.

Now fashion a handle for getting a comfortable hold on the table. I find a long, ¾-in. dowel held at each end by blocks to be good enough. All that remains is to make a platen from soft pine. It ought to be about 5 in. wide and 7 in. long and slightly beveled at the ends. Attach a handle that pleases you and when in use rub the contacting surface occasionally with a cake of beeswax.

Because this machine generates a lot of dust, I recommend that you hook it up to a dust-collection system of some kind. I have made an inexpensive dust-collection head from downspouting and scrap pieces of sheet metal, and connected the head via a flexible hose to an old blower that I scavenged from an oil burner.

Sanding belts—I use Norton Adalox 60-grit production paper, which can be purchased in 6-in. wide rolls from most industrial-supply stores and is cheaper than cloth belting. To determine the length of the belt, prop up the tracking idler and measure the distance around the pulleys and the idler with a steel tape. Add 2 in. to this and you've got the length of your belt. Now splice the ends together. Both of the ends should be cut at complementary 60° angles, using a sharp knife; these angles must be exact or the belt will not run true. Dimension two clamping blocks (2½ in. by 9 in. by ¾ in. thick) and, to pad the clamping blocks, cut 20 pieces of newspaper the same size.

With the smooth side up, bring the two ends of the belt together, and place one of the clamping blocks evenly under the joint, having first covered the block with one piece of newspaper. Using two short, thin brads, tack the belt onto the block. Then carefully butt the other end to the first and brad it in place.

Tightly woven linen makes the best splicing material. Cut two strips of the cloth 9 in. long, one 1 in. wide, the other 2 in. wide. Spread a thin coat of white glue on the narrow strip and lay it evenly across the joint; coat the wider strip with glue and lay it evenly over the narrow one. Center the pad of newspaper over the splice, and clamp the second block on top of the pad. Allow this to sit overnight, and then remove the clamps, carefully lift the belt from the brads and trim off the excess cloth. □

Andy Marlow is a consulting editor to this magazine.

Methods of Work

Sharpening jointer knives—two ways

Here's how I sharpen jointer or thickness-planer knives on the table saw. Mount a 6-in. medium-grit emery wheel on the saw's arbor. Then clamp a straight-edged guide board across the table in front of the wheel. Fit the knife in a block that's been grooved along one edge. Be sure the groove is uniformly deep and parallel to the opposite edge of the block, and that the knife is firmly seated at the bottom of the groove.

Adjust the height of the emery wheel to touch the center of the knife's bevel. Keeping the block flat against the table, pass the knife slowly back and forth across the wheel. Take the lightest of cuts. Duplicate this on the other knives. Slowly raise the wheel until each knife is ground to a feather edge. Honing the knives on an oilstone completes the sharpening.

—*Charlie K. Thorne, San Luis Obispo, Calif.*

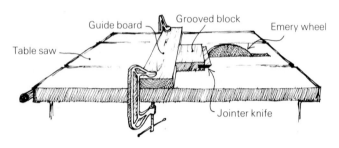

Table saw — Guide board — Grooved block — Emery wheel — Jointer knife

I sharpen jointer and planer knives on the table saw using the miter gauge. The approach offers several advantages: The knife edges are stronger (because they're straight-ground rather than hollow-ground), the grinding angle adjusts easily and the fixture handles long knives (up to 24 in.).

To make the fixture, drill and tap two holes in the slide of your miter gauge and fasten the plywood base of the fixture to the slide with machine screws. Now screw the top part of the fixture to the base so that the blade is sandwiched and clamped snugly in place. Install two adjuster bolts from the back edge of the fixture into nuts that have been mortised and epoxied into the base. Turn these bolts to adjust the first knife into perfect position. The bolts provide a reference for the last two knives so they will be ground exactly like the first.

—*Jack Down, Maseru, Lesotho*

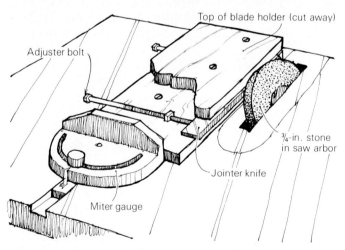

Adjuster bolt — Top of blade holder (cut away) — ¾-in. stone in saw arbor — Jointer knife — Miter gauge

Improved knife-sharpening fixture

When I tried to adapt James Gier's drill-press jointer-knife sharpening fixture (Methods, *FWW* #23) to the small knives in my 8-in. jointer, I ran into several problems. The biggest problem was positioning a row of thumbscrews to hold the narrow knife so they wouldn't interfere with the cupstone. I modified the design as shown above right.

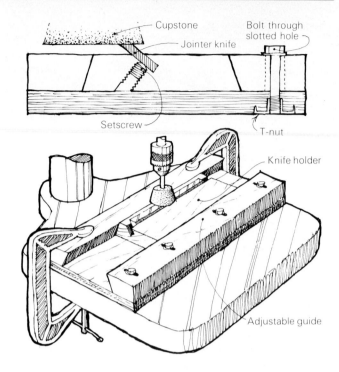

Cupstone — Jointer knife — Bolt through slotted hole — Setscrew — T-nut — Knife holder — Adjustable guide

First I replaced the top-side thumbscrews with hex-head setscrews tightened from the bottom side of the sliding knife-holder block. Second, I beveled the edges of the block and the guide channel for a dovetail arrangement, so the block won't tip as it runs under the cupstone. So it can be adjusted, the rear guide is fastened with bolts through slotted holes to T-nuts in the base. For a first-rate job, use Rosann inserts (available from Constantine) to hold the setscrews. Take extremely light cuts and preserve the setting of the first knife with the quill-stop.   —*Tom E. Moore, Springfield, Va.*

Other router-table improvements

I see the advantage of mounting an extra router base under the router table, but instead of groping around under the table to release the router or feel for switches and adjustment knobs, I've installed both an aluminum insert and a switch-controlled receptacle so I can perform all those operations up front with greater convenience and safety.

I made the 10-in. square table insert from ¼-in. thick aluminum plate. I chose aluminum over mild steel because it's easier to drill out the mounting and spindle hole and, if polished, is almost friction-free. The insert is held with two

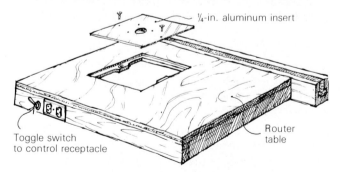

¼-in. aluminum insert — Toggle switch to control receptacle — Router table

countersunk flat-head machine screws into *T*-nuts in the table top. An accurately inlaid insert won't vibrate.

I mounted the switch and receptacle on the front of the router table. You can use any type of switch—just make sure it will carry the amperage. You will find plenty of other uses for the switch-controlled outlets (drills, sanders, etc.). Just unplug the router when you don't want it to run.

—*D. B. Neagley, Groveland, Calif.*

Cutting circles on the bandsaw

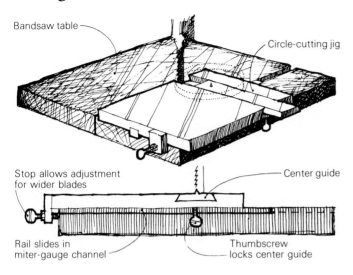

Bandsaw table

Circle-cutting jig

Stop allows adjustment for wider blades

Center guide

Rail slides in miter-gauge channel

Thumbscrew locks center guide

The circle-cutting jig I use in my shop offers several advantage. First, because the jig uses the miter-gauge slot in the saw's table, no clamps are necessary. This not only saves time but also guarantees perfect size duplication even if the jig is removed from the saw. Second, since the jig's base stays in a fixed position relative to the blade, you can put marks on the base to calibrate circle sizes. Third, you can reverse the sliding-dovetail center guide to cut large circles. And last, an adjustable stop can easily be added on the front of the jig so it can be used with a variety of blades. The stop ensures that cutting always takes place at the true tangent of the circle.

To use, set the center guide to the desired radius, lock it in place with the setscrew and place the circle blank on the center pin. If the blank cannot have a center hole in it, then cut a dummy disc from plywood and secure the blank to the dummy disc with double-sided tape. With the jig's rail riding in the saw's miter-gauge slot, ease the jig straight into the blade until the stop contacts the front of the saw table. Then turn the blank until the circle is completed.

Although you can make the jig from solid stock, it is easier to make the dovetail slot if you laminate the base. My jig is made of acrylic plastic, threaded for the two thumbscrews. If you use wood, epoxy in square nuts for the thumbscrews.
—*Thomas G. Marston, Mill Creek, W. Va.*

Follow-up on stroke sanders

Andy Marlow has a nice homebuilt stroke sander (p. 35). But I must take exception to the business of crowning the main drums. About 15 years ago, I built a 4-in. wide two-drum stroke sander. At the time of construction, I had the pleasure of meeting Dick Merrill of Woodcraft Supply, the innovator of their Mark II sharpening system. His advice was, "use only one crowned pulley, and the longer the belt, the better." I built my sander with a flat driver and a slightly crowned "cocking" pulley. It worked flawlessly. Since then, I've seen more problems associated with multiple-crowned pulleys in a drive. With more than one crowned pulley, it's virtually impossible to align the imaginary centers of the pulleys to each other. As a result, the various crowns fight each other, causing erratic side-to-side belt motion. Observe the commercial sanders. The driving pulley is flat, the idler pulley crowned. Incidentally, too much crown will break the back of the belt, so don't crown over ⅛ in. per foot each side of center. For optimum traction, lag the driving pulley with rubber. Crosswise strips glued on are almost as good as a solid sheet, particularly if you can't grind the surface flat. There are several graphite composites available to apply to the stroker to reduce heat and increase belt life. Also, design your drive to run the belt faster than 1500 surface feet per minute for optimum belt life.   —*W.B. Newbold, Milford, N.H.*

In A.W. Marlow's article on the stroke sander he discusses splicing the sanding belt and the importance of cutting the same angle on both ends. The desired result can be obtained by laying the two ends of the strip on top of one another after giving one end a single twist, thus placing the abrasive side of one end adjacent to the back side of the other. Align the edges of the two ends over a distance of 18 in., then cut through both with the same cut of a sharp knife. No matter what angle is cut the ends will fit and align perfectly.
—*C.D. Iddings, Tulsa, Okla.*

Here are a few notes for another approach to stroke-sander design. I made my drums from ¾-in. plywood rings with solid plywood end plates (two layers at each end). The shaft is locked to the drum by two steel cross-pins inserted through a hole in the shaft and sandwiched in a recess between the end

plates. The pin at one end is set at 90° to the pin at the other.

The tracking mechanism shown in the photo consists of a turnbuckle on each side of the idler drum, with a pivoting angle-iron arm. This arrangement allows accurate tracking adjustment and belt tightening, and quick belt changes (a wing nut releases the turnbuckle from a stud screwed into the sander frame). I mounted the sliding table rails on vertical shelf standards, permitting gross table-height adjustment for sanding work of various thicknesses, such as completed drawer assemblies. The top portion of the sanding belt rides over a 12 in. by 48 in. hardwood platen, providing a sanding surface for hand-held objects.

I purchase rolls of floor-sander abrasive belts (12 in. wide), glue them into stroke-sander lengths, then rip the belt down the center for two 6-in. belts. For the joint, I use an overlapped angled splice with silicone caulk as adhesive. Scrape off the abrasive in the splice area. Finally, put the power switch at the tracking-adjustment end of the sander. Otherwise, one does a quick sawdust shuffle from one end of the machine to the other after replacing a belt and trying to reach the adjustment device before the belt runs off the drum.
—*Bruce Bozman, Addison, N.Y.*

HAND TOOLS

Grinding
Use your tool rest only as a fence

by Frank Klausz

Grinding is the first step in shaping the bevel on a cutting tool. It makes the edge straight and square and puts the bevel at the proper angle. It is not necessary to regrind every time you sharpen; a properly ground edge can be honed many times. I grind damaged tools and new tools that have been incorrectly ground. I also regrind tools after repeated sharpening has flattened the hollow grind; it's easier to hone a hollow grind. In my apprentice years, we did not use a motorized grinding wheel. We had a flat, rough whetstone about 8 in. by 4 in. by 3 in. that sat in a wooden basin with a couple of inches of water. I spent many hours at that stone, and every week the worst job in the shop was to change the water and clean out the wooden basin so you could see the bottom. Flat grinding on such a waterstone and honing on a fine, grey stone produces the best edge, and it holds up longer than a hollow-ground edge, but if you have to remove a lot of metal, it takes a long time to do and a lot of sweat.

For faster, easier grinding, use an electric grinder with a 60-grit aluminum-oxide wheel, rotating toward you at 3,000 RPM. I prefer a 1-in. or wider wheel at least 6 in. in diameter. Wheels smaller than 4 in. in diameter give too deep a hollow grind. I keep the wheel clean and dressed with a carborundum block; a glazed stone will not cut well, and can overheat the tool. My grinder has a cover around the back of the wheel and a transparent shield on top. I get gooseflesh when I see a grindstone spinning freely with no cover and no safety glass for the operator. Protect your eyes.

My grinder also has a standard tool rest whose angle and closeness to the wheel are adjustable. But I never change it. The only part of the tool rest I use is the lower edge, as a guide for my right index finger. The tool need not lay flat

against the surface of the tool rest. If it did, you'd have to adjust it for each tool, depending on the steel and the work. Less dense woods require more acute angles, and hard steel can hold its edge ground to such smaller angles. Chisel and plane blades should be ground to 25° or 30°. To determine these angles, compare the width of the bevel with the thickness of the blade. The face of a 30° bevel is twice as wide as the thickness of the blade; a 25° bevel is two and one-third times as wide as the thickness of the blade. By the time you get the tool-rest angle right, you can have finished grinding, if you use the tool rest only as a one-point guide.

Hold the blade in your right hand between your index finger and thumb, about in the middle of the blade. Lay the tool on the tool rest and bring the edge toward the wheel until your index finger touches the back edge of the tool rest. If the wheel touches only the tip of the blade, move your finger down a bit. If the wheel touches the blade before your finger touches the tool rest, move your finger up a bit. Once you've found the right place, keep your finger there and use it as a stop to slide against the tool rest. Move the blade right and left, applying light pressure on the blade with the fingers of your left hand. There are only two supports for the blade— the index finger at the bottom edge of the tool rest and the wheel itself. This ensures that the hollow grind will be even. Keep the blade moving back and forth across the wheel and dip the edge often in water. When the beads of water on the tool evaporate, dip again. Don't get any blue mark on the chisel because that means you have raised its temperature to where it has lost its temper and however sharp an edge you get, it will dull easily. As the grind nears the edge of the tool, the danger of burning increases because the thin metal heats up fast. This metal will be your cutting edge and its temper is critical. You should get sure enough of the position of the blade in your right hand to be able to free your left hand to spray the edge with water from a spray bottle as you grind. It takes practice, but no jig will provide the feelings you will learn to recognize when you are grinding properly.   □

Frank Klausz builds and restores furniture in Bedminster, N.J. For more on his methods, including his sharpening techniques, see FWW #18, Sept. '79.

 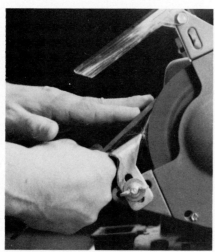 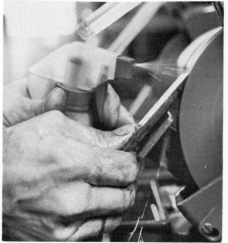 

The proper position for the index finger of the right hand, which rides against the bottom of the tool rest, will produce an initial grind mark about in the middle of the bevel, left. If the grind mark is too high, lower your finger; if the mark is too low, raise your finger. While grinding, second photo from left, the blade does not necessarily rest on the flat of the tool rest; the position of the index finger determines the bevel angle. As the grind nears the edge of the blade, it becomes easy to overheat it. Learn to control the tool with only your right hand, freeing your left to spray the edge with water as you grind, second photo from right. At right, the hollow-ground bevel directly off the grinder.

How to Sharpen
A keen edge makes all the difference

by Ian J. Kirby

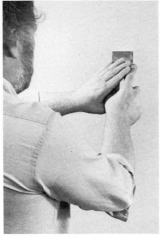

Putting the cutting edge on a chisel or plane iron causes confusion, doubt and fear in many beginning woodworkers. Yet once the tool's edge has been ground (to the appropriate angle and square to its long edges), sharpening takes only about one minute. A sharp tool is the difference between despair and delight—you need to sharpen often and without any fuss. After sharpening, a plane not only feels different as it cuts, it also sounds different—when it's blunt it cuts with a dull and heavy tone, but when it's sharp it sings.

What is it we have to do by sharpening? The diagram below shows a magnified section through a blade. The rounded edge at A is blunt; B, with the surfaces meeting at a straight line, is sharp. If we remove metal in the shaded area (C), we will have a sharp edge. But if we first grind the tool to a 25° angle and then sharpen to a 35°angle, we can accomplish the same thing more efficiently by removing a very tiny amount of metal (D). The grind can be hollow or flat; it matters little. What does matter is the 35° sharpening angle. The amount of metal we have to remove is measured in angstroms—at most, a few thousandths of an inch. In order to sharpen the blade, there is really very little work to do.

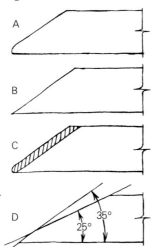

The important considerations in learning how to sharpen are how to hold the tool, how and where to stand, and how to use your body to move the tool over the stone. The photos at right give these answers. One of the things we have to achieve is controlled pressure across the cutting edge; the other necessary control is maintaining the constant angle between blade and stone. The grip shown in the photos provides both of these controls. With either chisel or plane iron, the index fingers of both hands are on top of the tool. Pressure can be exerted uniformly, or on one side of the blade or on the other side— whatever the tool requires. Angular control also comes from this two-hand grip, from the wrists, and subsequently from the shoulders, but the key to it is the thumb of the left hand. It acts as a fulcrum or back rest, and with the hand spread this way it is easy to keep the left thumb solidly locked in position. You find the angle in the first place by feeling for the grinding bevel, or by checking against a block of wood cut to 35°. Then, the left hand becomes a very sensitive jig.

What kind of stone is best? The type of stone you use is a matter of preference. You really need only two stones, a medium and a fine, provided you have some other way of grinding the edge (and if not, a coarse stone and some elbow grease will do it). They can be either oilstones or waterstones, although it's unwise to have one of each. The function of the

For chisels or plane irons, the sharpening grip is the same. Grasp the blade in the right hand, far enough forward to plant the index finger atop the edge (above left). This hand holds the iron and provides both power and pressure. Then make an L of the left hand, place the fingers atop the blade, and the thumb underneath (above right). This hand holds the angle, and also provides controlled pressure. This grip thus allows you to maintain and control both angle and pressure. Most left-handers find they can adopt this grip without reversing hands. Stand with your feet apart, parallel to the edge of the sharpening bench but far enough away to throw your shoulders forward, knees flexed slightly (photo below). Lock your wrists to maintain the sharpening angle as you move the iron forward and back on the stone. A wooden angle block, shown on table, can be used to check your position.

The main difference between sharpening a chisel and a plane iron is the pressure applied to the tool. The hand position, as shown in the two photos at right, is basically the same. Bear down hard on the wide iron, varying the pressure from left to right every few strokes, to round the edge slightly. Maintain constant, light pressure on a narrow tool. Here, Kirby uses a Japanese waterstone, kept wet by squirts from a plant sprayer.

lubricant is to keep the edge of the tool cool, to smooth the sharpening action, and to float away metal and stone debris, thereby helping to prevent plugging or glazing of the stone's abrasive surface. If you have oilstones, the type of oil is also a matter of preference. A light machine oil such as 3-in-1 is good. Motor oil cut with kerosene is popular, and straight kerosene is suitable on a fine stone.

The bench or shelf on which you keep your sharpening stones is a vital element of the workshop. It should be sturdy and built for the job. The surface should be easy to clean—Formica is ideal. There should be a cover over the whole thing or else covers for the individual stones, to protect them from dust, which clogs them and destroys their cutting action. Choose a bench height to suit your own body—34 in. is a good place to start. The stones should be mounted with their long ends at right angles to the front of the bench, and held firmly in place between small blocks fastened to the bench. When planning the bench, don't forget that you need about 10 in. to the right of each stone to clear the tool handle when backing off. Keeping stones in a toolbox is not good practice because sharpening is too important and too frequent an operation to be hindered by having to dig them out and set up some temporary work station. It's also bad to spill dirty water or oil on your workbench.

How much pressure to exert? The pressure varies with the blade you are sharpening—the wider the iron, the more pressure. With a 2⅜-in. plane iron, apply almost as much pressure as you can deliver, while still being able to move. With a ¼-in. chisel, apply very little pressure. The ¼-in. chisel is probably the most difficult tool to sharpen while retaining the right-angularity of the edge, and the usual fault is too much pressure. With narrow tools, you must take care to move around on the surface of the stone as you sharpen, to keep from wearing a groove in it. Some people avoid this problem by turning the stone on its edge.

Should the tool be held askew to the long edges of the stone? If the blade is narrower than the stone, you should keep the edge at right angles to the edge of the stone and to its direction of travel. In this way you will have to consider and practice a uniform grip and stance, and you will be more likely to get uniform results. Wear on the stone will be more even, and sharpening time will be minimized. When sharpening a plane iron that is wider than the stone, it's common to sharpen aslant, so the whole edge is on the stone. However, because plane irons are usually sharpened with a very slight

curve, more pressure is exerted on the left side of the iron for a half-dozen strokes, then on the right for a half-dozen strokes.

How long a stroke do I take? Learn to use the whole length of the stone, reversing direction an inch or so from each end. This keeps the stone flatter and speeds the process along. Maintain the pressure in both directions, forward and back.

How do I know when to stop? If you visualize what you are trying to do, you'll realize that once you've removed the face of metal that includes the rounded portion, then the edge is sharp. However, you can't know when this has been achieved, so you go a bit beyond. The effect is that the unsupported metal at the very tip of the edge collapses and bends over—a burr or wire edge forms. When you can feel the burr by running your thumb off the flat side (back) of the blade, it's time to stop. Now, turn the blade over flat on the stone and remove the burr by "backing off." No matter what, keep the back of the tool flat on the stone. If you lift the tool to an angle to remove the burr, you've changed the sharpening angle. Correcting the fault wastes both time and metal.

Backing off should be done only on the fine stone. The sequence of events, if all goes well, is this: Sharpen on a medium stone at a 35° angle until you just detect the burr, go to the fine stone and sharpen at 35° until you have polished out the scratches left by the medium stone, turn the blade over and back off. Don't back off on the medium stone before going to the fine stone, it's an unnecessary step. The back of the chisel or plane iron should touch only your finest stone.

There is no need to raise a huge burr, although it's possible to sharpen to the point where, as you back off, a visible wire of metal detaches itself. This may look impressive but actually you've removed about five sharpenings worth of metal, shortening the life of the grinding angle. You should expect to get 20 or 25 sharpenings between grindings, the first taking the fewest strokes, the second a few more, and so on.

What if, after backing off, the burr is now on the beveled (face) side? It frequently happens that way, and you simply turn the tool over, take a few light strokes, then back off again. You must persevere until, when running the thumb off either side of the blade, no burr can be felt.

How do I know the blade is sharp? There are two simple ways. A 10-power or 15-power hand-lens should be part of every woodworker's tool kit. A look through the lens at this stage is dramatic. What you thought to be a smooth surface turns out to be something like the surface of a worn phonograph record. With × 15 magnification you'll be able to see

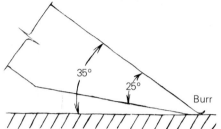

Sharpen at a 35° angle (right) until you detect a burr. Turn the tool over and back off on a fine stone. When backing off, the iron must lie flat on the stone (as shown at left and above). Use the fingers of both hands to press it down evenly.

whether the edge is a clear intersection between the sharpening angle and the back side of the blade. The other way to check is to feel that there is no burr on either side of the blade, then to offer the tool very carefully and gently to your thumbnail, as shown in the photograph below. The lower the angle you can achieve between thumbnail and sharpened edge, the sharper it is. This may seem dangerous but it has plenty of historic precedent: Silversmiths and engravers use the method to check the edge on gravers, and metal-lathe operators frequently employ it too. If you're still uneasy about pointing a sharp edge at your cuticle, set your thumbnail vertically on the bench and approach from the knuckle side.

If you are shopping for stones, I'd suggest a medium India (a man-made stone) from a reputable firm like Norton or Carborundum. For the fine stone, a soft or hard Arkansas *(FWW #12, Sept. '78, p. 68-71).* It's best if both stones are the same size and not too small—9 in. by 2½ in. is ample. If a large Arkansas is too expensive, get the largest you can afford. These two stones will last the rest of your life.

Japanese waterstones are gaining popularity. Although the edge produced by an Arkansas oilstone has long been a standard of sharpness, I find the waterstone to be even better—another level of quality that's really quite extraordinary. Japanese waterstones come with instructions for care and maintenance; they're used the same way as oilstones, and again, a medium and a fine stone are all you require.

Whatever the stone, unless it's kept flat in its length and its width, it's of little use. To check, clean and dry the stone by pressing it into a paper towel, then hold it to the light against a straightedge, just as you would check a piece of wood. If the length shows a hollow of 1/32 in. or more, or if you see any hollowing in the width, it's time to flatten.

Flattening a waterstone is simple. Place a piece of plate glass about 20 in. square on a flat surface. On it put a piece of 220-grit wet/dry sandpaper. Flood the paper and the stone with water, and grind the stone on the paper using as much of the paper's area as you can. Wash the stone and paper often by dipping them into a bucket of water, and dry the stone before you check it with a straightedge.

To flatten an oilstone, use a different piece of plate glass in a similar way. Sprinkle about ¼ cup of 80-grit carborundum powder (available from lapidary shops) onto the center of the glass, and pour about ¼ cup of water into the grit. Grind the stone in a circular motion, using as much of the glass area as

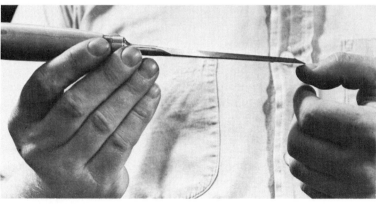

At left, the sharp edge. Find out how sharp by gently offering the blade to your thumbnail, below. The lower the angle at which it will catch, the sharper it is. At right, the sharpening bench in Kirby's shop is sturdy and easy to clean.

you can. Keep heavy pressure on the stone as you grind. It's easiest to flatten your coarser stone first, while the grit is cutting fastest; a fine Arkansas can take a long time to flatten, especially if it's been allowed to become much hollowed. To check the stone, scrape off the grit slurry, wash the stone, dry by pressing into a paper towel and test with a straightedge. After flattening a dozen stones, you'll probably notice the glass becoming hollow. Get a new piece of glass.

Problem tools. The spokeshave is awkward to sharpen because of its short blade. You can do it by holding it in your fingers but a better way is to make a wooden block about 5 in. by 2 in. by ¾ in. Saw a kerf in the end so that the spokeshave blade can be inserted about an inch into the block. You'll be able to exert ample pressure and still keep good control.

Carving tools can be sorted into three types: flat chisels, gouges and veining tools. Flat chisels are sharpened like bench chisels but on both sides. Thus to keep the same 35° angle you'd have to shoot for 17°30′ on each side, practically impossible. Since carving is such a variable process, just sharpen on one side until a burr is raised and then sharpen from the other side. A carving chisel usually has to be sharpened more often than a bench chisel.

The carving gouge is held the same way as a bench chisel but people often move it in a figure eight across the stone, rolling it as they go, to sharpen each part of the edge. A disadvantage of this method is that wear in the center of the stone is double, and it's soon hollowed. I find it better to work in a straight line along one edge of the stone, or with the stone turned up on edge, rolling the gouge to reach its whole edge. Once a burr has been raised on the inside, you'll need a slipstone to deal with it. Slipstones are usually small and handheld, not mounted. They're made in a variety of shapes, from flat like a miniature oilstone to cylindrical to conical with a conical hollow on the back side. The conical sort is most common, but cylinders are more useful, although you'll need a variety of cylinders to fit a variety of gouges. Most carvers collect them over the years, the same way they collect gouges. Choose a slip of smaller radius than the gouge, and work it flat on the inside face of the gouge to remove the burr.

An in-cannel gouge is a special problem calling for a cylindrical stone of its exact radius. Brace the butt of the gouge on the bench and work the slip in and out, rotating it at the same time, and maintaining the 35° angle with the tool's back. Then backing off can be done on a normal flat stone.

V-tools and veiners are similar to flat chisels, and most of the trouble comes on the inside, where the two faces meet. First sharpen both outside faces on a flat stone in the usual way, but then to remove the burr from the inside you'll need a stone shaped to an angle that will reach the bottom of the V. Usually a small slip can be ground to the necessary angle.

Many carvers avoid the problem by buffing their tools on a cloth wheel charged with rouge or tripoli. This will produce an extremely sharp edge, but it's haphazard and offers little control of angle. It's also difficult to shape a wheel so it will fit inside a gouge or V-tool. This lack of control usually does not matter to the carver, but the cabinetmaker needs precise angular control and an absolutely flat back, and for these reasons I advise against buffing. It's cheaper, easier and better to learn how to sharpen on flat stones.   ☐

Ian Kirby teaches woodworking and furniture design at Kirby Studios, North Bennington, Vt.

Japanese Blades
Traditional sharpening methods

by Toshio Odate

Although most woodworking apprentices begin training at the age of 13 or 14 years, I was 16 when my parents decided I should apprentice to a *tategu-shi*, the craftsman who makes doors, *shoji* (screens) and room-dividing panels. My starting master was my stepfather, which was unusual. It was common to be sent to apprentice with another craftsman for at least the first two to three years for spiritual as well as technical training. My stepfather was very strict and believed a father could not teach his own son. The first day he said to me, "From this day on we are total strangers. I will treat you like a common apprentice, maybe harder. You should call me master, not father." He did as he said.

A *tategu-shi* apprenticeship lasts five years. Two additional years, the first and last, are done as a service to the master, extending the relationship to seven years. The first year is spent working in the household and studio doing errands and assisting the master's wife. At this time you are beginning to learn the manners and attitudes of a craftsman through observation. The seventh year is spent working as a craftsman without salary to show appreciation to your master.

An experience in my third year that is still important to me helps to illustrate the relationship a craftsman has with his tools. I had saved a little pocket money given to me by my master and other craftsmen for doing errands. But as my daily needs were taken care of by the master, there was little reason to have or spend money. On the first and fifteenth day of the month we would take a half day off, but only after the master's tools and my tools were taken care of and the shop was cleaned. I was finally free around two o'clock. You can imagine just how precious those hours were to me. One afternoon I took the train to a store that was well known for its fine tools. There I purchased a plane that had been made by a famous blacksmith. At the time I did not know his name or the fine quality of his tools. All I knew was that the plane was expensive. On the train I was so overjoyed I unwrapped the plane and held and looked at it all the way home. I knew I couldn't show the plane to anyone because people would laugh at me—I was still a novice. I couldn't even keep it in my toolbox for fear someone would see it. I enjoyed the plane every evening while in my room. After the lights were turned out, I kept the plane by my bedside.

One day it was raining, and everyone was fixing tools. I don't remember why—it wasn't a day off—but my plane was now in my toolbox. I was pretending to fix my tools but was really looking at my plane. All of a sudden my master was standing behind me. It was too late. He asked, and I had to tell him I had bought it. He took the plane and showed it to the other craftsmen. They, too, thought it was a wonderful tool but teased me because I still did not know how to appreciate its greatness. They took the blade out of the block and examined it carefully. They talked about it for a long time, then gave it back to my master. My master came to me holding the plane in his hand and told me simply that the plane was too good for me. He took it away, and I never saw it again. I had expected that to happen.

Tools are made to be used, and great tools have to be used by great craftsmen. The plane was not for me and should not have been mine only to keep in a cabinet. I should have had greater respect for the tool and the craftsman who made it. It was a very painful and expensive lesson, but I learned.

Sharpening Japanese blades—Most Japanese woodworking tool blades are made by laminating steel (figure 1). High-quality Western blades also used to be made this way. The edge of the blade is thin and extremely hard and is supported by a thick, soft steel. The center of the back of the blade is hollowed-out to facilitate keeping the back completely flat. Most blades are beveled on one side, except for ax-like tools, which are beveled on both sides with hard steel laminated in the center. Plane blades, chisels and knives are made in the same manner, and the methods for sharpening them are similar. Once you have learned the techniques of sharpening plane blades, which are the most complicated, you will be able to sharpen any flat blade.

A new plane is usually ready to use, but most Japanese craftsmen will recondition it to suit their own preference. The optimal bevel angle depends on the quality of the blade and on the kind of work you are doing. Until you know otherwise, it is best to maintain the original bevel angle of the blade.

If the edge of the blade is not finished when purchased or is badly chipped, a grinder can be used to start the sharpening process. When I worked in Japan I did not have a grinder and always used a coarse stone, as was the custom. Mechanical tools were generally not used. Today a wide variety of machines and tools is available to make dressing or redressing a blade faster and more accurate, but sharpening itself, honing the final edge, has to be done by hand.

There are oilstones and there are waterstones; in Japan we used only waterstones. Many Japanese craftsmen prefer natural stone, but it is difficult to find large stones that have an even consistency. Today, manufactured stones are readily available at an affordable price. Three stones (coarse, medium and fine) are needed. When sharpening (and not redressing) a blade, only the medium and finishing stones are used.

When using a waterstone, water must be added constantly, or the pores of the stone will clog. Keeping the surface of the stone clean gives a faster grind. Japanese craftsmen keep a bucket of water next to the stone, or they have a sink-like wooden box beneath the stone (figure 2).

In sharpening, be sure to wipe the blade before changing to a finer grade stone to keep from transferring coarse particles. Before changing stones you should allow the stone you're on to dry during the last few strokes. This results in a smooth transition to the next stone. As the stone dries, the pores of the stone clog slightly, thus acting as an intermediate grit.

How the blade is held during sharpening is important. The plane blade is held in the palm of the right hand with the index finger extended (photos, right). Place the first two or three fingers (depending upon the size of the blade) of your left hand in the space created by the right thumb and index finger. Your fingers will maintain pressure on the blade so as to steady the bevel. The left thumb, placed under the blade, will provide support for the back.

The angle of the blade on the stone has to be constant

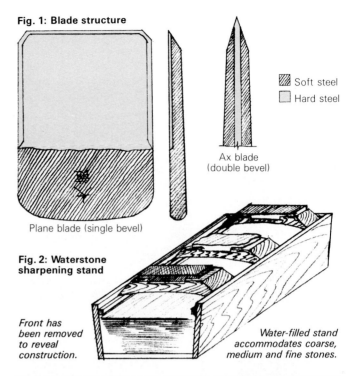

Fig. 1: Blade structure

Soft steel
Hard steel

Ax blade (double bevel)

Plane blade (single bevel)

Fig. 2: Waterstone sharpening stand

Front has been removed to reveal construction.

Water-filled stand accommodates coarse, medium and fine stones.

To sharpen the bevel, hold the blade in the right hand, index finger extended to press in back of the bevel. The fingers of the left hand fit between the index finger and thumb of the right hand, also pressing in back of the bevel. Position the thumb of the left hand to support the blade at the back. Keep the angle of the blade on the stone constant while rubbing back and forth.

49

Fig. 3: Bevels

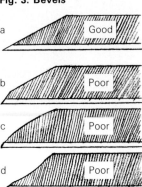

a — Good

b — Poor

c — Poor

d — Poor

Fig. 4: Plane-blade bevel

A plane blade must be sharpened flat from the edge to the top of the bevel but slightly convex across its width, to keep the corners from digging in. Roughing-plane blades should be more convex than smoothing-plane blades. The convexity shown is exaggerated for illustration.

When a burr has been raised on the flat side of the blade from sharpening the bevel on the medium and fine stones, flip the blade over and hold it with the fingers of the right hand around the back and the thumb extended to press on top of the bevel. Lay the blade flat on the fine stone and bring the thumb and fingers of your left hand to bear on the corners of the bevel. Rub hard back and forth until the burr has been bent back to the bevel side. Continue to rub the blade alternately on the bevel and the flat side until the wire edge falls off.

while sharpening; the surface from the edge of the blade to the top of the bevel must be perfectly flat (figure 3a). This is particularly important for chisels, which are sometimes used like planes, with the bevel riding on the wood—the flatness and smoothness of the bevel help to control the cut and also contribute to the strength of the edge. A double bevel or a convex bevel (figures 3b and 3c) will cause plane blades to skip when cutting hard grain or knots. If the beveled surface is slightly concave (figure 3d), maximum control and also support for the fragile hard-steel edge are sacrificed. Hollow-ground bevels are easier to hone, but there are disadvantages: They do not produce the strongest edge, and they are especially bad for laminated blades.

While the bevel must be perfectly flat from the edge to the top, plane blades require additional shaping: The edge must be slightly convex (figure 4) to prevent the corners of the blade from cutting into the planed surface. The shape is produced by subtly varying the pressure on the blade from side to side during the stroke. The convexity of the edge of a roughing-plane blade should be more pronounced than that of a smoothing-plane blade.

Japanese craftsmen sharpen not on a bench, but with their stone, or their stone stand, on the floor. The squatting position allows you to bring your weight to bear on the work. The orientation of the blade on the stone depends on the size of the blade and the training of the craftsman. Some craftsmen

are taught to sharpen with the edge of the blade always perpendicular to the stroke. This probably produces the strongest edge, but it requires keeping the elbows in close to the body, not their most natural position. I usually sharpen with the blade angled at about 30° to the stroke. This allows me to lock my hands and wrists and still move freely from the upper arms. Another advantage of this position is that it provides greater support for the bevel on the stone to steady the angle during the stroke. The greatest support comes from holding the blade parallel to the direction of the stroke; then there's little chance of rocking the bevel. To hold the blade this way, the stone must be at bench height, and you stand alongside the stone, rather than behind it. I use this position for very thin blades and also for gouges.

The blade should be sharpened on the coarse or medium stone, rubbing back and forth until a burr appears across the edge. To detect the burr, rub the back of the blade gently with your finger; it should not be quite visible. Switching to the finishing stone, sharpen in the same manner until the whole bevel is mirror-smooth. Turn the blade over and hold it with the fingers of your right hand around the back and your thumb extended to press on the top of the bevel. Bridge this thumb with the fingers and thumb of the left hand, pressing on the corners of the blade (photo, left). Rub 15 to 20 times with the back flat on the stone until you can feel the burr bent back to the bevel side. It is important not to sharpen the back of the blade until this time, and only on the finishing stone. Repeat the finishing process back and front until the burr falls off. Resist the temptation to peel the burr off as this will leave a raw edge. Sharpening is now complete.

Maintaining the flat back—The back surface of Japanese blades is unique in that the flat between the hollow grind and the blade edge is extremely narrow. It is common knowledge among Japanese craftsmen that the blade performs best just when this flat is narrowest. After repeated sharpenings finally make the flat disappear, a new flat has to be created. If the blade is wider than ⅜ in., Japanese craftsmen usually strike the edge of the soft steel with the corner of a small hammer on the bevel side of the back so as to bend the steel down slightly. It requires considerable skill to do this right because the hard steel of the back of the blade can crack from the slightest vibration of a misdirected blow. Most Japanese craftsmen have had this experience, including myself. I can remember hiding a blade from my master. If one wants to acquire the skill, one must take the chance and practice. I prefer using the corner of a hard wooden block, but some use the corner of an anvil. Either way, place the back of the blade on the corner, making contact ¼ in. to ⅜ in. down from the edge in the middle of the blade, exactly opposite where you will strike with your hammer. Tap lightly and repeatedly along the center two-thirds of the width of the blade (photos, opposite page), moving the blade between taps to position the corner underneath the hammer. Depending on the thickness of the blade, 15 to 25 taps should push out the hollow in the back enough to produce a flat at the edge after grinding.

Grinding is accomplished with a flat steel plate 2 in. by 8 in. by ¼ in. (stones are not flat enough), a pinch of carborundum powder (silicone carbide grain, grit #46) and a few drops of water. Mix the carborundum and water on the steel plate and rub the back of the blade, giving little pressure at the beginning, keeping the carborundum paste under the

Left, after repeated sharpenings, the narrow flat at the edge of the hollow grind on the back of the blade is worn away, and the hollow grind must be tapped out to provide enough metal to produce another flat. Back the blade on the corner of a wooden or steel block and tap lightly and repeatedly with the corner of a small hammer in the center of the bevel. Be sure the blade is supported directly behind where the hammer strikes; vibration can easily crack the blade. Below, when enough of the hollow grind has been tapped out, the back must be flattened on a steel plate sprinkled with carborundum and water. Use a length of wood to back up the blade and to provide leverage for gradually increasing the pressure on the blade as you rub it vigorously back and forth. As the carborundum and water become a fine paste, your whole weight is brought to bear. The result is a narrow, mirror-smooth flat at the edge of the blade. You can then sharpen the bevel and the flat on stones.

Fig. 5: Plane-sole contours

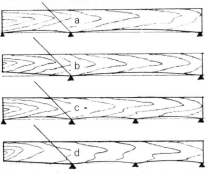

For truing (a), the sole is relieved so the plane contacts the work only at the front, the blade and the back. For roughing and smoothing (b), the whole back is relieved so the plane contacts the work only at the front and the blade. Both of these basic contours can be modified (c and d) to include more than one contact point in front of the blade. Exaggerated for illustration.

blade. Then slowly increase the pressure. Keep the surface of the plate moist, and maintain even pressure on the blade with both hands. For leverage place a piece of wood about three times the length of the blade over it and grip the wood and the blade together. Use the wood as a handle and rub hard for a few minutes, then wipe the carborundum paste off the blade to examine the back. If it's even but dull and rough, and you have a flat at the middle of the edge about 1/16 in. wide, then gather the carborundum paste at the center of the plate and add a few more drops of water. This time press and rub as hard as you can until the paste is completely dry. Here's where working on the floor allows you to get your whole weight on top of the blade (photo, above). Look once again and if the back, all of it except for the hollow grind, is flat and shiny as a mirror, the work is done. If it is not, repeat the process. This is important because the more shine the edge has the sharper it will be. Western flat-back blades should be ground this way as well, so that the blade will keep its edge longer.

For a very narrow chisel (less than 1/4 in.), it is not necessary to strike with a hammer. Use the carborundum powder and the steel plate. Obviously, the hollow grind will be shallower, but it will do the job.

Next, the corners of the blade are ground to an angle in order to prevent shavings from jamming in the plane body. Then the beveled edge is sharpened as described earlier. The dimples left in the beveled surface from tapping out the hollow grind will disappear within two or three sharpenings.

Plane preparation—Sharpening is only part of the story; the plane body too must be prepared. The article by Ted Chase (*FWW* #20, Jan. '80) gives some good information. To it I should add that there are two basic contours for the sole of the Japanese plane—one for truing and one for roughing or smoothing. For truing, the sole is relieved so the plane contacts the work at the front, at the blade and at the back (figure 5a). This contour planes a perfectly flat surface because it removes only the high spots of the work, its depth of cut being limited both in front and in back of the blade.

For both roughing and smoothing planes, the whole sole behind the blade is relieved (figure 5b). Thus the plane contacts the work at only two points: at the front and at the blade. This configuration can take much larger shavings. In smoothing planes, the same contour allows the plane to follow the surface exactly, leaving a consistent shine to the wood. Both these configurations can be modified according to the requirements of the craftsman to include more than one contact point in front of the blade (figures 5c and 5d). □

Toshio Odate, of Woodbury, Conn., is a wood sculptor who teaches art at Pratt Institute in New York City. This article was prepared with the help of his wife, Audrey Grossman.

Slow-Speed Sharpening
Lessening the chance of burning your tools

by Mark White

To reduce the risk of friction-caused heat drawing the temper of my tools, I designed a simple-to-make sharpening system that incorporates a vertical shaft turning slower than 300 RPM. The horizontal wheel, which allows flat grinding rather than hollow, may be a conventional grindstone or a flat wooden plate covered with an abrasive disc. For stropping, I use a crowned wooden disc covered with leather and charged with an abrasive compound.

The heart of the system, shown below left, is a laminated disc bolted to a standard pipe flange, which is in turn screwed to a short length of 1¼-in. pipe. The pipe turns in two bearings made of 4-in. by 4-in. by 9-in. chunks of hickory. I bored the holes for the bearings with an adjustable bit set to bore about ¹/₁₆ in. larger than the pipe's diameter, to compensate for swelling of the block and tightening of the hole when oiled. If you drill oversize and experience wobble in the shaft, you can cant the blocks until they bear upon the shaft. The hole in the upper block should pass entirely through it. The lower block should be drilled 1 in. short of going through, so that the shaft has a full inch of wood to rest on as it turns.

To make the pulley, I bandsawed two 14-in. discs and one 12-in. disc from ⅝-in. plywood. I marked and drilled the centers of these discs to take a ⅜-in. bolt and used these center holes to position the discs during glue-up, sandwiching the smaller disc between the two larger ones.

Next I lag-bolted the bearing blocks to the front edge of my workbench, lubricated them with chainsaw oil and inserted the pipe with pipe flange. I positioned the laminated pulley on top of the flange, and marked, drilled and bolted it in place.

The vertical-shaft motor I took from a junked washing machine. I mounted the motor on the workbench, hooked it up to the pulley and let it run for about 30 minutes in order to wear in the hickory bearings. The face of the flange did not run perpendicular to the axis of rotation, but a bit of fiddling with a couple of cardboard shims between the pulley and the flange leveled the disc.

A conventional grindstone could be mounted right on the pulley, but I chose to use my system for stropping. I stacked and glued a few more plywood discs to the top of the pulley, switched on the motor and turned the head with a sharp gouge to a rounded, conical shape. (Leather yields under pressure, and if the leather were applied to a flat surface, a tool pressed to the leather would sink in and the tool bevel would become convex.) Sanding completed the shaping of the head, and a heavy coat of paint sealed the wood. From a local leather shop I picked up a piece of ³/₁₆-in. thick shoe-sole leather, soaked it in hot water and molded it in place over the head. A nut and washer hold the leather in the center, and a ring of aluminum tacks holds down the perimeter. The leather can be charged with various grits of aluminum-oxide buffing compound; the distance you hold the tool from the center of the disc also affects the speed of the sharpening action. Because the head is crowned slightly, wide-edge tools are easier to sharpen. Attention can be concentrated on a small section of the edge, while the ends clear the perimeter and hub of the wheel. Always hold the tool on the plate so the rotation is away from the cutting edge; otherwise the tool can grab and cut the leather.

The system can be varied to incorporate a large flexible sanding disc which, if run at 800 RPM would be useful for sharpening axes, adzes and drawknives. A reversible motor would be useful for knives and other two-edge tools. □

Mark White teaches woodworking in Kodiak, Alaska.

White's horizontal sharpening system, which rotates at only 300 RPM, can be fit with a grindstone, an abrasive disc or a leather-covered stropping wheel. An old washing-machine motor provides power.

Another of White's slow-speed sharpening arrangements has a 2-in. by 9-in. aluminum-oxide wheel on a ¾-in. mandrel powered by a 1,725-RPM motor. A 3-in. pulley at the motor and a 10-in. pulley at the mandrel yield a grindstone speed of about 500 RPM, fast enough to remove metal with reduced risk of burning the tool.

Chisels, and How to Pare

Master the grip and stance before tackling joinery

by Ian J. Kirby

The first step in learning to work wood by hand is mastering the three basic cutting tools: the chisel, the plane and the saw. Each tool requires its own hand grip and body stance for the most effective transmission of power to the cutting edge. The best way to acquire skill is to practice using each tool until the proper techniques become second nature. In this article, I'll illustrate these concepts by showing how to use woodworking chisels.

I cannot overemphasize the importance of practicing fundamental tool skills before you attempt to make joints, let alone whole pieces of furniture. I constantly find beginning woodworkers who are struggling to learn some vital technique in the course of making furniture, with no attempt to develop and perfect their skills before the main event. The result will at best be a nondescript article of furniture that prominently features the scars of its maker's struggle, and at worst it will be failure and disillusionment. Either way, it seems futile. On the other hand, once you have learned how to use the tools, making joints is a simple procedural application of those skills; making furniture is, in large part, the application of jointmaking skills. No manipulative skill is acquired without practice. The potter, the dentist, the athlete—indeed, anyone wanting motor skills—must practice, and practice hard. The woodworker is not exempt.

Fortunately, all of woodworking can be broken down neatly into a series of skill-development processes. In particular, total control of the chisel can and should be learned by diligently practicing horizontal and vertical paring, nothing else. The photo essay on p. 54, therefore, proceeds first through horizontal paring, then vertical paring, and then shows the application of these techniques (plus sawing) to the through dovetail joint. I can only urge you to accept that it will be worth your while to practice with the chisel until you have mastered it before you spoil any good wood.

Central to becoming skilled with the chisel is learning the proper hand grip, and from that point on, going right through the body to the soles of the feet, learning the relationship of each part of the anatomy to the next part. After the grip, we must be concerned with the forearms and upper arms including the shoulders, next the trunk in relationship to the arms, then the pelvic girdle and legs, and finally the feet. To achieve just what's wanted at the cutting edge, the whole body must participate and be in accord. I find that most beginners are conscious of their relationship with the tool up to the shoulder, where their awareness seems to end.

Since there are two main ways of paring with the chisel, there are two different grips and stances to learn. Note that in either mode, both hands are kept behind the cutting edge. There are not too many universal rules in woodworking, but

this has to be one of them: when using a chisel, power it with one hand, guide it with the other, and avoid a nasty cut by keeping both hands behind the cutting edge. It goes without saying that your chisels must be perfectly sharp.

Although many different chisels are available on the market, when you are deciding which to buy, there are only a few factors to consider. In terms of blade section, there are just two types: the square-edged or firmer chisel and the bevel-edged chisel. The firmer can do heavier work, and can even be pressed into service for mortising. The bevel-edged chisel (there is no standard blade thickness or bevel angle) can get into such tight places as pin sockets between dovetails and is most suitable for furniture-making.

There are three common blade lengths: patternmaker's (8 in. to 10 in.), bench (5 in. to 7 in.) and carpenter's or butt (3 in. to 4 in.). Patternmakers need a long chisel to reach into deep, awkward places. I prefer the long blade's feel and balance, and it seems easier to control. Patternmaker's chisels are nearly always bevel-edged, and are also made with a cranked handle for paring far out on a flat surface. The bench chisel is commonest amongst furniture-makers, whereas the butt chisel, a phenomenon of American mass manufacture, is the least useful.

For handles, the most prized commercial wood is boxwood; the usual alternatives are ash and beech. The handle is generally driven onto a tang that has been formed atop the metal

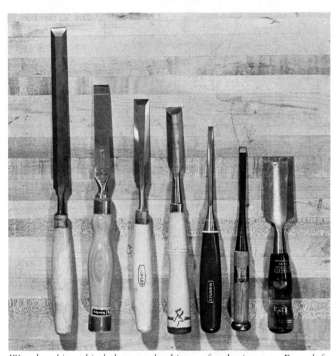

Woodworking chisels have evolved into a few basic types. From left, patternmaker's chisel, firmer, standard bevel-edged chisel with boxwood handle (the choice of many furniture-makers), socket bench chisel, Blue Chip, Japanese and butt.

Ian Kirby teaches design and woodworking methods at his studio and workshop in North Bennington, Vt.

blade, and seats against a bolster formed between tang and blade. Firmers, in order to withstand pounding, generally have a thick leather washer between bolster and handle, plus metal ferrules top and bottom. Paring chisels, which are not to be struck with a mallet, usually have a single ferrule (at the bottom of the handle) and no washer. A third style, called a socket chisel, in which a tapered cylinder turned onto the handle fits a conical socket in the end of the blade, can also absorb heavy pounding. Handles made of high-impact plastic are quite as good as wood. They are generally formed around the tang and have no ferrule. Even so, they can be driven with a mallet. Once there were numerous handle shapes, and chisels were named after them. Today manufacturers seem to have settled on relatively simple turned forms for both wood and plastic, although recently plastic handles have been injection-molded into new shapes as a result of research into effective grips for maximum control. The Marples Blue Chip, a rounded square in section, is one example.

The Japanese chisels now available generally follow the form of Western chisels, with one exception. The back of the blade is hollowed out, except at the cutting edge. This makes stoning the back of the blade a little easier.

When buying chisels, you get what you pay for. I'm inclined to stay with the well-known manufacturers because they use steel of appropriate and reliable quality. On a tight budget, I'd start with bevel-edged bench chisels in widths of ¼ in., ⅜ in. and ¾ in., filling out the set as need arises and finances permit. Since plastic handles are molded in place, they are usually in line with the blade from top and side views. This is not always so with wooden handles, so be sure to check. Also, examine the back face (flat side). Except for Japanese chisels, it should come ground absolutely flat, although it is often made convex by overly enthusiastic finishing at the foundry. Having to flatten the back can cost you hours of work at the sharpening stone. To avoid slicing the left-hand index finger, which guides the chisel, always take the sharp edges off the length of the blade. Place the chisel at 45° to its back on a medium stone and give it about ten light strokes. As with any tool, buy the best you can afford. One good chisel is better than two poor ones.

Horizontal paring

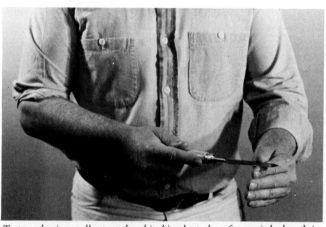

To pare horizontally, put the chisel in the palm of your right hand, index finger extended, photo above. (Kirby is right-handed; left-handers will have to reverse.) Line up blade, finger and forearm—this is the line that transmits the body's power. Rest the back of the chisel blade on your left forefinger, thumb on top, back of hand toward workpiece. This hand guides, and brakes, the cut. Now stand at the vise, take a step back with your right foot, and turn the foot so it's almost parallel to the bench edge, photo right. Bend at the waist and lock your right arm so your elbow is on or near your hip. Now push off with your right foot so the whole movement comes from your lower body and legs—your arms and trunk stay locked. You'll quickly find the most comfortable link of arms and body to suit your physique.

Horizontal paring is done on end grain when cleaning out dovetails (p. 57, step 7), and on cross grain when cleaning dadoes and crosslaps. In either case, the wood fibers must first be severed by sawcuts down to a gauge line. Then the waste comes out in stages, half from one side, half with the work turned around. The pattern of paring is the same, cross grain or end grain. To practice, mark out and saw a cross-lap housing in a length of 2x2 hardwood. Pare horizontally to just beyond the middle of the work, but tip the chisel alternately left and right so you reach the gauge line at the sides while leaving a peak in the middle. The drawing at right shows this strategy of approaching the line in controlled stages.

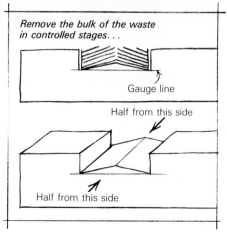

Remove the bulk of the waste in controlled stages...

Gauge line

Half from this side

Half from this side

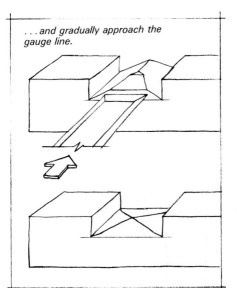

. . . and gradually approach the gauge line.

Remove the peak by holding the chisel flat, but with the handle about 10° below horizontal. As you approach the gauge line, the cut will slope upward away from you. Click the chisel edge right into the line for the last cut, but maintain the upward slope. Then turn the work around in the vise and repeat from the other side.

At this point the waste will be all gone, except for a small pitch in the middle of the housing. Remove it by raising the handle closer to horizontal with each cut, until on the final pass you feel the chisel go onto the gauge line on your side and see it exit on the gauge line at the far side. A little nibbling to clear out the corners, and you're done.

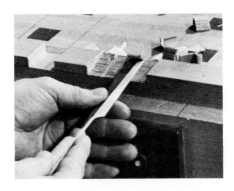

To cut a wide housing, saw the shoulders and saw a series of crosscuts spaced a little less than a chisel width apart. With the handle lower than horizontal, work a flat slope from one side and then the other, leaving a center pitch. Take small bites. The final cuts, as before, go from gauge line to gauge line. You'll find that this grip and stance provides ample power and control—the chisel should never come flying out of the wood on the far side. If it does, take smaller bites to get control of the relationship between the hardness of the wood, the sharpness of the tool, and your own strength.

Vertical paring

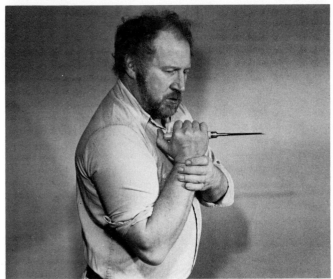

Vertical paring requires an entirely different grip and stance. Hold the chisel as if it were a dagger, thumb on the handle's end. Try to tuck your thumb into your shoulder joint. Rest the back of the chisel's blade on the middle part of your left index finger, left thumb on top of the blade. Stand with your left foot forward, and bend from the waist so the back of your left hand rests on the work. Lock your arms, rock your weight onto the forward foot, and flex your knees. All downward power comes from the hips and shoulders, not from moving your arms. Your head should move only as far downward as the chisel's edge moves, and no farther. (continued, next page)

This grip enables you to concentrate the whole power of your body onto the cutting edge. The left hand, braced on the work, provides fine control and acts as a brake. Practice by paring the corner off a block of wood—you'll readily see, quickly learn to sense, any variation from the vertical.

Vertical paring is how we usually clean up tenon shoulders. You can practice on the walls of housings cut in the horizontal paring exercise. With a ¾-in. chisel, place about half the blade's width in the knife line and pare straight down. Move over half the chisel's width for each subsequent pass, using the knife line and the surface previously cut as your guides. Try to sense how every part of your body functions in relation to the tool, the workpiece and the bench. Practicing these basic techniques is worth all the effort you can muster, for confidence here will make joinery an automatic and simple procedure, not the tense and chancy event that discourages many beginners.

Chisel skills and the through dovetail

Paring with the bench chisel is one of the prerequisite skills for making through dovetails. The other major skill is sawing, which I've discussed in my articles on the mortise and tenon joint (*FWW* #13, #15 and #18), but which I'll review in the following photo sequence. I suggest that you practice dovetailing with hardwood stock about ⅝ in. thick and 4¼ in. wide. From the start, get into the habit of preparing the ends of the stock clean and square, by crosscutting with a carbide blade or else by knifing deeply around and hand-planing the end grain. When making drawers and casegoods, this end-grain surface is the register that governs final fit (*FWW* #21, March '80, pp. 73-76).

It's possible to start the joint with either the tails or the pins, but I prefer to begin sawing the tails. This is because the tails are not cut straight down, but to an angle, and the saw is liable to wander. It doesn't matter whether the angles are constant, only that all the cuts are straight. If you make the pins first and transfer their angle to the tails, then you must cut a constant angle to a line—a constant angle not on the line won't do. If you have never practiced sawing down a line, draw a multitude of lines on scrap and just make cuts. It's worth emphasizing that the joint is made entirely from the saw. There's no need to chisel or file the side grain of the pins or tails. Although the joint has been elevated to a sort of ultimate standard, it's in reality simple—in no way

as difficult to make as the mortise and tenon. Don't be afraid of the dovetail.

Begin by gauging a line just less than the thickness of the stock at the ends of both pieces. After assembly, the outside surface of the stock will be planed to this thickness. Hold the wood upright in the vise. Using ¼-in. and ¾-in. incre-

ments, square lines across the end grain of the tails piece with a sharp pencil. I set the sliding bevel to a slope of one in six to mark the lines down what will be the outside of the joint (for practice, mark both sides). I carry these lines several inches below the gauge line to make it easier to sight the saw.

1. *Sawing stance is not unlike that for horizontal paring. Three fingers grip the saw, with the index finger extended. With feet well apart, wrist locked, power comes from the shoulder and upper arm. The other hand guides the saw into the work. A good preparatory exercise is to grasp the saw, close your eyes, and attempt to set the teeth down on the bench—level and square. Open your eyes, check with a try square, and try again.*

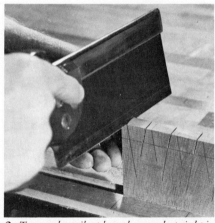

2. *To saw the tails, place the wood upright in the vise. Square lines drawn right on the vise make this easy. Some people put the wood at an angle so they can saw straight down, but it's better in the long run to learn control. Start the cut with the saw at the tail angle, on the far edge of the wood. Spend the first strokes bringing the kerf across the end grain, then bring the sawteeth to level. Saw down the outside of the pencil line, leaving no wood between line and saw. Don't try to adjust the angle mid-way—you must have a straight cut. Do try to keep the sawteeth horizontal. When you are down to the gauge line at the front, you will also be down to the line you can't see at the back.*

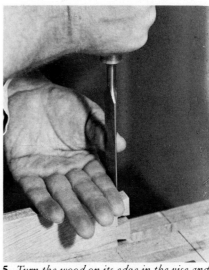

3. *Leave the wood upright in the vise and, standing as at left, remove the bulk of the waste with the coping saw. Its blade should slide easily into the kerf, down to within ⅛ in. of the gauge line. Rotate the saw's frame to twist the blade in the kerf, and it will turn the corner in its own thickness.*

4. *With practice, it's easy to keep the saw horizontal, and to cut very close to the gauge line, below. Some people chop all the waste out with a chisel. This is laborious, and some woods crumble so badly that the chisel pulls material out of the root of the joint.*

5. *Turn the wood on its edge in the vise and saw out the waste where the half-pins will fit. Clean up this shoulder by vertical paring, before turning the wood to do the other edge.*

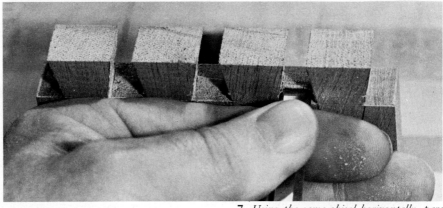

6. *To clean up the bottom of the joint, select the widest bevel-edged chisel that will fit between the tails and lay the wood flat on a cutting board. Pare down from both sides with the chisel about 10° back from 90° (left), until you can place the chisel into the gauge line. What's left is a small pitch in the middle of the joint. To remove it, place the wood upright in the vise.*

7. *Using the same chisel horizontally, pare straight across from gauge line to gauge line. The resulting surface will be flat and square, exactly where it should be. There is no virtue in undercutting the end grain, and no need to do so. Among other things, you lose the positive nature of the internal fit. Note that the initial incision made by the cutting gauge is where you finally place the chisel. An important part of the joint was completed at the start of marking out—a common condition in woodworking.*

8. *Now put the pins piece in the vise, projecting ⅛ in. above the bench top, and align the tails piece on it. You can adjust the fit of the joint according to the density of the wood by moving the tails piece minutely backward or forward. A tight joint in mahogany, which crushes easily, would be too tight in hard maple. Use a sharp knife to transfer the tail profiles, bearing down hard toward the outside corner. Then, with a square, pencil these lines several inches down the wood.*

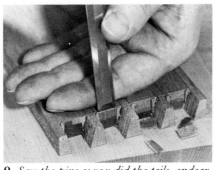

9. *Saw the pins as you did the tails, endeavoring to split the knife line. If you fear the line, study what you are doing through a magnifying glass. You'll see that it's quite possible. A method of reminding yourself which side is the waste side is to leave the tails piece in position on the bench. Remove the waste with the coping saw, then pare the end-grain flat. Use the widest chisel that will fit the narrow side of the aperture, and sweep it askew to reach the whole surface.*

10. *Tap the joint home with a hammer, directing each blow to the center of each individual tail. You don't need a block of scrap to protect the wood, and you shouldn't substitute a mallet because it's liable to damage the work. On a wide joint, you'll hear a change in pitch as the hammer strikes a tight tail. This is the best way to isolate just which part of the joint needs adjustment.* □

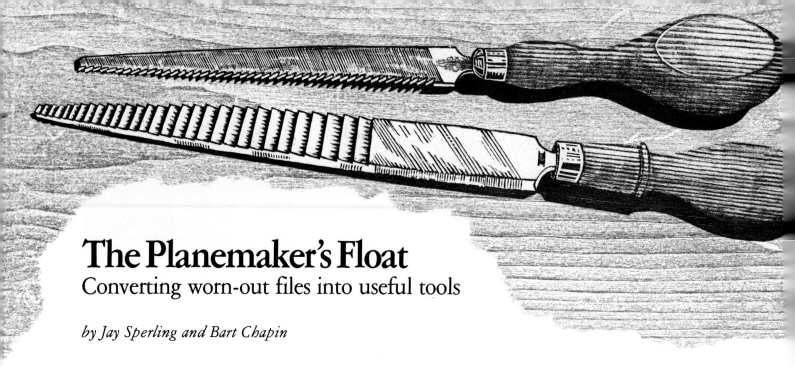

The Planemaker's Float
Converting worn-out files into useful tools

by Jay Sperling and Bart Chapin

Floats are toothed, file-like tools used in making wooden planes. They were widely used when cabinetmakers built their own planes, but now this versatile tool has been almost forgotten. A float cuts faster than a file and cleaner than a rasp. It's particularly adept at removing wood from hard-to-reach spots. Though chiefly used for wooden planes, it can do various jobs requiring controlled stock removal.

Traditionally made in a variety of shapes, floats are of two basic types: edge floats and flat-sided floats. Edge floats are fairly narrow in section and have teeth on their edges. They look like fat sawblades, and can cut narrow grooves and slots in tight quarters. The planemaker would saw each side of the wedge slot and then remove the waste between the two kerfs with the flat float, which he could also use to trim the walls to fit the wedge.

Unhardened, a float is quite easy to sharpen, and one sharpening is usually sufficient for making one plane. We'll give directions for making the flat-sided float, since it's more useful than the edge float. You can make the edge float following the same methods.

Make the blank from a worn-out flat file. You will have to soften (anneal) it by heating it red-hot with a torch and letting it cool gradually. If the file overheats and sags, pound it flat.

Next, grind off the file teeth. Select one side for the new teeth and take care to keep it perfectly flat. Remove any ripples with a flat mill file. Most planemakers didn't taper the thickness of floats, but a tapered tool is easier to use in tight places. Grind away enough

metal to form a gentle taper toward the tip. The float must be stiff along its entire length, so don't taper it too thin. (Edge floats must have a uniform thickness.) Beware of hard spots in the steel.

Flat-sided floats taper in plan pretty sharply toward their tips. A typical float 7 in. to 10 in. long and ¾ in. wide should taper to ⅛ in. at the tip. Edge floats taper in elevation from about ½ in. to ¼ in. at the tip. You can adjust these dimensions to suit the use of the tool. When grinding down the sides of the blank, keep the edges smooth and equal on both sides. Then fair the edges with a mill file and emery paper so they won't scratch your work. The edge float has a straight cutting edge. Grind and file it flat, referring to a straightedge regularly.

Although the teeth on traditional floats are uniformly spaced, I prefer to graduate the distances between teeth; this helps to make the tool cut more smoothly and eliminates chatter. At the tip of the tool the teeth are a little less than ⅛ in. apart; this distance increases in approximately 0.005-in. increments until the teeth at the back are close to ¼ in. apart. This allows a fine starting cut and greater stock removal afterward. Laying out the teeth for the first time, you should use a rule to graduate the distance between the teeth. Using a carbide-tipped scriber, etch in the lines at right angles to the centerline of the blank. Do this by clamping the blank near the edge of a worktable (centerline parallel with the

edge) and striking off the lines with a square. Flat-sided floats are toothed for only about two-thirds of their length, while edge floats are toothed along their entire length.

To cut the teeth you will need a pair (one large, one small) of triangular files and a file card. The file card is essential as the files can clog quickly. Clamp the blank down, and beginning at the tip and working back, thicken the scribed line with a couple of strokes of the file (step 1). Then, using the larger file on all but the smallest teeth, deepen the V-groove, while forming the relief angle on the back of the previous tooth. Stop filing the gullet when the file just nicks the top of the previous tooth (step 2). If you cut further, your teeth will not be level. With your last few strokes, push the cutting corner of the file toward the back, beginning the process of forming the tooth behind. As you work up the blank and the spacing increases, cuts will become deeper and wider. Don't overcut. You can always go back and correct the tooth shapes. When done, check the level of the teeth with a straightedge.

Now take your smaller triangular file and finish filing the teeth to get a 0° rake angle on each (step 3). Continue filing until the teeth are sharp. Recheck the teeth for uniform height a last time, and you're ready to fit the handle to the tang. To resharpen, repeat the process of filing the teeth backs with the large file and filing the face of the teeth with the small one. □

Jay Sperling is a freelance writer and Bart Chapin is a cabinetmaker. Both live in Bath, Maine.

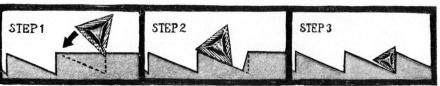

Woodcuts: E. Marino III

A Pair of Panel-Raising Planes

Two is more than twice as good

by Robert Bourdeau

In a recent project, a Louis XV armoire for my daughter, I used the shaper to raise the many panels for the doors and case sides. I was disappointed with the results—especially with tear-out both across and along the grain. Quite a bit of sanding was required to eliminate the pits and gouges; further, the crisp look and feel of cleanly cut wood was gone.

When it came time for me to begin work on my son's roll-top desk, and I wanted to raise its panels with double bevels, I discovered that the appropriate shaper knives would have to be custom-ground at a high cost. There had to be a better way, so I decided to make myself a pair of panel-raising planes, a left-hand and right-hand, which would allow me to plane in the direction of the grain regardless of the side of the panel I might be working on. This meant that I could keep tear-out and splintering under control, minimizing the amount of sanding I'd have to do.

I had never made a plane before, but after studying K.D. Roberts' *Wooden Planes in 19th Century America* and reading Norman Vandal's "Paneled Doors and Walls" (*FWW* #18, Sept. '79) and Timothy Ellsworth's "Hand Planes" (*FWW* #1, Winter '75), I felt I could make the pair of panel-raising planes by laminating the bodies. I began with a full-

Tear-out from planing against the grain, always a problem when using a single panel-raising plane, is minimized by having two, a left-hand and a right-hand model. No matter how the grain runs, one plane or the other can follow it.

scale sectional drawing of the panel I wanted (figure 1); the double bevel would form a tongue on the panel's edge and make for a nicer fit in the frame grooves than would an unrelieved wedge. Using ¾-in. stock, I divided the thickness of the panel into even thirds and decided to cut a ¼-in. by ⅜-in. rabbet along the back edge of each panel to form the back side of the ¼-in. tongue. When captured in the grooves, there's a resulting ⅛-in. wide gap between the vertical shoulder of this rabbet and the inner edges of the frame. This means that the panel can expand a full ¼ in. before it exerts any pressure against the frame, a sufficient allowance for most panels, unless they are exceptionally wide or made from an unstable wood. For a pleasing appearance, the back edges of the panel can be chamfered or slightly rounded over, as can the inner edges of the frame.

Since the profile of the panel's field, shoulder and bevel is the exact complement of the plane's sole, it was an easy matter to draw the plane in section atop the panel (figure 2) just as though the plane were making its final pass down the edge. By laminating the body of the plane with two sides, or cheeks, and a three-part core (a front block, an adjustable shoe and a rear block), the task of shaping the sole to the required angles was made much easier and simpler than would have been the case had I tried to make the entire body from a solid block in the traditional way. I beveled the bottom of the inside cheek at 6° off perpendicular and did the same to the outside cheek, the only difference between the two being that the outside cheek projects below the sole, while the inside cheek does not. See figure 2 for an elevation view of these parts. This arrangement determines the angle of the bevel and the final depth of cut, though these can be varied by altering the thickness of the shim, which is clamped to the bench along the edge of the panel and which stops the cut when the bottom edge of the outside cheek contacts it.

I set the two cheeks aside and turned to making the blank for the three core pieces. I laminated the blank from face-glued lengths of ½-in. thick maple. When the glue was dry, I dimensioned the blank 14 in. long by 2¼ in. high by 1¹³⁄₁₆ in. wide, this last dimension being final and the other two slightly oversize. Since a ¼-in. strip along the outside edge of the sole must be beveled at 6°, I set my jointer fence at 84° and took a few light passes until the jointed surface was exactly ¼ in. wide. This is the part of the sole that conforms to the second bevel, the face side of the tongue.

I reasoned that the iron should be skewed at 30° in the body of the plane and that its cutting angle should be 35°, though 45° is common on traditional planes of this type. This meant that the face of the rear block that would support the iron would have to be cut on a compound angle as shown in figure 4—60° in the horizontal plane, 35° in the vertical. You can make this cut by angling the miter gauge and tilting the arbor on the table saw, or by setting up the radial-arm saw for cutting a compound angle. From the toe of the angle to the rear of the blank should be about 9 in. You must orient the blank correctly when cutting; its 1¹³⁄₁₆-in. width is a finished dimension. The height and length will be trimmed after the body is glued up. The inner face of the forward block must also be cut at a compound angle—120° in the horizontal plane (to complement the 60° skew angle of the rear block) and 65° in the vertical plane. Since the core blank is about ³⁄₁₆ in. too high, you can rip off a ¾-in. thick slice from the beveled sole to produce the adjustable shoe. Make a

smooth cut, so that the sawn surfaces will mate uniformly.

As a final step before gluing up the body, cut a ½-in. wide tapered dado in the inside cheek about 1 in. forward of the mouth. I also cut a ½-in. wide dado ³⁄₃₂ in. deep in the corresponding place on the side of the forward core block. When the parts were glued together these two dadoes formed the tapered slot for the scribing spur and its wedge. The purpose of the spur, which I made from a length of ordinary hacksaw blade, is to score the wood in advance of the cutter when planing across the grain, thus to eliminate tearing the stock.

Now the body can be glued up (with the movable shoe left out). Be sure to position the rear and forward blocks so that if the angled face of the forward block were extended, it would intersect the face of the rear block at the surface of the sole. The acute angle on the adjustable shoe will be pared back at a later time to make room for the extended iron (figure 4, detail A). And the throat opening can always be enlarged by adjusting the shoe. Be careful about positioning the cheeks in relation to the core blocks when gluing up. You may want to use pins to help locate the parts and to keep them from swimming out of alignment under clamping pressure.

When the glue has set, plane the top edges of the core blocks flush with the top surfaces of the cheeks. The movable shoe is secured by means of a ¼-in. machine screw that passes through a slotted hole (⅜ in. by ¼ in.) in the forward block and screws into a T-nut set in a plugged counterbore in the shoe. You can make the slotted hole easily by boring two ¼-in. dia. holes and chiseling out the waste between. The washer can either be let into the block or sit proud of the surface.

I made the handle to fit my hand and working posture. The angle between the handle and the body of the plane (and also its point of attachment) determines how efficiently your muscular energy is transmitted to the cutting edge, so it's a good idea to experiment with several angles and shapes before making a final decision on the handle design that's correct for you. The handle is attached to the body by a long ¼-in. screw or bolt that extends through a hole bored through the full length of the handle and is screwed into a T-nut in the rear block. This T-nut, like the one in the movable shoe, is retained in a plugged counterbore.

The cutter has to be ground to conform exactly with the profile of the sole. This is critical. To ensure this conformity, I inserted the iron blank in the body and traced the profile of the sole with layout dye onto the steel and then traced again with a sharp machinist's scribe. I used a jig for grinding (see photo, next page) and I made periodic checks, re-inserting the iron into the body, to make certain the shape was being properly formed. I ground the bevel on the iron to 30°, which provided a clearance angle of 5°.

I made the chip breaker from ⅛-in. mild steel, which I first hacksawed and then filed to the final shape that is shown in figure 3. I used a small, round file to form the groove across the face of the chip breaker where it bears against the steel retaining pin. I drilled and tapped the upper part of the chip breaker to receive a ¼-in. thumbscrew. A square, steel pressure plate, countersunk to receive the end of the thumbscrew, presses against the iron when the screw is tightened. Even greater pressure is levered against the toe of the chip breaker where it contacts the iron just above the cutting edge. You may want to use the traditional wedge here, which should exert uniform pressure along the length of the iron.

The iron should be ¹⁄₁₆ in. narrower than the opening in

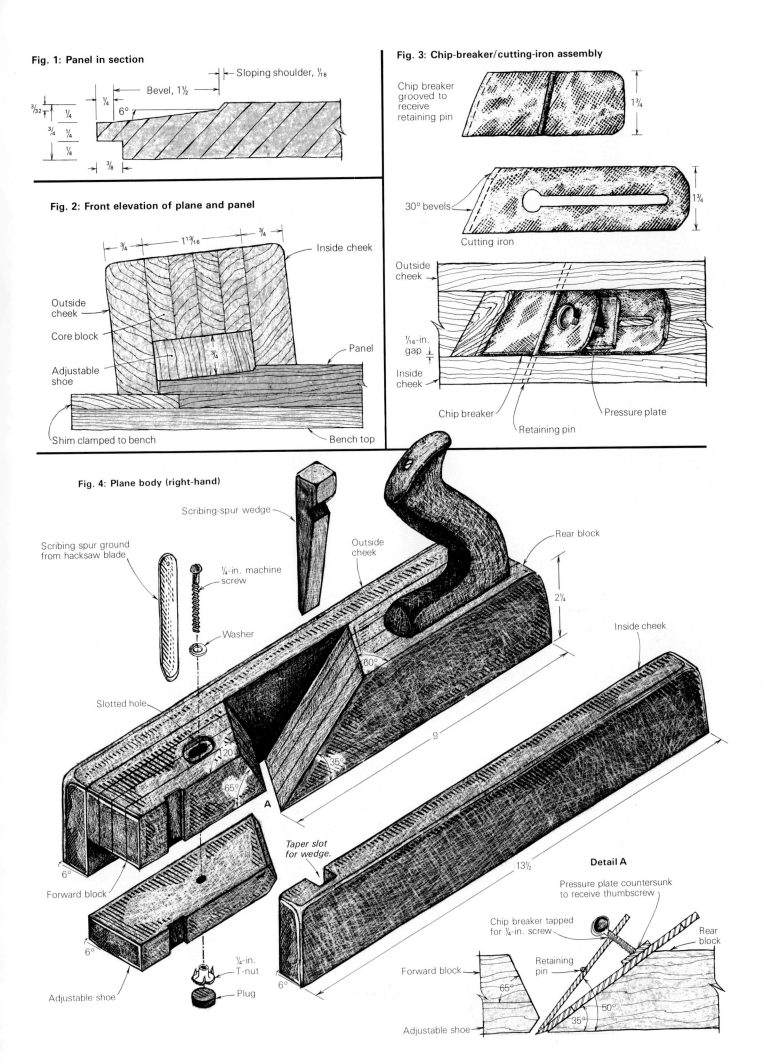

Fig. 1: Panel in section

Sloping shoulder, 1/16

Bevel, 1 1/2

6°

3/32
3/4
1/4
1/4
1/4
3/8

Fig. 2: Front elevation of plane and panel

3/4   1 13/16   3/4

Inside cheek

Outside cheek

Core block

3/4

Panel

Adjustable shoe

Shim clamped to bench

Bench top

Fig. 3: Chip-breaker/cutting-iron assembly

Chip breaker grooved to receive retaining pin

1 3/4

30° bevels

Cutting iron

1 3/4

Outside cheek

1/16-in. gap

Inside cheek

Chip breaker

Retaining pin

Pressure plate

Fig. 4: Plane body (right-hand)

Scribing-spur wedge

Scribing spur ground from hacksaw blade

1/4-in. machine screw

Washer

Outside cheek

Rear block

2 1/4

Inside cheek

Slotted hole

60°

9

120°

35°

65°

A

6°

Taper slot for wedge.

13 1/2

Detail A

Pressure plate countersunk to receive thumbscrew

Chip breaker tapped for 1/4-in. screw

Rear block

Forward block

6°

1/4-in. T-nut

Plug

Adjustable shoe

6°

Forward block

65°

Retaining pin

50°

35°

Adjustable shoe

61

Author's grinding jig holds the iron at a fixed angle (top photo), yet its base is unattached, allowing the profile to be shaped freehand. In raising the panel, the plane is first canted to the outside to take several narrow shavings (center photo). Then it's canted to the inside for several passes, and then several cuts are taken down the middle of the bevel. Only when making the last two or three passes is a cut taken the full width of the iron (bottom photo). This method reduces the chance of tearing the grain and is less tiring than taking a full cut with each pass.

which it rests, and it should fit snugly against the inside of the outside cheek. This leaves a 1/16-in. gap between the iron and the inside cheek, which makes room for the sloped shoulder to be formed. Looking back at figure 2, you will see a small triangular space between the edge of the panel and the inner edge of the outside cheek. Imagine the plane just beginning to make its first pass along the flat edge of the panel. The plane's body would be oriented at 90° to the panel's surface. With each successive pass and the removal of a single shaving, the plane's body cants more and more to the outside of the panel, and with each pass the cutting toe of the iron changes its attitude and its distance from the original shoulder line. The triangular space between cheek and panel edge widens and deepens as the bevel is cut. As the plane's body cants and the iron is pulled more to the outside, the sloping shoulder is formed.

I ground the scribing spur to a round-nose shape only after experimenting with several other cutting configurations. The round-nose spur need not be inclined forward in the body as shown in the photos. Care must be taken to set the spur at the exact depth of the iron. If set even slightly deeper than the iron, it will leave ugly lines in the sloped shoulder; if set higher than the iron, it will not sever the tissue through to the depth of cut, and tear-out and splintering could result.

The left-hand plane is made exactly like the right-hand one, only everything is reversed as in a mirror. The iron, of course, must be ground to precisely the same profile as on the other plane, as you may very well be planing the same bevel with both planes, since the grain direction can reverse in the middle of a board.

In use, I have learned that long, uninterrupted strokes are best, beginning at one end and going right through to the other. The outside cheek should always be kept snug against the edge of the panel when planing. To save your strength and to proceed at a workmanlike pace, begin cutting first to the outside, removing several narrow shavings (center photo, at left). Then cant the plane to the inside for several passes; then take a couple down the middle. Don't try to take a cut across the full width of the bevel until you make the last several passes (photo, bottom left). In a dense wood it uses a lot of energy to take a cut 1¾ in. wide, and I can now understand why in the old shops two people—one pushing, another pulling—were required to manage a large plane.

I have learned quite a bit from the experience of making these two planes, enough to realize that much lies ahead, for now I've got plans to make all of my planes for molding, rabbeting, jointing and other tasks. For those woodworkers who have never tried making planes, I would add that given a reasonable amount of technical reading, careful measuring and thoughtful joining, the plane's secrets unfold like the story in a good book.   □

Robert Bourdeau, 42, is an accountant and an amateur woodworker in Laval, Quebec.

A Cabinetmaker's Tool Cabinet
Updating a traditional design

by David Powell

When I first started making furniture in Edward Barnsley's workshop, the tool chests used by the craftsmen there were of the traditional sort. They were simplified versions of a design that had developed over centuries, originating probably as medieval oak chests or coffers. All of them were rectangular boxes that sat directly on the floor. Their lids were hinged in the rear and locked in the front to discourage borrowing and pilfering. The underside of the lid was fitted to hold tools, and the inside of the chest contained one or two banks of drawers which faced each other and opened into a central well (see drawing below). Under the drawers there was usually a space to hold tools too large or awkward to fit into any of the drawers or to hang from the lid. These tools might fit into partitioned compartments or just be wrapped in cloth and placed into an undivided bin. At the bottom of some chests there would be a wide drawer that opened to the outside, so a person could get at its contents without having to rummage inside the main part of the chest.

By the late 18th century cabinetmaker's chests had evolved into refined pieces of furniture. Though outside they remained plain and unadorned, the interiors of these chests were often finely fitted, veneered, inlaid and otherwise decorated. Such refinements proclaimed the skill of the maker to a prospective customer or employer, and no doubt brought a sense of satisfaction to the cabinetmaker who had to live with the chest and work out of it.

When I decided to make my own tool case about 25 years ago, the chests I saw around me in Barnsley's shop were superbly straightforward and well made, but without any in-

terior inlaying, decoration or veneering. Looking at these chests, it seemed to me that their big disadvantage was that too many of the tools they held were not easily accessible. A lot of the tools were stored below the drawer cases, which could mean having to move a whole bank of four to six drawers to get the shoulder plane you wanted. And then perhaps you'd have to go to the added trouble of unwrapping it. Retrieving a tool from the bottom of the chest was about like resurrecting a mummy.

Another disadvantage with these chests was that they were low to the ground. You had to do considerable bending and crouching to fetch and replace your tools. Finally, I felt that there was much wasted space in an already confined area inside these chests, because the well between the facing drawer units had to be left clear to allow the drawers to be opened.

I wanted to have my tools as readily accessible as possible, while still having a case that I could close and lock. I also wanted it to be reasonably transportable, and to fit into my workplace unobtrusively. An upright tool cabinet seemed to be the answer. Sitting on a squat base, such a cabinet when fitted with a bank of drawers would hold all my tools at a comfortable height and would minimize the amount of stooping I'd have to do, and I wouldn't have to remove some tools to get at others. Having a pair of doors would give me two large surfaces on which I could mount saws. And below the drawers, I decided to build pigeonholes for my planes.

Initially, I tried to measure every tool or set of tools I owned and to assign a place in the chest or a drawer for each. This, of course, proved impossibly complex, and couldn't take into account future acquisitions. So I designed the bank of drawers to general dimensions that seemed likely to accommodate my smaller tools, and in particular to keep together sets of related tools such as squares, chisels and gauges in a single drawer, or in a group of drawers. Then I estimated what further small tools I was likely to buy and added drawers for these. This estimate has fallen sadly short of the mark, and after 25 years the drawers are overflowing with tools.

Next, I got out all my planes and lined them up, measured them and assigned each a place in the bin below the drawer case. I also made allowance in this allotment of space for planes I knew I would buy later, and have found to my pleasure that all my planes still fit neatly where I planned for them to go. Then I fell into the trap of including an open well above the drawers. At the time I conceived the design, I reasoned that this space could contain tools that didn't fit conveniently anywhere else in the cabinet, and I could use the underside of the lid for hanging more tools. Over the years this well has collected a pile of tools and dust, and has become something of a junkheap from which it is difficult to disentangle a tool I want. This is exactly the feature in the traditional tool chests that I had wanted to avoid.

Now I'm redesigning the cabinet and will make a new one

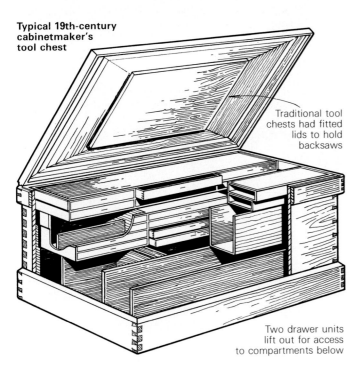

Typical 19th-century cabinetmaker's tool chest

Traditional tool chests had fitted lids to hold backsaws

Two drawer units lift out for access to compartments below

without the well in the top. The area it would have occupied will be taken up by additional drawers. The drawers' basic dimensions won't change, and I will still provide fitted spaces for indispensible tools, but will create more in the way of flexible space for new tools.

Building a tool cabinet brings all of your joinery skills into play, and gives you the chance to make one large case and a lot of little drawers. Make the main case from 4/4 pine. If you want to omit the upper tool well and devote this space to drawers as I plan to do, then you can through-dovetail the four sides of the case together, cutting the pins on the top and bottom pieces. Groove the inner rear edges of the case to receive a ¼-in. plywood back panel. The main horizontal divider, which separates the drawer unit from the pigeonhole section below, is through-tenoned into the case sides, with three wedged tenons on each end. This divider stiffens the sides of the case and supports the drawer unit as well.

If you are tidy, you might find the upper well useful. To make it you must let two wide rails into the sides of the case with through wedged tenons on each side as shown in the drawing on the next page. The bottom inner edges of these rails must be grooved to house the bottom panel, which is best made from ½-in. plywood. Also, the bottom edge of the rear rail is grooved to accept the ¼-in. plywood back panel.

The drawer unit includes two vertical dividers which are housed at the bottom in dadoes cut across the horizontal divider and in dadoes in the top of the case (in notches in the two rails if you build in the top well). These dividers are made from ¾-in. thick stock, and have ¼-in. deep, ¾-in. wide rabbets cut along both of their front edges. These rabbets accommodate the ¾-in. thick drawer fronts, which overlap the drawer sides ¼ in. The side of the case must also be rabbeted in the same amount to make room for the overlapping drawer fronts at the extreme ends of the unit.

The drawers slide in ¼-in. deep, ½-in. wide dadoes cut into the two vertical dividers and in the case sides. The dadoes are hidden by the overlapping drawer fronts, which also obscure the drawer runners. These are ¼-in. thick, ½-in. wide strips that are screwed to the sides of the drawers. When fitting the runners in the grooves, you'll probably need to plane a shaving or two off their width to get an easy sliding fit.

The drawers themselves are joined in a straightforward way. The sides fit into vertical stopped sliding-dovetail housings in the drawer front, and the back is joined to the sides with through dovetails. The ¼-in. plywood bottom is glued and bradded in a rabbet cut into the drawer front. The back and sides are cut narrow to ride entirely over the bottom, and therefore don't need to be rabbeted.

The three drawers across the bottom are really not drawers at all, but French-fitted trays for holding drill bits and wrenches. It's frustrating to go rummaging through a pile of wrenches when you're looking for just one, but in a fitted

To hold his cabinetmaking tools in a convenient and organized way, author built this tool cabinet, making maximum use of its interior space. Its design evolved from those chests he saw while an apprentice in Edward Barnsley's shop, and is well adapted to studio woodworking.

64

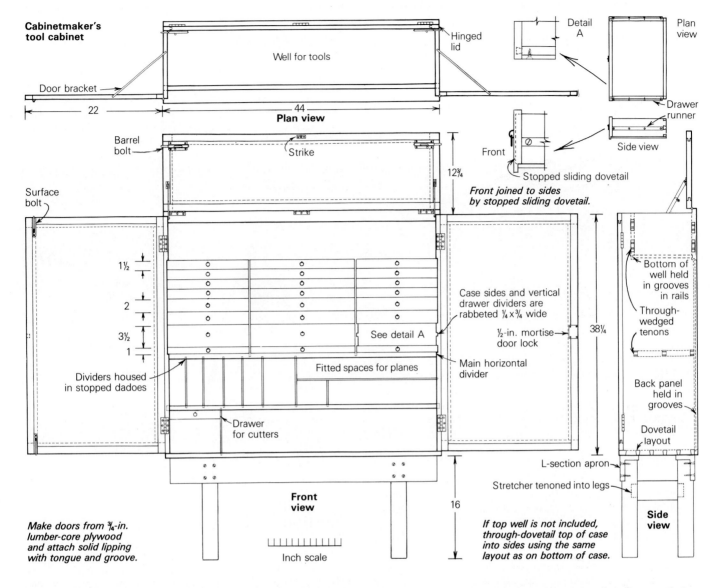

Cabinetmaker's tool cabinet

Door bracket

Well for tools

Hinged lid

22 — 44

Plan view

Detail A

Plan view

Drawer runner

Barrel bolt

Strike

12¾

Front

Stopped sliding dovetail

Side view

Front joined to sides by stopped sliding dovetail.

Surface bolt

1½

2

3½

1

Dividers housed in stopped dadoes

See detail A

Case sides and vertical drawer dividers are rabbeted ¼ x ¾ wide

½-in. mortise-door lock

Main horizontal divider

Fitted spaces for planes

Drawer for cutters

Bottom of well held in grooves in rails

Through-wedged tenons

Back panel held in grooves

Dovetail layout

38¼

L-section apron

Stretcher tenoned into legs

Make doors from ¾-in. lumber-core plywood and attach solid lipping with tongue and groove.

Front view

Inch scale

16

If top well is not included, through-dovetail top of case into sides using the same layout as on bottom of case.

Side view

---

drawer, you can pick out the right wrench at a glance. I used ½-in. thick pine for the tray, and cut out the spaces for the wrenches and other items with a jigsaw. Then I applied the fitted tray over a ¼-in. plywood bottom, and edged both sides with solid lipping to which the runners are attached. The front edge of the tray fits into a groove in the drawer front.

The pigeonhole unit has two levels, and the top one is divided into nine bins that are dimensioned to hold planes of various sizes. The shelf that separates the upper and lower sections is housed in dadoes in the sides of the case, and the vertical dividers are secured in stopped dadoes in the shelf below and in the main horizontal divider above. The bottom half of this area is left unpartitioned, except for a single pigeonhole on the left and a little drawer I built to hold cutters for my router plane and electric router. Note that the drawer fronts and pigeonhole dividers are recessed 2 in. into the case to make room for the tools that will be mounted on the inside of the cabinet doors.

I made the two doors from lumber-core plywood and edged them on all four sides with solid wood. This lipping has a tongue milled onto one edge that fits into a corresponding groove cut in the edges of the plywood. The solid lipping wears better than the raw edge of the plywood and keeps the face veneer from snagging on a shirtsleeve and tearing up. Also, it's more attractive, and will hold screws better. The doors are hung to overlap the sides of the case and are secured

with butt hinges mortised into the edges of the case and the door. If you choose to make a top well, then edge its lid with solid lipping and attach it with inlet butt hinges.

To hold the doors open so they don't flop around when you remove and replace the tools mounted on them, you can fashion brackets by bending the ends of a ³⁄₁₆ in. dia. metal rod to fit into sockets in the top edge of the case and the top edge of the door, as shown in the drawing above. These brackets can be put away when the cabinet is closed. The lid for the top well is secured by a pair of barrel bolts (one on each side), and the left-hand door locks top and bottom by means of two surface bolts (the strike for the top one is screwed on the underside of the lid). A half-mortise drawer lock installed on the right-hand door secures the entire cabinet.

The base I made from pine lumber also. The side stretchers are tenoned into the legs and the L-section aprons are held with screws and glue in notches cut into the tops of the legs. You could add a shelf to the base for holding tools and other items you don't mind having exposed to the outside. The cabinet sits unattached on the base; its weight is sufficient to keep it stable and in one place. This arrangement makes it easier for me (with some help) to move the cabinet whenever the need arises. □

David Powell is a designer and cabinetmaker, and the proprietor of Leeds Design Workshops, Easthampton, Mass.

Methods of Work

Inexpensive workbench

This simple workbench uses two pipe clamps for the vise. The size of the bench, quality of material and construction

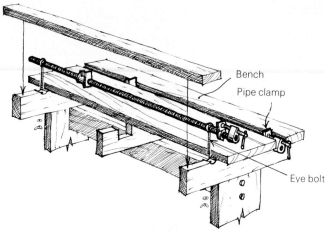

Bench

Pipe clamp

Eve bolt

design can all be varied to suit the needs of the builder. My choice is the trestle-leg design shown; others may want to use four corner legs to provide a mounting location for a leg vise. (For a pipe-clamp leg-vise design, see Methods of Work, *FWW* #11, Summer '78). The major drawback to this design is the non-adjustable dog height. To overcome this problem, preset the dog height at ¼ in. or ½ in. Then, to surface thin stock, shim it off the table with thin plywood.

—*J. Butler, Hubbardston, Mass.*

Improved leg-vise adjustment

On all the leg vises I've seen, to change the jaw opening you have to wiggle a pin out of a hole near the floor and fiddle it back into the next hole. Here's a design with fixed pins you can work with your foot—just step on the adjustment foot and it disengages, then kick the bottom of the moving jaw to where you want it.

The trick is to make the adjustment foot not out of wood but out of ¼-in. aluminum plate scavenged or from a sheet-metal dealer. To make the slots, drill a series of holes in the plate and saw into them from the edge with a hacksaw or a bandsaw. You can saw most aluminum alloys on the bandsaw with regular wood-cutting blades. You can saw most aluminum alloys on the bandsaw with regular wood-cutting blades. Aluminum tends to grab drill bits, so clamp the adjustment foot down before you begin drilling.

—*Geraldo Bennuccio, Oakland, Calif.*

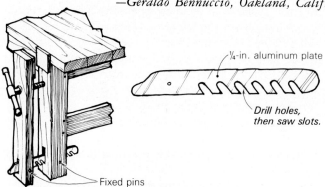

¼-in. aluminum plate

Drill holes, then saw slots.

Fixed pins

Cutting wooden threads

To cut perfect wooden threads, immerse the dowel in hot paraffin for ten minutes prior to threading. Thread while the dowel is still warm. The shavings roll out of the die in a neat string, leaving a perfect thread base. The method works even on hard-to-thread woods like oak.

—*Al Grendahl, St. Paul, Minn.*

Carver's stand

Woodcarvers will find this carver's stand useful—especially for sculpture and figures in-the-round. An old bowling ball at the heart of the stand forms what is, in essence, a universal joint. The carver can rotate his work or incline it at any angle, thus permitting easy access to all areas of the carving. Hardware consists of a long lag bolt mounted through the bowling ball into the work and two 24-in. long, ½-in. threaded steel rods. When the carver has his work in the desired position, he simply tightens nuts on the threaded rods to lock the bowling ball in position and also to make the stand rigid.

—*M.B. Hansen, Huntsville, Texas*

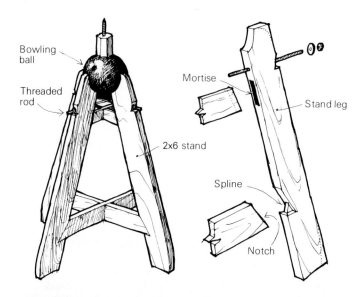

Bowling ball

Threaded rod

2x6 stand

Mortise

Stand leg

Spline

Notch

Horizontal vise

This horizontal vise, installed on a workbench, is indispensable for sanding, routing, carving and planing. For many operations it holds the work better than bench dogs. The vise consists of three simple parts: a bench screw, an oak jaw and a wooden step-block. Mount the bench screw's nut to the bench from the bottom so that the surface will be flat if you remove the vise. Cut the 2-in. thick jaw about 20 in. or so

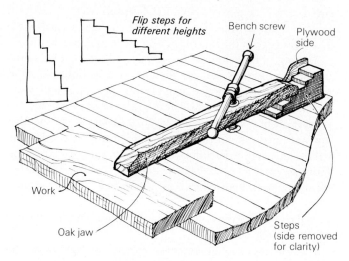

Flip steps for different heights

Bench screw

Plywood side

Work

Oak jaw

Steps (side removed for clarity)

long. Drill an oversize hole in the jaw about 7-in. from the back and fasten the bench screw through the hole. Bandsaw the step-block from a 4x4. Cut the steps taller one way than the other so you can flip the block and use it both ways. To keep the back end of the jaw from slipping off the sides of the step-block, glue a piece of plywood to each side.

—*Pendleton Tompkins, San Mateo, Calif.*

Grit-slurry sharpening

Here's yet another sharpening method to add a bit more lore to the subject many craftmen approach with almost mystic reverence. The method uses a slurry of loose grit on a flat glass plate. It is the same method laboratories use to sharpen the microtome, an instrument that slices tissue into thin sections for microscopic examination. The method is effective for sharpening woodworking tools, particularly plane irons. Start by dumping a half-teaspoon of #400 grit on an 8x8 pane of glass, adding several drops of light machine oil to make a slurry. Hone the plane iron as though you were using a bench stone. When you obtain a good bevel, wipe the glass clean and repeat the process using #600 grit to obtain the final cutting edge. For optimum results, polish with a polishing compound or give the blade a few strokes on a leather strop.

This method is superior in several ways to sharpening on a stone. The glass is flat and wears little even with much use, and the large surface area allows for a more comfortable hand motion. The large surface is particularly suitable for the use of a roller device to hone the iron at a constant angle. Finally, you can buy a wide range of abrasive powders at hobby shops that deal in lapidary supplies (one source is Grieger's Inc., 900 S. Arroyo Parkway, Pasadena, Calif. 91109). A small investment in materials will allow you to perform work that would otherwise require several different grades of stones.

—*George Mustoe, Bellingham, Wash.*

Edging with a leathercraft tool

To break the sharp, hard corners on straight or curved boards I use a simple tool that leather workers will find familiar. It's called a leather edger and is available in several sizes wherever leatherworking tools are sold.

If you're not near a source of leatherworking tools the edger is easy to make at home. Start by inserting one end of a 4-in. length of drill rod in a handle. Shape the other end of the rod into a curved fork with two tines about ⅜ in. long. Use the edge of a small rectangular file to cut the slot from the top and to form the appropriate cutting angle. Sharpen the cutting edge between the tines from underneath with a thin, rounded slipstone.

To use, push the tool along an edge with the grain. It should remove a thin, curled shaving and leave a delicately rounded edge in one pass.

—*Norman Odell, Quathiaski Cove, B.C., Canada*

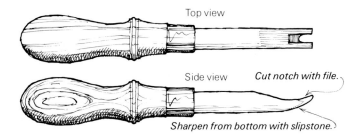

Top view

Side view   *Cut notch with file.*

Sharpen from bottom with slipstone.

Modifying twist drills for wood

A worn-out twist drill can be modified to perform much better in wood. First grind the tip flat. Then, using a cone-shaped stone in a hobby grinder or the rounded-over corner of an abrasive wheel, grind two hollows—one on each side of the center. The hollows form a center spur and two outer spurs. Be sure to bevel the hollows so that the back side of the flutes will clear the wood.

In use, the center spur holds the bit stable and keeps it

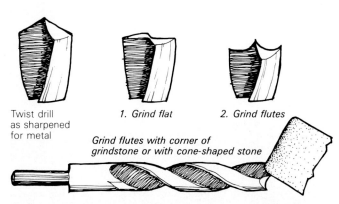

Twist drill as sharpened for metal   1. Grind flat   2. Grind flutes

Grind flutes with corner of grindstone or with cone-shaped stone

from wandering. The outer spurs cut the wood's fibers in advance of the cutting edge to give straight, clean holes.

—*Stanley F. Kayes, Richmond, Va.*

Shop-made counterbore

Here is an easily made counterbore for bolt heads, nuts and washers. With it you can avoid the problem of centering a second bit over a previously drilled bolt hole. Make the tool

Rod   Split washer   Weld

from a length of steel rod the same size as your bolt stock. Find a flat washer that just slips on the rod, saw a slot in it and twist the washer apart slightly. Weld the washer to the rod about 1 in. from one end with the lower edge of the split facing clockwise. File the pilot end of the rod for proper clearance and sharpen the cutting edge of the washer with a file.

—*Carl Meinzinger, Guemes Island, Wash.*

Recycling old blades as scrapers

An excellent cabinet scraper can be made from a section of a 1-in. or wider bandsaw blade. Just cut the blade to 9-in. lengths, grind off the teeth and round the ends to get the shape you need. Because the blade flexes you can scrape hard-to-finish surfaces like handrails and cabriole legs.

—*John E. Freimuth III, Peoria, Ill.*

Hazardless honing

Here is a simple combination storage box and jig that will enable you to use your oilstones more effectively and safely. What makes the box unique is a wide tongue cut into the bottom. In use, the tongue is secured in a woodworking vise, ensuring a stable, firm foundation for the oilstone.

To make the box, cut blocks for the base and cover from any hardwood. Use a drill press with a multispur or Forstner bit to remove most of the waste. The cavity in the base should be about half as deep as the stone. The cavity in the cover should be ⅟₁₆ in. or so deeper to provide clearance. Chop out the remaining waste with a chisel, making sure the stone fits snug in the base and doesn't rock. Saw away the bottom corners to leave the tongue. —*Al Ching, Fullerton, Calif.*

To use, clamp tongue in vise.   *Optional chamfered edge protects knuckles.*

JOINERY

Spline-Mitered Joinery
Concealed strength for fine lines

by Eric Hoag

Some years ago I solved a few design and construction problems with leg-and-apron structures using splined miters. Since then I've applied the technique to a number of projects, and after seeing these pieces exposed for several years to New England's fluctuating humidity, I believe the principles involved are sound. I was looking for a structure that would not be affected, visually or mechanically, by wood movement resulting from end grain butting long grain in the typical leg-and-apron joint. I also wanted to produce an unbroken, sweeping line from the bottom of one leg, up and across the apron, and down the other leg. Finally, I had to have strength in the joinery that would not be obtrusive or detract from the delicate appearance I was after.

The technique I worked out calls for mitering the leg-and-apron joint, which is reinforced with a blind spline, and also for joining the two halves of the legs with a splined miter (or bevel). The procedure I'll describe is for making a table like the one shown below, but you can modify it to build chairs, cabinet bases and other structurally similar pieces.

To establish the curves of the legs and aprons and to proportion the widths and thicknesses of these members, I start with an elevation drawing, fitting the end or side view within a square or rectangle of predetermined dimensions. Since the eight identical leg halves in the table must be uniformly cut, I

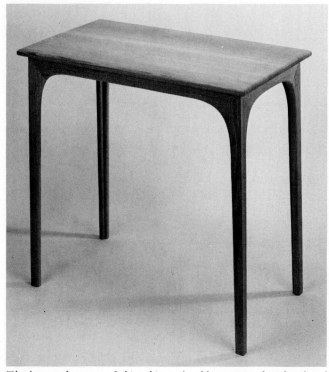

The legs and aprons of this white oak table are joined with splined miters. The delicate appearance of the piece belies the inherent strength of its joints. An additional advantage is that the whole assembly can be glued up with a minimal use of clamps.

make a Masonite pattern for these (photo A, facing page). Though adjacent aprons may be different lengths, I make only one pattern, which I lengthen or shorten in the middle (where the line is straight) as required. In proportioning the longer apron, pay close attention to its depth lest it produce, when shortened, a clunky, heavy-looking shorter apron.

Once the patterns are made, I joint and thickness-plane enough material for the four aprons and eight leg halves before tracing the layout lines onto them. Be sure when tracing that the straight edges of the patterns are flush with the jointed edges of the stock. Then bandsaw the inner curved and straight edges of the separate pieces.

Next, cut the miters for the leg-and-apron joints using an accurately set miter gauge in your table saw. The aprons must be mitered to finished length at this point (opposites must be identical), but the legs are left long at the bottom and cut to final length after assembly. Now the bandsawn edges are given a final rough shaping and smoothing to eliminate the need for too much of this kind of work when the pieces are assembled and more unwieldy. Some of the sweat can be taken out of shaping the legs by trimming the straight tapered edges on the table saw using a taper jig and stopping just shy of the curve.

Before cutting the spline slots for the leg-and-apron joints, I study the grain and color of all the pieces and decide which leg halves will go together and which aprons will go with which legs, and I determine the face side of each piece. Then I mark them all accordingly. Once I have this information marked on each piece, I cut the spline slots using a router table and straight-face bit of the appropriate diameter—usually one-third the thickness of the stock. The advantage of the router table is that you can adjust the depth of cut without disturbing the fence setting. This allows you to make a series of progressively deeper cuts when routing these slots—a safer and more accurate way to get good results than cutting to full depth all at once.

I set the fence on the router table to precisely half the thickness of the stock, measuring from the center of the cutter. Also, I project the centerline of the cutter onto the fence, using a square and pencil. With this line as a central reference, I mark on the fence two sets of diagonal lines that will show me where to position the stock for the initial plunge of each cut and where to stop advancing it into the cutter (photo B). The distance between these diagonals (one pair for each orientation of the stock) is determined by the length of the miter involved in the joint. Keep in mind that it's necessary to leave more space at the top of the slot (where the angle is acute) than at the bottom. If you're not careful you could cut all the way through the stock at the tip of the miter.

For spline material I often use plywood, as it allows me to rip a piece the desired length of the splines and to crosscut them to width. Because the router bit leaves the slots rounded at their ends, the splines must be rounded or chamfered to fit (photo C). After dry-fitting all the joints to check for proper tightness and accuracy, I glue each leg-and-apron assembly together. If the joints fit well to begin with, the miters need not be clamped, only forced together by hand and secured with several strips of tape across the joints on both sides. Sometimes unequal stresses exerted by the tapes cause the joints to rock and cure out of square. This can be remedied by tacking three carefully positioned strips of wood on a flat surface at right angles to one another. The three members can be clamped to this U, which will keep them square while the glue sets. Remove the tape as soon as the glue dries or it may pull up bits of wood when you peel it off.

Scrape and sand the area of the joint when the glue has dried; then smooth out any irregularities in the curves where the legs and aprons meet. My preference is to round these inner edges with my router, using a quarter-round bit with a ball-bearing pilot. This rounding also helps with the final shaping, as it eliminates a goodly amount of the edge I have to file and sand to get a finished contour.

Ultimately, these four leg-and-apron assemblies will be joined together with splined miters running almost the entire length of the legs. But before proceeding further, you should provide some means of attaching the tabletop support stringers to the inside of the aprons. I use a pair of stringers, with slotted expansion holes for screws (photo D) to attach the top. These stringers have tenons that are housed in shallow mortises cut into the upper inner faces of the long aprons. It's best to rout these mortises before gluing the separate assemblies into a single unit.

I cut the leg miters (bevels) on the table saw (photo E, next page). First I tilt the arbor to exactly 45°, checking with a combination square, and then lower the blade below the insert. Next I attach a straight wooden auxiliary fence to the saw fence, which I set on the left side of the blade, and with the saw running, I raise the blade slowly so that it just nicks the bottom outside edge of the wooden fence. The setup is checked by making a partial cut into scrap stock. The blade should enter the stock on the edge side, not the face side, and should leave behind a very narrow flat or land on the edge. This is necessary for holding the stock against the fence and keeping the beveled edge from creeping under the fence dur-

A. *Author traces interior curve and taper of half a leg from Masonite pattern. Only one apron pattern is needed, since the line between the curves can be lengthened or shortened as required. Straight side of the pattern must be registered along a jointed edge of the stock.*

B. *Diagonal lines on router-table fence show where to position stock and where to stop the feed for cutting blind spline slots in leg-and-apron miters. There are two pairs of diagonals, one for each orientation of the stock.*

C. *Corners of spline must be rounded or chamfered to fit into the rounded areas at the ends of slot. The slot must be stopped at least ¾ in. short of the miter's toe to prevent the bit from cutting through the edge of the stock.*

D. *Tabletop support stringers are slotted for screws and mortised into the ends of the long aprons. Screw slots allow the top to expand and contract without bowing or cupping. Mortises are routed before table frame is completely assembled.*

E. *Wooden auxiliary fence guides bevel cut on legs. A push stick is used for the last several inches of the cut, and care is taken to keep stock from being burned or gouged by the blade.*

F. *A wide fence on router table is used to guide stock when slotting the miter down the length of the legs. The extra-large fence gives needed support to the leg-and-apron assembly and ensures accuracy in cutting.*

G. *The legs should fit together easily, and the mating surfaces should have no gaps for an ideal interface. When the glue is applied, the joints are assembled by hand, pressed together and secured with clamps and tape at frequent intervals along their length.*

ing the cut. When two leg halves are assembled, these lands will create a small chamfer down the outside corner of the miter. This may be eliminated by planing or filing, or you may choose to increase its width or to round it over. Use a push-stick for the final 6 in. or so of the cut and take care that the work doesn't lurch against the blade as the cut ends, as this will create a gap in the joint.

Though you can cut the grooves for the splines on the table saw, I prefer to use the router table, which I equip with a high fence, angled accurately at 45° (photo F). Cutting the grooves this way allows you to stop them easily, and the high fence gives good support for the stock, ensuring accuracy. I cut the splines from scrap stock planed or resawn to the proper thickness, or I cut them out of plywood. With the splines in place, I dry-fit all four assemblies together (photo G), looking for a fit that is snug, with all joining surfaces in contact. The fit should not be so tight, however, as to require force to get the whole thing together. Use a band clamp around the top and C-clamps or spring clamps on the legs, working from top to bottom to ensure proper glue squeeze-out. Then I reinforce the joints with tape, where possible.

Depending on the piece of furniture you are making, there are additional steps prior to final assembly. A chair or a stool with a drop-in seat will need a groove near the upper inside edge to accommodate the tongue of a frame to support the seat. An inset tabletop will require a rabbet along the top inside edge. Although I've never had to use stretchers with this design, an end table with a shelf may require making some joints to receive the shelf supports. Lastly, in the case of a large piece (or one that will get rough treatment), corner braces may be necessary. Where they are placed will depend on where the increased stresses are expected. I mortise them into the structure, usually across the mitered joint between the leg and apron at an angle that will conceal their presence so they don't detract from the appearance of the curve. These corner braces can be decorative as well as functional in tables with inset or overlapping glass tops.

As I said earlier, I like to cut the legs to final length after assembly, whenever this is feasible. After the glue is cured, the tape removed and the excess glue scraped away, I set the fence on the table saw to the finished length of the legs and make the cuts by running the two long aprons against the fence. Before cutting, however, I wrap some tape around the foot of the leg where the sawblade will exit. This helps keep the wood from chipping out as the blade comes through. □

Eric Hoag, 37, is a professional cabinetmaker. He lives in Branford, Conn.

Routing Mortises
A simple fixture and the right router

by Tage Frid

A mortising machine is an important piece of equipment, and in a cabinet shop with several workers one might be a good investment. Whatever kind you buy, a chain-saw or a hollow-chisel mortiser or a long-hole boring machine, you can expect to pay a lot for it, $2,000 or more. But by building a simple fixture for holding the stock to cut the mortises with a plunge router, you can have a mortising setup that works just as well as an expensive machine. The cost is only about $350, and you'll have acquired a heavy-duty router for general shop use.

Two makes of plunge-type routers are sold in the United States—The Stanley (models 90303 and 90105) and the Makita (model 3600 B). The Stanley plunge-base routers are production tools specifically designed for rough cut-out work, like cutting out holes in countertops for kitchen sinks or lavatories. They plunge to a set depth and lock automatically, but can't be locked at any depth in between. Stanley, by the way, has recently sold its power tool division to Bosch Power Tool Corp. (PO Box 2217, New Bern, N.C. 28560), although the tools will still be sold under the Stanley label for the next two years. The Makita router is similar in design to the Elu router, which is a popular tool in Europe but isn't sold in this country because it has a 220v, 50-Hz. motor, and would burn out if plugged into an American outlet.

Several things about the Makita model 3600 B make it a good router for mortising. It's a plunge-type router with a 2¾-HP motor. The body (motor/spindle assembly) is attached to a rectangular base by two ⅞-in. dia. steel posts. These fit into sleeves in the body, which can slide up and down on the posts (against spring tension), and be locked at any height. Plunge routing lets you begin and end a cut in the middle of a piece of stock without having to lower or lift the base from the work. With the motor running you can lower the bit into the wood by pushing down on the router's handles.

The Makita is pretty heavy (11 lb.) and well designed. The switch can be worked without having to move your hand from the handle, but it's not located right on the handle where you might turn it on accidentally when picking up the router. The body is locked on the posts by a latching lever instead of a knob, and you can reach this lever to raise or lower the bit without having to take your hand off the handle. An adjustable knob on the top stops the upward travel and also controls the depth of cut for ordinary routing.

For plunge routing there are two depth stops that let you

For cutting clean, precise mortises quickly, Frid uses a Makita plunge router with an easy-to-build fixture (below, left) for holding the stock and guiding the tool. Using appropriately sized or contoured supports, almost any piece of stock, like the curved chair back shown here, can be mortised in this fixture. At right, Frid tightens one end stop, which, along with the other, will limit the travel of the router and determine the length of the mortise.

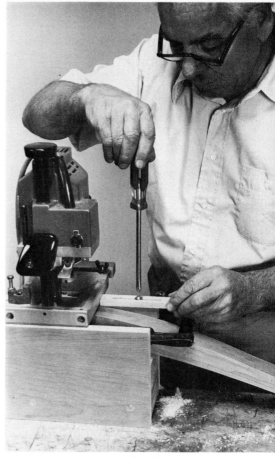

remove stock in two passes rather than in one, and the stop rod is capable of both fast and fine adjustment. You can also control the depth of cut when plunge routing without using the stops. Just turn on the router, release the lock lever, push the bit down to the desired depth and lock it. The fence is secured with only one wing nut and is easy to set. The Makita router comes with ¼-in. and ⅜-in. adapter sleeves for its ½-in. collet, so you can use different bit sizes and cut mortises of almost any width and up to 2⅜ in. deep. By turning the stock over you can produce a through mortise up to 4¾ in. deep. The weight of the machine makes it stable while running and helps give you a smooth cut. You might find that the posts bind in the sleeves if you try plunging the router when the motor is not running. But when the motor is on, the vibration allows the body to move smoothly up and down on the posts.

The mortising fixture I made looks like a big miter box. Its length and depth can be varied to suit your needs, but for general use it should be 20 in. to 36 in. long and about 4 in. deep. This will let you mortise everything from chair legs to bedposts. Regardless of the length, the inside width of the fixture should not be more than 3¼ in., or else the router base will not rest on both side pieces. Make the bottom of the fixture from two pieces of ¾-in. plywood. It needs to be thick to give the sides of the box a large gluing surface and to hold them stiff with a minimum of flex. The edges of the bottom piece must be a true 90° to the face, or the sides will not be perpendicular and your mortises will be askew to the face of your stock. When gluing up, be sure the bottom edges of each side are flush with the bottom of the base. Locating pins will help hold the sides in alignment when tightening the clamps. Solid wood could warp, so you might want to make the sides from ¾-in. plywood with solid lipping on the upper

edges where the router base rubs. When the glue is dry, check the two upper edges with a square; they must be perfectly parallel. If they are not, take light passes on the jointer until the edges are square and parallel, or use a hand plane to do the same thing.

You need to install lateral end stops on the top edge of the inboard side of the fixture. The two stops are slotted strips of wood with shallow grooves on their bottoms to fit over and ride along the edge. The slot in each strip rides around a 3/16-in. stove bolt which engages a T-nut embedded in the side. A barrel nut would prove even more durable and easier to install. Also, you could drill pilot holes in the upper edge of the inboard side for hanger bolts; use wing nuts with these to tighten down on the stops.

To cut the mortises in a piece of regular dimensions—a straight table leg, for example—raise the workpiece in the fixture so it's almost flush with the top edge. Center the area to be mortised in the middle of the fixture and clamp it to the inboard side. Set the stops on both ends to contact the router base so the bit can travel the full length of the mortise in one pass. With the fixture held in a vise, set the fence on the router the right distance from the bit and butt the base against the left-hand stop. Switch on the power, release the lock lever and lower the bit into the wood. For a ⅜-in. bit, a ¼-in. depth of cut would be safe. Then pull the router to the right. Don't start at the right-hand stop and push the router to the left. By pulling the router left to right, the rotation of the bit will hold the fence against the side of the fixture, which will give you a good, straight cut.

During routing, dust and shavings can get compacted on the ends of the stops where the router base makes contact. If you don't keep this debris cleaned off, your mortise will get

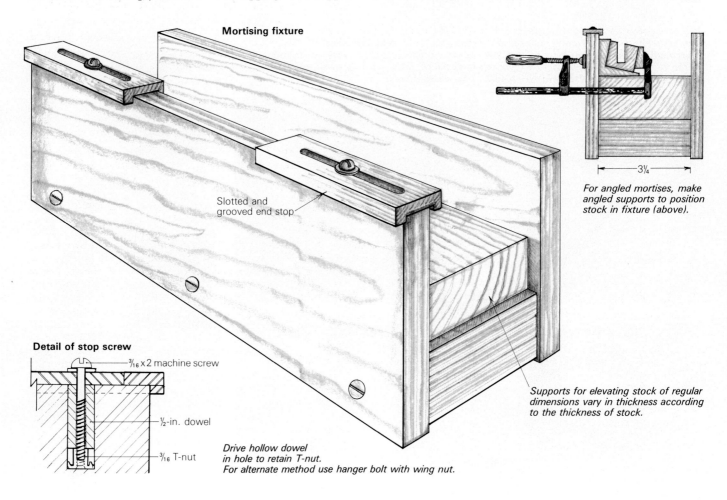

Mortising fixture

Slotted and grooved end stop

For angled mortises, make angled supports to position stock in fixture (above).

3¼

Supports for elevating stock of regular dimensions vary in thickness according to the thickness of stock.

Detail of stop screw

3/16 x 2 machine screw

½-in. dowel

3/16 T-nut

Drive hollow dowel in hole to retain T-nut. For alternate method use hanger bolt with wing nut.

The fixture shown here was made especially long for mortising bedposts. The stock is held in place by a wedge at either end, and the lateral end stops are set to limit the length of the mortise. By making a full plunge cut at the extreme ends of the mortise and routing out the waste between with a series of shallow passes, mortising proceeds with speed and precision.

Equipped with a spiral end mill, the Makita model 3600B router is an excellent tool for mortising. But its powerful motor and square base make it also well suited for clamping upside down in the tail vise of your bench, where with the proper fence it becomes a spindle shaper.

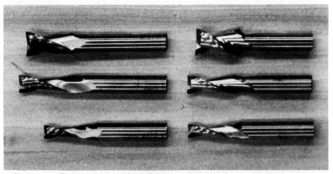

These two-flute spiral end mills were designed especially for routing wood. Bits with cutting diameters of ½ in. or more can cut as deep as the bit will plunge, but bits with cutting diameters smaller than ½ in. are limited in their depths of cut by the diameter of the shank. The bits on the right in ⅜-in., ½-in. and ¾-in. cutting diameters are made by Onsrud Cutter Mfg. Co. The bits on the left, in corresponding cutting diameters, are made by Ekstrom Carlson Co. Their longer shanks give them greater depth-of-cut capability.

shorter as the cut gets deeper. One way to avoid the problem is to make an initial plunge cut to full depth with the router held against the left stop and then against the right stop. Then you can rout out the waste between in several passes without having debris pack up against the stops.

The depth of each cut depends on the hardness of the wood you are cutting and on the size and kind of bit you use. Make repeated cuts, always left to right, lowering the bit between passes, until you have reached the desired depth for your mortise. All this might sound complicated, but you will be surprised at how fast it works. I have found it faster and cleaner cutting than the hollow-chisel mortiser.

To cut angled mortises in regular stock, like those in chair legs to receive tenons on stretchers and rails, make angled supports to hold the stock in the correct relation to the bit. To mortise curved pieces—a chair back, for instance—bandsaw a piece to fit the side of the curve opposite the cut and use it to support the stock when clamped in the fixture. You can place the curved support under the stock for mortising on one side. To mortise the adjoining face, support the stock from the inboard side of the fixture using the same curved piece, and a flat support on bottom.

For general mortising, I use two-flute, straight-face bits with ¼-in. shanks. High-speed steel, straight-face bits will work, but they will get dull faster than carbide bits. For mortises ½ in. wide or more, you can use bits with ½-in. shanks, which will perform better than bits with smaller shanks because they are stiffer and will chatter less. The best bits for cutting large mortises are two-flute spiral end mills with ½-in. shanks. They are especially designed for plunge cutting and for fast chip removal, and because of their spiral form they have a shear-cutting action. When wasting the area between the two plunge cuts, spiral bits can make passing cuts as deep as ⅜ in. without protesting. But they will start to scream when you make a passing cut that's too deep, and you will find yourself forcing the bit into the work. This is not good. Spiral end mills will cut effortlessly in a straight plunge and when taking a lateral pass that's not too deep.

You can get spiral end mills made for routing wood from Onsrud Cutter Mfg. Co., 800 E. Broadway, PO Box 550, Libertyville, Ill. 60048 and from Ekstrom Carlson & Co., 1400 Railroad Ave., Rockford, Ill. 61110. Costs vary, but generally ½-in. dia. and ⅜-in. dia. bits are under $10, while ¾-in. dia. bits run about $20. □

NOTE: The business of setting the router stops and of locating stock in the fixture can become tedious when cutting a lot of mortises. Here is a solution: First, knife a vertical line on the inside face of the fixture, near its center. This is the primary reference for subsequent measurements. Next, scribe a stop line on the top edge of the fixture, to the left of the centerline, the precise distance from the cutting edge of your mortising bit to the edge of the router base. With the left-hand stop locked at the stop line, a knife line on the stock marking the left end of the proposed mortise can be brought to the vertical centerline. Now, with the router placed against the left-hand stop, measure over on the fixture's edge, from the right side of the router base, the length of the proposed mortise minus the bit diameter. This locates the right-hand stop. To set the depth of cut, lower the adjusting knob until the cutter grazes the stock surface. Then set the depth screw to the depth of the mortise above its stop. Finally, back off on the adjusting knob so the bit will clear the stock. To make all of these measurements quick and reproducible, you can mill a set of hardwood gauge blocks. Instead of measuring, you simply insert the correct gauge block between the router base and end stop, and between the depth screw and depth stop. In addition to cutting mortises, these gauge blocks will come in handy for other setups in the shop.

Cutting Box Joints on the Radial-Arm Saw

Sliding jig moves workpiece into blade for safe, precise cuts

by Ken Mitchell

Sooner or later, the owner of a radial-arm saw will want to use this machine for some operation that will tax both patience and ingenuity. My challenge arose when I wanted to make a substantial number of box (finger) joints for drawers, quickly. The obvious method—clamping the work on edge to the fence, running the blade parallel to the table, and lowering (or raising) the arm for successive cuts—soon proved impractical. If you have ever tried this method, which most owner's manuals recommend, you'll know that it is slow and deplorably imprecise.

Resolving to find a better way, I decided that the blade should remain fixed and that the stock should be raised in precise increments for each cut. The first requirement in working this out was finding a way to guide the work along the table for each pass into the dado head. Table saws have miter-gauge slots for guiding the stock into the cut, and I reasoned that such an arrangement could be worked out for a radial-arm-saw table. To make this guide slot, I first attached skirts to the sides of the table, and to these I screwed a guide rail parallel to the front of the table. As shown in figure 1

Ken Mitchell, 49, an amateur woodworker, is an engineering supervisor for AT&T in San Francisco, Calif.

(facing page), the slot is created by a spacer glued along the bottom inside face of the guide rail. This spacer holds the rail a consistent ¾ in. away from the front edge of the table.

Next I designed a sliding jig for holding the stock on edge while it is being fed into the dado blade. The jig's travel across the table is guided by a bar that rides in the slot. To make the work go faster, I made the jig big enough to hold eight pieces of ¾-in. by 6-in. stock, which meant that I could cut the joints for four boxes at once. The jig (figure 1) consists of a plywood base, a guide bar that rides in the slot, a fixed fence, an adjustable fence and a stop block (for determining the depth of cut) that travels along a slotted rail and is secured at the appropriate setting with a wing nut.

To make the jig, first dimension the base to a size that is suited for your project and glue and screw the guide bar in place. Install the fixed fence on the base with glue and countersunk wood screws through the base. Make sure you brace the fence with blocks as shown, and be certain that the fence is precisely perpendicular to the base. The adjustable fence is made so it can slide toward and away from the fixed fence, sandwiching the stock in between. The distance between the two fences depends upon the thickness of the stock and the number of pieces being cut at one time. So it can

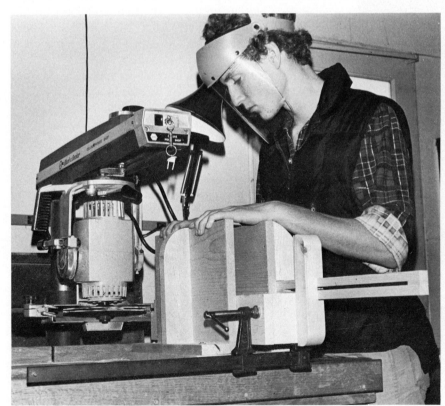

With the stock aligned and clamped together between the two fences on the sliding jig, the work is passed through the blade. The jig is guided by a bar that rides in a slot at the front of the table. The adjustable stop block is secured in place along the slotted rail and determines the depth of cut. Photos: Ken Mitchell.

Here the stock is positioned for making a third pass into the blade. Successive fingers are cut by stacking precisely thicknessed shims under the stock, thus elevating it in precise increments.

These crisp finger joints were cut quickly and accurately on a radial-arm saw, using the author's modified saw table and special jig for feeding the work into a stationary blade.

slide right and left, the adjustable fence has a base with a slotted hole at each end, through which ¼-in. hanger bolts protrude. The fence is fixed in position by tightening wing nuts down on the hanger bolts.

The slotted rail for the stop block is screwed to the fixed fence. Don't glue it, as you may want to add longer or shorter rails for different projects. The stop block should be almost the same height as the fences. Dado the block so it will slide along the rail and bore it for a ¼-in. hanger bolt.

Now that you have a means of holding the stock on edge and feeding it accurately into the blade, the next step is choosing the size of the fingers to be cut. The depth of cut will determine the length of the fingers, which should be just slightly longer than the stock is thick. With all pieces cut to final length, clamp opposite sides of the drawer or box together with ends flush. With the depth of cut scribed on one board, move the stock horizontally in the jig between the fences until the tip of the blade is aligned with the mark, as shown in figure 2. Now tighten the adjustable fence snug against the stock and bring the stop block into contact with the ends of the boards and secure it in place.

You must decide on the thickness of the fingers and proceed to cut a number of shims, which will be placed under the stock to elevate it for each successive cut. For ¼-in. thick fingers, the shims must be exactly ½ in. thick. For ⅜-in. thick fingers, the shims must be ¾ in. thick. The width of the shims is slightly less than the distance between the fences, and their length is the same as that of the fences. Shims that are too short and too narrow could allow the stock to wobble in the jig. In addition to the shims that are twice the thickness of the fingers you want to cut, you'll need one or two that are the exact thickness of the fingers. Take care to thickness the shims to the exact width of the cut made by the dado blades

mounted on your arbor. Don't assume because the chippers are supposed to be ⅛ in. thick that your blades cut in precise ⅛-in. increments. Make a sample cut with your blades and thickness your shims according to the width of this cut. If you don't have a thickness planer, you can rip the shims oversize and finish them with a hand plane, or you can rip them to final thickness if your saw is capable of fine adjustments.

Begin by cutting the sides that have fingers on their top edges (figure 3). With the saw carriage secured on the arm, the blade parallel to the table and the depth of cut established by the stop block, lower the column until the blade lightly touches the top edge of the stock. Return the jig; then slide a ¾-in. shim under the stock, switch on the saw and pass the stock through the blade. This produces a ⅜-in. pin (finger) on the top edge of the box sides. For the second cut, insert another ¾-in. shim on top of the first shim, replace the stock and pass it through the blade. For each cut, repeat this procedure, adding as many shims as the width of the stock requires. If tear-out is a problem, back the stock with a piece of scrap.

The other two sides must be notched on their top edges to receive the pins just cut. I insert a ⅜-in. shim under the stock for this first cut (figure 4) and then make all the subsequent cuts by adding ¾-in. shims, as I did previously.

I've used this system frequently and have found that it produces close-fitting joints. And it's fast, especially once you've established a rhythm in performing the discrete little parts of the process. Another virtue is that the slot at the front of the table can be used for other purposes. I've made a number of cut-off and mitering jigs that ride in this slot, and they give more accurate results than rotating the arm on the column and pulling the saw into the work. The point is that a radial-arm saw will perform more accurately if the blade is stationary than it will if you move the carriage along the arm. □

Fig. 1: Modified saw table and box-joint jig

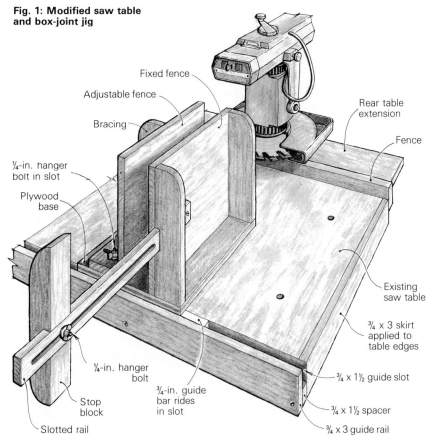

Fixed fence

Adjustable fence

Bracing

¼-in. hanger bolt in slot

Plywood base

¼-in. hanger bolt

Stop block

Slotted rail

¾-in. guide bar rides in slot

Rear table extension

Fence

Existing saw table

¾ x 3 skirt applied to table edges

¾ x 1½ guide slot

¾ x 1½ spacer

¾ x 3 guide rail

Fig. 2: Setting up the blade and jig

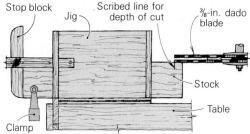

Stop block

Jig

Scribed line for depth of cut

⅜-in. dado blade

Stock

Table

Clamp

Lower column until blade touches the top edges of the stock, then align tip of blade with scribed line for proper depth of cut.

Fig. 3: Cutting the pins first

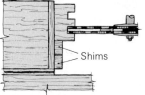

Shims

Make initial cut by inserting ¾-in. shim under stock. Add a second ¾-in. shim for the second cut, a third one for the third cut, and so on.

Fig. 4: Cutting the notch first

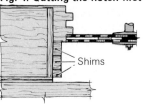

Shims

Cut notch at top edge of stock by inserting ⅜-in. shim beneath stock. For all following cuts, add ¾-in. shims under stock.

77

Template Dovetails
Another way to skin the cat

by Charles Riordan

Tools for template dovetails.

For centuries the dovetail joint has been the most satisfactory method of joining two pieces of wood meeting at the end grain. It's especially appropriate for drawer and case construction. The joint is strong, durable and decorative, one of the hallmarks of the master craftsman. However, the tyro need not approach dovetailing with a faint heart. There are indeed many ways to divest a feline of its fur; I believe using templates is the best way to produce dovetails. The method described in this article, with special attention to drawer construction, owes its inspiration to Andy Marlow, whose *Classic Furniture Projects* (New York: Stein and Day, 1977) describes a similar approach.

Templates can be made quickly and easily using the sheet aluminum stocked by almost any hardware store. The photo top right shows the tools I use. The scratch gauge, photo right, is a machinist's gauge made by Starrett Tools (Athol, Mass. 01331), and I use it for both laying out the templates and marking the boards for the dovetails. Over the years I have found this marking tool easier to use and more accurate than the conventional cabinetmaker's marking gauge.

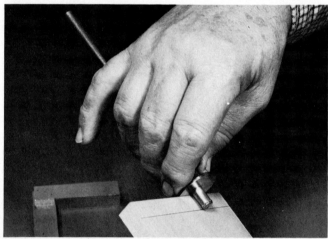

Charles Riordan makes period furniture in Dansville, N.Y.

Machinist's scratch gauge marks wood and metal.

To make the template, cut a piece of aluminum about 4 in. wide and long enough to span the width of the stock you are joining. Make sure that the bottom is square to both sides. Don't count on the sheet you buy at the hardware store being square at each corner; check it. Set the scratch gauge to the thickness of your drawer-side stock, or the stock you will cut tails in, and mark the sides of the template. You will be able to make two templates from this one

sheet, one on each long side.

Determine the number of pins necessary for the depth of the drawer and mark their centers on the template using either a rule at an angle or the dividers, starting so the bottom pin just misses the groove for the drawer bottom. I use the bottom of each board as my reference edge for marking the pieces. With the proper pin spacing marked, set the bevel to the desired angle, usually 15°, and mark the pins

on the template. Leave just enough space at the points to allow the jigsaw blade to enter. Take a sharp-pointed knife and score the bases of the pins (A). Laying the top blade of the tin snips in the scratched lines, cut the sides of the pins slightly through the baseline (B). Then, with the long-nosed pliers, grasp the waste metal at the pin baseline and carefully bend it back and forth until it breaks off (C). A little touch-up with a fine file and your template is ready.

A. *Scoring the template baseline.*

B. *Snipping the template.*

C. *Breaking out the waste.*

Hold the boards to be marked for the tails firmly on your bench either by clamping or with bench dogs. Leave enough space above the dog to hold the square against the bottom and end of the board, and butt the template against the square (D). Hold the template firmly and mark the tails (E). It's important here that the scratch awl be sharpened to a needle point and that it be held at the same angle for each marking, an angle that will ensure that the point follows the template cutout unerringly. Observe the grain direction and mark so that the grain will force the point of the scratch awl against the guide. The consistency of the marking will determine the accuracy of the joint.

To mark the pins, I place the board to be marked in the vise with a flat back-up board extending slightly above it. If your vise is too narrow to exert pressure across the whole width of the board, use a C-clamp or two to make sure there is no gap between the back-up board and the piece to be marked. Place the template on the end of the board to be marked and firmly against the back-up board. Abut the template against a stop held against the lower edge of the piece to be marked (F) and mark the pins. Here again I must stress the importance of the angle at which the scratch awl is held; a few degrees variation will result in a poorly fitting joint, especially if the errors are additive.

With a small square and the scratch awl, mark the inside face of the drawer back (or front) for the wide side of the pins. I find that it helps also to mark the narrow side of the pins on the outside face for through dovetails, especially if the wood is not fairly straight-grained. Now take a soft, black pencil that has been sharpened to a chisel point and trace lightly over the scratch marks (G). This will leave the center of each scratch line clearly defined as a thin, light line between the black pencil lines.

To cut the pins for a lipped (rabbeted) drawer front I use a router, with the drawer front clamped vertically in the vise (H). To give the router a firm base I clamp a piece of hardwood 3 in. thick, 4½ in. wide and 12 in. long to the face side of the drawer front. I also clamp a stout piece of hardwood to the inside of the drawer front both to protect the piece from clamp marks and to act as a stiffener. Instead of using the router guide fence I use a fence (or back stop) fastened to the heavy base board. I find that this gives firmer control over the router and less chance for tipping or wobble when routing end grain. This is

D. *Positioning template on tail board.*

E. *Marking the tail board.*

F. *Positioning template on pin board.*

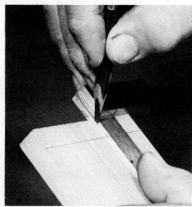

G. *Squaring down the pin lines.*

H. *Routing waste for half-blind dovetails.*

important because the router bit is extended to include the depth of the drawer lip as well as the pins and is otherwise unstable.

Do not attempt to rout all the way to the pin lines. Come as close as you feel is

safe, leaving a shaving or two to clean off later with the chisel. Of course, the depth of the pins and their width is taken care of by the depth of the router bit setting as well as by the positioning of the fence. →

The next step is to cut the tails and rough out the pins of the drawer back (I) on the jigsaw. A band saw can be used, but a jigsaw will give better results. Use a sharp, fine-toothed blade, ³⁄₃₂ in. to ⅛ in. wide, tensioned enough not to wander. Don't depend on your unmagnified eyesight here. I use 4× magnifying glasses and seldom have to touch a chisel to the tails or pin bases after jigsawing. Saw just to the waste side of the scratch-awl markings on the inside face highlighted by the pencil.

After the pins are cut on the jigsaw they will, of course, be square pegs that must be brought to their final triangular shape with a paring chisel. Don't try to chop down in one or two large bites. Nibble off fine shavings as shown (J). The chisel must be as sharp as a razor. The first cut will give the indication of which direction the grain is going. If the grain runs into the pin, pare in horizontally from one face or the other, holding a stout piece of wood against the opposite face of the pin so the wood will not break out as the chisel cuts through. Here again, use the magnifiers and place the chisel in that fine, light line between the pencil markings to make the final shave.

To cut away the shavings and clean up around the base of the pins, I use a spear-pointed chisel I made from a ¼-in. straight chisel by grinding it to a 30° point (K). It is much better than a skew because it cuts on both sides and can be held flat on the pin baseline while severing the shavings. Its usefulness is fully appreciated when cleaning up the pins for a blind dovetail joint, as no square-edged chisel can quite get into the acute corners.

Now that you have carefully followed that fine, light line with sawblade and chisel and a careful inspection shows no more trimming to be necessary, you can assemble the pieces (L), and tap the tails home using a hammer and a block of wood. If you have done all your cutting with the care needed to make a dovetail joint, the pieces should go together with a firm "thunk" and you'll have to go out and buy a new hat because your old one will never again fit.

Glue up only after you're sure all the parts fit with no binding or excessive pressure being brought to bear. Apply glue to the pins only and clamp with just enough pressure to snug up the joints. Too much will cause bowing and will produce an out-of-square drawer or case with poor joints. Use a try square on the inside corners to make sure this is not taking place. □

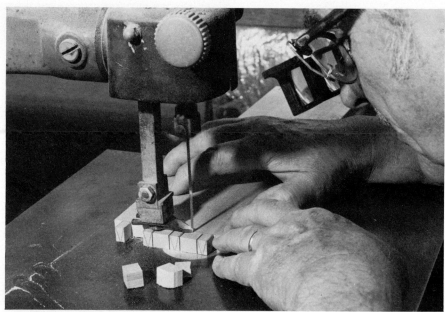

I. *Sawing waste from through dovetail pins. Do the tails the same way.*

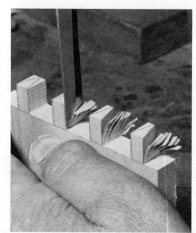

J. *Paring the pins.*

K. *Cleaning pin bases with spear-pointed chisel.*

L. *The completed joint.*

Greeno interlock joint

The development of a genuinely new wood joint is worthy of notice. In the shop of Jerry Green, the furniture maker with whom I apprenticed, we often worked with a tropical wood called partridge wood. Dramatic color made the wood popular, but it was prone to checking and honeycombing in thicker dimensions. Green's designs, nevertheless, frequently called for 2-in. and thicker material, so we laminated ¾-in. stock. Capitalizing on this, Green invented this highly deco-

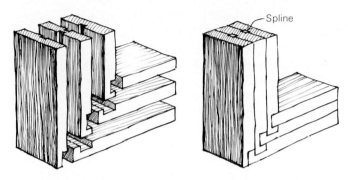
Spline

rative, extremely rigid and (since it requires only one setup) easy-to-machine joint. Because the joint is self locking, it must be assembled while laminating. After the glue sets, scrape and belt-sand the surfaces. To register the laminated boards we often added splines, as shown in the sketch.

In memory of its inventor we came to call this joint the Greeno interlock joint.

—*John W. Kreigshauser, Kansas City, Mo.*

Three-member lap joint

Here's a variation of the lap joint I discovered while trying to find a way to connect three stretchers on a three-legged table. The joint is attractive and strong. Each member overlaps the other two members with a large edge-grain glue surface.

To lay out the joint, scribe a centerline on both faces and both edges of all pieces. Set a bevel gauge to 60° and use it to mark the diagonal lines shown in the sketch. Saw away what waste you can, then finish chopping out the waste with a chisel. Take care to keep the glue surfaces flat and the edges that show crisp.

By changing the angle of the layout you can adapt this joint to any number of members, odd or even.

—*David Nebenzahl, Flagstaff, Ariz.*

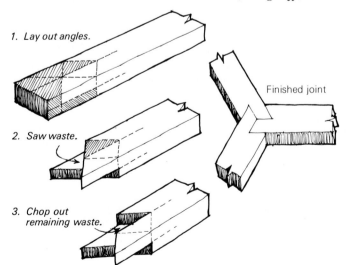
1. Lay out angles.
2. Saw waste.
3. Chop out remaining waste.
Finished joint

Routed box joint

I enjoyed Patrick Warner's article on the box joint (*FWW* #14, Jan. '79). I like the visual results, strength and ease of assembly the joint allows. Like Warner, I use a router to cut box joints, but my technique is different. I have installed a guide block on the base of my router that acts as a jig for accurately spacing the finger cuts. The setup does not limit me in width, angle or length of project. I have made jigs to fit several common-size router bits but I usually prefer the ½-in. setup for most work. The sketch shows how to mount the guide block for ½-cuts. The accuracy of the joint depends on

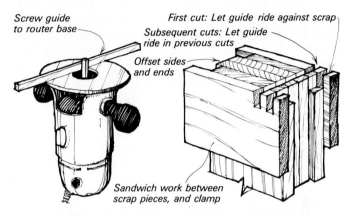
Screw guide to router base
First cut: Let guide ride against scrap
Subsequent cuts: Let guide ride in previous cuts
Offset sides and ends
Sandwich work between scrap pieces, and clamp

how carefully you position the guide in relation to the bit. Drill the screw holes in the router base a little large to give yourself some adjustment room.

To use the guide, sandwich the box sides and ends between two pieces of scrap, offsetting the sides from the ends ½ in. and the ends from the scrap ½ in., as shown. Now chuck a carbide bit in the router and make the first cut with the guide sliding against the scrap pieces. For the second cut, just slide the guide in the newly cut groove. Continue the process across the ends of the boards for the rest of the cuts. It's like climbing a ladder. Wax the guide to slide easily in the grooves.

—*George Persson, Star Lake, N.Y.*

Routing tongues

I cut the tongues for tongue-and-groove joints with a router. There are faster methods, but the router's precision depth adjustment produces a fit that's unbeatable. First set the router depth by trimming the edge of a scrap board. Flip the board over, trim the other side and test the resulting tongue in the groove (which has been previously cut). Make fine depth adjustments and continue to rout test tongues until the fit is perfect. To cut the tongue, first measure the distance from the router base to the bit. Then clamp a fence to the work this distance from the tongue. Gently tap the fence into perfect position with a mallet, checking the measurement with a steel ruler.

—*Jeffrey Cooper, Portsmouth, N.H.*

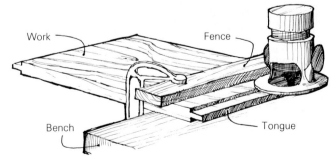
Work
Fence
Bench
Tongue

Decorative Joinery
Leading the eye around the piece

by John E. N. Bairstow

The most important element in the craftsman's repertoire is the wooden joint. Although its functional development has been extensive, fascinating possibilities remain unexplored for using the joint in a decorative capacity. Historically, decoration has more often been supplementary, applied to the piece of furniture, rather than integral with its construction. Carving, inlay and marquetry have been used extensively in various forms, while joinery, although potentially the most interesting element, remains quiescent. Few historical examples exist where the method of construction plays a major visual role in the finished work. Thus the designer has become accustomed to creating an attractive piece of furniture using shaped and decorated parts, while sticking to standard joinery beneath.

I choose to start designing a piece of furniture by considering the decorative possibilities of its joinery. This approach makes it possible to use fairly simple forms, and to create the initial visual impact through the joint. Most standard carcase joints, the dovetail and the finger joint, for instance, rarely relate well to the form of a piece of furniture because they concentrate all the interest along the corners. This is fine if you are close to the piece and can appreciate the proportion and accuracy of the joints, but if you are viewing it from more than a few feet, then the most striking thing will be the overall form and not the beauty of the detail. By designing decorative joints that extend beyond the locality of each corner, it is possible to stimulate that first impression at the joint yet bring the viewer's eye around the rest of the piece.

Each of the joints discussed on the following pages is an elaboration of a basic joint, in most cases the finger joint. I do not set out to design a decorative joint with a particular machine or process in mind, but I do try to produce them all with equipment usually available to the designer/craftsman. Small-workshop machines, particularly the router, are versatile, and we should look to them to help carry out creative processes rather than sticking to their conventional functions.

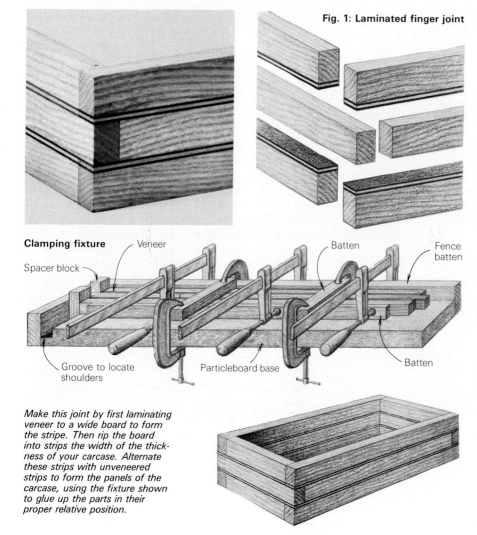

Fig. 1: Laminated finger joint

Clamping fixture — Veneer — Batten — Fence batten

Spacer block

Groove to locate shoulders — Particleboard base — Batten

Make this joint by first laminating veneer to a wide board to form the stripe. Then rip the board into strips the width of the thickness of your carcase. Alternate these strips with unveneered strips to form the panels of the carcase, using the fixture shown to glue up the parts in their proper relative position.

The first joint, illustrated at left, is probably the simplest both visually and constructionally. To make it, begin by laminating veneer to the face of a wide board to produce the stripe in the panel. The thickness of this board, including the veneer combination, will be the width of the laminated fingers in the joint and is therefore an important dimension. When the glue is dry, rip the board into strips, the widths of each will be the thickness of the panel. Each panel (case side) is made from a combination of these strips and of unveneered strips. They are crosscut to alternate lengths; the shorter ones determine the inside dimension of each side of the finished carcase, and the longer ones determine the outside dimension.

When all the strips have been prepared, a simple fixture is required to glue up the panel while maintaining the staggered formation at the ends. It may be difficult to get each strip to lie flat with only side pressure of the clamps. I have used a press that provides both vertical and horizontal pressure, although it is possible to surface and thickness-plane these panels after glue-up without affecting the joint, provided that the grain of all the strips runs in the same direction.

Make this joint by first shearing off the corners of the components on a guillotine miter box, shaper or table saw. Then slot the components with a router, a shaper or a table saw, and as-

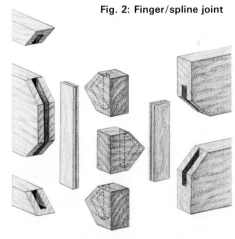

Fig. 2: Finger/spline joint

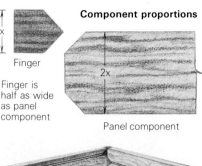

Component proportions

Finger

Finger is half as wide as panel component

Panel component

semble using plywood splines. A veneer strip can be added between the panels, as shown in the drawing at right, to visually link the corners of the carcase.

The second example, illustrated above, is again basically a finger joint, but its construction is entirely different from the previous one. Visually, the joint is confined to the corner, which is something I try to avoid. This drawback can be overcome by gluing up the panels with veneer between the components, so that thin lines connect the V-shaped "fingers" from corner to corner.

Cut your stock to the required length, width and thickness. The length is the distance between shoulders of the constructed panels (the inside dimensions of the carcase). The width of each com-

ponent is twice that of the finger in the joint. If you want to use contrasting lines to visually link the corners, apply them to the edges at this stage. The thickness of these veneers should be included in the width of the components. Next, cut off the corners of each component at 45°. To achieve the accuracy this joint requires, I recommend using a guillotine miter box and making a pattern to clamp to the top of each piece against which you can locate the guillotine blade. Alternately, you can clamp all the components together face to face and remove the corners in one operation

on the spindle shaper or tilting-arbor table saw. The contrasting fingers can also be cut in one of these ways. The panels are glued up with the aid of a fixture like that shown on the previous page for constructing the first joint. With the panels assembled, groove their ends, as well as the end of each finger, for the plywood spline. You can cut the grooves using a router, shaper or table saw; in the latter two cases, cut the groove before gluing the outer components to the panel, and finish by hand. A jig is required to hold the fingers while carrying out this operation.

The third joint, shown at right, employs dovetail pins to lock a miter joint in both directions. You can vary the length and width of these pins for decorative effect. Prepare each panel to the correct length, width and thickness and construct the carcase using a simple miter at each corner. Depending on the size of the carcase, the dovetail slots are cut using either a router table (or shaper) with a dovetail cutter, sliding the carcase over it, or a portable router in conjunction with a simple jig to guide the router over the carcase.

After you have cut the slots, make sliding dovetail pins to fit into them by cutting one angle on the jointer and then cutting to rough width at the opposing angle on the table saw. I next secure each pin to a block and run it through the shaper, though the pin could as well be hand-planed to final fit. The slots can end square or be rounded off. If you prefer the latter, you can round the pins to match on the disc sander.

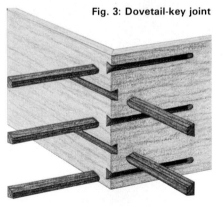

Fig. 3: Dovetail-key joint

This joint is basically a miter into which you rout dovetail slots to fit dovetail keys. The size of the keys can vary. The photo, lower left, shows this same feature used in a finger joint.

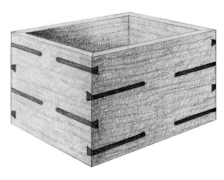

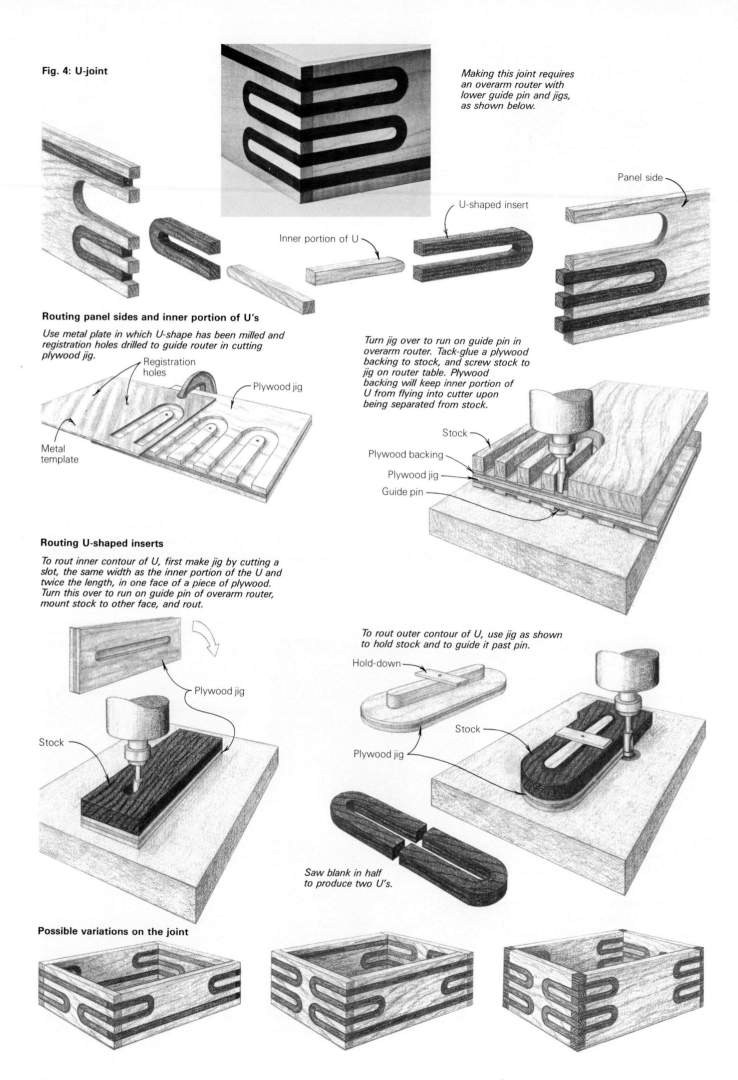

Fig. 4: U-joint

Making this joint requires an overarm router with lower guide pin and jigs, as shown below.

Panel side

U-shaped insert

Inner portion of U

Routing panel sides and inner portion of U's

Use metal plate in which U-shape has been milled and registration holes drilled to guide router in cutting plywood jig.

Registration holes

Plywood jig

Metal template

Turn jig over to run on guide pin in overarm router. Tack-glue a plywood backing to stock, and screw stock to jig on router table. Plywood backing will keep inner portion of U from flying into cutter upon being separated from stock.

Stock

Plywood backing

Plywood jig

Guide pin

Routing U-shaped inserts

To rout inner contour of U, first make jig by cutting a slot, the same width as the inner portion of the U and twice the length, in one face of a piece of plywood. Turn this over to run on guide pin of overarm router, mount stock to other face, and rout.

Plywood jig

Stock

To rout outer contour of U, use jig as shown to hold stock and to guide it past pin.

Hold-down

Stock

Plywood jig

Saw blank in half to produce two U's.

Possible variations on the joint

84

Probably the most successful of all my decorative finger joints is shown on the facing page. It uses contrasting inserts to create a pattern that flows around the corner, continually leading the eye to and away from the joint. It is possible to link all the joints of a carcase by taking the line the length of the panel. The joint requires the overarm router with the aid of a jig constructed using a metal template. On the milling machine, cut one U-shape into a metal plate and drill the centers for the radii of the remaining U-shapes. From this, rout the plywood jig with all the necessary U-shapes. To retain the inner part of the U, which would otherwise fly into the cutter upon being separated from the stock, glue a thin plywood backing to the stock before routing. Allow for this thickness when setting the cutter depth. Secure the stock to the reverse side of the jig, and place the jig over the guide pin in the overarm router table. Make the initial cuts with a cutter smaller in diameter than the guide pin, to waste most of the stock. After routing, the plywood backing can be pried off the stock and the inner portion of the U's retained. To make the U-shaped inserts, rout the inner contour in an oversized blank (large enough to accommodate two U's, which will later be sawn apart), then use this negative space to locate the blank on a jig that guides the router around the outside contour.

When all the components have been made, it remains only to glue them back into the voids in the panels. The inserts are of such length that the joint is created in this operation. Because the contrasting U also forms a finger in the joint, visual continuity is interrupted by the end grain. This can be overcome by mitering each insert, leaving the end grain of the light wood only. This reduces the gluing area of the joint but not enough to jeopardize its strength.

Fig. 5: Segmented finger joint

Make this joint of any number of finger/panel components, angling the ends to form the pattern. Tack-glue the lengths together before gluing up the panels, which can be done in a jig similar to the one shown in figure 1.

The final joint, above and right, is the most time-consuming to produce, but the many variations possible make the effort worthwhile. The length and cut-off angle of the fingers can create any pattern the designer wishes. Basically, each panel is made from a number of strips with the alternate ones creating the pattern. Each strip is milled to the dimension of the finger in the joint. The decorative pieces are then cut to length and the required angle cut on a guillotine miter box. In this example, each consecutive strip varies by an angle of 15° to produce the curved effect. The contrasting pieces are tacked together with glue, end to end, which holds them until the panels are constructed. The end of each plain strip forms the shoulder of the joint, so the length of the strips should be finished to the inside dimension of the carcase. Each panel can then be glued up as for the joint shown in figure 1, p. 82.

These are just five of the many joint variations I have designed—all give a decorative effect when used on anything from small boxes to the largest of cabinets or tables. There are many other ways to use joints decoratively, and no matter how bizarre any idea may seem, it might be quite effective put to proper use. I always make a sample of any joint I design to assess its visual effect, experience the problems it will give in production and decide how it can be efficiently made. Of course, these joints take longer to produce than conventional ones, but the advantage is that any decoration needed in a piece of furniture is already built in. □

John Bairstow designs and builds furniture in Loughborough, England.

Curved Dovetails
Secret miter is the key

by John F. Anderson

Through dovetails with curved baselines can enhance case joinery and provide visual interest. Making pins and tails a different thickness from the stock being used involves cutting a curved secret miter on the inside corner of the joint.

The appearance of through dovetails is ordinarily determined by the thickness of the pieces being joined, and the exposed end-grain surfaces of both pins and tails usually make a straight line parallel to the corner of the joint. But this baseline need not be straight. By varying the thickness of the pins and tails, you can create curves along both sides of the joint. Curved dovetails open up new design possibilities. Incorporated into a cabinet, drawer or box, this joint can enhance and accent the overall composition.

The procedure for making curved dovetails is basically the same as for cutting regular ones. But there are two notable exceptions—you need a curved template block for laying out the curved baselines and for chiseling, and you have to cut a curved-bottom blind miter along the inner edges of the joint. You'll need a sharp pencil, a marking gauge, a dovetail saw, chisels and mallet, and a good eye.

The inside miter is the key to curved dovetails because it lets you make pins and tails that are thinner in section than the thickness of the stock and thus permits a wide range of curves to be used. They can be either concave, convex or reversed, symmetrical or asymmetrical, and the thicknesses of the pieces joined need not be the same. The curves on each side (pin and tail) need not be the same either, though to accomplish such a joint you need to make two templates and to lay out the curved cuts alternately (figure 5). The procedures described below will work for any curve, so long as the miter is cut properly.

First make the curved template block from a piece of wood at least ¾ in. thick. It should be large enough to be clamped firmly to the workpiece (without the clamp getting in the way) and precisely the width of your case sides, for ease of alignment. After laying out the curve, take care in cutting it, making sure that the curved end-grain edge is perpendicular to the bottom face. You'll use this edge to guide your chisel when making vertical cuts, so it has to be a true 90°.

Next, set a marking gauge to the thickness of the stock and score the inside faces of the work in the usual way (*FWW #2*, Spring '76, p. 28). The inside faces should be finish-planed or sanded to avoid knocking off the edges of the curves after the joint is completed. Don't strike a baseline across the outside face of the stock; rather, score marks at the outer edges that will allow you to position the curved template. Trace the curve from the template onto both faces of the stock, using the straight baselines for registration; also trace the curve onto the end-grain edges (figure 1). After careful consideration, mark out the pins first; I do this freehand, but you can use any means you like. Clamp the piece in a vise and saw down the waste side of each pin to the curved line.

Sawing done, lay the piece, outside face up, on the bench and clamp the template on top in its original position. Using the edge of the template as a guide for the back of your chisel (figure 2), chop into the waste deep enough so that no chip-

ping or tear-out will occur when you finish chiseling through from the other side. Turn the piece over, clamp the template into position on the inside face, and chop straight down, removing chips near the edge of the template with oblique paring cuts (figure 3). Don't go any deeper than the curved line marked on the end-grain edge, and don't try to remove the waste between the pins just yet. Clean up the bottom of the cut by paring in from the edge with a narrow chisel or incannel gouge. This must be done acurately because the results will determine the fit of the miter on the inside corner. Now remove the template, secure the workpiece again to the bench and cut this miter using a sharp chisel, beginning at the baseline and paring to the intersection of the vertical shoulder and the curved bottom (figure 4). This will automatically produce a miter at the proper angle.

Now that the miter has been cut, return the template to its former position and use it as a guide for removing the waste between the pins. Cutting the miter comes before this because the entire bottom curve is still visible then, making it easier to cut to this line, which is partially obliterated when the waste between the pins is removed.

Now lay out the tails from the pins as in standard practice. Saw down on the waste sides of the tail lines to the curved line. Then simply repeat the procedures used for mitering the inside corner described above, chiseling out the waste between the tails last. The pieces should fit together correctly, leaving no gap on the inside of the corner.   □

John Anderson, a cabinetmaker, lives in Bottineau, N. Dak.

**Fig. 1:
Laying out
the curve**

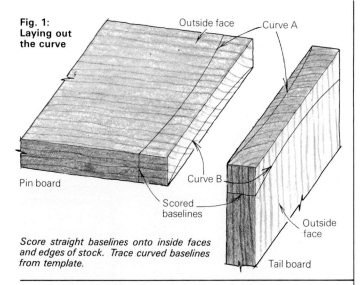

Outside face

Curve A

Curve B

Scored
baselines

Pin board

Outside
face

Tail board

*Score straight baselines onto inside faces
and edges of stock. Trace curved baselines
from template.*

Fig. 2: Preparing the outside face

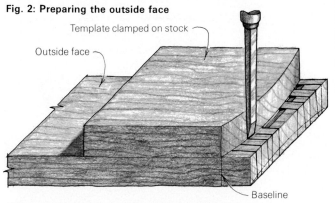

Template clamped on stock

Outside face

Baseline

*Using template edge to guide chisel, sever the waste tissue across the
grain to prevent tear-out when chiseling from the reverse side. Note that
tail board (photo below), which will be marked from completed pin board,
is prepared similarly.*

**Fig. 3: Cutting the
inside curves**

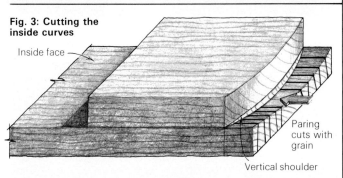

Inside face

Paring
cuts with
grain

Vertical shoulder

*Again using template as a guide, cut the curved vertical shoulder and
pare away waste along curved line on inside face of pins. Photo below
shows tail-board shoulder similarly cut.*

**Fig. 4: Cutting
the inside miter**

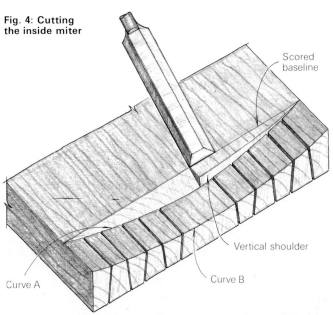

Scored
baseline

Vertical shoulder

Curve A

Curve B

*Cut the miter from straight baseline to curved one. Remove waste
between pins only after cutting miter.*

*Curve A and curve B need not be the same. If they are, as in the exam-
ple above, then the miter is a true 45°. If curves A and B are dissimilar,
as in the drawing below, then the angle of the miter will vary along the
length of the joint, like a slightly twisted ribbon.*

**Fig. 5: Laying out
two different
curves**

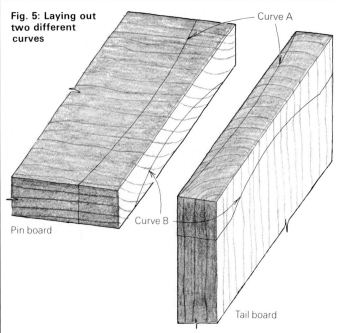

Curve A

Curve B

Pin board

Tail board

Curved Slot-Mortise and Tenon
Contoured joinery for enhancing frames

by Ben Davies

Design decisions in woodworking cannot be made entirely for aesthetic reasons. Wood is not a plastic medium but a rigid one, and we usually shape it by removing portions of it. Our designs are thus limited by the capabilities of our cutting tools and our skill at using them. To achieve new shapes—to experiment with line and form and the basic geometry of joining wood—we either develop specialized tools or adapt our old tools to perform in innovative ways. Highly specialized hand tools, like molding planes, have limited applications, while more versatile modern tools, like computer-controlled carving machines, can be afforded only by industry. So there's considerable reward for the craftsman in being able to extend the use of general-purpose tools—the router in particular—in imaginative ways.

The following description of making a curved joint is not meant to be definitive. Rather, it is a tentative first step toward adding a dimension to our work when struggling to achieve a balance between geometric and organic forms. When we build we are faced with a dichotomy—crisp and differentiated forms on the one hand, soft and flowing forms on the other. Consider the rigid control exemplified by Shaker and Cubist formalism contrasted with the flowing asymmetry of Art Nouveau. The dichotomy transcends woodworking and the visual arts. For more, read Nietzsche's discussion of the Apollonian/Dionysian duality in his essay "The Birth of Tragedy from the Spirit of Music."

Using a router equipped with an ordinary straight-face bit and a pair of guide bushings, plus a shop-built fixture to hold the work and a bearing template to guide the router cut, you can quickly contour the adjoining shoulders of rails and stiles with little chance for error. But making the fixture and template requires careful planning and accurate work.

Preparing the stock

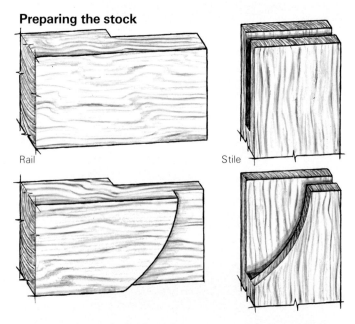

Rail

Stile

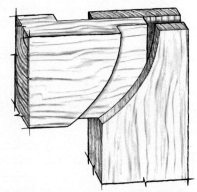

Facing shoulders of joint are contoured; rear shoulders remain square. This compensates for the loss of mechanical strength that comes from reducing the gluing surface on the front cheek of the tenon. To prepare the stock, dimension frame members and cut to length. Slot the ends of the stiles as though making an ordinary slip joint; then cut a tenon cheek on the rear face of each rail, but don't remove any stock from the front faces, as these will be routed to produce the curved shoulder shown.

Reverse curve defines joining shoulders of rail and stile, left. A variation of the technique can produce a curved half-lap joint, right.

The door on this cabinet shows how contoured joinery can be used to advantage. The wood has been carefully selected so the grain conforms to the curvature of the joint, which repeats the gentle curve made by the bottom sides of the cabinet. The two bottom joints of the door frame have been cut square, complementing the upper corners of the case.

Making the fixture—This part of the system consists of a plywood base and four rabbeted cleats as in the drawing at left. Its job is to hold the rails and stiles and to support the bearing template. The base should be made from a piece of ¾-in. plywood about 15 in. to 24 in. square, a suitable size for joining the frames of cabinet doors. The cleats should be cut from stock whose thickness equals the thickness of the frames plus the thickness of the bearing template, usually ½ in. If you're joining ¾-in. thick frame members, the cleats must be 1¼ in. square, rabbeted to an exact depth of ½ in. and to a width of about ½ in.

To set up the fixture, position the cleats, rabbets in and up, on the edges of the square base; use a true framing square to orient the cleats at precisely 90° to one another (other angles are possible), and screw them to the base with countersunk wood screws. The cleats should not meet at the corners; you have to space them far enough apart so your stock will slide easily through the gap.

The guide bushings—Most routers are designed to accept standard guide bushings generally available as accessories. With a ½-in. bit, use a ⅝-in. O.D. bushing with your router, but any bushing of this general size will do. Because the bushing bears against the curved template when making a cut, and because you're cutting complementary curves using the same bearing template, the line of the cut must be offset from the curvature of the template, and two bushings are required—a large-diameter one for making the cut on the rail,

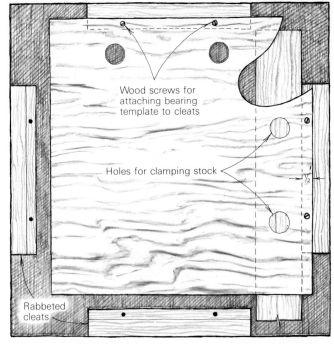

Fixture Plan view showing bearing template screwed in place

Wood screws for attaching bearing template to cleats

Holes for clamping stock

Rabbeted cleats

Fixture in elevation

Rabbeted cleats   Bearing template   Cleat

¾-in. plywood base   Stock (rail or stile)

89

and a small-diameter one for cutting the stile (as is the case with the examples here).

Purchase two ⅝-in. guides from the manufacturer; one will serve permanently to hold the outer bushing (epoxied to it), the other as the inner guide bushing. The outer bushing should be turned from brass or aluminum. It is necessary to observe the following mathematical relationship between the diameter of the cutter (D_c), the O.D. of the inner guide bushing (D_{ib}) and the O.D. of the outer guide bushing (D_{ob}): $D_{ob} = D_{ib} + 2(D_c)$.

The bearing template—This step involves making three separate templates: one that exactly duplicates the curved line of the joint, another whose profile is offset from this curve and parallel to it, which serves as a pattern for the third tem-

Guide bushings

Section through router base and bushings

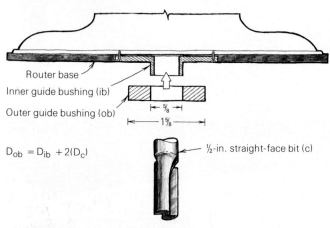

$$D_{ob} = D_{ib} + 2(D_c)$$

½-in. straight-face bit (c)

Guide bushings in use

Rout shoulder on rail using outer guide bushing.

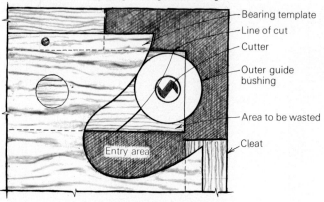

- Bearing template
- Line of cut
- Cutter
- Outer guide bushing
- Area to be wasted
- Cleat
- Entry area

Rout shoulder on stile using inner guide bushing.

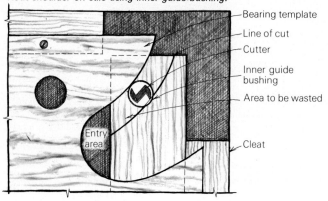

- Bearing template
- Line of cut
- Cutter
- Inner guide bushing
- Area to be wasted
- Cleat
- Entry area

Making the bearing template

Step 1: Joint-line template

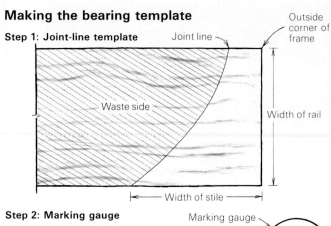

Joint line — Outside corner of frame — Waste side — Width of rail — Width of stile

Step 2: Marking gauge

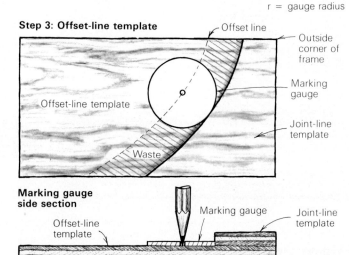

Cutter (c) — Inner guide bushing (ib) — Marking gauge — Hole in center for pencil point

$$r = \frac{D_{ib}}{2} + \frac{D_c}{2}$$

r = gauge radius

Step 3: Offset-line template

Offset line — Outside corner of frame — Marking gauge — Offset-line template — Joint-line template — Waste

Marking gauge side section

Marking gauge — Joint-line template — Offset-line template

Step 4: Bearing template

½-in. plywood bearing template — ¼-in. plywood offset-line template — Ball-bearing pilot

Screw offset-line template to bottom of bearing template to guide router-bit pilot during cut to produce a smooth, precisely vertical edge.

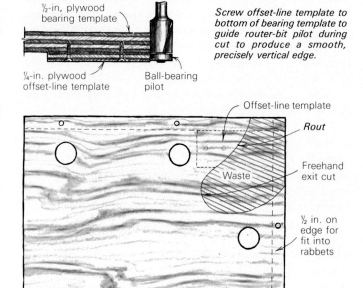

Offset-line template — *Rout* — Freehand exit cut — Waste — ½ in. on edge for fit into rabbets

plate, the bearing template itself. After composing the curve of the joint on paper, taking into account the width of the rails and stiles, transfer the line to a piece of ¼-in. plywood; then cut along this line with a band saw or jigsaw and smooth the contoured edge with a file. This becomes the joint-line template (step 1 in the drawing at left).

The next thing to do is to make a marking gauge that will allow you to scribe a line on a second template parallel to the curve of the joint-line template. The gauge is made from a plastic disc with a hole in the center for a pencil point, as in step 2. The distance from the outside of the gauge to the pencil point equals the distance from the cutting circle of the router bit to the opposite outside edge of the inner guide bushing (r), which also defines the smallest possible radius of curvature in the joint.

Cut along this offset line and smooth the sawn edge with a file. For the bearing template itself, dimension a piece of ½-in. plywood so that it is slightly smaller than the inner dimensions of your fixture and so its corners are absolutely square. On two adjacent sides, scribe lines that are exactly ½ in. in from the edge and parallel to it. These lines mark the boundary defined by the inner edges of the cleats on the bottom of the bearing template. Now position the offset-line template as shown in step 3 and screw it to the bottom of the bearing template. It should abut one of the cleat lines and be positioned out from the joint line (drawn on the bearing template) with the help of the marking gauge. Using a straight-face flush cutter with its pilot bearing against the offset-line template, cut the curve in the bearing template (step 4). It may seem like a lot of trouble to make one template just to cut another, but only by routing the curve on the bearing template can you get walls that are smooth and perpendicular to both faces.

Next bore four 1¼-in. diameter holes in the bearing template; these permit you to clamp the rails and stiles into place for routing. Also bore four pilot holes for wood screws on the template's edges and countersink them on both sides—top and bottom. This completes work on the fixture and bearing template.

Routing the joints—After preparing the stock, place the frame members in their respective positions and mark each end as shown in the drawing at right so you can orient them properly in the fixture. With the bearing template screwed into position, clamp one of the stile ends (S1) into place so it is flush against the inside cleat and so the end-grain edge is lined up with the inside edge of the top cleat. Attach the inner guide bushing to the router, and set the bit to a depth that equals the thickness of the cheeks of the mortise on the stiles. Insert the bit and bushing into the entry area and rout towards the corner, holding the bushing firmly against the bearing template. Make only a single, careful pass when routing the shoulders on the stiles. Now rout the opposite end of the other stile (S3).

Remove the inner bushing and attach the outer bushing. Insert one of the rail ends (R1) into the fixture so it is flush against the top cleat and its end-grain edge is in line with the inside edge of the right-hand cleat. Rout the tenon on the rail, first wasting most of the stock and finally making one decisive pass with the bushing pressed firmly against the curve of the bearing template. Now rout the tenon on the opposite end of the other rail (R3).

Positioning of stock for routing sequence

Cut tenons on rails (R)

Cut slots in stiles (S)

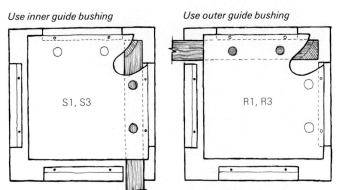

Use inner guide bushing

Use outer guide bushing

S1, S3

R1, R3

Flip bearing template diagonally.

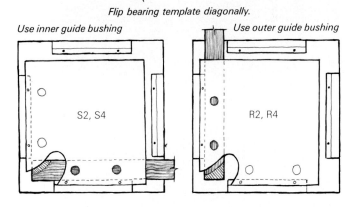

Use inner guide bushing

Use outer guide bushing

S2, S4

R2, R4

At this point you've cut half the joints for one frame, and they are diagonally opposed to one another. To cut the other pair of joints, you will have to flip the bearing template and screw it in place on the opposite corner of the fixture. Then repeat the entire process described above, now for S2, S4, R2, R4. On the back side of the frame the joints are left square, which increases the strength of the joint. When you're done, all four joints should fit snugly, and their curves should match up without a flaw. ☐

Ben Davies, 35, owns and operates Muntin Woodworks in Chattanooga, Tenn., where he designs and builds furniture and doors.

The Mosaic Door
Possibilities of the plywood sandwich

by James Rannefeld

Many woodworkers have become dissatisfied with the design limitations imposed by the typical frame-and-panel door, while others are frustrated by the structural problems of the batten door, which weathers rather poorly. There's another way to make a door, one that presents new design possibilities and offers structural improvements over traditional methods. For the past six years I have been refining a technique for building the mosaic door. Essentially a three-layered composite structure with a dimensionally stable

Mosaic technique offers strength, dimensional stability and design versatility. Playing on Art Deco motifs, this design required joining the central components with splined miters.

plywood panel as its core, this particular type of door can be treated in an endless variety of ways—even made to look like the traditional frame-and-panel door it supplants.

The core panel itself is best made from a single sheet of ½-in. exterior-grade plywood, which is overlaid front and back with solid wood. Though similar in several respects, my doors differ considerably from the two-layered doors that have been made traditionally in New Mexico by Spanish craftsmen, who typically nailed a rail-and-stile facade over a tongue-and-groove panel, or covered the panel with applied trim. These doors often become leaky from wood shrinkage, not only around the jambs, but also between boards in the door. It was this problem that led me to sandwich a stable plywood core between two outer layers of solid material of virtually any thickness.

An exterior door must withstand great stresses. On the inside, the home environment is typically warm in winter and cool in the summer—the exact opposite of climatic conditions on the outside of the door. Normally the home is uniformly dry, while winter snows and summer rains lash the door's exterior. Yet the greatest problem is direct sunlight on the door, which raises the temperature of the outer surface considerably higher than the ambient temperature, especially when dark woods are used.

Because of these conflicting stresses, I spline together adjoining mosaic pieces on the outer surfaces in addition to laminating them onto the stable core. Even under optimal laminating conditions using a press, there is often enough cupping in larger mosaic pieces, or enough variation in the plywood core, to create a less than perfect bond. But with a matrix of splines covering the whole surface, it is virtually impossible for any single piece to become dislodged from the panel. The splining technique also accommodates the expansion and contraction of individual pieces that may be of different species with differing expansion coefficients.

Overlaying the surface with individually splined pieces allows not only mixing wood species, but also using various thicknesses in the composition, sculpting, carving and shaping them at will or whimsy—as long as the spline grooves are in alignment. Additional possibilities include piercing the door and incorporating glass mosaics in the design.

My technique for making mosaic doors is not unlike that used to make stained glass windows. First I design the patterns for the panel surface (inner surface too if it's different) and lay out the design full-size on paper. Then I cut to rough size the larger mosaic pieces, where the same species and lumber thickness will permit. Next the mosaic pieces are bandsawn out and touched up where necessary with a belt or drum sander to achieve an optimal fit along their contoured edges. This part is like making a giant jigsaw puzzle, fitting the pieces together on top of the paper cartoon.

Then I relieve the adjoining perimeters of the pieces on my

shaper, though the same thing can be done with a router, using a chamfering or rounding-over bit. You may, of course, want to sculpt each individual piece with hand and power tools in whatever combination suits you. When all the pieces are shaped, I use my shaper to cut a groove ½ in. deep by ¼ in. wide all the way around their edges. Rather than using a standard depth collar for this, I recommend a ball-bearing collar. Again, a router equipped with a proper slotting cutter can do the same job. Remember, all the grooves must be cut a uniform distance from the bottom of each piece. Next I cut the contoured splines from tempered hardboard or plywood (dark-colored splines look best), but you could use other suitable materials for this.

I cut the plywood panel for the core oversize, and after trial-fitting all the pieces, I start gluing them to the panel, beginning flush at one edge of the design and proceeding outward from there. Then I put the whole thing in my glue press, which has enough screws to handle mosaic tiles of varying thicknesses, apply even pressure and let it sit overnight. The next day I repeat the process on the door's other face, which might have a totally different pattern.

With gluing complete, I cut the mosaic panel to finished size, allowing the core to protrude ½ in. on all four edges. I used to allow a ¼-in. thickness of the mosaic tiles to remain flush with the edges of the plywood, in effect rabbeting them, but the size of the groove this requires in the frame leaves too little stock overhanging the panel sandwich. So now I cut back the tiles to allow only the plywood to protrude. Then I groove the rails and stiles to fit snugly on the "tongue" that's been formed by the protruding core. The joinery of the frame members themselves can vary according to your preferences—½-in. by ½-in. tongue-and-groove plus ¾-in. through-dowels do nicely, though sometimes I spline them together. Next I finish both sides with two coats of a 50/50 mixture of exterior polyurethane and Watco Danish oil and follow these with additional applications of exterior Watco.

I recommend keeping the mosaic pieces reasonably small so that expansion and contraction are minimal. The only problem I have experienced to date has been with a mixed-wood mosaic—a couple of walnut pieces loosened up. At the time I was using a dry marine resin glue. Now I use a resin-emulsion type glue called WP-2200 made by National Casein, 3435 W. MacArthur Blvd., Santa Ana, Calif. 92704. It's a fast-cure (closed assembly time of 20 min.), exterior Type 1 bond that's ideal for doors.

No matter how tight the joints or how good the gluelines between the laminations, the spaces between mosaic pieces on the exterior side of the door will grow and dwindle with seasonal changes—just as a loose panel will move around in its enclosing frame. However, by chamfering or otherwise relieving the edges of individual mosaic elements, these changes appear minimal and often enhance the overall textural quality of the surface.

Recently I have begun to treat the individual mosaic pieces sculpturally, and this has widened the horizons for my designs. Now I'm using the technique on headboards, murals and tabletops. And I'm contemplating the use of stone, ceramics, plastics and glass as potential materials for overlaying wood. □

James Rannefeld (JAWAR), 33, designs and builds furniture and architectural components in Taos, N. Mex.

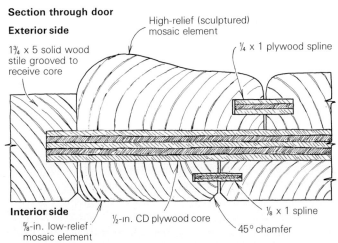

Section through door

Exterior side

1¾ x 5 solid wood stile grooved to receive core

High-relief (sculptured) mosaic element

¼ x 1 plywood spline

Interior side

⅝-in. low-relief mosaic element

½-in. CD plywood core

⅛ x 1 spline

45° chamfer

Gap between mosaic pieces is determined by season and location of manufacture, and by the relative size of the individual elements.

The mosaic pieces on this door, called Curvilaminar II, are of different thicknesses; individual press screws with padded feet apply uniform pressure to each piece.

Gluing Up
How to get a strong, square assembly

by Ian J. Kirby

Gluing up is unique among woodworking operations. It's an irreversible, one-shot deal and has to be got right. You may have done accurate work up to this point, only to find that a small error in assembling or clamping has produced all sorts of inaccuracies that will be difficult, perhaps impossible, to fix. A common lament in woodworking is that "everything went perfectly until glue-up, then everything went wrong." When you think about it, this is not surprising. How often do we systematically consider gluing up, and how much time do we give to dry clamping? Usually very little, and then halfheartedly.

To get the best results, we should bring a studied method to this operation and practice it more. We ought to have a table especially prepared for this purpose, its top surface flat, clear of debris and well waxed to resist glue penetration. A piece of varnished plywood over your benchtop will do, but a sturdy table, 36 in. high with a Formica surface, is better.

Before gluing up, you should dry-clamp each assembly exactly as you would clamp a glued assembly. This means positioning and tightening all the clamps, with correct glue blocks, and checking the whole assembly for accuracy. Gluing should proceed calmly, in an atmosphere of preparedness, with the glue and necessary applicators ready, clamps standing by, and you and your assistant decided on the order of events. The time of day you glue up is important. Most woodworkers like to glue up in the evening and let the glue set overnight. To meet this goal, a lot of work often gets rushed, dry clamping gets short-circuited and we have all the necessary ingredients for a disastrous glue-up—fatigue, unpreparedness and anxiety. The only reason to proceed under such conditions lies in the spurious notion that glue cures only while the moon is out.

Consider the alternative. Leave the work dry-clamped overnight. The next morning, check the clamping to see if everything is still properly aligned. Then collect all the tools and materials you need and begin to glue up. The light is better, your mind is fresh, the pressure to complete the job is gone. If you can't leave the work dry-clamped overnight, at least let it sit for an hour while you attend to other things.

Gluing up actually begins with a decision about what to glue together and in what order. The more subassemblies you can get together, the easier the total operation will be, especially the final glue-up. But before gluing any parts, always clean and prefinish surfaces that cannot be reached later with a plane. It's much easier to work on a piece of wood while its entire surface is exposed and accessible than to try to remove mill marks and other blemishes once other parts are permanently in the way.

You must also weigh the inconvenience of having three or four finishing sessions as the job proceeds against one grand and difficult cleanup after final assembly. Prefinished surfaces will resist glue penetration from squeeze-out. When the

excess glue is dry, simply lift it off with a sharp chisel. When finishing prior to gluing up, take care to keep the finishing material off joint interfaces.

Bar clamps—The type of bar clamp you use has considerable bearing on the ease and accuracy of the glue-up. For general cabinetmaking applications, quick-action bar clamps with a circular pad at the screw end are no substitute for a standard bar clamp. A good clamp should sit on a glue table without falling over at the slightest touch. The bars should be identical in section, and the heads should move easily, but not flop around. When pressure is applied, the face of the head should be at 90° to the bar—this way we know exactly where pressure is transferred. A collection of clamps is an investment no matter which you choose, but it is a long-term investment you can make by purchasing one or two clamps at a time. The combined value in the end may equal that of two major machines. The best choice in the main is between Jorgenson, Wetzler and Record clamps. I prefer the last.

Applying the glue—The amount of glue squeeze-out is an important signal. Since it is waste, it is best to have as little as possible, but we still want assurance that there is sufficient glue in the joint. The smallest bit of squeeze-out is enough. This results from getting the glue in the right place in the right amount. For different jobs you will need different applicators. White glue (polyvinyl acetate) and yellow glue (aliphatic resin) can be stored in and dispensed from a squeeze bottle. But a squeeze bottle is not a good applicator, and won't guarantee that the surfaces being joined are completely wetted by the glue. There is no reliable adhesion if joining surfaces don't get completely wetted.

Since the future of the piece depends on the quality of its joints, we need to take a close look at the business of applying the glue. Manufacturers try to lower the surface tension of the glue so it will spread easily. Nevertheless, the glue should be rubbed or rolled on, not merely squeezed out onto the surface. A set of stiff-bristle brushes of different sizes (I use plumber's flux brushes) will suffice in most instances. If you use white or yellow glue, brushes can be stored in a jar of water, but it is just as easy to wash them out and begin next time with a dry brush. If you use urea-formaldehyde glue or resorcinol, you must clean the brush after each use, for these will set hard even in water.

When edge joining boards, white or yellow glue can be squeezed from a plastic bottle onto one surface. If the boards are clamped or rubbed together and the clamps are removed immediately and the joint broken, chances are you will find that the glue has covered both surfaces uniformly. That this happens in edge joining does not mean that it will happen in other joining situations. In fact, it's not a good method for edge joining either. A better way would be to run a very light

The size and position of the clamping block can make the difference between success and failure when gluing up. The block should be the same dimensions as the section of the rail, and placed directly opposite the shoulder area, centering the clamping pressure on the joint.

bead on each surface, and then with a 1-in. wide paint roller, spread the glue thinly. Now we know that the surfaces are evenly wetted and that when the joint is clamped we won't have gobs of the stuff dripping on the floor, the table and the clamps. Spreading glue with your fingers is a bad practice. You need fingers for other things, and the grease and dirt you add to the glue won't help adhesion. If you insist on using your fingers, wash your hands first.

Edge gluing—When gluing up several narrow boards to make a case side, tabletop or framed panel, there are four important considerations: the position of each board in the composite piece, the grain direction of each, the number of clamps to be used and the means for aligning and registering the boards to keep them from swimming about when pressure is applied. Assuming that all of the boards are dimensionally stable and free of defects, the first thing to decide is how to arrange them to get the best appearance. This involves shuffling the pieces around to achieve visual harmony and continuity in the figure. Remember that after gluing up you will have to clean up the surfaces with a smoothing plane, so try to decide on an arrangement that permits the grain of all the boards to run in the same direction. If this is not possible, then you will have to plane in both directions and carefully avoid tearing the grain on an adjacent board.

Having decided on their arrangement, mark the boards so their order can be recalled when they are put in the clamps. Dry clamping will determine the number of clamps you need and where to put them. As shown in figure 1 on the next page, clamping pressure is diffused in a fan of about 90° from the clamp head. You will need enough clamps to ensure that the lines of diffusion overlap at the first edge joint. The number of clamps then is a function of the length of the boards and of the widths of the two outer boards. Since the boards themselves transmit and spread the pressure, clamping blocks are unnecessary in edge gluing. Plan to joint and rip the composite piece to width after glue-up. This will remove any depressions the clamps leave.

When you know how many clamps the job calls for, put half the number (half plus one if the total number is odd) on the table, evenly spaced. If the bars are not bent or damaged, they will register the boards in the horizontal plane. Coat each edge to be joined with glue, wetting all the surfaces thoroughly and uniformly. When the boards have been put

into the clamps and slight pressure applied, place the remaining clamps over the top of the panel and begin to tighten all the clamps. Having an equal number of clamps top and bottom prevents the panel from bowing under pressure.

Ideally you should be able to edge-glue boards without having to rely on any mechanical means of holding them flush. But when the boards are even slightly warped this isn't possible. It is common to use dowels for aligning and registering boards; if you're going to do this, use a doweling jig to align the holes. Another method for registering edge-glued boards is the Lamello joining plate (or biscuit joint); the machine that cuts the slots is expensive, but worth the investment for the professional woodworker. The quickest solution is to lightly clamp battens across the width of the panel. Don't overtighten the bar clamps. This can squeeze out most of the glue and starve the joint. Moderate pressure is all that is needed when edge gluing.

Gluing up mortise-and-tenon joints—Mortise-and-tenon joints usually get little attention when gluing—most woodworkers want to assemble them as fast as they can. But the pace ought to be less hurried; ideally there should be two people at a glue-up, one to direct the order of events and to tighten the clamps, the other to manage the shoe end of the clamps. Both apply the glue. One coats the tenons thoroughly while the other puts glue in the mortises. Because the mortise and tenon goes together in a sliding fit you can't expect to apply glue to the tenon alone and still have enough in the joint. You will have to spread glue in the mortise as well. Don't just squirt in some glue and push it around with a stick or pencil, because the excess glue can impede fitting the joint. Visualize the glue as a fluid pad of considerable thickness. The pressure exerted by an excess on one side of a tenon can misalign the members. So apply glue thinly and evenly to all surfaces. Better than squeezing lots of glue into the mortise and stirring it with a stick is using a stiff-bristle brush.

During dry clamping pay close attention to dimensioning and positioning the clamping blocks. Their purpose is not so much to protect the stock as to transfer the pressure from the clamp to the workpiece in exactly the area required. The fact that the clamp heads can lean away from a right angle under pressure, that they may have been put onto the work slightly askew and that the workpiece may not have edges perpendicular to its face, are all things you must consider when direct-

Fig. 1: Edge gluing

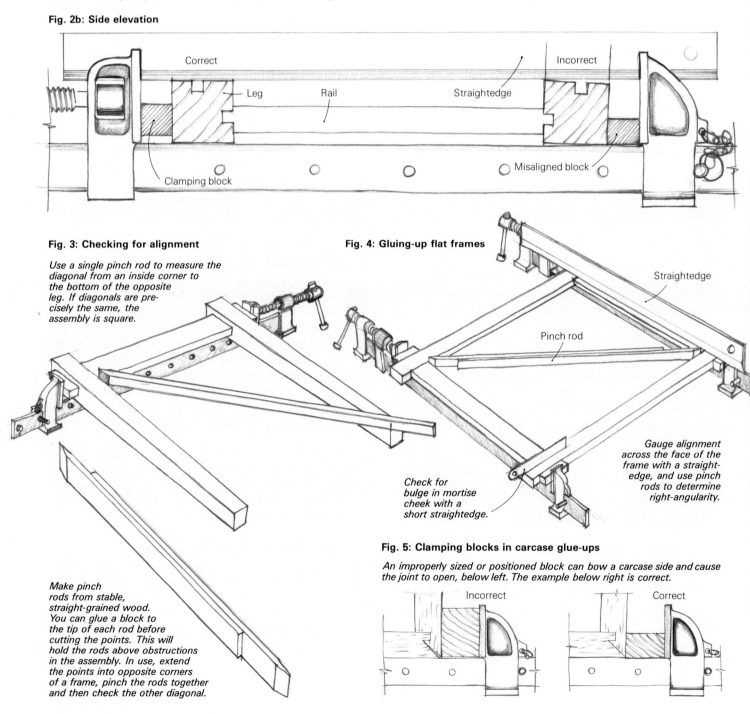

Shaded areas show diffusion of clamping pressure. Use enough clamps to ensure that lines of pressure overlap at the two outer joints. An equal number of clamps above and below the panel prevents bowing.

Fig. 2a: Gluing leg/rail assemblies — Plan view

Horn

A properly sized and positioned block is essential to an accurate glue-up. To keep the leg from canting and the joint from gapping, the centerline of the rail must bisect the angle of pressure diffusion.

Position the blocks initially by eye, but check across the inside surface of both legs with a straightedge to make fine adjustments in their final placement.

Fig. 2b: Side elevation

Correct

Incorrect

Leg

Rail

Straightedge

Misaligned block

Clamping block

Fig. 3: Checking for alignment

Use a single pinch rod to measure the diagonal from an inside corner to the bottom of the opposite leg. If diagonals are precisely the same, the assembly is square.

Make pinch rods from stable, straight-grained wood. You can glue a block to the tip of each rod before cutting the points. This will hold the rods above obstructions in the assembly. In use, extend the points into opposite corners of a frame, pinch the rods together and then check the other diagonal.

Fig. 4: Gluing-up flat frames

Straightedge

Pinch rod

Check for bulge in mortise cheek with a short straightedge.

Gauge alignment across the face of the frame with a straightedge, and use pinch rods to determine right-angularity.

Fig. 5: Clamping blocks in carcase glue-ups

An improperly sized or positioned block can bow a carcase side and cause the joint to open, below left. The example below right is correct.

Incorrect

Correct

ing clamping pressure. Putting a piece of plywood between the workpiece and the clamp shoe or head isn't enough.

In gluing up leg/rail or rail/stile assemblies, the size of the glue block that distributes the pressure to the shoulder line of the joint is important. Providing that the grain of the block runs lengthwise and it is thick enough not to distort under pressure, the block should be about as long as the rail is wide, and about as wide as the rail is thick, as shown in figures 2a and 2b. With the right clamping block, pressure can be placed where you need it by moving the block slightly to one side or another or up or down the legs. If you attempt to glue up without clamping blocks, there's little chance of directing pressure where it is required.

The parts of a correctly glued-up assembly or subassembly should not twist or wind in relation to one another. They should be aligned and at right angles to one another. Joint lines should close up tightly. When assembling two legs and a rail, as in a table frame, cut the legs ¾ in. longer than the finished length. This excess, called the horn, is left at the top of the leg, where it can reinforce the mortise and help keep the end grain from splitting during dry clamping and gluing up. The horns are cut off later when the glue has cured. On rail/stile assemblies, where you have mortises at both ends of the vertical members, add 1½ in. to the length of the stile, making a ¾-in. horn at each end. When laying out the joints on legs, measure from the bottom to the top, not from top to bottom. This way you won't have to cut the legs to final length after assembly. When laying out the joints on stiles, clamp the two members side by side and lay out the final cut to length at the top (striking across both at once); then measure down from these to lay out the finished length at the bottom. Use a try square and a layout knife for the best results. Then you can accurately check the work when gluing up.

Checking for alignment—The legs should be sighted with winding strips to make sure they are in the same plane. Don't try to sight tapered legs on the tapered side. To correct twist or wind in the assembly, one person holds it down tightly on the clamp bed and slackens off the clamping pressure. The second person, holding one leg in each hand, moves the legs into proper alignment. Then the clamps are retightened.

Right-angularity between legs and rail is frequently overlooked. This is best checked by laying a straightedge across both legs as shown in figure 2b. To correct misalignment, the clamping block must be raised or lowered to redirect clamping pressure. If this isn't done, the rails will go off at odd angles at the next glue-up when the subassemblies are joined by two more rails. Then the finished piece will be under constant tension and the rails may bow. Using the straightedge as a reference, shift the clamping blocks in the appropriate direction. Here dry clamping will tell you ahead of time where to position each block. Remember to dimension each block carefully, as improperly sized blocks are difficult to position and can misalign an accurate joint by putting pressure in the wrong place.

Next check for overall squareness in plan. A try square is hardly adequate for checking this sort of right-angularity. On assemblies with long legs and rails, it can gauge only a fraction of the lengths involved, and if the legs are curved or tapered, or if the rails aren't straight across their bottom edges, a try square won't work at all.

Squareness is best determined by taking diagonal measurements from the top inside corners to the inside bottom corners of the legs. If the diagonals are equal, the assembly is square. You can make these measurements with a long rule, though take care to place the rule at the same depth in the two corners. A flexible metal tape can also be used, but this requires two people for accurate results. One holds the one-inch mark in precise alignment with the corner, while the other pulls the tape taut to measure the distance to the bottom inside of the leg.

Traditionally, diagonal measurements are taken with pinch rods. Shown in figures 3 and 4, these are similar to the two sticks described in *FWW #6*, Spring '77, p. 46, only their ends are pointed to fit into corners, and stepped so they can span obstructions like center stiles and stretchers. Considering their high degree of accuracy and the small amount of effort needed to make them, there's little reason to use anything else to measure internal diagonal distances. We should find the diagonals equal if the clamp holding the assembly together is in line with the rail member. If they are not equal, reorient the clamp and the blocks in such a way that the members will creep into square with one another.

Assembling frames—When gluing up a flat frame, as for a door, employ the same checking procedures and assembly methods as you would for a leg/rail assembly. But because a frame is closed on four sides and relatively thin in section, it calls for some special attentions. The flatness of the gluing table is particularly important. If we are using identical clamps and we press the frame down onto the clamp bars, we will get a twisted frame if the table we are working on has a twisted top. Usually the cheeks of a mortise in a frame are fairly thin, and the glue in the joint migrates to the center where it can cause them to bulge outward. Avoid this by clamping across the cheeks with a C-clamp and properly sized blocks.

Gluing up carcases—A situation where improperly dimensioned clamping blocks can be dramatically counterproductive is in gluing up carcases. Too large a block, as shown in figure 5, can misapply the pressure, cause the sides to bow like crazy and open the joint on its outer edge. For clamping case sides tightly against an internal shelf or other member, we have little choice other than to use cambered cauls *(FWW #23*, July '80, p. 12).

Gluing dovetails is totally different from gluing mortises and tenons. If the dovetail has been made so that the end grain of the pins and tails is below the surface on the adjacent boards *(FWW #21*, March '80, p. 75), then all that is required to glue a large carcase together is one clamp and two people. After the glue has been applied and the joint put together, the dovetails are clamped home individually. They will not spring back if correctly made, because there is considerable friction in the glue interfaces between the pins and tails. When the glue has been uniformly brushed on the long grain of the pins and tails, each part swells, making the close fit even tighter. Don't delay assembly after applying the glue, and don't try to hammer the parts home, as you quite properly did during the dry test assembly. Clamping is the proper means once the glue is applied, and it is sweet and easy to clamp each tail one after the other and see the glue come squeezing out at the bed of each pin. □

Ian Kirby writes frequently for this magazine.

Pole-and-Wire Joinery
The quick way to build

by Len Brackett

Almost everyone at some time needs a temporary building or shelter, but most structures on the market are both expensive and time-consuming to erect, plus awkward to store once their purpose has been served. As a carpenter's apprentice in Japan, I encountered a method that is simplicity itself—lashing poles together with wire into a scaffolding that can support a roof. Because joints can be lashed easily and quickly anywhere along the poles, structures can be adapted to any site, even to rough terrain where prefabricated buildings cannot be used. In Japan the technique is used primarily for scaffolding, but also for wood-drying sheds, tool storage, and even for enclosing an entire temple while it is being worked on. I built my own 40-ft. by 60-ft. workshop this way; other applications are craft-fair booths, lean-tos, covered woodpiles and trellises, to name but a few.

Materials—Japan is blessed with some of the richest forests in the world, and wood has always been the traditional building material. Straw rope used to be the traditional binding for pole construction, but #9 annealed iron wire (not common baling wire), which neither rots nor frays and is stronger and faster to wrap than straw rope, is the material of choice today. You can buy it at most hardware stores or at building and agricultural-supply outfits. Enough wire to make one joint (about 3 ft. to join 5-in. dia. poles) will cost about 3ᶜ. Be sure to get annealed black wire; galvanized wire is too highly tempered, too brittle and too stiff to work.

As for poles, straight ones with little taper work best. They are lighter in proportion to their strength and easier to store, transport and position than ones with a lot of taper. Almost any species will work. We like to use Douglas fir or ponderosa pine because they are straight, strong and locally available. Poles larger than 8 in. in diameter are heavy and awkward. A butt diameter of 4 in. to 5 in. is best. All poles must be peeled. Bark holds moisture inside the poles, which fosters fungus growth and insect infestation (boring beetles especially), both of which can dangerously weaken a pole. Beware of rot, knots or other weaknesses, particularly if the pole is to bear horizontal loads. Poles should be stored in a dry place, vertically for maximum ventilation if stored outside.

The only tools you will need are a wire cutter (preferably the kind easily used with one hand) and a sturdy tapered spike for twisting the loops of wire. You could use an ironworker's spud wrench, a large machinist's punch or even a very large nail.

The photos and sequence of drawings at right show how to wrap a joint and secure the wire knot. Practice a few times before you attempt to put up some structure—be sure you understand how the loop wraps around the tails, not vice-versa, or else the wire might fatigue and break off. Tighten the knot until the wire bites into the wood, then stop. Too much twisting will also weaken or break the wire. When

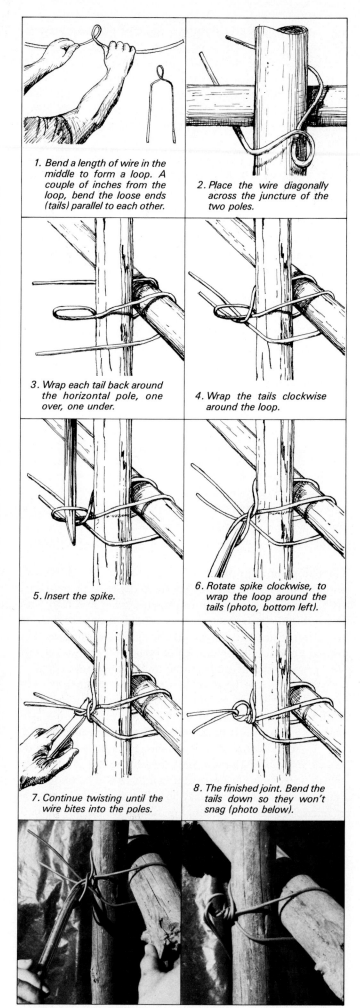

1. Bend a length of wire in the middle to form a loop. A couple of inches from the loop, bend the loose ends (tails) parallel to each other.

2. Place the wire diagonally across the juncture of the two poles.

3. Wrap each tail back around the horizontal pole, one over, one under.

4. Wrap the tails clockwise around the loop.

5. Insert the spike.

6. Rotate spike clockwise, to wrap the loop around the tails (photo, bottom left).

7. Continue twisting until the wire bites into the poles.

8. The finished joint. Bend the tails down so they won't snag (photo below).

Brackett's pole-and-wire shop is spacious and well ventilated; detail, left, shows cross-bracing at central post.

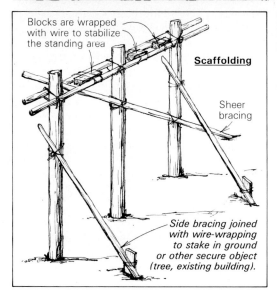

Blocks are wrapped with wire to stabilize the standing area

Scaffolding

Sheer bracing

Side bracing joined with wire-wrapping to stake in ground or other secure object (tree, existing building).

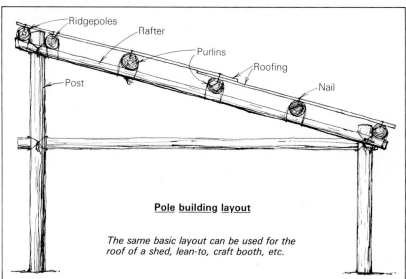

Ridgepoles
Rafter
Purlins
Roofing
Post
Nail

Pole building layout

The same basic layout can be used for the roof of a shed, lean-to, craft booth, etc.

done, bend the ends of the wire down to the wood, so they can't snag clothing or flesh.

With practice, you can make a joint in just a few seconds, especially if the wire is precut and hanging in your belt. The joints tend to self-tighten, but it's wise to check them periodically, especially if the poles are green or are exposed to humidity extremes. Poles shrink in dry weather, loosening the joint. You cannot tighten wire simply by pulling on a loose end, so wrap it tightly to start, as if it were wallpaper, smoothing out the wrinkles from the middle toward the ends. And of course, you should take the shortest and most direct route around the poles.

Building—Once you have mastered the way to twist the wire, you are ready to design a building. The following suggestions should help you get started. Pole-building layouts look a bit goofy, but are really quite rational, even if the rafters do hang from the purlins, ridgepole and top plates. Improvisation is the key. The structure must be kept rigid. Be sure to fix the poles to a stake in the ground or to some solid object to keep them from falling over as you build. Later they can be shear-braced with diagonal poles.

Pole-and-wire joinery is a very fast way to make scaffolding. Begin by fastening two horizontal poles at the required height, one on either side of the verticals. Jam spacer blocks of wood between the horizontal poles at 6-ft. intervals, then lash the horizontal poles tightly together, as shown in the drawing above left.

Pole buildings usually have corrugated steel roofing running parallel to the rafters. In this case, the purlins must be placed on top of the rafters and midspan between the top plates and the ridgepole (drawing above), and at the correct intervals for nailing the steel roofing to them. Rafters are fastened to the posts below and up against the top plate. The ridgepole can be placed on top of the central post for a gable roof; better yet, two ridgepoles can be fastened, one on either side of the central posts and high enough so the posts won't protrude through the roofing material. Put in the shear bracing, nail on the roofing and the roof is complete.

My own 2,400-sq. ft. shop was put together by three men in 2½ days, not including the time it took to peel the poles. It ought to last 15 to 20 years, and it cost about $600 for wire and roofing in 1976. Building inspectors have nightmares about such buildings, which are out of keeping with a heavily industrialized, consumer economy. But they do go together fast to make a variety of structures, they disassemble quickly and the materials remain available, unimpaired, for future use. In today's throw-away society, the ingenuity, simplicity and economy of pole buildings have great appeal.   □

Len Brackett, 34, of Nevada City, Calif., apprenticed for five years with temple builders in Kyoto.

Methods of Work

Making dowels with the table saw

I prefer to make my own dowels for several good reasons. I can make any size dowel in any length from any wood. My system is simpler and certainly less expensive than the commercial dowel-making tools that are limited to only a few sizes. The drawings show the complete tooling required: a hardwood block and your table saw. The block size isn't critical, but it should be thick enough to clamp easily to the saw's rip fence and long enough to cover the sawblade in use. This last point is important because you'll need to reach across the saw to withdraw the finished dowel.

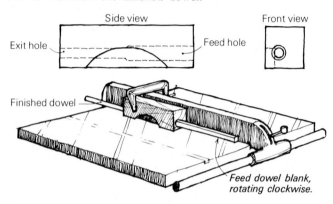

To construct the fixture, first drill a dowel-sized exit hole through the length of the block. Enlarge this hole from the front, halfway through the block, to produce a feed hole. The diameter of the feed hole should be the same as the diagonal of the square dowel blanks you plan to use. As a guide the diameter of the feed hole shouldn't exceed the exit hole by $\frac{1}{4}$ in. Now clamp the block to the saw's rip fence. Center the block over the blade. In a succession of cove cuts (made by raising the sawblade into the block) cut a channel from the edge to just into the wall of the exit hole. The best blade to use to channel the block and make dowels is a heavy, small-diameter carbide-toothed blade. Next rip the dowel blanks so they will turn easily in the feed hole. With the block clamped and the fence locked, start the saw and insert the blank. Rotate the blank clockwise and feed slowly until the blade starts cutting. Adjust the block's position with the rip fence until the dowel fits snugly in the exit hole. It's a good idea to withdraw the dowel and check the size of the first few inches.

In smaller sizes, which are difficult to rotate by hand, I cut a short dowel on one end. Then I chuck the short dowel in my portable drill. A slow feed and a slow rotation yield the smoothest dowels.   —Larry Churchill, Mayville, Wis.

Making dowels with the router

Here's how to make dowels of any size with a simple router setup. First drill a pilot hole through a 2x4 the same diameter as the dowel you want to produce. Chuck a core-box bit in your router, rout a recess in the front of the 2x4 just above the hole and clamp the router in position. Center the bit

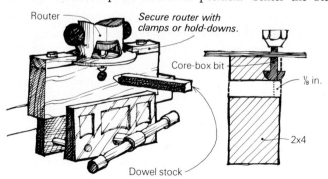

right over the top of the hole with the shaft of the bit inset about $\frac{1}{8}$ in. into the 2x4. Make sure the leading edge of the bit is precisely at the circumference of the hole. Now turn on the router and push the dowel blank into the hole, rotating the blank with a hand drill. Taper the front of the blank for easier starting.   —G. Weldon Friesen, Middlebury, Ind.

Cutting round tenons on slats

With a metal pipe, a simple jig and my radial-arm saw, I solved the problem of cutting round tenons on the ends of slats for the sides of a cradle. Find a 6-in. length of pipe that slips snugly over the slats (my slats are $\frac{3}{4}$ in. wide by $\frac{3}{8}$ in. thick). Add masking tape to the slats to tighten up the fit if they're loose. Build the simple jig shown in the sketch below and clamp it and the stop block to the saw's fence. Carefully adjust the stop block so that the tenons will be the right length. Mount a sharp plywood blade in the saw and center the blade over the slat location. Now push a slat into the pipe and place the pipe in the jig with the slat up against the stop. Lower the blade until it just touches the flat side of the slat (this will result in a slightly undersize $\frac{3}{8}$-in. tenon). Rotate the pipe to cut a clean shoulder on the slat. Work the pipe back and forth under the blade, slowly rotating the pipe. A round tenon will result. This process leaves the tenon a little bit rough, but so much the better for gluing. After you're set up, you can cut the tenons on 20 or 30 slats in an hour.

—George Eckhart, Kenosha, Wis.

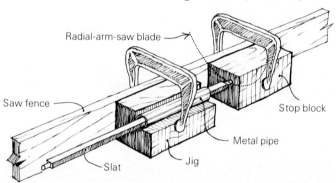

Chair-rung tenons on the bandsaw

Here is an easy method of using the bandsaw to make tenons on round pieces such as chair rungs. Take out the saw's miter gauge, put it in backwards (with the face toward you) and clamp it to the table with a C-clamp. Position the gauge so that its face is the same distance from the cutting edge as the depth of the desired shoulder on the tenon. Deep shoulders

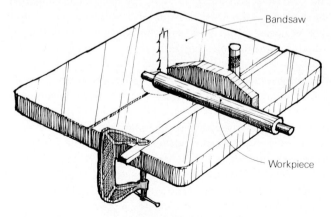

may require two or three passes. With the saw on, rotate the workpiece against the face of the miter gauge. Done properly, the result is a smooth, properly sized tenon.

—George Kramer, Santa Rosa, Calif.

Slot-mortising table

I cut slot mortises on my radial arm saw using this two-way sliding table. The table consists of three separate ¾-in. thick plywood or particle-board sections. Cut the middle and top sections wider than the bottom to leave room for clamping stop blocks. To get the two-way sliding action, cut tracks and set rails in the parts, as shown in the sketch. I used ¾-in. square, waxed hardwood rails glued into grooves cut just less than ⅜ in. deep. The shallow grooves will separate the sections a little so the surfaces won't rub. Notch the back corners of the top section (so you have a place to clamp stop blocks) and add fences, handles and work hold-downs as needed.

To use the table, mount an end-mill cutter in a chuck on the saw's spindle and set the height and depth of cut with the saw's adjustments. Clamp the stop blocks in place to control side-to-side movement. Now you're ready to mortise. Secure the work in position, turn on the saw and move the table from side to side as you slowly push the work into the cutter.

—*Bill Horton, Chino, Calif.*

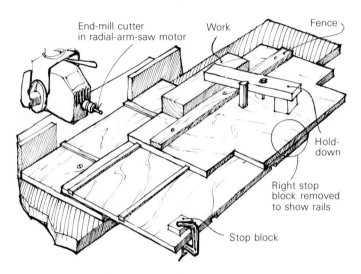

Drill-press mortising fixture

Here's a fixture for cutting mortises on the drill press using fluted end-milling cutters. A lateral control mechanism, made from ⅛-in. steel plate, pivots at three points and gives the fixture the back-and-forth movement needed to cut the mortise. The stop mechanism is a ¼-in. rod that passes through a collar piece that is screwed to the base. Two sliding collars, fastened in place on the rod with setscrews, limit the movement of the sliding table. To use, clamp the fixture to the drill-press table. Clamp the work to the fence and set the stop collars for the size mortise needed. Your right hand, on the drill-press feed, controls the depth of the mortise, while your left hand controls the lateral movement for the length of the mortise.

—*Mario Rodriguez, Brooklyn, N.Y.*

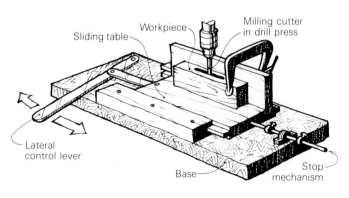

Glue spreader for lamination

This glue spreader makes easy the tedious job of covering thin laminations with just the right amount of glue. The heart of the spreader is a cork-covered cylinder. The cork has the right

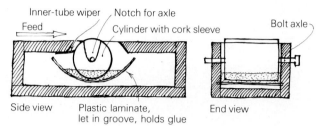

texture to pick up and deposit the right amount of glue. Make the spreader frame from plywood. Cut a semicircular groove in each side of the frame to hold a piece of plastic laminate which acts a a glue reservoir. Notch the sides of the frame so the glue-spreader cylinder can be removed for cleaning. Tack a piece of rubber innertube to the frame so that it will scrape excess glue from the cylinder as it rotates. I use commercial white glue mixed with water to get a better consistency for spreading.—*Rod Davidson, Port Angeles, Wash.*

Dadoing guide

Sketched below is a quick setup I use for repeated dadoing operations with my router and portable workbench/vise. It's so simple, yet it's more accurate and quicker to use than the fence-clamped-to-the-board approach. Make the parts from the stock the same thickness as the boards you're dadoing. Clamp the fence atop two guide blocks to form a bridge over the work as shown. Shim the fence off the two guides with cardboard or veneer. This should leave enough clearance so the stock will slide in under the fence easily. Now just push the workpiece in under the bridge, snug against the stop. Clamp the workpiece to the workbench somewhere behind the fence, set the router to proper depth and go to town. The guide blocks not only guide the workpiece, they also support the router base near the edge of the board.

—*Josh Markel, Philadelphia, Pa.*

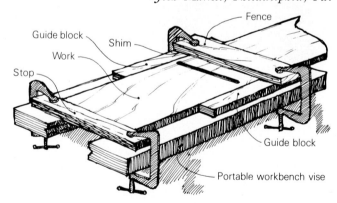

Sanding small pieces in the clothes dryer

I needed radiused edges on both ends of a thousand ½-in. long pieces of ½-in. diameter dowels. I lined the insides of three 5-lb. plastic peanut-butter buckets with 100-grit sandpaper, tossed in about 350 dowels per bucket and secured the lids with masking tape. Then I put the buckets into my clothes dryer along with a couple of heavy towels to aid the tumbling action. I set the dryer to air fluff and turned it on. In only ten minutes the job was done.

To protect your dryer, be sure to use only "soft" containers, secure the lid, add towels and use a no-heat setting.

—*Marilyn Warrington, Tiro, Ohio*

TURNING

Five Basic Spindle Laminations
Glued-up turnings produce various patterns

by Ted Pack

Ernest Hemingway used to argue there were only four plots in American novels. If you want to turn out a lamp, rolling pin, inkstand, candlestick or weed pot instead of a novel, your range is increased; I count five basic spindle laminations: the sandwich, the stack, the multiple sandwich, the checkerboard and the chevron.

The sandwich (figure 1) is the easiest lamination. You face-glue a series of boards together, let the glue dry overnight, trim the block and turn. The outer layers follow and accent the piece's curves, making a bull's-eye effect on the front and back; the sides look striped. Making the outer layers thinner than the inner ones will emphasize the bull's-eye effect; making the inner layers thinner emphasizes the striped sides. You can use a range of wood colors, from front to back or from the center slab out, and you can alternate thick slabs of dark wood with thin slabs of light—it's still a sandwich.

Turn a sandwich on its side and you get a stack (figure 2). It's made of short pieces of wood face-glued to one another, with the grain direction alternated for strength. This means your cutting tool will jump from end grain to side grain all along the piece, making this one more difficult to work on. Keep a firm grip and a sharp tool. You can vary the colors and thicknesses of the laminations on this one, too, just like the sandwich. It's a good way to use up ends of boards too short to join and too pretty to throw out.

The multiple sandwich (figure 3) has the bull's-eye effect on all sides, and no striped sides. There are a number of ways to build up the multiple sandwich. I usually turn lamp bases out of them, and so start with a 6-in. by 6-in. core. This can be a solid piece or a glued-up block trimmed square. I laminate to it a thin layer of contrasting wood on each side, then

add a thin layer of the core wood on top of that. This is a good way to use up thin pieces of figured wood. I do not overlap the laminations at the corners, and thus the largest diameter that the finished turning can be is slightly less than the diagonal of the core. This method produces equal-size bull's-eyes on four sides without having to miter the corners of the laminations, which is another way of building up a multiple sandwich. Mitered corners are trickier to cut and glue, but they give you more possibilities for the thickness of the laminations and their proportion to the size of the core. Three, six and eight-sided sandwiches are possible, but the more sides you have, the closer your polygon comes to a circle, and the thinner the laminations will be after turning.

The checkerboard (figure 4) is the most exacting of the five designs. To make a block with, say, five strips per side, start with 25 strips planed exactly as wide as they are to be in the final block, and ¼ in. thicker than they are wide. Glue them across the width to make five striped boards, two with a dark strip in the center and three with a light. When the boards are dry, plane down the extra ¼ in. in thickness, to make each board as thick as the strips are wide. Now glue the five boards into a block, being sure the ends make a checkerboard pattern. Apply clamping pressure slowly and evenly; I usually put a light clamp at each end and then apply the clamps from the center of the piece out to both ends. (For an alternate way of making checkerboard patterns, see Methods of Work, *FWW* #22, May '80.)

The procedure is the same for any number of squares, but if you pick an even number the center will be in the joint, not the center strip. You can vary the checkerboard design by making the outer layer on all four sides a solid board, the

---

The Overlapping Multiple Sandwich

Paul Darnell of Phoenix, Ariz., sent us yet another method of gluing up the multiple sandwich, the third of Ted Pack's five basic spindle laminations. Darnell begins with a square core and laminates first only two opposite sides of it. When the glue has dried, he planes the glueline faces and laminates these, overlapping the edges of the first laminations. This process can be repeated until he reaches the limit of his lathe's swing. It produces different-size bull's-eyes on the four "corners" of the turning, as shown in the sample of his work at right. □

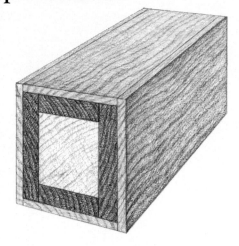

Paul Darnell

| Sandwich | Stack | Multiple sandwich | Checkerboard | Chevron: two views |

Fig. 1: Sandwich

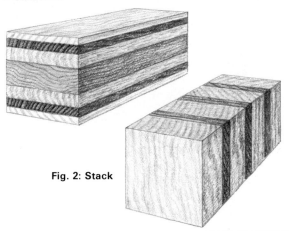

Fig. 2: Stack

Fig. 3: Multiple sandwich

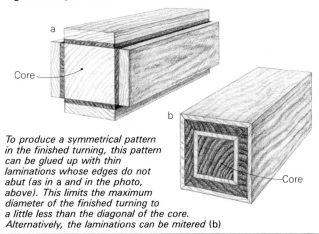

a

Core

b

Core

To produce a symmetrical pattern in the finished turning, this pattern can be glued up with thin laminations whose edges do not abut (as in a and in the photo, above). This limits the maximum diameter of the finished turning to a little less than the diagonal of the core. Alternatively, the laminations can be mitered (b)

Fig. 4: Checkerboard

To make the checkerboard design, first glue up five striped boards. . .

. . .then glue these into a block.

To vary this pattern enclose the checkerboard with solid boards. This produces accents at the smaller diameters of the finished turning.

Fig. 5: Chevron

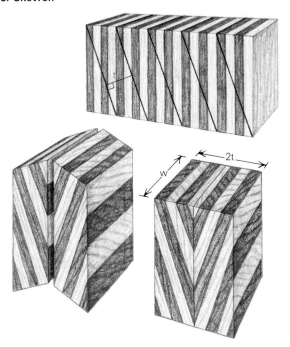

t

2t

w

For this pattern, make the angled cut through the slab so it passes through an even number of laminations. Otherwise the contrasting laminations of the half-blocks will not align when reversed and glued up. To produce a square turning block, the thickness (t) of the half-blocks should equal half the width (w) of your laminations.

result being that the interior checkerboard will produce minor accents as it is revealed in turning.

The chevron (figure 5, preceding page) is easier to glue up than the checkerboard, but it takes more time and planning. Face-glue a number of thin slats into a slab, then cut the slab at an angle to make thick slices. Reverse every other slice and glue them into turning blocks two by two. If you've ever made a herringbone cheeseboard you'll recognize the technique.

There are several things to mull over with pencil and paper before you start making noise and sawdust. First, the triangular pieces at the ends are waste, no matter how many turning blocks you get from the middle. For economy, consider making at least two blocks from each slab. Second, to have the light and dark laminations meet in your turning block, you have to cut each half-block so it contains an even number of laminations; the half-blocks in the models and the drawing are four laminations wide.

Look at the sketch again. The true thickness of each half-block will be the altitude of a parallelogram—the line marked t in figure 5. This will be less than the thickness of four slats because of the angle, and the steeper the angle, the more pronounced the difference. The true thickness of two half-blocks should be close to the width of the slats you begin with, to end up with roughly square turning blocks.

After planning your blocks out on a piece of paper, cut the slats and glue up the slab. Let it dry, then plane the top and bottom flat and square with the ends. Now cut the half-blocks, using a bandsaw if possible. Be sure to start and end each cut on a slat of the same color. Plane the sides of each half-block, flip and glue. If you didn't get the bottom quite square, or the bandsaw was a little out of true, the blocks will not match in front and back; at this stage the best you can do is make a perfect chevron in the front and keep the back of the finished piece turned to a wall. Wait for the second application of glue to dry overnight, trim the ends of each block square, and turn.

You can vary the thickness and color of the laminations in this configuration, but you have to do so carefully. If you use very thin slats of maple alternated with thick slats of cherry, for example, you still must have an even number of slats in each half-block. If you use three woods you must maintain the same sequence throughout the slab, and you must have a multiple of three slats in each half-block. The same holds for four, five or more woods.

All of the patterns are easier to do if you have, or have access to, a thickness planer. The checkerboard, in particular, is almost impossible to do without one. If you don't have one, and can't see spending $1,500 to get one, consider signing up for woodshop at your local junior college or night school. School shops usually have a planer, a bandsaw and a lathe. The cost is minimal—I've paid from $3 for an entire semester to $20 for 10 nights—and the teachers do not confine your choice of projects or tool use, once you've demonstrated a reasonable familiarity with basic shop safety.

The best glue joints are produced between freshly planed surfaces and between woods of similar density. Maple, cherry, walnut and koa work well together, as do pine and redwood. I've always thought the pattern, not the wood, was the focus in a laminated turning, so I usually use plain, unfigured wood, and let the lamination speak for itself. ☐

Ted Pack lives in Riverbank, Calif.

106

Methods of Work

Two steady-rests

The homemade stabilizer device shown below allows me to turn four-poster beds and architectural columns on my 9-ft. lathe. The stabilizer eliminates the whipping and vibrating that accompany long-stock turning. The brace bolts to the lathe bed at about the midway point. A long upward-pointing handle is hinged to move the cast-aluminum stabilizer back and forth so it can ride against the stock. The stabilizer has several different diameters to fit different-sized turnings. The aluminum, coated with a little beeswax where it rubs, effectively carries away the heat. The brace adjusts against the stock through a spring-loaded device that moves an old file against a stack of hacksaw blades.

—*Deloe Brock, Chattanooga, Tenn.*

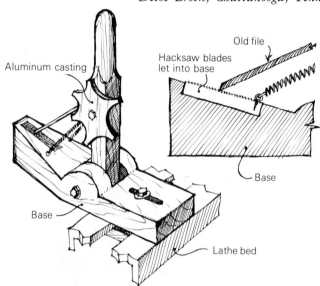

Here is an economical steady-rest made from three sections of 2x4, a carriage bolt and two plastic casters (drawing below). Cut and join the wood to fit your lathe bed, then drill the bolt hole the same height as the center spindle. The base clamps to the lathe bed and adjusts in or out for large or small work. The roller arm pivots on the bolt to provide a fine-tune adjustment to the changing diameter of the work in progress.   —*James Ulwelling, Coon Rapids, Minn.*

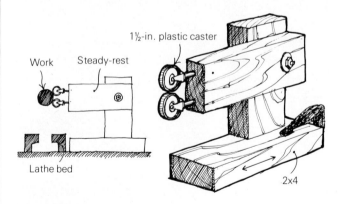

Faceplate scraping

A curved cabinet scraper works extremely well for the final shaping of bowls and other faceplate turning projects. The scraper easily smooths end-grain areas where turning tools tend to tear out splinters and chunks. It also eliminates the need for coarse grades of sandpaper that put in those hard-to-remove, concentric scratches.

—*John Rocus, Ann Arbor, Mich.*

Turning for Figure
Some design considerations when making bowls

by Wendell Smith

Recent articles about woodturning emphasize the techniques of turning. Discussions of grain and figure are generally found in books about wood or timber. The purpose of this article is to bring these two subjects together and to discuss some aesthetic aspects of bowl turning which depend upon grain and figure in wood. You can predict and control the figure that will appear in a completed piece by considering how your proposed bowl shape relates to the original orientation of the blank in the tree. The same blank can yield several types of figure, depending on how you orient it on the lathe and the radius of curvature you choose for the turning.

In this discussion, the words grain and figure will be used

Wendell Smith, who lives in Fairport, N.Y., is a research scientist and woodturner.

in the technical sense. Grain refers to the orientation of wood cells with respect to the axis of the tree. Authorities generally distinguish six types: straight, wavy, interlocked, irregular, spiral and diagonal. The first four are the most common. Figure is the surface appearance of the wood's anatomical features, including grain, which results from cutting or machining. In the same turning blank, tangential, radial and transverse surfaces display different figure, as shown on p. 108.

You can obtain many interesting effects using straight-grained wood by varying the orientation of the growth rings. Bowls can be turned with the growth rings "concave up" (the ring curvature running in the same direction as the bowl curvature) or with the growth rings "concave down" (with the ring curvature running opposite the bowl curvature). Some people find these relationships easier to visualize in terms of the bark side and the heart side of the wood. A bowl turned with the growth rings concave up opens toward what was the center of the tree, while one turned with the rings concave down opens toward what was the tree's bark.

Whether you turn with the rings concave up or concave down changes the appearance of a bowl or tray. I turned two cherry trays from blanks cut from adjacent segments of a single board, but I flipped one blank over before turning. A predictable pattern of concentric ellipses was produced on the tray blank oriented with the rings concave down (photo above left), while a hyperbolic pattern resulted when the rings were oriented concave up (photo below left). A striking example of hyperbolic figure is shown in the tulipwood bowl below. Turning concave up or concave down is a matter of personal preference, although I think that the former emphasizes flat-

Cherry trays, left, from the same board show growth-ring figure from turning concave down (top) and concave up (bottom). Above, hyperbolic figure on tulipwood bowl by Brian Lee.

Photos: Wendell Smith

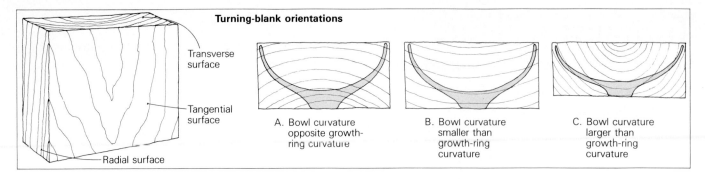

Turning-blank orientations

Transverse surface

Tangential surface

Radial surface

A. Bowl curvature opposite growth-ring curvature

B. Bowl curvature smaller than growth-ring curvature

C. Bowl curvature larger than growth-ring curvature

ness, while the latter accentuates roundness and depth.

These examples of growth-ring figure are really special cases of a more general rule. If the radius of curvature of a bowl is opposite to (A, above) or smaller than (B) the radius of curvature of the growth rings, a pattern of concentric circles or ellipses will result. If the radius of curvature of a bowl is greater than the radius of curvature of the growth rings (C), a hyperbolic and/or parabolic figure will result. Thus, under certain circumstances turning with the rings concave up can lead to either figure, as shown at right and below, on the butternut bowl. The base of the bowl has a greater radius of curvature than the rings, while the sides of the bowl have a smaller radius of curvature. Therefore, what begins as a hyperbolic pattern in the bowl bottom becomes a concentric pattern at the sides. The result is a set of rings that progresses across the bowl, a figure enhanced, in the case of butternut, by the characteristically scalloped annual rings of the species.

Many of the bowls shown here I purposely turned for symmetry. If symmetry is eliminated, the relationships discussed will still apply. Thus trial and error, and careful observation, can lead to turnings that fully reveal the beauty of the wood.

Two anatomical elements which are present to different degrees in all hardwoods are vessels and rays. Broad rays are characteristic of woods such as oak, beech, planewood and lacewood, regardless of the presence or absence of fancy grain. When rays are exposed on a radial surface, flake (or ray-fleck) figure results, which can be an interesting design element. Rays can be seen in radial and tangential section in the block of European planewood, left.

The planewood bowl, below, was turned from a quartersawn board. Because of this, the flake figure is revealed in the center of the bowl, but is lost toward the sides. At the lower left is a tangential (end on) view of the rays, and at the upper right, a transverse view. In fact, this photograph illustrates on a single surface of wood every conceivable ray figure that can be exposed in European planewood.

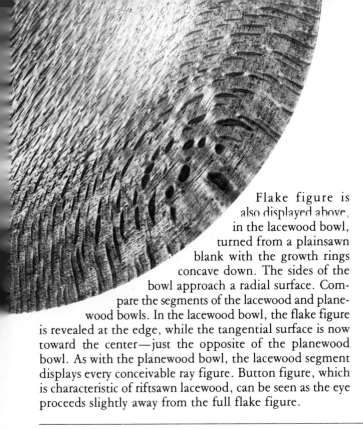

Flake figure is also displayed above, in the lacewood bowl, turned from a plainsawn blank with the growth rings concave down. The sides of the bowl approach a radial surface. Compare the segments of the lacewood and planewood bowls. In the lacewood bowl, the flake figure is revealed at the edge, while the tangential surface is now toward the center—just the opposite of the planewood bowl. As with the planewood bowl, the lacewood segment displays every conceivable ray figure. Button figure, which is characteristic of riftsawn lacewood, can be seen as the eye proceeds slightly away from the full flake figure.

In transverse sections of certain species of hardwoods, such as elm and osage orange, the latewood pores appear as wavy, concentric bands (see "Two Neglected Woods," *FWW* #25, Nov. '80, pp. 86-87). A tangential surface which cuts across the tops of the waves will lead to a figure resembling bird feathers, which is called partridge-breast figure. This figure is illustrated in the elm tray, above. I turned this tray with the rings concave up because the surface of the tray would be very close to tangential. In a perfectly tangential cut the figure is rather diffuse.

Orientation is also important with woods having a fancy grain, such as wavy or interlocked. Wavy grain leads to a figure known as curl, which is best displayed on a radial surface. The curly maple bowl, left, was turned with the rings concave down. Consequently, the figure is slightly more pronounced at the sides of the bowl (radial cut) than at the base (tangential cut).

The same considerations apply to turning woods with an interlocked grain as apply to those with wavy grain. Interlocked grain, which is typical of many tropical woods, occurs when fibers of successive growth layers spiral in opposite directions. This results in a figure on quartersawn surfaces known as ribbon, or stripe, of which striped African mahogany is probably the classic example. To display this figure in a plainsawn board it is best to turn with the rings concave down. Alternatively, the combination of a quartersawn board with maximum radius of bowl curvature would also lead to maximum stripe figure. The combination of interlocked with wavy grain can lead to several other figures, many of which are better displayed on a radial surface.

Irregular grain is the fourth type considered here. One example, caused by localized swirls in the grain, is bird's-eye. Because bird's eyes develop radially within the tree, a tangential cut best reveals the ends of the eyes. Thus, turning concave up may be preferred, as in the bird's-eye maple bowl at left (turned by Al Stirt). On the other hand, bird's eyes can also be attractive in cross section, which calls for cuts that expose a radial surface.

The most frequently encountered irregular grain occurs in the vicinity of crotches. Boards which at first sight might be rejected because of unwanted knots can be used to turn beautiful objects. A blank removed from a board by sawing close to but not including a knot will usually lead to a figure with chatoyant swirls. The ultimate in crotch figure is generally taken to be a full-feather crotch, shown at left. To obtain this figure, however, bowl design really must begin when the log is cut. For more on cutting wood for figure, see "Harvesting Green Wood" by Dale Nish, *FWW* #16, May '79. □

Inlaid Turnings
Decorating with plugs

by Fran William Hall

Several years ago the harvesters came through my section of southern Minnesota looking for black walnut veneer logs. They scoured the woods, buying trees and then taking only the straight bole for shipment to Germany, where, I am told, they cut veneer half again as thin as we do in America. After removing the boles, they left the rest of the trees to rot in the woods. I got permission from the farmers, most of whom I had known most of my life, to go in and remove whatever was usable. In several weeks time I had chainsawn more than 200 chunks of this lovely wood. I waxed the ends with paraffin and stored them in a shed to dry. At the end of two years I cut circle blanks from each good chunk and again waxed the perimeters to prevent checking.

I've made many bowls from this wood. The pieces that are highly figured I let do their own talking. Those that are plain I usually decorate. I first turn the bowl to a rough shape, then lay out a pattern using the indexing head of the lathe. A simple pattern, for instance, would consist of a single line of plugs all around the bowl. If the pattern is to be complicated, I must do one set of dots at a time, gluing in the plugs and then waiting for the glue to set before turning them down with a very sharp tool and the lathe running at a high speed.

To bore the plug holes, I first mark the bowl surface with a sharp punch to keep the drill from wandering. I clamp the work in a machinist's vise on the drill-press table and use multi-spur machine bits, running them at high speed. The hole must be clean and crisp its full depth, or turning will reveal ragged edges. I usually drill the holes about ¼ in. deep, but this depends on the thickness of the bowl-to-be and on what the wood looks like.

For the plugs, instead of using a plug cutter, I turn dowels. If the dowel is to be of small diameter, I use short lengths to minimize whipping, which can produce an oval section. I turn the dowel slightly oversize, then sand it with a wide piece of sandpaper (80 grit) to minimize irregularities, and gauge it to make sure its diameter is exact. Dowels must fit their holes perfectly. I never smooth-sand the dowels because a rougher surface makes a better glue joint. I use yellow glue. I cut the plugs on a bandsaw, holding them in a V-trough if they are small. I cut plugs approximately the depth of the drilled holes and, with a disc sander, put a slight bevel on each plug to facilitate entry into the hole. To prevent splitting, it is important that the plugs not be so long that they stick out any distance from the bowl. Cut them the right length and tap them in so they are level with the bowl wood or flush them off after assembly by sanding. Once again, run the lathe at high speed, use a sharp tool and take a light cut. If the plugs have been fitted properly, you should feel no crack when you rub your fingers over the finished design. □

Fran Hall is a travel lecturer whose home and home shop are in Northfield, Minn.

Inlaying decorative plugs begins with marking the bowl blank for bore centers on the lathe, using the indexing plate, top. The hole locations are center-punched and the holes are drilled with a spur bit at high speed, the blank held in a machinist's vise, center left. Center right, the holes are filled with plugs cut from lathe-turned dowels. It is important that the plugs be flush with the surface of the bowl blank, or they will split during turning. Above and right, completed bowls display the flawless surface that a sharp tool taking a light cut at high speed can produce. The bowls are of walnut, decorated with holly and blackwood.

Sanding and Finishing on the Lathe

by David Ward

The first step to a good finish is a good sanding job: beginning with a coarse grit and not skipping grits. Sanding lathe work involves unique problems because it is impossible to sand with the grain while the lathe is running. Consequently, a lot of time is spent removing cross-grain scratches.

This problem can be solved on convex surfaces by using an orbital sander. With a sander, the grit does not remain in one place long enough to create scratches. Another advantage of an or-bital sander is that it won't dip into soft spots in the grain the way hand-held sandpaper will. The technique works so well that in sanding decayed wood, the edge of a void can become too sharp and need softening by hand, with 320 grit or so. Areas of the turning not accessible with the sander can be reached with strips of sandpaper reinforced with clear Mylar packing tape.

I don't have any magic answers for sanding inside surfaces, but the process can be made less painful by spraying sheets of sandpaper with pressure-sensitive adhesive (3M's #75) and sticking them together back to back. Tear off pieces, and the grit on one side keeps the sandpaper from slipping off the finger while the other side sands.

Another technique that I find essential in achieving a good sanding job is something I call flip-flopping—spinning the piece in one direction and then in the other while sanding. Wood fibers tend to bend over rather than being cut off, especially on end grain. Reversing the lathe (see Methods of Work, *FWW* #16, May '79) bends them back and forth until they are cut off. Be sure the faceplate is tightened securely before trying this.

Once the piece is adequately sanded I use a finishing process that is a takeoff on French polishing. The ingredients are similar and so are the results, but the method of application is much different. The turning is first soaked with raw linseed oil. This brings out the color of wood better than any other oil or mixture I've tried. After a few minutes, wipe off the excess oil and apply liberally a mixture of about 25 parts orange or white shellac and 1 part raw linseed oil. The oil lubricates the finish when it is being buffed. Too little oil will cause the surface to drag, while too much will not permit the shellac to heat up enough. The proportions may need adjusting for a specific application.

After the shellac-and-oil mixture has dried for two to ten minutes, depending on how porous the wood is, run the lathe at a fairly high speed. Step to one side before doing so, however, to avoid a shower. Then hold a pad of folded soft cotton cloth firmly against the turning. Most of the excess shellac will be quickly removed, leaving a clear surface on the work. The surface must be burnished with increasing pressure until the finish ceases to migrate, as observed in the glare of a light. At this point any shellac remaining on the wood has been driven into the wood by heat and pressure.

I usually apply a final coat of clear shoe wax for extra luster and durability. The end result is a hard surface finish that does not coat the wood with plastic—a penetrating finish that will not dull with time and takes minutes rather than hours to complete. This finish works well on most hardwoods. □

David Ward is a turner in Glenwood Springs, Colo.

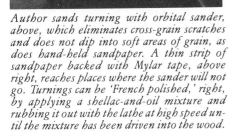

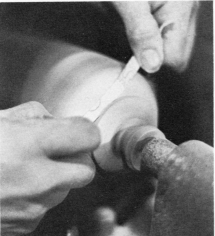

Author sands turning with orbital sander, above, which eliminates cross-grain scratches and does not dip into soft areas of grain, as does hand-held sandpaper. A thin strip of sandpaper backed with Mylar tape, above right, reaches places where the sander will not go. Turnings can be 'French polished,' right, by applying a shellac-and-oil mixture and rubbing it out with the lathe at high speed until the mixture has been driven into the wood.

Coopered Columns
Joining and turning large staved constructions

by John Leeke

Since leaving my father's woodworking shop ten years ago, I have made my living building furniture and cabinets and restoring houses. Occasionally I do rough carpentry for a regular customer, but I would rather stick to finish work. So I was something less than excited when I was asked to repair a porch. My attitude improved quickly when I learned that the house was listed with the National Register of Historic Places. A typical example of a 19th-century mill owner's house, the Goodall House in Sanford, Maine, is a mansard-style mansion with a Colonial Revival porch built in a simple classical style. One of the 9-ft. columns had rotted and needed to be replaced. I hadn't done any lathe work as large as this required, but thought that my small shop just might be able to handle it. Had I known then that in the end I would replace more than a dozen columns, I might not have taken the job.

Now I'm happy I did, for making columns has been profitable for my small enterprise. It took me 38 hours to build the first 9-ft. column. A subsequent run of six columns for the same house required 32 hours per column, and a recent run of six columns for another job took 26 hours for each. These figures include the time I spent developing techniques and making the special jigs and clamps that I'll describe below. The actual production time on the last run of columns was 20 hours apiece. At that rate I can make large columns that are comparable in cost, and at least equal in quality, to those produced by millworks and large manufacturers, even though I use only ordinary, small-shop machinery and tools.

The old columns were 13 in. in diameter and were built up stave-fashion like a wooden bucket. Made of cedar, their lapped tongue-and-groove joints had loosened over the years, even in columns not yet rotted. I decided to join mine with splined miters, and chose resorcinol-formaldehyde exterior glue to keep the joints together. Instead of cedar, I used pine.

Cutting the staves—To begin, I made full-scale drawings of the column in section and elevation (figure 1). The sectional drawing shows the finished diameters of the shaft and the dimensions of the 12 staves. The elevation drawing shows the shaft, plinth, base, bead mold and capital, as well as the curvature of the entasis, the barely perceptible swelling of the shaft towards the middle. In deciding upon 12 staves, I considered the higher cost for fewer staves of thicker stock against the extra labor involved in making more joints with thinner stock. Because a greater number of staves makes the column more stable, I used 12 of them, and as in the original columns, I oriented the annual rings at random.

I cut the rough stock to within 1 in. of finished length, which made it much easier to mount the coopered blank on the lathe. The width of the rough stave blanks was also cut oversize to allow for warping due to relieved stresses in the plank. After jointing one face and one edge on each, I leaned the staves up in a corner of the shop for a few days to allow

the stresses to equilibrate. I jointed them again just before cutting the bevel on their edges. The staves must be stable and straight, and should not warp after the bevels are cut, as this would alter the angle of the beveled edge.

For a 12-stave column the bevel is 75°. The accuracy of this cut is important because joints must have uniform contact their entire length. If a cumulative error of 1° is tolerable in the whole ring of staves, then each bevel cut must be within $\frac{1}{24}$ of a degree. To achieve this degree of accuracy I use the compounding-of-the-errors method. To do this, set the tablesaw blade to cut an angle slightly larger than 75° and the fence to cut about $\frac{3}{16}$ in. larger than final width. Then take a set of twelve staves, 10 in. long, and saw one bevel on each. On the first cut leave the blade low enough so the waste remains attached and doesn't get wedged between the blade and the insert (figure 2). Remove the waste by hand and cut the other bevel. Clean the sawdust off of the staves, set them on end on a true flat surface, and butt the edges tightly against one another. Usually a gap of about $\frac{3}{8}$ in. will appear (figure 3). Now reset the sawblade higher and for a slightly smaller angle, and the fence to a slightly narrower width. Pass the staves through the saw again and check as before. Repeat this operation, making minute adjustments in the blade and fence until the gap is closed. Then measure the diameter of the blank across the opposite faces. It should still be somewhat larger than required. With repeated checking and small adjustments to the width of cut, the diameter can be brought to the correct measurement. It usually takes me a couple of hours to get the saw set for this one cut. Once I am satisfied with the setting, I saw the run of staves.

The splines are $\frac{1}{4}$ in. by $\frac{5}{8}$ in. To make sure that the joints would close, I cut the grooves (figure 4) just slightly deeper than needed and wide enough for each spline to be pushed into its slot with my thumb. If the grooves are so narrow that the splines must be tapered or forced into place, final assembly will be very difficult because the glue will swell the splines slightly, making the fit even tighter.

Gluing—I begin by gluing up pairs of staves; then I glue two pairs together to make a third of the column. Finally, I glue the one-third sections together to make the whole shaft. In all the gluing operations I use a clamp every 12 in. when possible and keep the ends of the staves flush to make it easier to mount the shaft on the lathe. When clamping it is best to tighten or loosen each clamp a little at a time.

Gluing up pairs of staves is fairly simple. I made special fixtures with blocks to match the angles of the staves where they meet the clamp jaws. Two sets of clamp heads on each fixture speed handling throughout the production run (photo, top, next page). The one-third sections require clamping pressure from above, as well as from the edges. This is applied by using a frame in which a $\frac{1}{2}$-in. lag bolt is screwed into a hori-

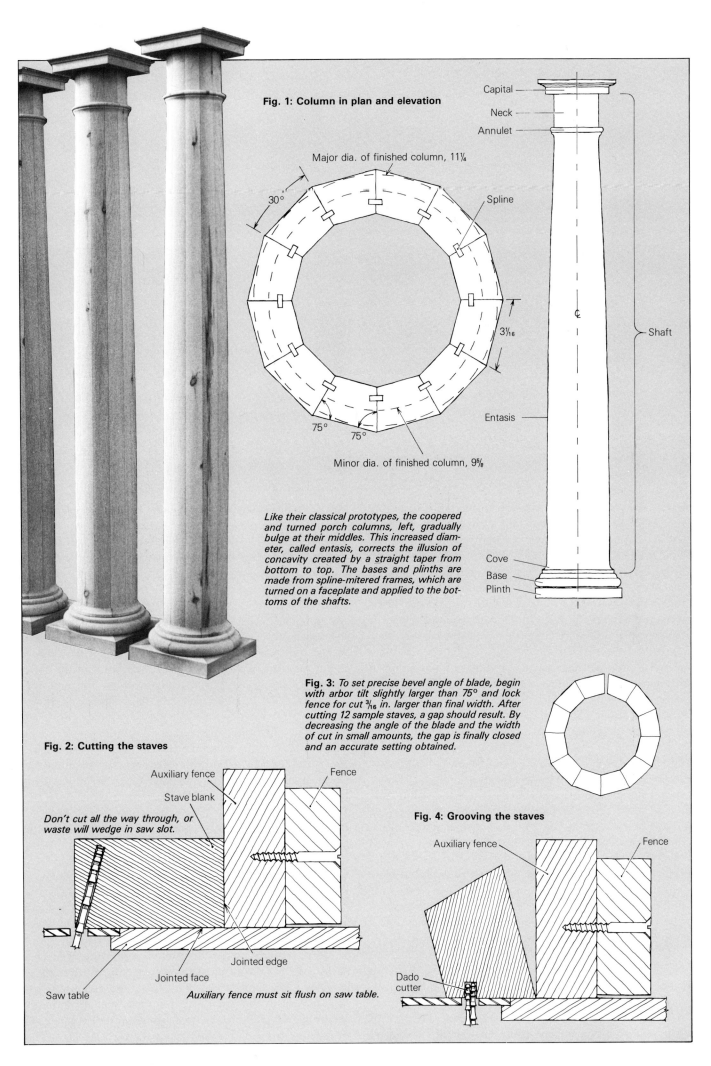

Fig. 1: Column in plan and elevation

Capital

Neck

Annulet

Major dia. of finished column, 11¼

30°

Spline

3¹⁄₁₆

Shaft

Entasis

75° 75°

Minor dia. of finished column, 9⅝

Like their classical prototypes, the coopered and turned porch columns, left, gradually bulge at their middles. This increased diameter, called entasis, corrects the illusion of concavity created by a straight taper from bottom to top. The bases and plinths are made from spline-mitered frames, which are turned on a faceplate and applied to the bottoms of the shafts.

Cove

Base

Plinth

Fig. 3: To set precise bevel angle of blade, begin with arbor tilt slightly larger than 75° and lock fence for cut ³⁄₁₆ in. larger than final width. After cutting 12 sample staves, a gap should result. By decreasing the angle of the blade and the width of cut in small amounts, the gap is finally closed and an accurate setting obtained.

Fig. 2: Cutting the staves

Auxiliary fence

Fence

Stave blank

Don't cut all the way through, or waste will wedge in saw slot.

Fig. 4: Grooving the staves

Auxiliary fence

Fence

Jointed edge

Jointed face

Saw table

Auxiliary fence must sit flush on saw table.

Dado cutter

Pairs of splined staves are glued up using notched blocks and clamping heads (available from Woodcraft Supply Corp., 313 Montvale Ave., Woburn, Mass. 01888). Using two sets of clamps per bar makes handling easier and gluing faster.

To glue up a one-third section of a column, pressure atop the center joint is applied by a hanger bolt with a knurled face, which is screwed into the top crossmember of a clamping frame. Dry-clamping is necessary to get the adjustments right so the joint will close properly when horizontal pressure is applied by the clamps.

zontal clamp bar, which is fastened to the lower clamp bar with ⅜-in. machine bolts and four ½-in. by 2-in. pieces of hardwood (photos, above left and right). The joints of the frame are left somewhat loose so that vertical pressure from the lag bolt can be applied directly over the glue joint. When pairs of glued-up staves are put into the lower clamp bar and the rest of the clamping frame assembled around the staves, the joint is left open at the inside. This gap closes as the screw is tightened and pressure builds up against the lag bolt, flexing the upper horizontal member. If the joint does not have enough pressure when the gap is closed, loosen the clamp and turn the lag bolt down to make the gap bigger. Once each lag bolt is set, it should be correct for the rest of the run. The lag bolt has a knurled pattern filed into it so that it will not slip off the joint. After the clamps are tightened, the width of the section should be checked. Also, check the angle of the two edges with a bevel. If the angle is wrong, more or less pressure can be applied with the clamps to correct it.

After the one-third sections come out of the clamps, the angles should be checked again. Any irregularity along the beveled surface should be corrected with a jointer plane equipped with an adjustable angle fence.

For assembling the thirds into the whole shaft, I first developed a rather clumsy system of forged rings and wedges. This worked well for the first single column, but by the time all of the rings and wedges were set in place and driven up tight I was nearing the end of the glue's closed assembly time. I replaced the forged rings and wedges with clamps made from length of ⅜-in. chain and tightened with 1-in. machine bolts. Each clamp head consists of five parts—a bored steel block through which the bolt passes and to which one end of the chain is welded; a steel nut with a hook machined onto its bottom side so it can grab a link of chain; two steel flanges that are welded to the sides of the bored steel

block; and the 1-in. by 6-in. bolt. Pressure is exerted by tightening the bolt with a wrench, drawing the ends of the chain together. The links will press into the wood quite a bit, but this causes no problem since the outer part of the column is wasted in turning.

On the first couple of shafts, I dry-clamped to make sure everything fit well. Then I spread glue on two joints and set two one-third sections together in semicircular holders. I put glue on the two remaining joints and set the top one-third section on. It took a little jiggling and coaxing with a mallet to get the splines lined up. I placed the heads of the chain clamps on alternate joints around the columns. The semicircular holders made it easy to rotate the columns while clamping.

Setting up the lathe—Few lathes will handle a 9-ft. spindle between centers. To give mine this needed capacity, I hacksawed the ways away from the headstock and mounted the two components the required distance apart on a long, wide bench. You may not want to saw your lathe in half, but if you want to turn long pieces, it's not as destructive an act as you might initially think. The headstock can be bolted firmly in place, the tailstock can still travel back and forth along the detached ways, and the distance between centers is limited only by the size of your shop. It's also quite convenient to have a highly portable headstock for faceplate turning.

I don't particularly like to have large, heavy objects moving at high speeds in my shop. I was concerned about the ability of my lightweight lathe to handle such large stock, so I decided to reduce the rotational speed of my lathe. I made a 22-in. idler pulley out of plywood with a bronze bearing in its center. I glued to the side of it a 4-in. disc, and V-grooved both for belts. The drive belt runs from the motor pulley around the 22-in. pulley; the 4-in. pulley in turn is connected by a belt to the 3-in. mandrel pulley (figure 6, p. 116). This

A jointing plane with metal fence, top left, is useful for correcting any irregularity in the joint interface. Leeke prefers the hand plane over his power jointer for this operation. For gluing and clamping the one-third sections into a full cylinder, Leeke devised and fabricated chain clamps like the one at left from ½-in. chain, steel plate, solid mild steel (for the tapped hook block) and a 1-in. bolt for tightening the chain. The clamp heads are staggered around the column, above, to help equalize the pressure and keep the column's diameter from being squashed into an ellipse.

slowed the lathe down to 100 RPM. I devised a sliding carriage that allowed me to use my router to do the cutting as the stock turned at a slow speed (figure 5, next page). The router (base removed) is equipped with a ½-in. cove-cutting bit and is mounted on a cradle-like block with a 4-in. dia. hose clamp. The cradle is screwed to the plywood carriage. The near end of the carriage is guided by a guide bearing that rides against the edge of a ¼-in. plywood or Masonite pattern board. A rabbeted wooden retainer or metal bracket helps keep the carriage from riding up off the pattern. The far end of the carriage slides underneath an elevated keeper board, which is screwed into the bench top.

Mounting the column—I mounted the columns on the lathe by screwing plates made of ¾-in. hardwood plywood to the ends of each one with 2-in. sheet-metal screws. The screws should pass through the end plate and into the inner one-third of the column wall. These plates have a ⅜-in. hole at the center and were turned and accurately sized to the finished diameter at each end of the column. The column is mounted on the lathe between 60° centers and driven by an angle-iron dog screwed to the plywood head plate, as shown in figure 5 (next page). The dog rides loosely in a slot on the faceplate, which I wrench tightly onto the mandrel as I sometimes use it as a brake during turning to keep the column from rotating too fast. Using this method of driving the shaft, the head plate does not have to be exactly perpendicular to the axis between the centers. In fact, it can be off quite a bit and the column will still turn true because it is held rigidly only between the two 60° centers. This works better than just screwing the faceplate directly to the end plate.

Making the pattern—Specific rules and formulas for developing the proportions and shapes of classical columns can be found in old pattern books, though you may simply reproduce existing columns as I have done. The shaft of the column has a curved outline (entasis), a cove and a fillet at the bottom and an annulet or neck molding near the top. To make the entasis, and to make all the columns in a run the same, a guide template (pattern) is used. To lay out the entasis, mark radius measurements of the finished shape at equal intervals along the pattern perpendicular to a line that is parallel to the axis of the lathe. Connect the ends of these, cut out and smooth the shape with spokeshave and file, and screw the pattern to the bench as shown in figure 5. For long runs, coat the pattern lightly with varnish to preserve the surface, and then wax it.

Turning—Prepare for turning by properly attaching and adjusting the eccentric guide bearing on the sliding carriage. To do this, draw a line on the pattern board that is perpendicular to the axis of the lathe. Now, for optimal cutting angle, slant the sliding carriage at about a 55° angle to the perpendicular, as shown, and bring the router bit into contact with the center of one of the column staves. Clamp the carriage to the pattern board, turn the guide bearing until it contacts the edge of the pattern and then tighten the screw. (Figure 5 shows where to position the guide.) Its eccentric shape will allow you to make fine adjustments in the depth of cut. Now unclamp the carriage, and you're ready to begin turning.

While turning use extreme caution. You have to keep track of two machines, and the exposed router bit is a real hazard. Ear protectors, goggles and a dust mask are essential. I also wear a leather glove to protect my left hand from the downward spray of chips.

Run the lathe for a while to make sure everything is operating correctly before turning on the router. Hold the router assembly firmly against the edge and top of the pattern board

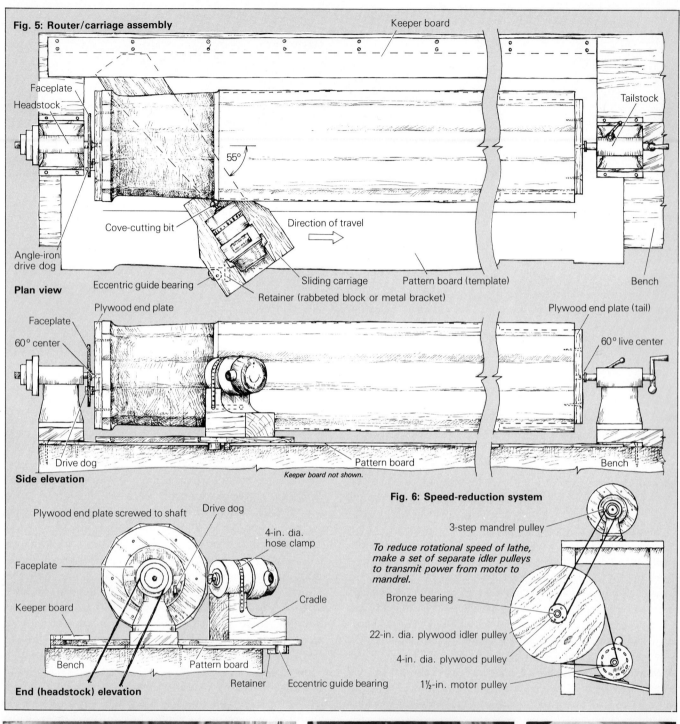

Fig. 5: Router/carriage assembly

Keeper board

Faceplate
Headstock

Tailstock

55°

Cove-cutting bit

Direction of travel

Angle-iron
drive dog

Eccentric guide bearing

Sliding carriage

Pattern board (template)

Bench

Retainer (rabbeted block or metal bracket)

Plan view

Plywood end plate

Plywood end plate (tail)

Faceplate

60° center

60° live center

Drive dog

Pattern board

Bench

Side elevation

Keeper board not shown.

Plywood end plate screwed to shaft

Drive dog

Fig. 6: Speed-reduction system

4-in. dia.
hose clamp

3-step mandrel pulley

*To reduce rotational speed of lathe,
make a set of separate idler pulleys
to transmit power from motor to
mandrel.*

Faceplate

Bronze bearing

Cradle

Keeper board

22-in. dia. plywood idler pulley

Bench

Pattern board

4-in. dia. plywood pulley

Retainer

Eccentric guide bearing

1½-in. motor pulley

End (headstock) elevation

Routing from headstock to tailstock, with the router carriage canted at 55°, causes the cove-cutting bit to push itself away from the cut instead of digging into it. At left and center, the staved shaft is being roughed into round in a single light pass. At right, the completed shaft is sanded using a belt sander turned upside down and slid along the column as it turns.

116

Fig. 7: Cutting the base

To produce a perfectly flat, perpendicular bottom, the router carriage is bolted to the bench at its far end, and the router is pivoted into the work (drawing, left), cutting through the base plate into the shaft. The carriage is clamped into position and the column is rotated by hand. The straight-face bit is set to cut one-third of the way through the column wall (photo, below), and the cut is finished with a handsaw, which is guided by the inside wall of the groove.

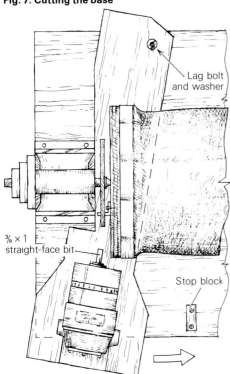

Lag bolt and washer

3/8 × 1 straight-face bit

Stop block

Fig. 8: Plinth and base
Leave square for making plinth. For making base, bandsaw a rough circle, mount on faceplate, turn round and turn molding.

Spline   Molding profiles

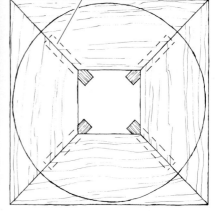

with the left hand. Then turn the router on and position the right hand as shown in the photo, facing page, far left. With the guide pressed against the edge of the pattern, start from the left end, and round off the entire shaft in one pass. The cut should be made by sliding the carriage slowly towards the tailstock. When the router bit is cutting on the right side of its center axis and the router assembly is moving towards the tailstock, the bit tends to push itself out of the cut, instead of digging in, and is easier to control. Avoid sliding the carriage from right to left, because this could damage the workpiece or cause injury.

Once the column is cylindrical, you're ready to turn it to its finished diameters. Adjust the eccentric guide bearing for a deeper cut, and begin to waste the bulk of the wood with short cuts, beginning about 10 in. from the tailstock and routing to the right. Then move to the left 10 in. from the beginning of the previous cut and rout again to the right. Continue along the entire column, roughing it to within 1/16 in. of its finished diameter. The final cut is made in one long, uninterrupted pass from left to right, having made a last adjustment in the eccentric guide bearing.

The column's neck and base moldings are not featured on the pattern. I marked out their positions and leave unwasted stock for them when making the rough and final cuts. Then I clamp a tool rest to the bench atop the pattern board and form the moldings with scraping tools sharpened to a rough-ground edge.

The router bit leaves a rough surface that must be sanded. I use a belt sander, sliding it upside down along the top of the pattern board, with the sanding belt working against the column as it turns. Making one pass with a 40-grit belt and another with an 80-grit belt will leave a surface that is good for painting.

In order for the column to stand up straight, the bottom must be cut so that it is exactly perpendicular to the axis of the shaft. Make this cut with a 3/8-in. by 1-in. straight-face bit

in the router. The depth of cut should be set to one-third the thickness of the column wall. Bolt the far end of the sliding carriage to the bench top, and clamp a stop block to the pattern board as shown in figure 7. Use the indexing pin of the headstock to lock the column in position. Holding the carriage down firmly on the pattern board, pivot the router toward the column, cutting through the plywood end plate and into the base of the shaft. When the carriage contacts the stop block, switch off the router, and clamp the carriage to the pattern board. Switch the router back on, release the indexing pin and slowly rotate the column by hand. This will produce a very accurate cut around the base of the shaft. Turn the column away from you while cutting, or the faceplate may unscrew. Take the column off the lathe and remove the plywood end plate. Using the inside wall of the groove for a guide, cut off the waste on the end with a handsaw.

Bases—I make the separate round bases and square plinths with splined-miter joints (figure 8). I make the bases by first roughing them into shape on the bandsaw and then truing them up on a faceplate, after which I turn the various molding profiles with scraping tools. On one run of columns, I needed extra-wide stock on the bottom for a cove molding. I trued the bottom of the columns before turning them and fastened on a 1½-in. thick base with screws and sealed it with butyl caulk, which allows the column to expand and contract.

To increase efficiency in the future and to expand the range of my work, I plan to develop an automatic travel for the sliding router carriage and a system for gluing up all the staves at once, instead of having to glue up each blank piece-meal. I am also working on a method for making tapered and bent-stave columns and on plans for a large router fixture that will let me produce fluted columns.   □

John Leeke, 31, assisted by his 10-year-old son Jon, works in Sanford, Maine.

Robert Yorgey's Hand-Carved Turnings
Making do with what you have

by Richard Starr

When Robert Yorgey shows his drop-leaf tables at a craft fair, people stop to admire the neatly turned legs and stretchers. But Yorgey didn't use a lathe to form the pretty vase and ring shapes; he carved them by hand. At 85, he's been at it for thirteen years.

"My granddad was a woodworker," says Yorgey. "Maybe I inherited something from him. He used to make the wooden screws and gears for the old forges, the old steel-rolling mills. That was back in the 1850s and 60s. He died around 1906—I was about 10 years old.

"My first encounter with woodworking was when I was 12 or 13. I attempted to make a boomerang, having read about them in some book. It was supposed to return to the thrower. Result was, when I threw it, it kept going. If I were superstitious, I'd believe it was coming back in my carvings now."

Yorgey lives near Reading, Pa., on the farm he has worked for most of his life. "When I sold the farm to my son in 1968, I called it 'I retired,' but I really didn't. I kept on working. I don't believe in that retirement business." Though still busy, he found time to take up woodworking.

One of his early projects was a magazine rack illustrated in William Klenke's book, *Things to Make and How to Make Them*. The rack had four short, delicately turned legs. "I had Klenke's book, but the only hitch was, I didn't have a lathe. Klenke didn't tell me one thing: how to do it with hand tools." Yorgey describes himself as being of "tough Pennsylvania Dutch stock." True to this, he carved the turned shapes with a chisel, a gouge, a coping saw, a Surform and a good deal of careful measurement. The results were convincing and pleasing. He was encouraged to try a more complex piece from Klenke's book: a gate-leg table.

"Listen, my first table I made all by hand. There was a walnut log up in the woods, 7 ft. long by 7 in. It was lying over and was pretty dry and I got it in the old summer kitchen, and I sawed it with a handsaw. Full length. It took me about two days to saw one trip through. I sawed it out in about 2-in. planks." He ripped the planks into 2x2s for the eight legs and six stretchers. Each piece was "turned" by hand using carving tools, with the work held in a vise.

Yorgey has made 22 gate-leg and trestle-style drop-leaf tables in a variety of local woods—cherry, walnut, butternut and dogwood—all with hand-turned parts. Each tabletop has its own corner shape. "I try to put different corners and colors in each table so I can say it's pretty near one of a kind." He

Graceful symmetry of Yorgey's table legs in dogwood belies its lathe-less origins.

carves the rule joint between the main top and the drop-leaf by hand and judges the quality of the table partly by how well this joint fits. "See, this one I didn't get quite as good as those; I don't get them all perfect. These latest ones I got pretty good because I had a little more experience."

With experience came the need to diversify. "I don't know what branched me off to the vises. I guess I wanted a challenge. The gate-leg tables weren't enough of a challenge for me." Yorgey cuts the wooden screws and nuts for his vises by hand. He uses a short piece of metal tape-measure as a flexible layout ruler, and carves the threads with a V-gouge. To make the nuts, he drills a hole in a block of wood, then saws the block in half through the hole. After gouging out the threads, he glues the block back together. Though Yorgey developed his own threading technique, it closely resembles the procedure described by Hero of Alexandria almost two thousand years ago. When simple vises were no longer challenging enough, Yorgey designed and built a vise whose moving jaw floats on a pair of opposite-threaded screws that are coupled together by wooden gears. Improved variations are now in the works.

Yorgey was invited to demonstrate his unique style of non-lathe turning at the March and June '79 turning symposia in Newtown, Pa. *(FWW #19, Nov. '79).* Surrounded by 20 growling lathes, he quietly chipped out screws and table parts, attracting a good deal of amused, though respectful, attention. "They were ribbing me about taking too much time and patience doing this. So I had to get back at them. I told them, 'I'm the original. You fellows are all copiers!'" Yorgey's message has a certain authenticity to it: perhaps the lathe was originally developed to mimic hand-carved objects. When he was reminded that the lathe is a very ancient tool, Yorgey replied, "Before the lathe were my tools."

Robert Yorgey came to his craft late in life; perhaps that explains the joy with which he works. But why the unusual methods? "You just want to try to see what you can do with what you have," he says. "Here's another reason; maybe you'll agree with me and maybe you won't. I went through the Depression and I guess that knocked a little patience in me, and a little endurance too." □

Richard Starr is Fine Woodworking's *New England correspondent. He lives in Thetford Center, Vt.*

With the work held in twin-screw vise, Yorgey shapes a leg with a Surform.

Yorgey at home with four of his gate-leg tables.

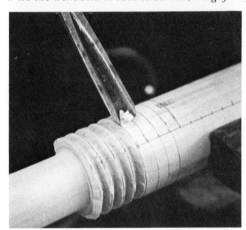

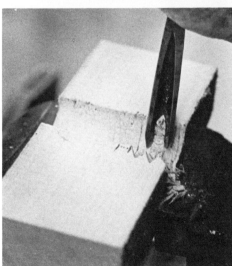

Yorgey lays out his screw threads with a flexible ruler and carves them with a V-gouge (above, left). The result is a spiral with a pitch of four to the inch. Nuts are similarly roughed out with gouge and mallet, left, but the stock must be drilled and halved first and the threads must meet when the halves are re-assembled. The finished twin-screw vise, above, is a monument to skill, patience and leisure time. Crank mounted on top screw is geared to opposite-threaded lower screw. Rear jaw has two threaded holes and moves on the screws as the crank is turned. Because simple wooden gears would be too coarse to work smoothly and finer gears would be too fragile, Yorgey mounted two gears on each screw, one-half tooth out of phase. The effect is as smooth as single gears with twice as many teeth, but is far stronger.

PROJECTS

On Designing Chairs
How to develop ideas into working drawings

by Alan Marks

Chairs obsessed my teacher, the Swedish designer Carl Malmsten. Starting with his prize-winning piece in 1916, he designed dozens of successful chairs, mainly for production. By nature a perfectionist, he continually revised his manufactured models, periodically updating his drawings, until his death in 1972. "It's not bad," he'd say, "but it could perhaps be made even better." His critiques of his students' work were sharp, and his criteria for good chair design were pointed: (a) Is it strong and practical? (b) Does it look good? (c) Is it comfortable, not only at first but also during a long sit? (d) Is it economically feasible to make?

This article is Part I of a series. Designing seating for comfort is the subject of Part II. Part III covers aesthetic concerns—making the chair look right. But the first thing to talk about, here in Part I, is how best to use paper and pencil to draw chairs, exploring the basics of chair design.

Before considering anything carefully, I play around with chair ideas in side elevation. These are rarely more than guidelines, and I try to make them as outlandish and unpremeditated as possible. After a dozen or so of these, I choose one to develop further. Probably the final design will bear no resemblance to it, but it serves as a starting point.

From the chosen idea I work up a drawing in 1/10 scale, in millimeters. I find metric dimensions easier to convert to full scale. Two millimeters on the small sketch become twenty on the large drawing. On the paper I mark off seat height and depth, back angle, overall estimated height and armrest height, if there are any armrests. I do the side elevation first. It is the most critical and will largely determine the appearance of the front and back. Into the limits marked out, I try to fit the most promising side view. This usually takes quite a bit of adjustment. Unless you are uncommonly sure of yourself, you

need to erase a lot. I use a light-grey, plastic eraser, as it doesn't smudge or abrade the paper the way pink or art-gum erasers do.

Translucent drafting paper is best for sketching. If you plan to have commercially processed copies made, you must use translucent paper. But it has another advantage: You can change the design without erasing the previous version. Simply tape a new piece of paper over the earlier version and trace it, changing as much of the design as you like. When you fold back the top sheet, you can make useful before-and-after comparisons. But even if the second version is better, don't discard the first. Build up as many thicknesses of changed sketches as needed, saving them all. Often an element you drop at one stage will be just what you want later on.

It isn't easy to reproduce complex curves in symmetrical pairs using standard flexible rules. A quick and accurate method is to use your translucent paper as if it were carbon paper. Lay a suitably sized piece over the curve and trace it using a 2B lead. Now turn the paper over and you have a mirror image. Position it on the drawing and trace heavily over it with your pencil. A light deposit of graphite will indicate the curve, and it can be drawn in darkly by hand.

Sometimes a preliminary drawing, of curved splats for example, turns out less than symmetrical for being drawn freehand. The halves are subtly different, like the halves of your face. Which looks better? To tell, hold a mirror along the centerline, mirroring first one half and then the other. The better version will usually be apparent. On paper, simply erase the less desirable half and use the copying method described above to transfer the better half.

Having done a preliminary sketch to your satisfaction, tape a large piece of paper to a drafting board and enlarge it to full

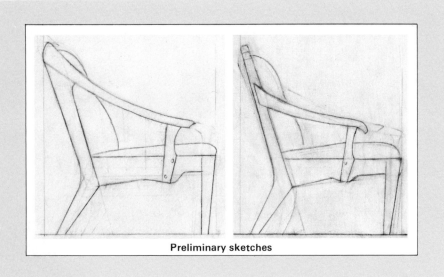

Preliminary sketches

Sketches of easy chair "Little Egypt"

450

scale. I use discarded roll ends of newsprint, had for the asking at the local newspaper press room. Since it doesn't cost anything (drafting paper is quite expensive) and because you're not doing a final drawing, you won't feel bad about consuming it. To enlarge, draw a vertical reference line alongside the side view and measure up from the floor line and over from the vertical to established points. This method is simpler and quicker than the standard grid method of enlargement. Probably, what looked great at ¹⁄₁₀ scale will need substantial revision in the blowup, so change whatever looks wrong, except the contour of the back, which is pretty much determined by human anatomy (which will be discussed in a later article). When the side view is satisfactory at full scale, reduce it back to ¹⁄₁₀ scale on drafting paper. Next to this drawing transfer with the T-square dimensions needed for a front view. Work on this until it seems right, then enlarge it to full scale on newsprint and refine it. When you are done, simply tape a piece of translucent paper over the newsprint and make a final working drawing.

For many one-off pieces of furniture—tables, cabinets and stands—you have the choice of making a full-scale working drawing or taking the particular planks of wood you will use and letting their size and figure shape the design. Of course, if the design is complex, a working drawing will eventually be necessary. Chairs are complex, and they must fit the human body, so working drawings are essential. Comfort can't be left to chance; it must be carefully engineered. An advantage of full-scale drawings is that during construction you can take measurements directly from them, with ruler or tape measure.

Still, a drawing has limitations. It is impossible to see from a flat drawing how a solid element will appear in fact. Thicknesses, curves and overhangs have an unpleasant habit of doing unpredictable things when seen in three dimensions. The width of a set-back table apron or of a chair's front rail may look fine on the drawing, but in the solid it disappears under the overhanging top or seat. It's difficult to guess from a drawing how much will remain visible. So no matter how final the drawing, it should still be seen merely as a guideline. I always have a black-line copy made of my "final" drawing, and then I pencil in the alterations as construction proceeds. When I have completed the piece, my copy reflects all revisions. I transfer these changes to my original drawing, discard

the copy, and have a new one made to keep on file for prospective clients and to enable me to duplicate the piece.

You can approximate the effects of perspective and of viewing at an angle if you stand the working drawing, mounted on the drafting board, vertically against a wall. It helps if you draw the piece close to the bottom of the paper and mount it close to the board's bottom edge. You can look at the views from above or at an oblique angle or at a combination of both. This strategy assumes you have a board to draw on, not a fixed table. Use a piece of shop-grade birch plywood, 38 in. by 50 in. minimum. The 38-in. width will accommodate 36-in. drafting paper (which also comes in 42-in. and 48-in. widths). A 38-in. by 50-in. board is big enough for most chairs, though lounge chairs require a 48-in. by 60-in. board and wider paper. I lay my board on two work stands similar to the sawhorses shown in *FWW* #24, Sept. '80, p. 78.

Working drawings of chairs generally require three views, side, front and top, and they should be condensed and superimposed as much as is practical. Because the front view and the top view are symmetrical, I draw a vertical centerline to the left of the side view and show half of a front. Another centerline, drawn horizontally through the side view, either slightly above the seat or below it, locates the top view. It also is symmetrical, so only half of it need be drawn. The position of the halves depends on what's least confusing. Some designers superimpose all three views, but the advantages are dubious. Erasures become a complex nightmare, and it is sometimes difficult to indicate clearly all the necessary information, because so many lines crisscross. I transfer dimensions from view to view with a T-square and triangle. Partially superimposing and drawing halves cuts down on drawing time without sacrificing clarity, and it results in smaller drawings that are much less clumsy to handle in the shop. To depict the back of a chair, one side of the vertical centerline shows a front half and the other a back half.

While thinking about appearance, you must keep construction in mind. Plan to make things easy for yourself. On curved pieces, leave at least one surface flat as a reference for layout and machining. To determine the minimum dimensions of a blank, draw rectangles around the curved piece, in side and top views. I leave flats on curves at points, for example, where rails or arms attach to legs. Butting one flat sur-

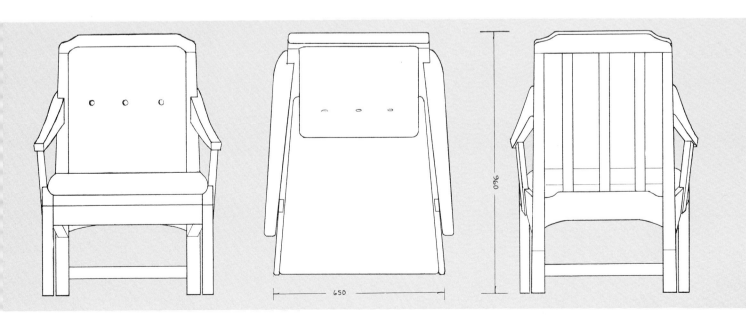

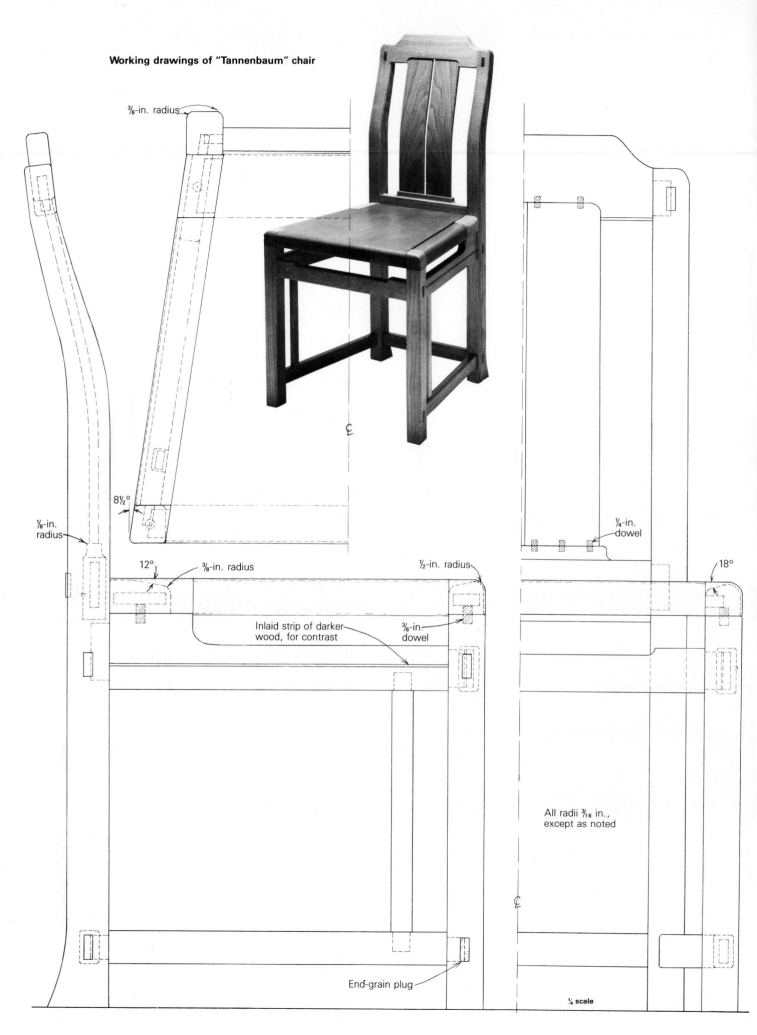

Working drawings of "Tannenbaum" chair

⅜-in. radius

8½°

⅛-in.
radius

12°   ⅜-in. radius

½-in. radius

Inlaid strip of darker
wood, for contrast

⅜-in.
dowel

¼-in.
dowel

18°

All radii ³⁄₁₆ in.,
except as noted

End-grain plug

¼ scale

face against another is easier than mating to a curved surface.

When designing arms for easy chairs or sofas, where a large curve can be pleasing, or when drawing curved legs, it is important to design with regard to available stock. If you chainsaw-mill your own lumber you can write your own ticket. But commercial wood in 12/4 planks is scarce. Bent laminations or steambent parts are more practical when their shape integrates two or more functions, such as combined front-leg/back-leg/armrests. An alternative to laminating, bending or stacking, is splicing. Often a spliced joint can be a decorative feature. Sometimes you can find grain curved to match the shape you need, but most often pieces must be sawn from straight-grained planks. Because chairs take a real beating, areas of grain running across a curve should be avoided. Thus, curves can't be too radical in solid stock.

Curves are most efficiently cut using a shaper jig. Jigging ensures exact repetition of dimensions and guarantees squareness. You can rely on the consistency of pieces through subsequent machining operations. I prefer not to settle on the final appearance of curved chair arms until after I've made a prototype of the whole chair. I hand-shape the arm at that point and transfer its shape to my drawing. Then I make jigs.

Some complicated shapes can be done only by hand, but drawing them facilitates repetitions. At appropriate intervals on the drawing, revolved sections, usually crosshatched, show the shape. Templates made from these revolved cross sections can be saved for the next run.

In the drawing stage, the strength of joints has to be kept in mind as well. Depending upon the relative stength of the wood used, dimensions will vary. Oak is stiff and strong, and furniture of oak could be made very slender. Pine, on the other hand, must be used lavishly.

Major weaknesses in chairs show up when the back is leaned upon heavily. People love to tilt back on a sidechair's rear legs after a good meal. This relaxes them at the chair's expense. Auxiliary rails between front and back legs alleviate the strain. Though it is conceivable to build a sidechair with seat rails wide enough to withstand the after-dinner tilt, I always suspect seat rails alone of being inadequate. Arms on chairs will provide the necessary bracing, but the method of attaching them to the rear legs should be carefully considered. Attaching directly to the front of the rear legs makes it likely that the joint will pull out. For maximum strength, an arm should attach from the side as well (see *FWW #12*, Sept. '78, p. 42). When the front leg does not serve as a riser to anchor the arm in front, a separate riser can be attached to the seat rail and an auxiliary side rail added below the seat.

Make sure your design will go together properly by imagining an assembly sequence as you draw. For a conventional chair, front legs with connecting rails usually get glued up as a unit, and back legs with splats and rails form another unit. The next glue-up occurs when front and back assemblies get joined by the side rails. Arms often get glued on as a final step. In rare cases, however, it may be necessary to assemble the back only partially, depending upon the splat and top-rail construction. The most complicated chair to design and assemble is an armchair whose rear legs splay outwards, at an angle to the seat rails. Knowing in what order a chair is to be assembled ensures that it can indeed be done. □

Alan Marks is a frequent contributor to this magazine. Photo and drawings by Alan Marks ©1977, 1980.

To produce curved parts, splicing is an alternative to laminating, bending or stacking. This splice between arm and back is from Hans Wegner's Classic chair (see FWW #21, March '80, pp. 36-42).

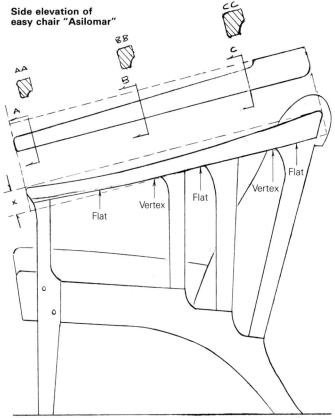

Side elevation of easy chair "Asilomar"

Note that only the top surface of the arm is curved. The bottom surface consists of three flats, facilitating the butt-joining of the verticals, while maintaining the appearance of a smooth curve. Revolved sections of the arm indicate otherwise difficult-to-illustrate transitions. Dashed lines around curved members determine blank size.

Strengthening chair structures

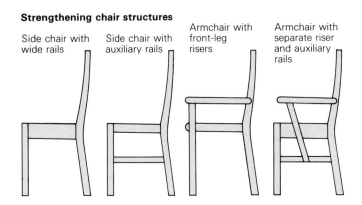

Side chair with wide rails / Side chair with auxiliary rails / Armchair with front-leg risers / Armchair with separate riser and auxiliary rails

Two-Board Chairs

Plans and methods from a Swiss woodworker

by Drew Langsner

The craftsmen of southern Germany, Austria and Switzerland have long been known for their fine sense of design and their excellent craftsmanship. From woodcarving to the magnificent log-and-timber-frame farmhouses, examples of their skill can be found throughout the Alps. This is also the region of the famous fairy-tale chair with the cut-out scrollwork back, painted or chipcarved with hearts, flowers, initials and dates. The chair is called a *Bretstuhl* (board chair) in Germany, or a *Stabelle* in the Swiss-German dialect, Berne Deutch. In English it is sometimes known as a two-board chair or fiddle-back. It ranks with the Windsor and the ladderback post-and-rung chair as a great example of folk furniture.

The construction is almost identical in chairs made throughout the region; individuality is emphasized in the contour and carving of the chair back. Most prominently defining a two-board chair is the beautifully simple manner in which the back and seat are joined—by two through mortise-and-tenon joints secured with tusk tenons under the seat. The backboard tenons pass through mortises not only in the seat board, but in battens in the seat bottom. These battens, which receive the leg tenons, are sliding dovetails, held in place by the backboard tenons. The battens are thicker than the seat board, but set back from the front of the seat to maintain

the overall appearance of lightness and simplicity. Their thickness allows the straight-tapered octagonal legs to be mounted free of stretchers.

These chairs can be knocked down for storage or shipping. The backboard comes loose by removing the two tusk tenons. The sliding-dovetail battens and legs can then be driven out of the tapered housings in the seat bottom, and the disassembled package measures 18 in. by 20 in. by 8 in.

My introduction to the two-board chair was in Switzerland, where I've twice had the pleasure of working with Rudolf Kohler, a cooper who also makes a fair number of these chairs each year. In the fall of 1980, Kohler and I took a break from coopering to build a chair together. Kohler gets the credit for the more difficult work, as he wanted to be certain that the *Stabelle* going to America would be a good one. The chair dimensions given in this article are in inches, and vary slightly from Kohler's metric measurements. Exact equivalents would be awkward, and they are not necessary. As chairmaker John Alexander says, "Chairmaking is an approximate craft." There can be considerable variation from one chair to another, even in a matching set.

Kohler's two-board chair is made from ten pieces of wood: The seat, the back, four legs, two sliding-dovetail battens and two tenon tusks. In the

Alps, two-board chairs are usually made from hard maple. Ash is sometimes used for the legs and sliding dovetails.

Kohler buys his chairwood in the form of plainsawn slabs from a local mill. He never buys edged boards, as every bit of wood is used. The slabs are stickered to air-dry in a drafty loft for at least two years. The wood we used had seasoned for eight years. Several weeks before starting a chair, Kohler moves his wood to the overhead racks in his shop. No moisture-content measurements are taken, but the shop is usually very dry. Most of Kohler's chair work is done during the long winter, when his shop woodstove burns every day. The warm shop acts as a kiln. Cold, dry air infil-

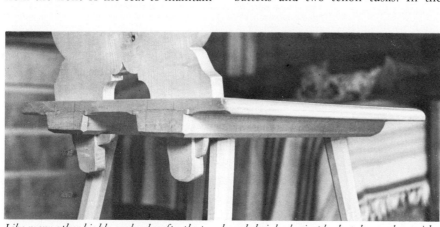

Like many other highly evolved crafts, the two-board chair looks simple, but demands considerable woodworking skill and attention to detail during construction. Its tusk-tenoned back and sliding-dovetail battens to receive the legs, above, make it a sturdy, yet light, knock-down design.

trates from outside. As the air warms inside the shop, it picks up moisture from the wood and then leaks out, letting in more cold, dry air. The relative humidity in the shop remains low.

Although the *Bretstuhl* design has been around for generations, the introduction of power tools has affected the actual construction methods. The most prominent machine in Kohler's tiny shop is a massive combination planer/jointer/shaper. Kohler also uses a bandsaw, a sabersaw and a router where a turning saw (a bowsaw with a narrow blade whose orientation can be varied) and planes were traditionally used. Leg tenons are turned on the lathe.

As is usual, the first step is milling the rough lumber. The planer is large enough to handle the 16¼-in. wide seat blanks and the backboards, both dressed to ⅞ in. The sliding-dovetail battens are planed to 1⅜ in. Kohler used to make these battens only ⅞ in. thick. In those older chairs the leg tenons were mortised through both the sliding-dovetail battens and the seat board. The tenon ends were then wedged from above. Kohler says that the thicker battens, which house stopped mortises, allow the seat board to move freely with moisture variation. Also, the end grain of the tenons is encased, making them less responsive to changes in humidity. After dressing both faces of the sliding-dovetail stock, Kohler joints one side. Using a bandsaw he rips the second side so that the width tapers from 3⅜ in. to 2⅞ in., then joints this resawn side to a finished width tapering from 3¼ in. to 2¾ in.

Dressing the leg blanks begins with planing all four sides to a 1⅜-in. square. To make the taper Kohler runs the legs through his planer on a wooden tray with a tapered bottom board that inversely matches the taper of the leg. The final dimensions taper from 1¼ in. to 1 in. square. Kohler turns the leg tenons 1⁹⁄₁₆ in. long with a diameter of ¹⁵⁄₁₆ in. He chamfers the end and the tenon shoulder at 45° for ³⁄₁₆ in. To size the diameter Kohler uses a test hole bored in a ¾-in. hardwood board. He likes a very snug (but not extremely tight) fit so the tenon squeaks when it is twisted in the hole. The legs are finished by hand-planing to an octagonal section, with proportions judged by eye.

Outlines for the bottom and backboards are transferred from cardboard patterns. Kohler has used the same patterns for over 30 years, with just one variation—the addition of three small curls to the C cutouts on the sides of the backboard. The outlines are traced with a pencil and sawn on the bandsaw. Small details of the back are shaped with an electric sabersaw. The scrollwork is dressed with flat and half-round rasps, then sanded smooth. The front edge of the upper section of the seat back is rounded, nowadays with a router, formerly by spokeshaving and sanding. The remaining scrollwork is dressed square to the faces. Edges are then softened about ¹⁄₃₂ in. with a piece of sandpaper. The tapered mortises through the seat-back tenons are made after the sliding-dovetail battens are fitted to the seat bottom.

The tapered housings for the sliding-dovetail battens are laid out parallel to the sides of the seat bottom after the

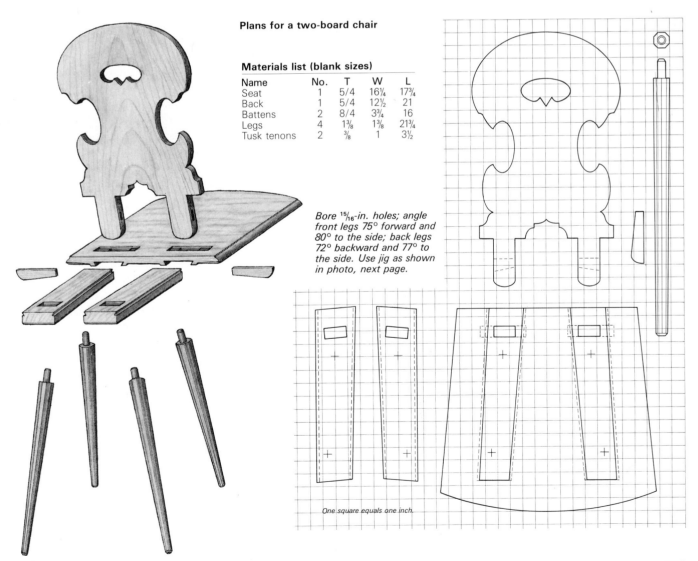

Plans for a two-board chair

Materials list (blank sizes)

Name	No.	T	W	L
Seat	1	5/4	16¼	17¾
Back	1	5/4	12½	21
Battens	2	8/4	3¾	16
Legs	4	1⅜	1⅜	21¾
Tusk tenons	2	⅜	1	3½

Bore ¹⁵⁄₁₆-in. holes; angle front legs 75° forward and 80° to the side; back legs 72° backward and 77° to the side. Use jig as shown in photo, next page.

One square equals one inch.

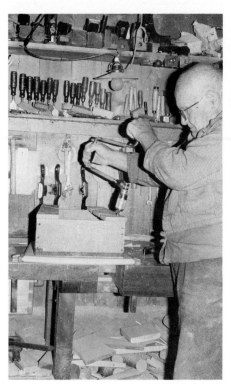
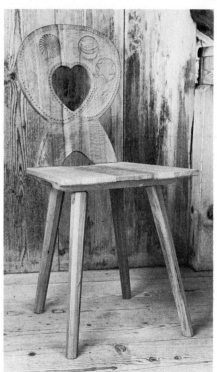

Kohler uses a wooden box with slots in boards across the top to jig his brace and bit to the proper angle for boring the leg mortises.

Design variations on the two-board chair include a slatted back, right, and battens running the width instead of the length of the seat, left. Note that the decorative cutout in the back serves also as a handhold. Photos: Armin Erb.

sides and back of the blank have been jointed, and the curved front dressed with a spokeshave. The outside edges of the housings should be 2½ in. from the sides. To excavate the housings, Kohler starts by chiseling out the last 2 in. before the front stop. He then uses a backsaw to cut the side kerfs at an 80° angle, 5/16 in. into the board, and cleans out the cavity using an electric router and a dovetail bit. The whole cavity could be excavated with the router and a fence, but instead Kohler uses his router freehand, and the saw kerfs are useful boundaries

The tapered sliding-dovetail battens are individually fitted to the finished housings. Kohler cuts the side angles using a router with a dovetail bit. A dovetail hand plane can also be used. The front of the dovetail tongue is cut back so that the end of the batten overlaps the chiseled stop in the housing. A simpler batten with beveled sides instead of a dovetail tongue is sometimes used on plainer chairs. This version doesn't require using a router or dovetail plane; the stock can be cut on a tilting-arbor saw or planed to shape.

Mortises through the seat board and battens are chiseled at an angle of 80°. They are cut a little wider than the tenons, to allow for expansion and contraction of the backboard, which runs cross grain to the seat board. In addition to

the through mortises, Kohler chisels a 1/8-in. deep housing for the shoulders of the backboard tenons. This conceals any gap between mortise and tenon. The backboard tenons are fitted, and the baselines for the tusk-tenon mortises are marked flush with the bottom face of the battens. The back is removed, and the tapered mortises are chiseled in the backboard tenons 1/16 in. inside the line scribed when the back was in place. Kohler makes these mortises ¼ in. wide, tapering from 7/8 in. to 5/8 in. The tenon tusks are 3½ in. long.

While the chair is apart (the sliding-dovetail battens are also removed), Kohler dresses the upper and lower edges of the seat board. He routs the upper edge with a beading bit. The lower edges of the front and sides are deeply chamfered with a plane, which adds to the visual lightness of the piece. The chamfers on the back of the seat are carefully shaped with a drawknife. All four lower edges of the sliding-dovetail battens are relieved by routing with the quarter-round bit.

Kohler bores the mortises for the leg tenons with the dovetail battens back in place. The front legs cant forward at 75° and to the sides 80°. The rear legs angle back 72° and to the sides 77°. For accuracy, Kohler uses a homemade boring jig (photo, above). The jig is a wooden box about 16 in. by 16 in. by 6 in. The

bottom of the box has a large trapezoidal opening that fits snugly over the mounted battens, and the top of the box has a central opening and four angled slots 5/8 in. in width. Kohler punches predetermined centers on the battens, the jig is fitted into place and correct angles are bored by holding the auger at the end of the slots. Kohler doesn't use a depth control, but he aims to stop just at the base of the battens.

Just before the final assembly, the separate chair parts are given a careful sanding. Fitting the legs is simply a matter of dabbing a little white glue on the tenons, then pounding the legs in place. After assembly, the legs are trimmed. On Kohler's standard chair the upper front edge of the seat is 18⅝ in. high. The seat angles downward slightly so that the upper rear edge is 18⅜ in. from the floor.

The next stage is decorating the back. Kohler is an excellent chipcarver, but that's a skill for someone else to write about. The *Stabelle* for America was finished, and we picked up where we'd left off with our coopering. □

Drew Langsner is director/instructor at Country Workshops, Rt. 3, Box 221, Marshall, N.C. 28753. Regular summer workshops include white oak basketry, country woodcraft, and post-and-rung chairmaking.

Tough finish for tables

I'm making a dining-room table, and would like to learn of a finish that would be tough and touchable. What would you recommend?

—John Millerd, Pembereton Meadows, B.C.

There are as many finishes for tabletops as there are finishers. But the one I have found to be both durable and attractive combines a prime coat of Watco Danish oil with following coats of Deft lacquer. Here's the method: Brush on a sloshing coat of Watco over the prepared surface, let it soak in and then wipe it thoroughly with a clean, absorbent lint-free cloth. Let it sit for at least 24 hours, and then rub it down with 4/0 steel wool, taking care to rub in the direction of the grain. Allow it to sit for another two to three days, depending on the humidity, until the Watco has gotten fairly hard and won't interfere with the adhesion of the Deft to come.

Now spray or brush on a thick, wet coat of Deft lacquer, as much as the surface will take without developing runs. When this coat is completely dry, sand it in the direction of the grain with 220-grit paper, using a padded block. Spray on another full coat, and when it is dry, sand with 400-grit paper. Repeat this step. The fourth coat is also a full-strength application, but it should be steel-wooled, not sanded.

—Morris Sheppard

Checks in burl veneers

During the past 20 years I have built a number of pieces of furniture using various crotches, burls and butts as face veneers. In almost every case, cracks and checks have developed in these veneers. What can be done to remedy this, or to avoid it in the future.

—Hal Halstead, Woodland, Calif.

Burls, crotches and butt veneers are usually wavy, ripply and brittle, and the grain runs in all directions with soft and hard areas. When these veneers are glued to a ground, any moisture that may have been present in them will dry out after a period of time, causing the veneers to shrink and check along the odd-formed figures.

These veneers are usually flattened by being sprinkled with water, then pressed in a veneer press or between two boards with heavy weights on top. Be sure to place several layers of newspapers over and under the veneers. If after a day the papers are still damp, replace them with dry ones. A couple of days in the press should do it. Many craftsmen put a backing on the veneer when it's dry before it can become wavy again. You can glue the burl or crotch veneer directly to a straight-grained, stable veneer such as mahogany. Apply the glue to the veneer only, then put it in the press immediately so the moisture from the glue does not penetrate and expand the burl or crotch veneer. Never use water-base contact cement for gluing veneers. Also, veneered objects should not be placed in areas with very dry heat. *—Peter L. Rose*

Finish for spoons

I am intrigued by Dan Dustin's finishing process for green wooden spoons (FWW #22, May '80, p.82). I wonder what proportion of beeswax and olive oil he uses to make the creamy mixture. How does he combine the ingredients? How long does the whole finishing process take?

—William C. Pellouchoud, Boulder, Colo.

When carving spoons from green wood, you can tell when the piece is about to check. Work in the shade, and take chances with only the poorest pieces. In time you get a feel for what's best. Carve the least stable woods outdoors on rainy days. Just before you think a piece is going to check, bury it in a pile of wet leaves or shavings or snow or under a wet towel.

When the going really gets rough (lilac cut six months ago will check in about five minutes once you start working it), I keep the whole batch in a tub of water, carving a minute or two in each piece and tossing it back into the water until I wind up with a tub full of spoons.

Then I oil the rough-carved pieces as often as they show the need until they won't take anymore. When they've shown a gloss for a week or two they are probably ready to fire.

For the third step, I fire in a mixture of beeswax and olive oil. I have never weighed or measured anything. I just melt the wax and add the oil until the cooled mixture can be softened by friction between the bare hands and the wood. The harder the mixture the better it is, as long as you are able to work it cold.

The spoons are immersed in this mixture at the minimum temperature required to vaporize the remaining moisture in the wood. You will see the surface of the liquid foam and roil. This process tires the mixture and, therefore, more wax must be added with every firing to keep it sufficiently hard. When it appears that all the moisture has been boiled out of the wood, I allow the oven to cool and remove the spoons from the wax/oil mixture just about as soon as I can with my bare hand.

Next, I lay the fired spoons outdoors for a week or two allowing the sun to draw out some of the oil (leaving, it seems, more wax behind). The longer you wait, the easier the spoons are to finish. As a last step, I finish by scraping and sanding, scrubbing well with soap and water and hanging each to dry before each sanding. Finally, I rub in some of the wax/oil mixture and polish with a cloth. *—Dan Dustin*

Front fence for radial-arm saw

The front fence for the radial arm saw, as described by Allen L. Cobb (FWW #26, Jan. '81, p. 8) appears to be a very good idea. In addition to saving fingers, it would put the work at the front of the saw (when ripping), where it can be seen and easily controlled by the operator. Could Mr. Cobb provide a sketch or a photo of this device to make it a little clearer?

—Victor H. Cahalane, Clarksville, N.Y.

Here is a rough sketch of the saw fence. My saw is set into the right edge of a 9-ft. storage counter. I installed the fence 25 years ago, and have found it very useful. *—Allen L. Cobb*

Rip fence for radial-arm saw

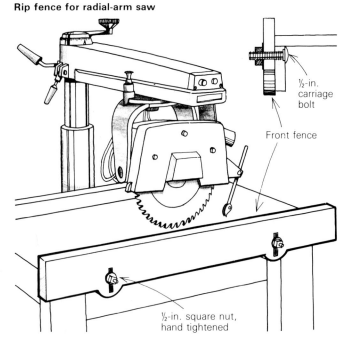

½-in. carriage bolt

Front fence

½-in. square nut, hand tightened

A Single Bed
Basic design develops joinery skills

by Kenneth Rower

This bed, built for my son, was made to fit a mattress 7 in. by 39 in. by 75 in. It can be viewed as a particular design or as a general method of making a bed out of heavy stock and one wide board. There is much room for variation without changing the construction. While the piece shown is for those who like rectangles, certainly the tops of the posts and the headboard could be shaped to taste, and the legs could be tapered or turned from square stock. A theoretical adaptation for stacking twin beds is shown in the drawing on the facing page.

Rails and posts are the same thickness, but the rails are set back about ½ in., thus emphasizing the separateness of the posts, and yielding integral ledger strips on the insides of the rails, needing only to be rabbeted to carry the platform. The shoulders at the ends of the long rails are unequal, the inner being housed ¼ in. in the posts to assist the bolted stub tenons. The short rails bear no load, are not rabbeted and do not have a housed shoulder.

The platform is of pine boards laid the short way and fitted loosely edge to edge. Other materials could equally well be used, for greater or lesser flexibility, and the rabbets could be altered to accommodate a different arrangement, for example a grid of boards running both ways.

In cutting out the rails and posts, consider which surfaces will be seen to relate, and arrange grains accordingly. For example, the front surfaces of the head posts will be seen with the front surfaces of the foot posts. The most convenient stock to work with, especially for the posts, is the rift cut (see inset in drawing), since all faces of a piece show about the same linear pattern. Plain or quartersawn stock, which shows bolder patterns that differ markedly on adjacent faces, can nevertheless be thoughtfully organized.

There are several kinds of mortise-and-tenon joints to be cut. To make the very long tenons at the headboard, true up one face and one edge of the stock. Square the ends exactly to the overall length including tenons. Gauge the tenon cheeks from the trued face and gauge the shoulders from the squared ends. Saw or plane grooves across the grain just on the waste sides of the shoulder lines, cutting to the depth of the cheek lines. Remove the waste and finish up with a rabbet plane. Then saw away part of the tenon to yield a long haunch. Make the other half of the joint by chopping the blind mor-

Child's bed, here in red oak, can be varied in size and adapted for bunk beds by lengthening the footposts and shaping them, along with the headposts, to interlock with the feet of a top bed, as shown in the drawing on the facing page. This clean, sturdy design incorporates various mortise-and-tenon joints, (as in the detail, right) housed, wedged and drawbolted for strength. Photos: Richard Starr.

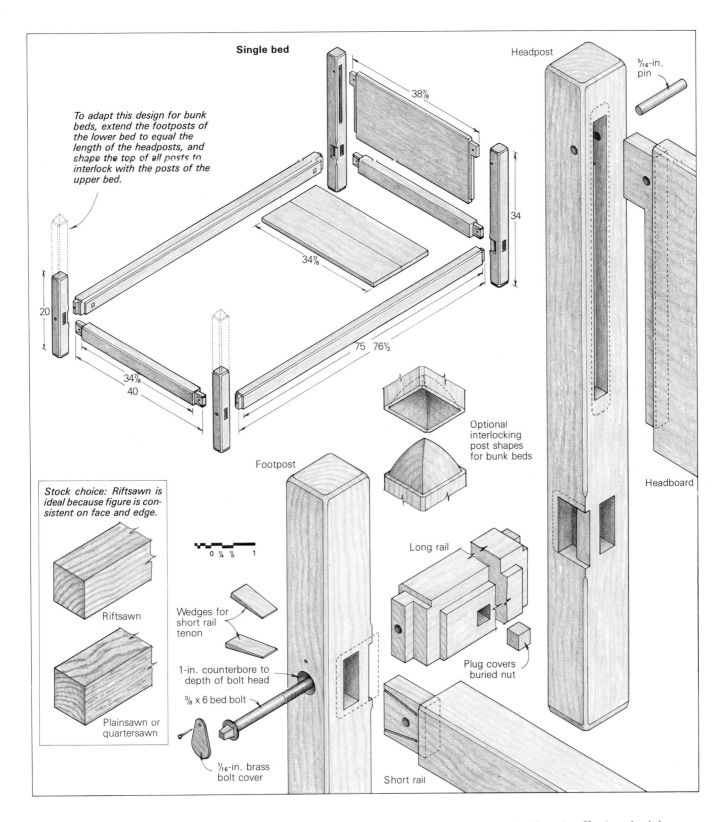

Single bed

To adapt this design for bunk beds, extend the footposts of the lower bed to equal the length of the headposts, and shape the top of all posts to interlock with the posts of the upper bed.

38⅞

Headpost

⁵⁄₁₆-in. pin

34

75 76½

20

34⅞
40

Footpost

Optional interlocking post shapes for bunk beds

Headboard

Stock choice: Riftsawn is ideal because figure is consistent on face and edge.

Riftsawn

Plainsawn or quartersawn

0 ¼ ½ 1

Wedges for short rail tenon

Long rail

Plug covers buried nut

1-in. counterbore to depth of bolt head

⅜ x 6 bed bolt

¹⁄₁₆-in. brass bolt cover

Short rail

tise first, then chopping or routing the groove. While the mortise should be as tight as possible, the groove should be a good deal longer than the haunch to allow for expansion of the headboard, and the shoulder below the haunch should be long enough to allow for contraction.

The mortises for the outside-wedged tenons can be made accurately with the aid of a guide block to chisel the desired slopes at the ends (see *FWW* #19, Nov. '79, p. 95). For a plainer appearance, blind tenons could be used here.

Notice that in laying out mortises, the gauge should bear on the inner faces of the posts, which have been previously trued and squared to one another. Thus, post sections may

vary somewhat without significantly affecting the joinery.

The order in which the parts are made does not matter, but it may be easier to bore for the bolts while the posts are free and before they are mortised for the short rails. First, working plumb, counterbore and bore the holes in the posts. Then clamp the posts to the long rails and use the holes to guide the bit into the end grain of the rails. If necessary, take away the post to finish the hole. Then, leaving the bit in the hole, draw a line on the inner face of the rail to show the actual path the bit has taken. Remove the bit and bore the crossing hole to house the square nut. As there is some danger of boring too deeply, it is prudent to stop a little short, square up

131

the hole with a chisel, try the nut, then deepen as required. When all is well, and with the joint bolted up, shim around the nut to keep it from shifting, and dry-fit a plug. It remains to complete the bolt holes through the short-rail tenons. Clamp up the end frames, mark the tenons from each side, then remove. Bore the holes a little oversize, lest eventual shrinkage pinch a bolt.

Matching the shoulder-to-shoulder lengths of the headboard and the headrail requires care. When testing the assembly, remember that because of moisture loss through freshly cut surfaces, post faces can deform after being mortised, and in order not to be misled, check these surfaces for truth before trying the matched pieces in place. The shoulder-to-shoulder length of the footrail, meanwhile, may differ a trifle without harm.

Before final assembly of the end frames, shape all arrises with a chamfer or radius, including those underneath. Children do crawl under beds, and planed oak can cut. The chamfer is perhaps more interesting to look at and to finger, the radius friendlier and more comfortable to lean against. The corners of the post tops can be worked with a finely set block plane, or they can be sanded with paper on a block. These corners can also be left sharp, straight from the chamfering of the arrises, for a pure if rather dangerous-looking detail.

During assembly, if the tenons make good friction fits in their mortises, very little glue is desirable. Put glue only on the tenon, and then only on the first inch or so next to the shoulder. Don't put glue on the haunches of the headboard: they must be free to shrink upward toward the fixed points at the top. The lower rail will keep the bottom tight. It is not necessary to glue the wedges, and more than a drop of glue can cause them to seize before they are driven home.

Simple bolt covers can be made of ⅟₁₆-in. sheet brass, using dividers, drill, hacksaw and file, or patterned ones can be obtained, along with the bolts, from Ball and Ball (463 W. Lincoln Hwy., Exton, Pa. 19341) or from Horton Brasses (P.O. Box 95, Cromwell, Conn. 06416).

To adapt the design for stacking twin beds, make all posts the same height, and carve all the post tops and one set of bottoms to make a gravity-locking joint. One way is shown in the drawing. A master set of male and female parts should be cut first to ease the job of fitting the actual posts. When the beds are stacked, additional racking strain on the joints of the lower bed would indicate widening the rails. Some compromise may be required here between acceptable sway and visually acceptable rail width. There seems no practical way to have matched bunk beds while preserving the interesting difference in height between headposts and footposts.

As for access, if the lower bed is placed head to foot with respect to the upper, steps for climbing will be found at 12 in. (footrail), 33 in. (headboard), and 48 in. (footrail). The second interval could prove too great for some children. Another approach would be to orient the beds normally and fit a two-step ladder between the lower edge of the upper footrail and the upper edge of the lower footrail, establishing 12-in. intervals for the climb. The ladder legs should be mortised in at the top end. Since mortises would be unsightly in the lower footrail when the beds were apart, the lower end of the ladder could be located by buttons fitted to the rail and shaped similarly to the post tops. ☐

Kenneth Rower makes furniture in Newbury, Vt.

132

Methods of Work

Cam hinge reveals hidden compartment

The sketch below shows how I used a modified hinged lid to construct a hidden compartment in the top of a bookshelf I was building. When the compartment is closed, there are no seams. The dowels lock down the front, making the top snug and tight. The pivoted cam rolls the top forward so it will clear the wall. —*James B. Eaton, Houston, Tex.*

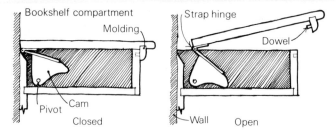

Bandsawn drawer bottom

By carefully bandsawing the center section from a solid-wood drawer at an angle, you can use a slice of the interior plug for the drawer bottom. If you intend to use the top face of the plug for a prescribed thickness of drawer bottom, carefully determine the cut angle using mathematics, a scale cross-section drawing or trial-and-error test-cuts on a piece of scrap. The proper angle varies depending on the thickness of the drawer blank, the thickness of the desired bottom and the width of the bandsaw blade's kerf. The method will not work with drawer shapes that reverse direction, as shown below. —*J.A. Hiltebeitel, S. Burlington, Vt.*

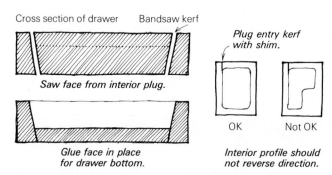

Installing glass for easy replacement

This method for securing glass in mitered frames makes it easy to replace the glass if it's ever broken. The key to the method is a special molding that fits in a groove cut into the frame. First cut a rabbet in the inside edge of the frame stock. Then cut a groove in the frame stock offset from the rabbet's shoulder by the thickness of the glass. Next mill the molding with a tongue that slips into the groove with a snug fit. Assemble the frame and molding as shown in the sketch with two pieces on the bottom. If you have cut and fit the pieces carefully you won't need any brads or glue to lock the molding in place. —*Douglas L. Wahl, Washingtonville, N.Y.*

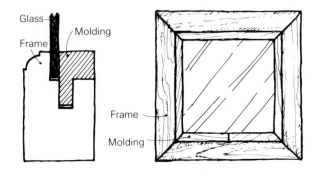

A Wooden Mechanism for Dropside Cribs

by Kenneth Rower

Cribs are often designed so the sides can be slid down to get the baby in and out. The proper metal parts might be hard to come by, and even then unsatisfying to see and use. But the whole mechanism—pins and grooves that allow the gates to slide and to be removed when the child outgrows the need for them, bolts that stop the gates in several positions, and springs that activate the bolts—all can be wood.

Fit upper and lower guide pins at each end of the gate to run in grooves cut in opposite posts. At the bottom of each groove, cut an escapement for the lower guide pin, to allow the gate to be swung outward. Once in this position, the gate can be removed entirely by tilting it, thus freeing the upper guide pins from the grooves.

Near the top of each leg, deepen the groove into a notch that will receive the spring-loaded bolt. Two such bolts, each passing through a bar and a stile of the gate, support the gate when up. A single-leaf wooden spring, housed in its own groove in the gate and retained at its lower end, presses the bolt outward into the notch. Drill a finger hole in the end of each bolt to make the bolts easier to retract.

Lower down in each groove, cut a notch to hold the gate off the floor. Slope the grooves for a short distance above these lower notches to allow the gate to be raised without having to retract the bolts. Cover the seats of the notches with thin cork to absorb shock.

To prevent a child from withdrawing the bolts, first at one end then the other, and bringing the gate down with resounding effect, fit locks across the bolts where they pass through the bars of the gate. These locks are simply dowel pins notched part way through for the thickness of the bolt, and shaped where they protrude on the outside of the bar to offer a finger-and-thumb grip. In one position the pin allows the bolt to move freely, but if rotated one-quarter to one-half turn, it locks the bolt in the mortise.

While there are no special pitfalls to

Kenneth Rower is a woodworker in Newbury Village, Vt.

the construction, groove and notch depth, bolt travel and bar centers in the gate must be carefully planned. The guide pins on the prototype are through-fitted dry, and thus adjustable as to projection, but you can cross-pin them once they are properly located in their grooves. Make the bolts and springs of straight-grained stock, and cut the mortise in the bolt for the spring deep enough so the spring can be pulled up past its retaining pin when installing or removing the mechanism. Mortises in the bars should be cut before the bars are shaped, and the whole system tested before gluing up the gate. The holes for the lock pins can be bored once everything else is in place. Locate them to put about less than half the diameter of the pin in the path of the bolt.

In order for the system to work smoothly the legs of the crib must be stout enough to resist spreading; otherwise the gate can jam. □

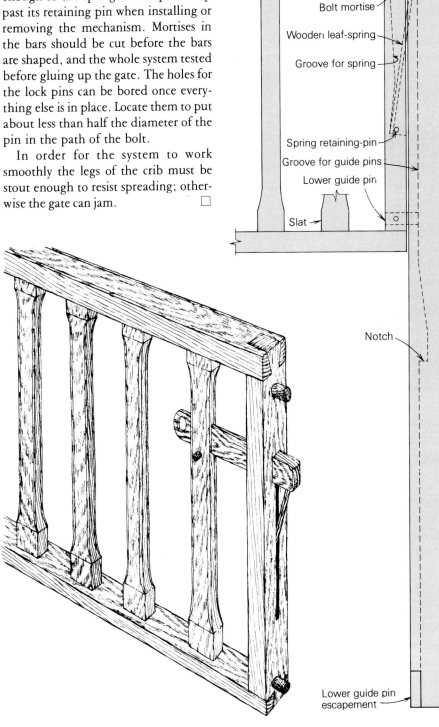

Side view

Bar
Bolt
Lock pin
Upper guide pin
Bolt mortise
Wooden leaf-spring
Groove for spring
Spring retaining-pin
Groove for guide pins
Lower guide pin
Slat
Notch
Lower guide pin escapement

A Spindle Cradle

by Dick Webber

The imminent arrival of our first grandchild recently forced me to put aside other projects and turn my attention to the design and construction of a cradle. An adequate supply of air-dried cherry, purchased eight yeas ago from a country sawmill, seemed an ideal choice of wood. My problem was the design. I wanted it to be practical, of a style that blended traditional lines, and of a construction that omitted metal parts yet allowed the cradle both to rock and to be removed from its stand. Too, it should be sturdy enough to last several generations. I am an amateur turner, and I got some assistance in designing the spindles for this cradle from a long-time turner, Walker Justice, of Vermillion Bay, Ont. He improved the spindle forms by suggesting more pronounced curves, perfectly semicircular beads and right-angled shoulders, exactly the sort of crispness that is usually missing from a beginner's turnings.

The stand—I wanted the effect of a single-post end support, but needed good lateral strength to withstand the racking stress of a rocking cradle. I decided to fasten two 8/4 turnings together, and left three parts of the turnings square for later gluing. The lower two receive the square tenons of the turned stretchers. The upper one receives the cradle-support pin (of oak, for strength), and is slotted accordingly. The bottom of the larger and smaller diameters of this T-shaped slot must conform to the size and shape of the pin. I started the cut by drilling a hole the size of the small diameter of the support pin into the face of the post where pin meets post. Then I chiseled down into the top the exact width of the diameters of the pin, making sure to position the mortise properly for clearance between post and cradle, and stopping at the centerline of the previously drilled hole. The last task here is to cut out the rounded part of the slot that receives the large diameter of the pin. I roughed out the space with a ¼-in. chisel, and finished by making a slightly smaller copy of the support pin, gluing sandpaper around the large end and turning my sandpaper peg in the slot with an

electric drill. Once the cradle was built, I drilled a hole in each end and glued in the support pins, waxing them with paraffin where they fit the T-slot for smooth, quiet operation.

I bandsawed the feet of the stand from 2x3 stock, then mortised for the posts and drilled for caster posts before rasping and sanding the feet to a pleasing rounded shape. Casters are optional, but I figured them in my overall height, so omitting them would necessitate adjusting the length of the posts or the shape of the feet.

The cradle—The construction of the cradle is post and rail, using mortise-and-tenon joints with framed panels at both ends. One-inch dia. spindles with ½-in. round tenons connect the top and

bottom rails before they are joined to the corner posts. I laid out the corner posts, then turned the ball at the top and the button at the bottom. I then mortised the posts for rails, and grooved them for the end panels. I joined the rails ⅛ in. from the outside of the posts in order to allow more depth for the tenons and to keep them from meeting.

Instead of molding them, I grooved the outside face of the top side rails and the top of the end rails using a ¼-in. core-box router bit. I sanded the edges of the grooves and rounded over the tops of the side rails to produce a section like that of a handrail.

I made the bottom of the cradle from ½-in. stock, notched to fit around the posts. The bottom rests on ⅜-in. by ½-in. cleats screwed to the inside of the

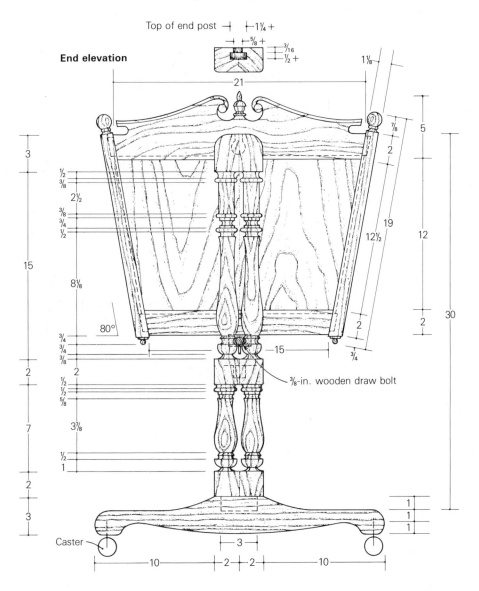

134

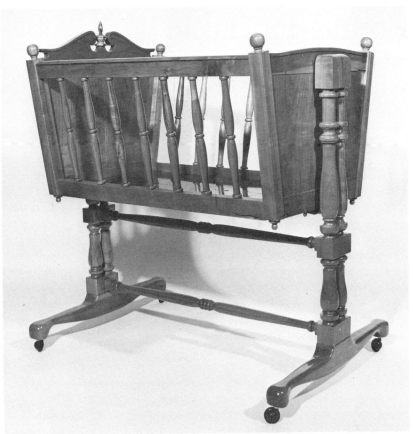

An ideal project for the turner, this cherry cradle uses twin 8/4 spindles for strong, stable posts. Instead of using metal hardware, the cradle pivots on an oak pin in a T-shaped slot, above, cut at the top of the posts. The cradle can thus be lifted easily from its stand.

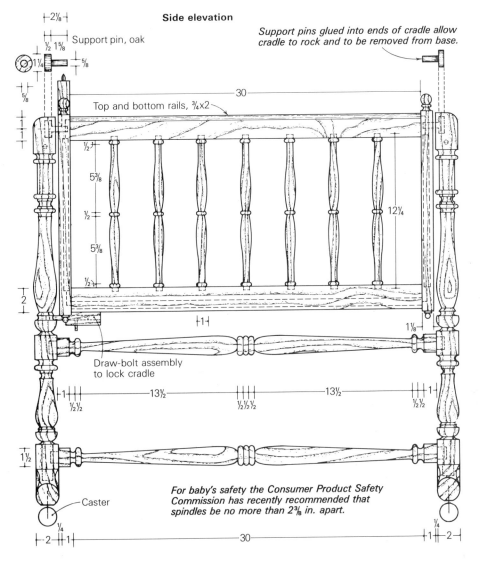

Side elevation

Support pin, oak

Support pins glued into ends of cradle allow cradle to rock and to be removed from base.

2⅛

½ 1⅝

1¼

⅝

⅝

30

Top and bottom rails, ¾x2

½

5⅜

½

12¼

5⅜

½

2

1

1⅛

Draw-bolt assembly to lock cradle

1 ——13½——— ½½½ ———13½—— 1
½½ ½½½ ½½

1½

Caster

For baby's safety the Consumer Product Safety Commission has recently recommended that spindles be no more than 2⅜ in. apart.

¼

¼

2 1

30

1 2

cradle, flush with the bottom of the rails. I chose not to fasten the bottom to the cradle thinking that, given the habits of infants, it might be handy to be able to remove it. A standard-size mattress fits into the bottom of the cradle.

To keep the cradle from rocking when the baby is left unattended, I made a wooden version of a draw bolt and fastened it to the bottom of the cradle. When extended, the bolt slips between the two turnings of the end post.

Finishing—Because so much of this project involved turnings, I finished the parts before assembly. I use Qualasole hand-rubbing lacquer (available from Woodcraft Supply, 313 Montvale Ave., Woburn, Mass. 01888). I begin by applying a generous amount with a cloth pad, making sure to saturate corners and crevices. As the finish builds, I apply lighter coats, increasing the pressure on the pad as the finish dries. When finishing on the lathe, I stop the lathe occasionally and rub longitudinally to prevent ridges from developing. The final coat should be a light application of Qualasole mixed 50/50 with thinner and rubbed vigorously until dry. ☐

Dick Webber is a real estate developer in Oklahoma City, Okla.

Round-Top Table
A piece that's subtle and direct

by Kenneth Rower

Here is a table capable of extensive variation in the shape of the legs, treatment of rails and outline of the top. It is straightforwardly built since all the joints are the same and the parts of the square frame are in two groups of four copies each. By altering the length of two rails, it is readily adaptable to rectangular or oval forms, and a rectangular section could be used for the legs. The top is quickly detachable via a locking system of dovetail pins cut on the leg tops and housings cut into the underside of the top.

The example shown here is in Georgia pine, with tapered, chamfered legs, chamfered rails and a 48-in. dia. top. The marriage of round top and square frame is not entirely serene, the difficulty being to make the frame large enough to seem right when viewed straight on, yet small enough not to seem bulky when viewed from a corner. The ideal stock for legs and rails is rift-cut, so that the grain is the same on all faces. A certain amount of heart figure can be included near the upper edges of the rails where it will be obscured by the overhang of the top. But do take the legs from near the edges of a flatsawn plank where the end grain shows the rings at about 45° to the face of the piece.

The thickness of the top should be less than half the thickness of the legs, but somewhere above two-fifths. Many arrangements are possible for the boards in the top. One good plan is to start with a long, thick plank and resaw all the pieces required, and then arrange them in a balanced pattern. Another approach is to use a fairly wide, flatsawn piece in the middle and build out to the edges with rift-sawn and quarter-sawn pieces. Given random stock, it is best to order the pieces to minimize discontinuities at the joints. There is normally no purpose in alternating heart and bark faces of the

boards except to gain a flowing appearance at the ends. Once glued up, the top is likely to curl upward at the edges regardless of the way the boards are laid. What counts most in the end is the appearance of the surface.

To make a top round by hand requires a compass or other coarse handsaw, a heavy spokeshave and an adjustable circular plane. Lay out the circle with a trammel. Saw away most of the waste, then set the top on edge in a bench vise, and work to the line with spokeshave and circular plane, exercising caution on the changing grain between quadrants. The goal is to achieve a fair curve kept pretty square to the top, free of perceptible irregularities. Some tearing is likely, and the edge will need to be sanded with paper wrapped around a thin, flexible stick about 6 in. long.

Frame size derives from the diameter of the top. A ratio of about five to eight is satisfactory if the top is round, but the frame would be somewhat larger under a square top because of the prominent overhang at the corners. Rectangular tops permit considerable variation in overhang without straining the eye. Comfortable rail depth for a table 29 in. high is about 4½ in. The leg section should be between 1¾ in. and 2½ in., assuming a thickness for the top from ¾ in. to 1¼ in.

Tenon thickness accords with leg section and the chosen system of mortising the legs. In this design, mortises are cut equal distances in from the leg faces and open into one another at the back. For tables of ordinary size the tenons should be ½ in. to ⅝ in. thick. Rail thickness, in turn, depends further on the style of the frame. If the rails are to be set flush to the legs, they must be twice as thick as the tenon in order to yield an equal amount of stock in the outer wall of the mortise. But if the rails are set in ¼ in. to create a strong

Close attention to joinery, proportion and grain orientation can make the difference between success and failure in the simple design of the table at left. Removable top is secured by dovetail pins, above, which are engaged in housings.

Round-top table

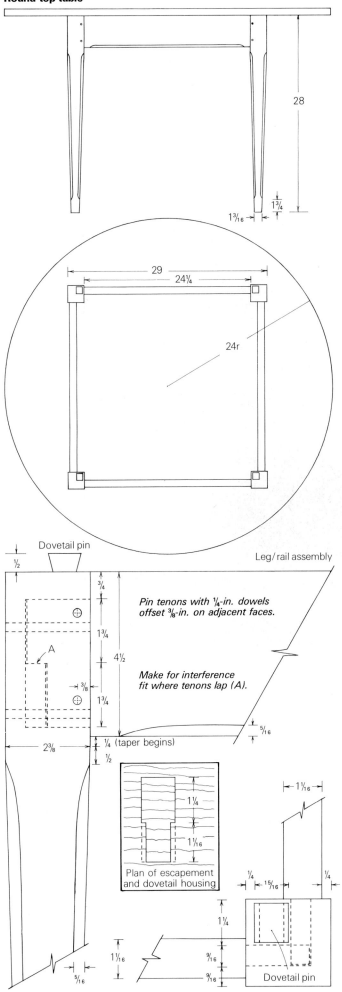

Dovetail pin

Leg/rail assembly

Pin tenons with ¼-in. dowels
offset ⅜-in. on adjacent faces.

Make for interference
fit where tenons lap (A).

¼ (taper begins)

Plan of escapement
and dovetail housing

Dovetail pin

shadow at the joint, they can be thinner by that amount, or the extra wood can be cut away to form an inner shoulder, certainly desirable in the absence of corner blocks. In any case, the mortises should not be cut closer than ¾ in. to the top of the leg, and it is good practice to reduce the mortise a little at the other end, allowing a small shoulder at the bottom of the tenon to conceal any bruising or shrinkage.

Tenons may be haunched or not, according to one's opinion of the relative importance of maintaining the integrity of the mortise, compared with keeping the rail flat and increasing the withdrawal resistance of the tenon. The latter is perhaps more definitely achieved by a pair of tight pins fitted across the joint close to the shoulders. But in the case of a frame with rails flush to the legs and not pinned, haunched tenons are well justified.

Taper in the legs may be scant or bold, inner faces only or all faces. The legs shown here are boldly tapered all faces, each face being reduced by half from a point a little below the joint to the bottom of the leg. This is a satisfactory proportion if the legs are to be chamfered. If they are to be left plain, it is better to use scant taper of about ½ in. for the inner faces, or ¼ in. on all faces. It may be that tapered legs yield a more durable frame than straight legs, since tapered legs are more flexible, and strains at the feet are distributed near the leg bottoms, rather than communicated fully to the joints.

Tapers and chamfers on the legs, and chamfers on the rails, should be cut after the joints are fitted and little further handling will be required. Stop chamfers can be cut with the drawknife (bevel down), and finished with rapid, firm strokes of the spokeshave. Entrances may need to be corrected with a sharp chisel. Tearing is a frequent danger. Lay out chamfers in pencil, because scribed lines cannot be removed without broadening the chamfer.

The construction of the frame does not preclude the use of turned or specially shaved legs, as long as the inner faces of the legs are flat and square in the area of the joints.

To assemble the frame, join two legs and their rail, repeat with the other legs and their rail and then join the assemblies to each other with the remaining rails. If there is plenty of friction when the joints are tested dry, glue only the first inch or so of the tenon nearest the shoulders since any glue at the back of the mortise will cause trouble if the leg shrinks.

The fastening system between frame and top consists of four dovetail pins cut on the tops of the legs and four housings with escapements cut in the underside of the tabletop. The method for cutting these is described in *FWW* #20, Jan. '80, p. 57. When cutting out the legs, leave stock at the top ends for the pins, which should be sawn after the legs are mortised but before the frame is assembled. This fastening system will not interfere with seasonal movement of the top, but when the top shrinks or swells in width, two of the pins will remain partly engaged when the top is slid over to unlock, and you can damage the pins when removing the top. The simplest solution is to lengthen the escapements away from their housings, those on one side accounting for expansion, those on the other for contraction. This method of joining top to frame offers no advantage of strength over the customary use of screws between rails and top. But it does allow quick removal of the top, and it satisfies a certain notion of pure construction. □

Kenneth Rower makes furniture in Newbury, Vt.

A Carver's Tricks
Three methods from a period-furniture maker

by Eric Schramm

One of the most valuable additions to my collection of carving tools is a set of four round-nose chisels. Originally they were ordinary butt chisels, but I re-ground them to rounded profiles and hollow-ground the bevels to a length of about ⅜ in., as the factory-ground bevel was too steep for carving. I use these four chisels in place of many gouges having different sweeps and widths. Used with the bevel down, the 1-in. and ¾-in. chisels are excellent tools for wasting wood fast in relief carvings as well as roughing-in a carving in-the-round. Used with the bevel up, all four chisels work well for shaping and smoothing convex surfaces. The ½-in. and ¼-in. chisels eliminate the need for a large number of gouges when setting-in a line. For example, setting-in a simple scroll can take up to eight different numbered gouges, as shown. But this scroll can be set-in using only one or two round-nose chisels.

To maintain a razor-sharp edge on my carving tools, chisels and plane irons, I made a rotary hone from a disc of ¼-in. plywood covered with 3⁄16-in. thick leather which is cemented in place. I bored a hole in the center of the disc and mounted it on a work arbor (available from Sears or a well-stocked hardware store); with the arbor chucked in my drill press and the leather stropping surface charged with white rouge (available from Sears), I can hone chisels and gouges quickly, without having to interrupt my work by getting out and setting up a lot of sharpening equipment. The drill press should run at its lowest RPM. You can also use tripoli or jeweler's rouge, but neither is as effective as white rouge.

For sanding sculptured furniture parts, I devised a pinwheel sander, which I make up from worn stroke-sander belts that I get free from a local cabinet shop. I cut the belt into 8-in. dia. circles and cut a ½-in. hole in the center of each. Then, using a paper pat-

tern and scissors, I cut eight evenly spaced slits from the outside toward the center. These stop about 1½ in. from the center hole. Next I fold one corner of each slit over the center and secure the pinwheel on a work arbor, whose collars hold the folded ends in place. A little piece of double-sided tape on the folded corner will keep the pinwheel together until it's secured on the arbor. Take care that all the folds go in the right direction in relation to rotation. □

For doing the work of many carving gouges—roughing-out relieved areas and smoothing convex surfaces—Schramm made this set of round-nose chisels by re-grinding standard butt chisels. The long hollow-ground bevels are especially well suited for carving.

To make honing quick and tidy, Schramm constructed this rotary strop (above left) from plywood and leather. He mounts it in his drill press and charges the surface with white rouge, a simple arrangement for keeping a razor-edge on all his tools, without the mess made by oilstones. Pinwheel sander (above right), when chucked in lathe or drill press, is good for finishing contoured furniture parts like cabriole legs.

Eric Schramm is a professional cabinet-maker who builds reproduction furniture in Los Gatos, Calif.

Pillar-and-Claw Table
Designs and methods for a period piece

by John Rodd

There is always a demand for small tables to put beside an easy chair or in a bare corner. One of the handiest types of these has been traditionally known as the pillar-and-claw table. The name is confusing, because the term claw refers to the whole leg and not to the foot, which may or may not be an actual claw of the sort that most of us are accustomed to seeing. So to avoid confusion hereafter, the claw will be called the leg. Before describing how to make one of these step by step, let's consider some of the historical variations on the three principal elements of the basic design—the legs, the pillar and the top.

The earliest and most common form of this table is the Queen Anne version shown in figure 1A. Fashionable from about 1700 to 1760, it's never entirely gone out of favor. Most of these were made of walnut and often had a shell carved on the knee. Instead of plain pads, the feet might be ball and claw as in figure 1B. Occasionally, tables with pad feet were "improved" by craftsmen who glued cheeks on the feet and then recarved them in the ball-and-claw style. This left the foot wider than the leg at the pillar and the result was horrible. Later, when mahogany became popular, paw-and-scroll feet were introduced.

Tables shown in Sheraton's drawing book have legs with continuous concave curves that sweep from pillar to foot. Examples of these often end in a brass paw carrying a caster (figure 1C). In America this form was perfected by Duncan Phyfe, whose designs combine beauty with stength in a most satisfactory way and should be studied by anyone who plans to work in the style. If you choose to make one of these, you may have difficulty trying to cut the reeds on the legs so they taper in the same proportion that the leg tapers. See the box on p. 85 for my method of doing this. The table shown in figure 1D is typical of those fashionable during the Regency (1811-1820). The legs are tapered, rectangular in section and terminate with involuted scrolls.

The lower end of the pillar is always a cylinder to which the legs are attached, usually with sliding dovetails, but sometimes with dowels instead. Above this there is usually a shoulder, next a waisted section and then an urn, which may be decorated with reeds, carved leaves or other ornament. The member between the urn and the top should be the longest part of the pillar, and spread to the maximum diameter at the top to give adequate support. It is often fluted and, in Victorian tables, worked with a tapered twist, a rather attractive detail that's fun to make. Examples of that period also may include a boss and pendant at the base, covering the dovetails and showing a bead at its junction with the pillar.

A common weakness in pillars of this type is that the waist

John Rodd's book, Restoring and Repairing Antique Furniture, *is available from the Van Nostrand Reinhold Co., 450 W. 33rd St., New York, N.Y. 10001.*

section below the urn has been turned too narrow. Not only is there danger of its breaking across the grain, but also any strain on the legs can cause splitting along the sides of the dovetail housings. These housings should be supported by a substantial amount of wood on either side and at the top. The fat pillar shown in figure 1B is less common, but in some respects to be preferred for its strength. Also, it shows classical details, as does the pillar for the table whose construction is described on the following pages (figure 2). The base of the pillar, like an Ionic column, consists of two beads with a hollow between, or as it was called, an upper and lower torus with a scotia between. The base of the shaft, in classical fashion, curves outward to meet the fillet above the torus. Turning a perfectly tapered shaft is more difficult than turning beads and coves. I once asked an old turner whether a pillar should have an entasis (a slight bulging in the shaft), thinking this was a feature that belonged only on a large architectural column (p. 112). I was surprised when he answered that to be correct it should, and that explaining the entasis made a good excuse if the customer complained that the shaft was barrel-shaped.

Unlike a classical column with its 20 or 24 flutes, table pillars have only 12, but the ratio of one part land or fillet to three parts flute is correct. However, having repaired so many

Fig. 1: Four basic table designs

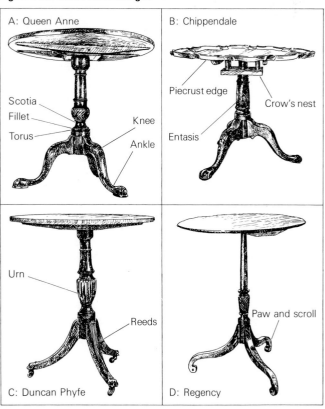

A: Queen Anne
Scotia
Fillet
Torus
Knee
Ankle

B: Chippendale
Piecrust edge
Crow's nest
Entasis

C: Duncan Phyfe
Urn
Reeds

D: Regency
Paw and scroll

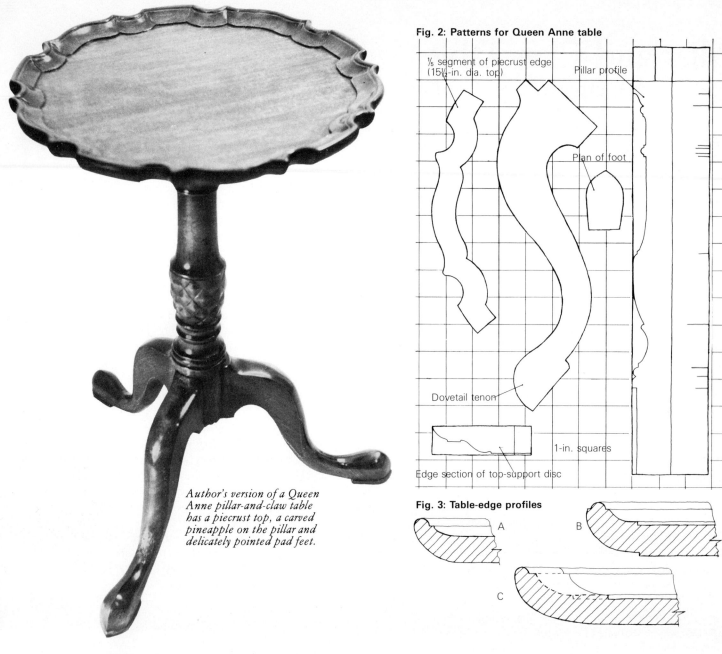

Author's version of a Queen
Anne pillar-and-claw table
has a piecrust top, a carved
pineapple on the pillar and
delicately pointed pad feet.

Fig. 2: Patterns for Queen Anne table

⅕ segment of piecrust edge
(15¼-in. dia. top)

Pillar profile

Plan of foot

Dovetail tenon

1-in. squares

Edge section of top-support disc

Fig. 3: Table-edge profiles

A

B

C

1"

thin fillets where they have been chipped out, I usually make them more substantial, sometimes as much as one part fillet to two parts flute.

A plain top with a slightly rounded edge is quite satisfactory, or with a double or triple bead around the edge. Dished tops (figure 3) are nicer, but should be turned from stock at least ⅞ in. thick, unless they are quite small; then the edge is usually like the one in figure 3C. The best of all, in my opinion, is the piecrust edge, about which I'll say more later. A top that is not intended to tilt should be supported by a turned disc that could be as much as half the diameter of the top. The disc will reduce the tendency of the top to warp and strengthen its attachment to the pillar. It's best to make the disc of the same wood as the top, and to orient its grain in the same direction. Tilting tops have a crow's nest, as in figure 1B.

Making a table—The style I like best is the Queen Anne table with pad feet and a piecrust top. Figure 2 shows the patterns for the legs, pillar, top-support disc, the foot and a one-fifth segment of the piecrust edge. Cut the patterns from ¼-in. plywood, hardboard or solid wood. Take care to fair and smooth all the curved edges, and make sure that the bottom of the foot is square to the back of the leg (what will become

the dovetail tenon). Next prepare the stock for the parts, using the dimensions given in figure 2. The top is 1 in. thick, the legs 1⅜ in. thick, and the pillar 3 in. in diameter. Bandsaw the top and the top-support disc to rough circles, ignoring the shape of the piecrust edge at this stage.

The legs—Now cut the three legs, having made sure that the grain in each runs at about a 45° angle from the foot to the back where it will join the pillar. Stack the three legs one atop another, align them carefully and clamp them together in a vise. Then plane the rear edges flat and flush. These surfaces will become the backs of the dovetail tenons, and the shoulders are gauged from them, so having all three in the same plane ensures that the legs will be square to the pillar when the dovetails are seated in their housings.

Gauge in from the backs ½ in. and score a line on all four sides of each leg to mark the shoulder lines of the joint. Then lay out the dovetail tenons. The accepted slope is 1:7, and they should be no narrower than ½ in. where they meet the shoulders. Saw right to the lines to minimize cleaning up of the cheeks with a chisel, but you must pare the end grain carefully to form the shoulders of the joint. Cut the top of the dovetail tenon back about ⅝ in., as shown on the pattern

With the leg secured to the bench with a holdfast, author, above, spokeshaves the leg in a gentle curve to form one side of the ankle. The penciled line on the leg marks the limit of cut. The other side (down) has already been shaved to the line. At right, holding the leg in one hand, a wide-sweep gouge in the other, Rodd pares the foot to bring it to a point. Note how the butt of the gouge is seated in the hollow of his shoulder and how his arm is locked in position, so the cutting force comes from the body rather than from the arm.

Author uses this marking jig, left, on his lathe to lay out complex patterns for carving and for turning, like this stylized pineapple. The jig consists of a base which sits flat on the ways, plus a post for holding a pencil. Attached to the outboard mandrel is the wooden indexing wheel and pin stop. At right, having set the diamond pattern for the pineapple, Rodd uses a shallow gouge to form the pyramid-shaped elements. The horizontal lines on the base of the pillar delineate the areas to be later flattened and mortised for dovetail housings which will receive the dovetail tenons on the legs.

above. This will make the housing stronger by leaving more wood at the top of the joint.

Now begin shaping the legs by fairing and smoothing the sweep of the curves top and bottom with a spokeshave. To make the ankle area about two-thirds to three-fourths the thickness of the foot and upper leg, pencil in a line from each side to mark the depth of cut. Hold the leg to the bench with a holdfast, and spokeshave it in a curve down to the line (top left photo). The curve should begin about midway between the shoulder and the foot and continue onto the foot itself. The ankle gets fully rounded, while the sides of the leg remain flat. The top surface of the knee is rounded, leaving a distinct corner at the top which fades about one-third of the way down. The spokeshave does most of the final shaping, though rifflers and large half-round files are useful in small, concave surfaces.

The pointed toe is roughed out with a large gouge (photo, top right). You can do this by eye or use the pattern provided and lay out the shape on the bottom of the foot. Note that the sharp ridge from the pointed toe dies out on top of the foot. Complete the shaping of the foot by carving a groove around the bottom with a V-parting tool and rounding the sides of the toe into it.

The pillar—Except for decorating the urn, turning the column is pretty straightforward and needs no comment. Urns were commonly ornamented with reeds, but I chose to carve a pineapple instead, and I'll describe how it's done. If your lathe is not equipped with an indexing wheel, make one out of wood, along with a pin stop. The wheel should fit friction tight on the outboard end of the mandrel. Laying out the pineapple calls for 18 equally spaced horizontal lines along the circumference of the urn, so bore a ring of 18 holes (each 20° apart) in the indexing wheel. To mark the 18 horizontals, make the simple jig shown above, at left. It consists of a base which sits on the lathe bed and a vertical post which holds a pencil, whose point is aligned precisely with the turning axis.

The next step is to mark the spiral lines on the urn. First draw on a single spiral line using a short length of flexible metal tape to guide the pencil. At each point where this initial spiral intersects the horizontal lines (there are five intersections in the example shown) you will draw a circle around the circumference of the urn, using the marking jig and rotating the stock into the pencil. Now you have a framework on which you can accurately mark out the rest of the spiral lines in both directions. Once this is done, you will have a grid of uniform diamond-shaped elements, and you can to set them

141

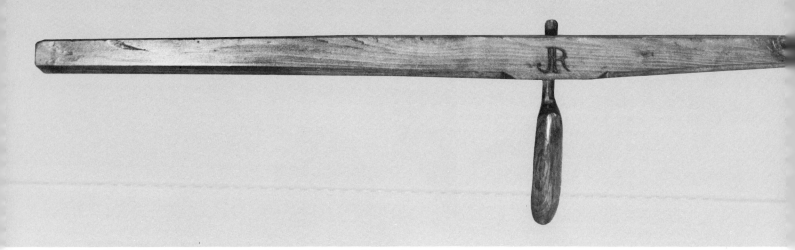

Used for cutting dished-out tops to final depth, after most of the stock has been wasted with a gouge, this depth cutter, above, is basically a hefty stick with a hole in it, through which protrudes a ½-in. gouge. The stick rides against the raised rim of the revolving top while the tool cuts the relieved area to a uniform depth. Below, for turning round tabletops, author made this tool rest from steel bar stock. It can travel laterally on the horizontal bar below, and is provided with an auxiliary rest for getting at the rim of the rotating stock.

in, cutting grooves along the spiral lines with a V-parting tool.

When these cuts are finished in both directions, start shaping the individual diamonds. With a fairly flat gouge, pare away the wood on the four sides of the center point to form a pyramid. Cut close but not quite to the bottoms of the grooves, and try to leave the intersections of the spirals plainly visible. Once the gouge work is finished, you should clean up the grooves with a small parting tool.

While the stock is still on the lathe, you will need to lay out the base of the pillar to receive the legs. This involves cutting three flat areas and the dovetail housings. First mark out the boundaries for the flats; these are 1⅜ in. wide and as long as

the shoulder on the legs. Use the indexing wheel to find the centerline for each land, and measure over $^{11}/_{16}$ in. on either side to establish the shoulder lines. Cut the flats by sawing a series of kerfs almost to the shoulder lines, then remove the waste between with a chisel. Finally, pare to the lines with a wide chisel or rabbet plane, and check for flatness using a piece of glass with crayon smeared over its surface. The color will rub off on the high spots, and you can level them.

To cut the dovetail housing, first bore a ⅝-in. hole on the centerline so the top edge of the hole is ⅝ in. below the top of the land. This area is not mortised because the dovetail tenon has been cut back ⅝ in. from the top. Position the end of the dovetail tenon as though it were going to enter the pillar, and trace around it with a sharp pencil or scriber. Carry the marks up across the face of the flat to the outer edges of the holes. With a dovetail saw or tenon saw, cut down the walls of the housing, finishing the cuts with the point of the saw. The hole at the upper end makes this job easier. Chisel out the waste between the cuts, making sure that the bottom of the housing is cut to full depth and is absolutely flat. Slightly bevel the two outside corners, then try the fit by inserting the tenon to about two-thirds its length and moving it in and out a couple of times. Check the walls of the housing for shiny spots to pare down. Repeat this until the leg can be driven home with a few light blows. The fit should be snug, and the shoulders should pull up tight.

At this point I find it convenient to glue the rough-sawn top-support disc to the pillar (you can reinforce the joint with a dowel), and turn it as part of the spindle, rather than as a separate faceplate turning. Then I sand the finished turning, taking care to avoid the urn. You'll ruin its appearance if you sand the points off the pyramids.

The top—The roughsawn blank for the top should be 1 in. thick and 15½ in. in diameter. The dished area will be ½ in. below the carved rim. Screw the top to a faceplate and mount it on the outboard side of the lathe. You will need a wide tool rest like the one shown at left, which you can fabricate from steel bar stock, or simply make out of wood for an occasional turning. To dish out the top I first remove most of the wood with a ½-in. gouge; then I use the depth cutter shown above, which I made myself. It consists of a long bar about 1½ in. square and three times as long as the radius of the largest top to be turned. The ½-in. dia. hole for the cutting tool, an ordinary ½-in. turning gouge, is bored about one-third the way from the one end, and the back of the bar should taper slightly from this area to the ends. The cutter (wedged in place) projects through the hole in the amount you want to dish out the top. In use, the bar is tilted back for the initial cuts and slid back and forth across the rim. Finally, the face of the bar rides flat against the rotating rim.

Before removing the top from the lathe, prepare a wooden straightedge of suitable length, cover it with crayon and hold it against the top as it revolves. High spots will show up as rings. The center portion can be leveled with a finely set block plane, and the outer part can be smoothed with a flat 1½-in. wide gouge which has been ground to an angle of 65° and honed absolutely sharp.

Next comes the piecrust edge. With a compass, describe a circle 15 in. in diameter and use it to register the pattern for the outside scalloped edge, which is marked out and cut with a bandsaw. Next fair all the curves with a large half-round file. This outer edge serves as a guide for making two more such edges, one within the other—the line to mark the upper edge of the cove, and the one to mark the lower edge of the cove. The curves and proportions of the piecrust pattern change as you move inward, and some freehand drawing is necessary to get things right. Once you do, make a cardboard template for these inner edges.

With the two inner edges marked out, begin setting in and grounding the cove, taking care to cut it to no more than half its final depth, and observing how the grain responds to your direction of attack. This is followed by a second setting in, us-

ing an almost flat 1¼-in. gouge, until the cove has been fully grounded. Both care and control are needed to avoid tearing the wood during final grounding, so remember how the grain behaved during the first stage of carving and adjust your direction of cut if necessary. Next cut the inside corners of the rim with a parting tool, using an easy sweep from top to bottom; then complete the cove, cutting into the corners with the flat gouge.

Use a small parting tool to set in and ground the little fillet that separates the cove from the bead which forms the top edge of the rim. Work the intersections (inside corners) with a spade firmer chisel. Finally round the bead with the concave side of a ¼-in. carving gouge, whose sweep should conform to the curve. These cuts are made from both directions with a rolling motion. This is particulary good exercise in handling carving tools because the angle of the grain is constantly changing, and cuts to both the left and the right are necessary. In doing this you will appreciate the small inner bevel you get if you sharpen your gouges properly.

Little now remains to be done. The underside of the outer edges must be rounded, the inner curve being started with a large gouge and finished with file and spokeshave. Lastly, the grounded areas of the top are smoothed with a cabinet scraper, and then the entire top is sanded before attaching the top-support disc with woodscrews. ☐

Cutting tapered reeds

Tapered table legs, whether curved or straight, are often decorated with reeds, which for a correct appearance must also be tapered in the same degree as the leg. Reeds can be tapered freehand with carving tools, but getting accurate and uniform results is tedious and difficult. The only specialized tool involved is a scratch stock, which you will find useful for other molding jobs. Mine is similar to the one described in *FWW* #11, Summer '78, p. 60, but has an adjustable fence, like a marking gauge, instead of a fixed fence. The adjustable fence isn't necessary; on a conventional scratch stock, you simply move the cutter in its slot and tighten the setscrews to reset the distance between the cutter and the fixed fence.

Two cutters are needed. One is ground to cut the vein between two reeds and half the profile of each (cutter A, shown at right). The other is ground to cut only the outside half of the outer reeds and the relieved area between it and the border on the leg (cutter B). You can make these from bits of hacksaw blade or other thin, suitable steel.

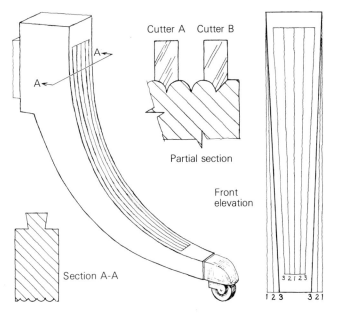

Cutter A   Cutter B

Partial section

Front elevation

Section A-A

I'll describe how to cut four tapered reeds on a curved tapered leg; the principles can be adapted to handle other legs or furniture parts and more or fewer reeds. First dimension the leg blank, bandsaw it to its proper profile and fair the curve, leaving the sides yet untapered. With a flexible metal tape, lay out the lines of the finished taper on the face of the stock. Now look at the wedge of wood on either side that will become

waste; at the bottom of the leg divide the wide part of both wedges in two. Draw a line from this midpoint to the top of the leg, bisecting the wedge of waste. Do this on both sides of the leg.

Install cutter A to take a cut down the center of the leg. Hold the fence against the side of the leg and cut in the middle vein and the two inner halves of the two middle reeds. Then handplane the taper on both sides to the first line. You now have a new edge on which to register the scratch-stock fence. Reset the fence to cut the veins between the two outer reeds and the two inner ones. When done you will have formed two tapered central reeds and the inner halves of the two outer reeds. Now plane the leg to its finished taper, install cutter B and form the outer halves of the outer reeds.

Cutting more reeds means tapering the leg in more increments. Cutting an odd number of reeds requires tapering the center reed by planing first to half the depth of the first taper line on both sides. To stop reeds, square off the ends of the veins with a parting tool. —*J.R.*

The American Harp

by Robert T. Cole

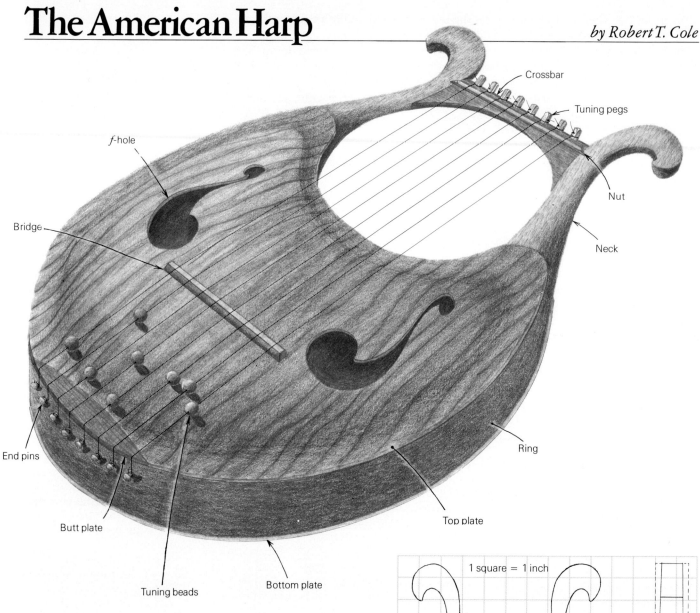

Crossbar

Tuning pegs

Nut

Neck

f-hole

Bridge

End pins

Butt plate

Tuning beads

Bottom plate

Top plate

Ring

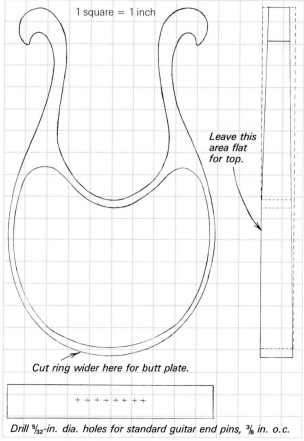

1 square = 1 inch

Leave this area flat for top.

Cut ring wider here for butt plate.

+ + + + + + +

Drill ⁵⁄₃₂-in. dia. holes for standard guitar end pins, ³⁄₈ in. o.c.

The lyre form of the harp is the most ancient of stringed instruments, and it has evolved into a variety of forms. I designed the instrument here to be used with high-tension steel strings; it is strong and stable, and it includes carved front and back plates. No other lyres have been built like this, so I call this the American harp. Regardless of the name, its function, as usual, is to encourage music at home and singing in particular. It can be tuned to many scales, so there's enough complexity to occupy the player for years.

Materials
1½ x 10 x 16 Philippine or
   Honduras mahogany
¾ x 10 x 20 Philippine or
   Honduras mahogany
1½ x 2 x 5 hardwood crossbar
Hardwood strips for nut,
   bridge and butt plate
¼-in. dowel, 10 in. long
Wooden beads (8)
Piano-tuner's pegs (8)
Guitar strings (8)
Guitar end pins (8)—you can
   make your own

The ring, shown in the drawing at right, forms the sides and necks of the harp. It may be cut out on a bandsaw or with a coping saw. It is then cleaned up using both a disc sander and a drum sander. The overall width of the harp may vary between 9½ in. and 10 in., and the thickness of the wall ranges from ¼ in. on the sides to ⅝ in. where the end pins will be drilled. Do not round any edges until the harp is glued up.

144

The crossbar should be made from a strong hardwood, like maple, oak or koa. Trace the inside curve of the necks onto the crossbar blank, then cut and shape it to fit. Bevel its two faces, and drill holes for the tuning pegs slightly smaller than the pegs. Tuning pegs can be had from a piano supply house, and a tap-wrench handle works well to adjust them. Glue in the crossbar, and when dry, drill and pin it with four ¼-in. dowels.

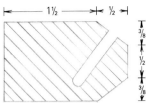

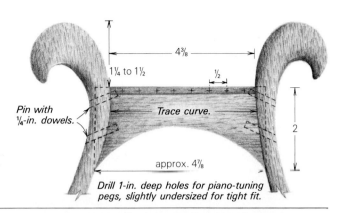

Pin with ¼-in. dowels.

Trace curve.

approx. 4⅞

Drill 1-in. deep holes for piano-tuning pegs, slightly undersized for tight fit.

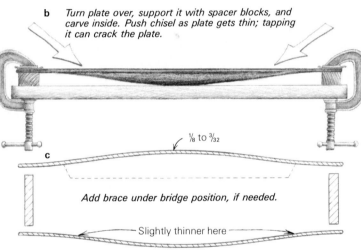

a   Carve outside first.

Leather pad

b   Turn plate over, support it with spacer blocks, and carve inside. Push chisel as plate gets thin; tapping it can crack the plate.

c   ⅛ to ³⁄₃₂

Add brace under bridge position, if needed.

Slightly thinner here

Now you can carve the plates. First saw the outline from the ¾-in. thick mahogany blank, leaving ⅛-in. trim. Clamp the blank to the bench, outside up, and fair the edges with a wide gouge (a). Turn the blank over, clamp it to the bench using spacer blocks, and begin carving the inside face (b). As the plate gets thin, push the chisel rather than tap it (or use a disk grinder), or you risk splitting the wood. Quite often you must unclamp and feel its thickness. It should approach ³⁄₃₂ in. near where it will be glued. If it deflects more than ¹⁄₁₆ in. under moderate pressure, you should add a brace under where the bridge will be (c). If you carve the plate too thin at any spot, glue on a wood patch.

Smooth the inside with sandpaper and refine the contour, Then cut the *f*-holes in the top plate—carefully, as it is easy to split the thin wood (d). Next cut out the space for the butt plate. This is where the strings will lay over the end, and they would cut through the softer mahogany.

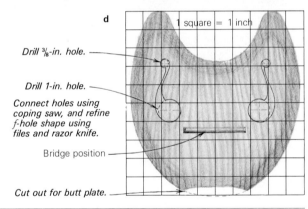

d   1 square = 1 inch

Drill ⅜-in. hole.

Drill 1-in. hole.

Connect holes using coping saw, and refine *f*-hole shape using files and razor knife.

Bridge position

Cut out for butt plate.

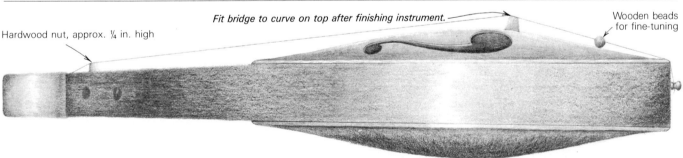

Fit bridge to curve on top after finishing instrument.

Wooden beads for fine-tuning

Hardwood nut, approx. ¼ in. high

Glue up one plate at a time, back, then front, checking first to see that the surfaces make good contact. I use aliphatic resin (yellow) glue and clamp with C-clamps every couple of inches, protecting the wood with leather pads. When the front plate is dry, glue on the butt plate and drill the end-pin holes. Round all the edges and finish-sand.

Make the hardwood nut about ¼ in. high and glue it to the crossbar. I finish the harp now using a brushing lacquer—three coats, sanding between coats and rubbing with steel wool at the end. Now fit the bridge to the curve of the top and slot it for the strings: Use regular guitar strings, as shown:

String	Tuning
0.046 wound	Bass C
0.036 wound	G
0.026 wound	C′
0.020 wound	E
0.016 plain	G′
0.012 plain	C″
0.010 plain	E′
0.008 plain	G″

Other tunings are possible. Bring all the strings up to tension, then fine-tune using the wooden beads between the end pins and the bridge. The first tuning takes patience because the instrument needs to adjust to the tension.

The harp can be played by plucking, or with hammer-dulcimer sticks made of felt, to produce the effect of a steel-string lyrical drum.   □

Robert Cole, of Santa Barbara, Calif., is a luthier.

Project: Music Stand

by John D. Freeman

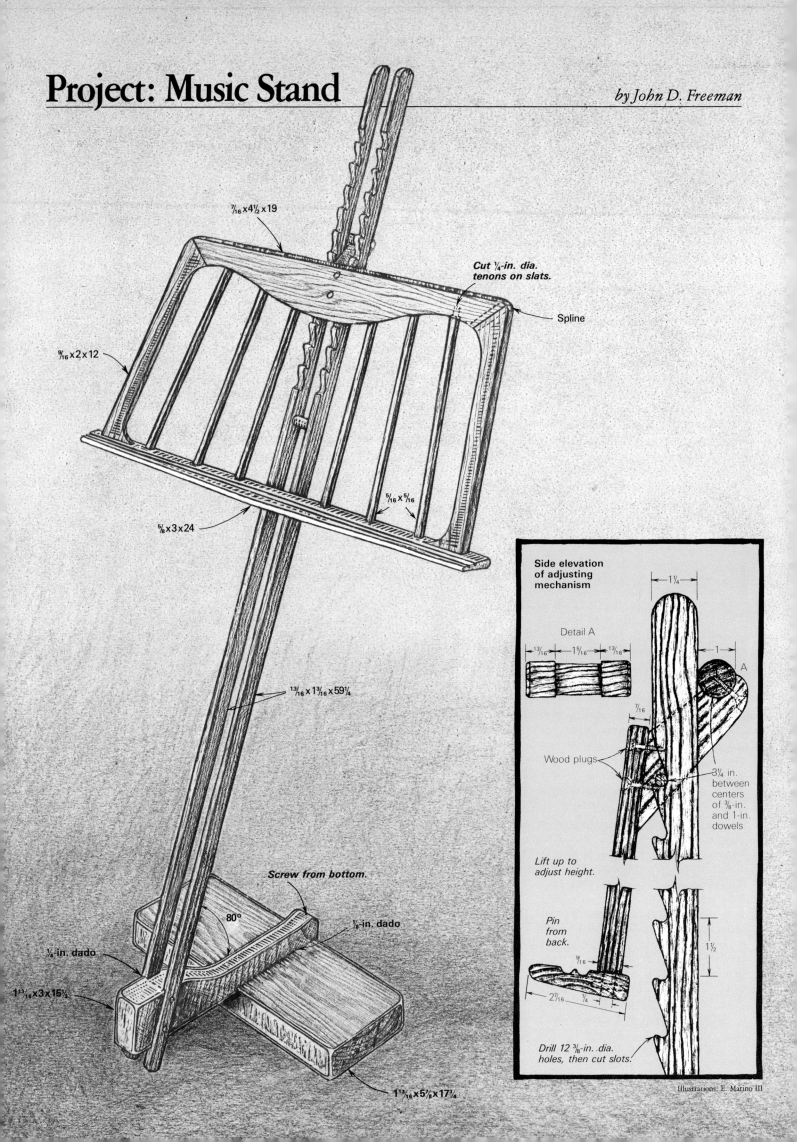

$^7/_{16}$ x 4$^1/_2$ x 19

Cut ¼-in. dia.
tenons on slats.

Spline

$^9/_{16}$ x 2 x 12

$^5/_8$ x 3 x 24

$^5/_{16}$ x $^5/_{16}$

$^{13}/_{16}$ x 1$^{13}/_{16}$ x 59¼

Screw from bottom.

80°

⅛-in. dado

¼-in. dado

1$^{13}/_{16}$ x 3 x 15½

1$^{13}/_{16}$ x 5⅝ x 17¾

Side elevation of adjusting mechanism

Detail A

$^{13}/_{16}$ 1$^5/_{16}$ $^{13}/_{16}$

1¼

1

$^7/_{16}$

A

Wood plugs

3¼ in.
between
centers
of ⅜-in.
and 1-in.
dowels

Lift up to
adjust height.

Pin
from
back.

$^9/_{16}$

1½

2$^7/_{16}$ ¼

Drill 12 ⅜-in.-dia.
holes, then cut slots.

Illustrations: E. Marino III

Tall-Case Clock
The typical 18th-century design

by Eugene Landon

During the 18th and early 19th century, tall-case clocks were made in infinite varieties, yet their basic construction is the same. They consist of a base, a waist section enclosing the weights and pendulum, and a hood, which houses the clockworks. The feet could be ball, straight-bracket, ogee-bracket, French or simply straight-turned. The base might have a plain board front, a raised panel and fluted quarter-columns, or a scalloped panel front. The waist could have a flat, rectangular door with a "bull's-eye" (a window to see the pendulum), a "tombstone" door or a carved arched door flanked by fluted quarter-columns. The top could be flat, stepped, broken-arched or bell-shaped. The combina-tions seem to be inexhaustible. By detailing the construction of one particular clock, Philadelphia style c. 1770 by James Gillingham (my reproduction of which appears at right), I will present the basic elements necessary in the construction of any typical tall-case clock of this period. Note that this particular clock is exceptionally tall, approximately 109 in. to the top of its carved cartouche. If the room in which this clock is to be used cannot accommodate such a height, obviously this piece must be scaled proportionately.

It is best to construct the hood first because dial size and shape determine all other dimensions. The dial size for the drawings that follow is the most frequently used size during the 18th cen-

Reproduction of tall-case clock (original by James Gillingham) follows typical 18th-century con-struction, as shown in the drawings on the following pages. The cartouche in place of the center finial and the applied carvings on the scrollboard are ambitious, optional embellishments.

tury, 12 in. by 12 in. with a 5-in. radius moon dial atop. Dials this size are available from James A. Zerfing, 123 Linden St., Williamsport, Pa. 17701, and high-quality reproduction clockworks from Merritts, RD 1, Douglasville, Pa. 19518. Begin with the base frame of the hood, which is mortised-and-tenoned together and mortised through its upper face to receive the hood sides (be sure to make a right and left side). Glue the hood sides to the base frame, set it aside and begin to construct the pediment box. The front of this box is called the scrollboard, and to it attach the moldings, rosettes and center cartouche. Note that the arch is cut in the scrollboard and its backing board before they are assembled as part of the pediment box. After gluing up the half-blind dovetails that join the pediment box together, you can apply the moldings. Over the years I have taken to making my moldings using the old wooden planes; however, one can use a shaper or other tools to make them. I carve the gooseneck molding of the broken pediment by hand, as shown in the drawing at left.

To attach the moldings I rough the glue surfaces with a toothing plane, glue them in place, and then brad them after the glue is dry. This is the way the old clocks were done, and reproduction brads are available from Tremont Nail Co., 21 Elm St., Wareham, Mass. 02571. To ensure that the miter will look tight, I relieve the surface behind the visible corner.

Next make the corner plinths and caps. Drill a ½-in. hole in each plinth top to receive the finials, which will be carved later. The plinth in the center of the broken pediment has the same molding as the scrollboard. Glue on all these pieces; later, when the pediment box is capped, you will mount a block behind the center plinth and bore it to receive the cartouche.

Now make the dial frame so that it will overlap the dial no more than ⅛ in. on all sides. The inside edge is molded with a thumbnail to match the front of the hood sides, and the corners are coped. Half-lap the frame together and cut the arch for the moon dial, also ⅛ in. smaller than the radius of the moon dial itself. Then carve the thumbnail molding into this arch. Slide the completed dial frame into the 5/16-in. channels in the hood sides; it will be secured in a moment.

Mount the pediment box on the hood sides. The front and rear of the hood sides are cut away, and the pediment box should fit snugly enough over the wide tongues of the sides that it must be tapped into place with a hammer and block. Secure the hood sides to the pediment box with glue and/or nails and screws from the inside. Also secure the dial frame to the backing of the scrollboard with small brads. It is not necessary to glue the sides or bottom of the dial frame because a good fit in the channels will secure it indefinitely—I've seen it so on many a tall-clock hood. Last, nail the top (use a secondary wood, such as pine) to the pediment-box sides.

The door is the next element of the hood to be made. Don't cut the arch until after gluing up; otherwise short grain in the top member makes clamping dangerous. Use a paper pattern to transfer the hood arch to the doorframe blank, allowing about 1/16 in. for clearance. Lay out the arch, the inside with a radius 2 in. shorter than the outside. Cut the thumbnail and the rabbet for the glass on the inside arch before cutting the outer arch; again, once the outer arch is cut, the piece is fragile. Now cut the outer arch with a bevel to correspond with the hood-arch bevel and fit the door. Its outer edge should line up with the shoulder of the dial-frame thumbnail. Brass hinges hold the door at the top and bottom so it swings from the right. I don't know why, but almost all tall-case clocks have hinges mounted to swing this way. I made my own clock-case hinges, but you can order them from Merritts.

Next the columns can be turned and fastened to the hood. Four freestanding columns can be used, or, as shown in the drawing, two freestanding front columns and two half-columns mounted on backboards applied to the side. I like to flute the columns with a 2-mm #9 gouge, though a scratch beader can also be used.

The rosettes can be carved and applied next. They start as turnings. Since I made two of these clocks concurrently, I varied some of their elements, the rosettes being among them. Two options are given in the drawing. Flame finials in the 18th century were usually made in three parts—the plinth, the urn and the flame, which makes the last easier to carve. The cartouche in place of a center finial and the applied carving of the scrollboard are ambitious embellishments that could be omitted.

Now that you have the hood finished, set it aside and begin construction of the base unit. Cut a rabbet in each of the side pieces to receive the back before dovetailing the two sides to the pine bottom. The bottom is to be flush with this rabbet and extend ¼ in. in front; the reason will be clear when

Carving the gooseneck molding

Lay out parallel lines of contour, and saw blank.

Grain

1. With ¼-in. firmer chisel, chop a curve along the face of the blank, overlapping the cuts. Then, with a ¾-in. chisel, pare in from the edge to remove the rabbet shown.

Chop contour

Pare rabbet

2. Remove, as in step 1, a second rabbet.

10 mm, #8 gouge
6 mm and 8 mm, #8 backbend gouge

3. Carve with gouges the ogee shape.

#8 gouge { 16 mm
18 mm }

4. Carve the large cove.

5. Carve the thumbnail. Smooth the whole molding with curved scrapers.

6 mm, #8 backbend gouge

Tall-clock-case hood

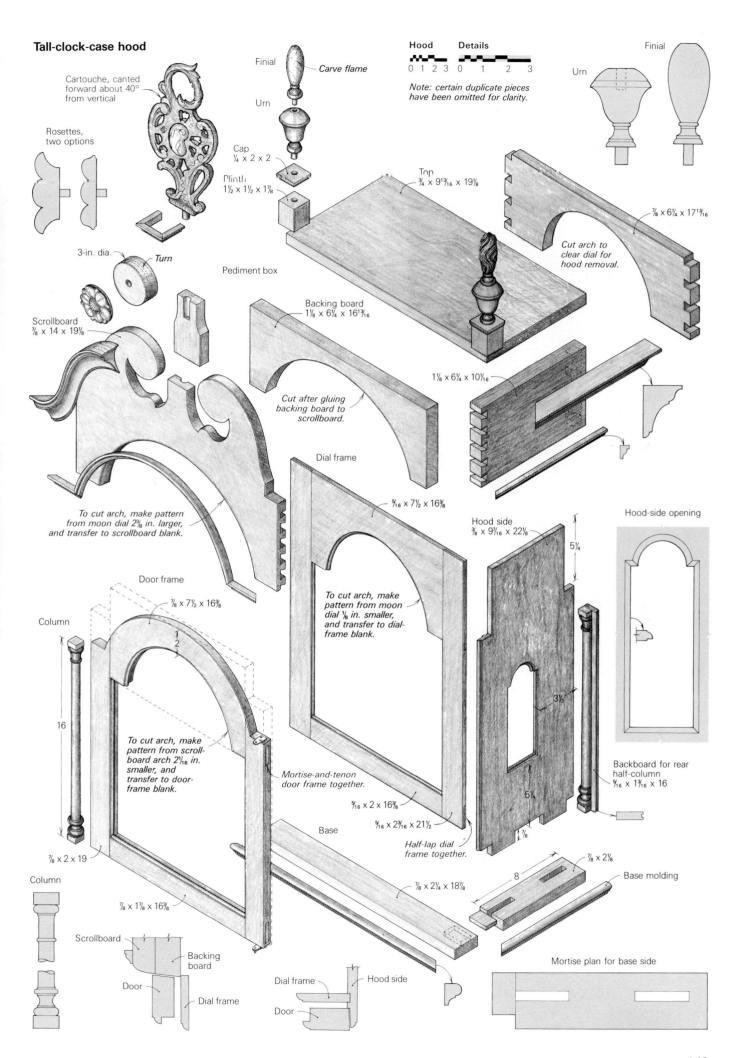

Cartouche, canted forward about 40° from vertical

Rosettes, two options

Finial

Urn

Carve flame

Cap
1/4 x 2 x 2

Plinth
1 1/2 x 1 1/2 x 1 7/8

Hood   Details

0 1 2 3   0   1   2   3

Note: certain duplicate pieces have been omitted for clarity.

Finial

Urn

3-in. dia.   *Turn*

Scrollboard
7/8 x 14 x 19 1/8

Pediment box

Top
3/4 x 9 13/16 x 19 1/8

Backing board
1 1/8 x 6 1/4 x 16 13/16

Cut after gluing backing board to scrollboard.

7/8 x 6 1/4 x 17 13/16

Cut arch to clear dial for hood removal.

1 1/8 x 6 1/4 x 10 1/16

To cut arch, make pattern from moon dial 2 3/8 in. larger, and transfer to scrollboard blank.

Dial frame

5/16 x 7 1/2 x 16 3/8

Hood side
3/8 x 9 7/16 x 22 1/8

5 1/4

Hood-side opening

Door frame

7/8 x 7 1/2 x 16 3/8

To cut arch, make pattern from moon dial 1/8 in. smaller, and transfer to dial-frame blank.

Column

16

To cut arch, make pattern from scroll-board arch 2 1/16 in. smaller, and transfer to door-frame blank.

Mortise-and-tenon door frame together.

5/16 x 2 x 16 3/8

5/16 x 2 3/16 x 21 1/2

Half-lap dial frame together.

3 1/2

5 1/4

7/8

Backboard for rear half-column
5/16 x 1 3/16 x 16

7/8 x 2 x 19

Base

7/8 x 2 1/4 x 18 7/8

8

7/8 x 2 1/8

Base molding

Column

7/8 x 1 7/8 x 16 3/8

Scrollboard

Backing board

Door

Dial frame

Dial frame

Door

Hood side

Mortise plan for base side

149

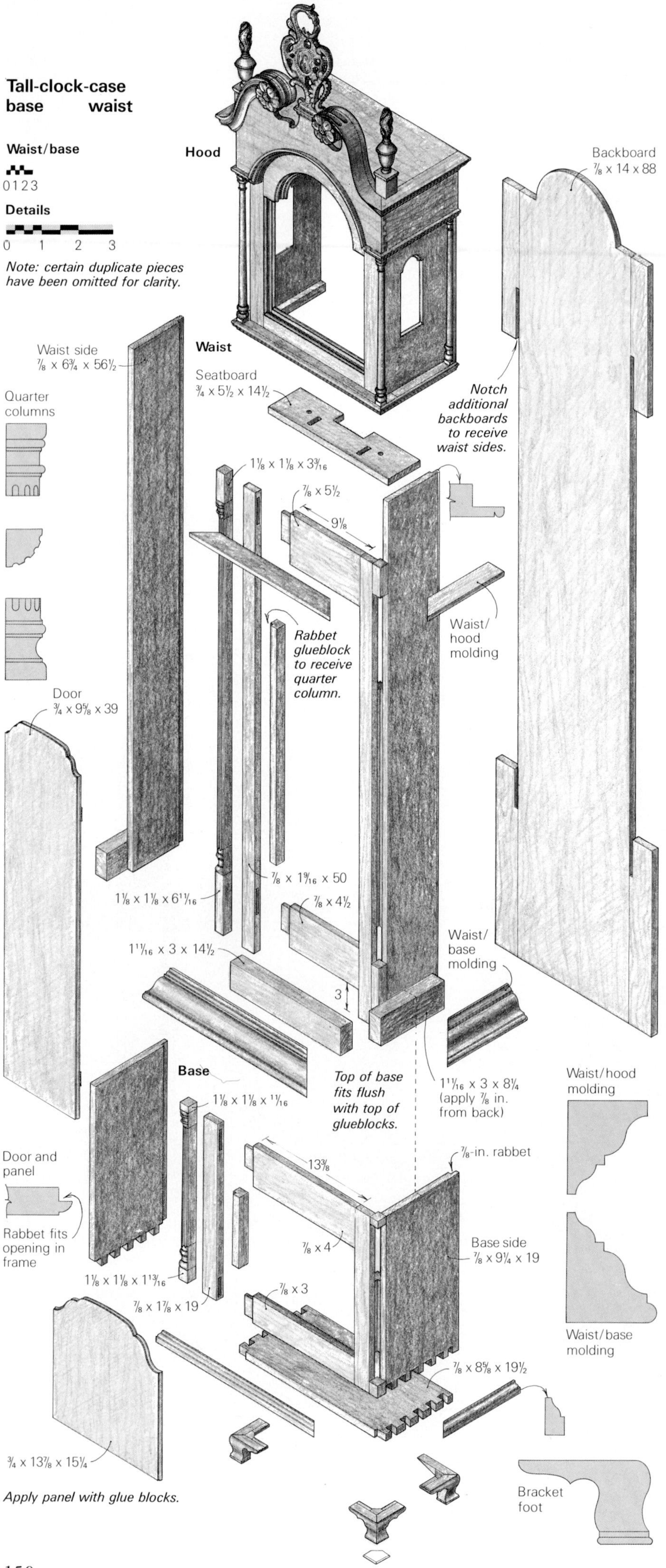

Tall-clock-case
base waist
Waist/base
0 1 2 3
Details
0 1 2 3
Note: certain duplicate pieces have been omitted for clarity.
Hood
Backboard
7/8 x 14 x 88
Waist
Waist side
7/8 x 6 3/4 x 56 1/2
Seatboard
3/4 x 5 1/2 x 14 1/2
Quarter columns
Notch additional backboards to receive waist sides.
1 1/8 x 1 1/8 x 3 3/16
7/8 x 5 1/2
9 1/8
Waist/hood molding
Rabbet glueblock to receive quarter column.
Door
3/4 x 9 5/8 x 39
7/8 x 1 9/16 x 50
1 1/8 x 1 1/8 x 6 11/16
7/8 x 4 1/2
1 11/16 x 3 x 14 1/2
Waist/base molding
3
Base
Top of base fits flush with top of glueblocks.
1 11/16 x 3 x 8 1/4 (apply 7/8 in. from back)
1 1/8 x 1 1/8 x 11/16
Waist/hood molding
Door and panel
7/8-in. rabbet
13 3/8
Rabbet fits opening in frame
7/8 x 4
Base side
7/8 x 9 1/4 x 19
1 1/8 x 1 1/8 x 1 13/16
7/8 x 3
7/8 x 1 7/8 x 19
Waist/base molding
7/8 x 8 5/8 x 19 1/2
3/4 x 13 7/8 x 15 1/4
Bracket foot
Apply panel with glue blocks.

the quarter-columns and front are attached. Mortise-and-tenon the front frame together, as in the drawing, and to it glue 1⅛-in. by 1⅛-in. blocks that will become the tops and bottoms of the quarter-columns. Then glue the frame to the sides and base using glueblocks with a rabbet cut along one corner to receive the quarter-column. The quarter-columns I turn from oversize stock, about 2¼ in. square (turn to 2⅛ in.), leaving an unturned square section at each end to support the stock while I flute and slice it, first in half, then in quarters, on the band saw. I then plane the two sawn surfaces until I have quarter-columns with 1-in. radii. Turn the quarter-rings that form the capital and base of each quarter-column from separate stock, 2½ in. square, then glue these to the 1⅛-in. blocks and mount the quarter-column between.

Apply the base molding around the bottom of the sides, covering the exposed dovetails, and to this molding apply the feet (for a way to make bracket feet, see *FWW* #21, March '80). Reinforce the feet with glueblocks. The front panel can now be attached to the base unit with glueblocks from behind. Choose attractively figured wood—bookmatching is common here. A thickness of no more than ⅜ in. should extend beyond the face of the frame; however, the panel can be made thicker with a rabbet around the sides. Now set the base aside and construct the waist portion of the clock.

First prepare the back and sides. The backboard is made of pine or some other secondary wood. Begin with a piece 88 in. long—the excess will be trimmed to fit under the dial arch later when the hood is slipped on from the front. Rabbet and bead the two walnut sides along their back edges and attach them to the backboard, 16 in. up from the bottom. Be sure the sides are square across from each other (scribe a line across the back of the backboard) as this will determine if the waist sits straight in the base. Along the lower edge of each side, on the outside face, apply a glueblock of pine ⅞ in. from the back to allow for the thickness of the backboard. To these blocks will be attached the base. Now make a front frame, which is joined with mortise and tenon like the frame used for the base. Again, attach 1⅛-in. by 1⅛-in. blocks to the corners for the top and bottom of the quarter-columns and apply this frame to the back/side assembly, keeping the frame and side bottoms flush. Make and apply the quarter-columns with quarter-ring capitals and bases, all the same in section as for the base. Cut the mortise for the lock, and mount the door using butt hinges, again on the right.

After completing the waist unit, the waist is slipped into the base, and the blocks previously glued to the bottom of the waist sides are now glued and clamped to the inside of the base sides. The backboard will extend to the bottom of the base, where it is nailed, but because it is only as wide as the waist, additional backboards must be fit to cover the extra width of the back of the base. Make and apply the waist moldings, upper and lower.

If you have bought an authentic reproduction clockworks, you will have to mount it on a seatboard, slotted for the cables and pendulum. Then you can fit the hood to the top of the waist. The base molding of the hood slightly overlaps the upper waist molding; if necessary, shave the edges of the waist molding, so the hood will slide over and rest on this molding. Note that the hood will not slide all the way on because the backboard and the back of the pediment box have yet to be cut. Remove the hood and place the seatboard, with the movement attached, atop the waist sides, which are over-long. Replace the hood, measuring the distance that the dial sits high in the dial frame. Remove the hood and the seatboard, and cut down the waist sides the distance the dial sat high plus ⅛ in. When you replace the movement and the hood, the dial should be properly framed in the dial frame. All that remains is to cut an arch in the pediment-box back and in the backboard, as shown in the drawing, so the hood will pass over both the dial and the backboard when being slid on and off. With the hood finally in place, glue additional backing boards to the backboard to cover the extra width of the hood.

After you have done all of the above, apply your favorite finish, and you should have something that resembles the clock for which James Gillingham was paid in 1770 the princely sum of 15½ lb. of veal. □

Gene Landon makes and restores period furniture in Montoursville, Pa.

Tall-case clocks are adorned in various ways. Hood of a Philadelphia clock (left) from the same period as the Gillingham example has basket of ferns for central finial and diminishing spirals in place of rosettes. Tobacco-leaf finials top country clock (right) from Reading, Pa., c. 1770.

Photos: Gene Landon

Philadelphia clock (1725), left, with step top and fretwork bell-speaker is high-style compared with Lancaster County clock, above, whose arched pediment is probably a country cabinetmaker's rendition of various elements he'd seen.

Cross-Country Skis, the Easy Way

by George Mustoe

Though it took me a long time to make the discovery, cross-country skis are relatively simple to make. Ski building originally seemed intimidating because of the numerous laminations and the long curve from the tips through the arched or "cambered" bottom. However, in a recent and inexplicable attack of common sense, I stumbled upon a simple method for building skis that requires only a bare minimum of materials and effort. Based on 1980 prices, a pair of skis will cost about $20 for materials.

Preparing the laminations—Figure 1 shows a ski whose upper and lower surfaces, along with the thin wedge that fortifies the tail, are made from hardwood; hickory is most common, but birch, ash and oak work well too. Select straight-grained lumber with no knots, cracks or other defects. The two core laminations are of softwood to minimize weight; spruce, cedar, fir or pine will do. The final ski will be a compromise between a heavy, mountain touring ski and a light, racing model. However, you can modify the thickness of the inner layers to obtain just about any degree of durability and rigidity.

Saw the hardwood strips to a thickness of ⅛ in. and the softwood core strips to a thickness of 3/16 in., both from stock 2½ in. wide. Plane and sand the sawn surfaces smooth.

The lamination lengths given in figure 1 will vary depending upon the length of your ski. Feel free to experiment; significant variation exists among the various commercial brands, so if your skis come out looking unusual, just act smug. Starting about 6 in. from the ends, plane the core layers to a gradual taper so they will make a smooth joint.

The bending form—This form consists of three separate units: the base plate, the T-shaped form used for the main body of the ski, and the form used to bend the tip (figure 2a). When in use these three parts are bolted together into a single unit. To manufacture skis of other lengths you will have to make other main body forms. However, the same base plate and tip-bending form can be used regardless of the ski length.

The base plate is made from a length of warp-free 1x4 lumber, at least 4 ft. long. Glue or nail several pairs of wooden blocks to it for attaching the main body with machine bolts.

The main body form is also made from a warp-free 1x4. Draw an outline of the ski bottom along one edge of the board. The recommended method is simply to trace the contour of a commercially made ski. If a ski of the appropriate length is not available, don't be afraid to make your own pattern. The main consideration is that you include a reasonable amount of curvature, or camber. You can draw a smooth curve by tracing along a thin strip of wood bent around a series of tacks in the body-form blank (figure 2b). Cut along the line using a jigsaw or coping saw, and smooth with a plane and a sanding block. Make sure this surface is square with the sides of the board.

Once the correct outline has been shaped, cut a number of notches at 4-in. to 6-in. intervals for inserting C-clamps during lamination. The form is completed by nailing on a 2¼-in. wide piece of ¼-in. plywood (figure 2c). Align the center of the plywood with the 1x4. The result is a form that is T-shaped in cross section. The upper surface is only ¼ in. thick, thus only small C-clamps are needed to assemble a ski.

The form used to bend the curved tip consists of a sandwich made from three layers of ¾-in. thick solid lumber or plywood (figure 2d). The curvature can be copied from a commercially made ski, or it can be drawn freehand. Try to achieve a smooth curve that rises about 2½ in. vertically in a horizontal distance of about 8 in. Note that the tip form is designed so that it slips over the front end of the main body form as shown.

Assemble the base plate, tip form and main body form using machine bolts. Sand the upper surface and apply one or more coats of shellac or varnish. When the finish has dried, rub on a coat of paste wax, to prevent the ski from sticking to the form during lamination.

Lamination—Begin by sorting out the pieces of wood you will need to build one ski. Dampen the first 12 in. or so of the hardwood strips using a rag dipped in hot water. This will reduce the amount of force needed to bend the curved tip. Coat one surface of each strip with glue, and place the resulting sandwich on the bending form, aligning one edge of the wood strips with one edge of the form. The strips should extend slightly beyond either end of the form. Tighten the clamps of the tip form so that the two hardwood layers are pressed against the form surface. Coat with glue both surfaces of the softwood core layers and the wedge-shaped tail piece, and slide them into position between the two hardwood layers. Use C-clamps with wooden pads to press all of these strips against the form. If you don't have enough C-clamps, you can cut C-shaped forms from scrap plywood that will slip over the clamping platform of the main body form (figure 3). Wedges between these C-shaped forms and the laminations will provide adequate clamping pressure. Avoid excessive pressure that would squeeze out too much glue and produce a weak bond. Remove exuded glue with a damp rag to make clean-up easier. Leave the ski on the form for about 12 hours to allow the glue to harden completely, although this time will vary according to the room temperature. Do not remove the ski from the form until you are certain that the glue has thoroughly cured.

Shaping—Use a coping saw or jigsaw to cut the tip to a point and to trim the tail to the exact length. Sand the ski to remove glue stains, and if necessary plane the edges parallel.

Next cut the center groove in the ski bottom using a router with an edge guide. This groove serves as a rudder to keep the ski pointed straight ahead as it glides through the snow; on most models the groove begins about 12 in. back from the tip of the ski for maneuverability. A straight, ½-in. dia. bit can be used for this task, setting the depth to about 3/32 in. Alternately, a core-box bit having rounded corners will make a more professional-looking groove.

Finally, it is necessary to plane the edges of the ski to obtain the proper

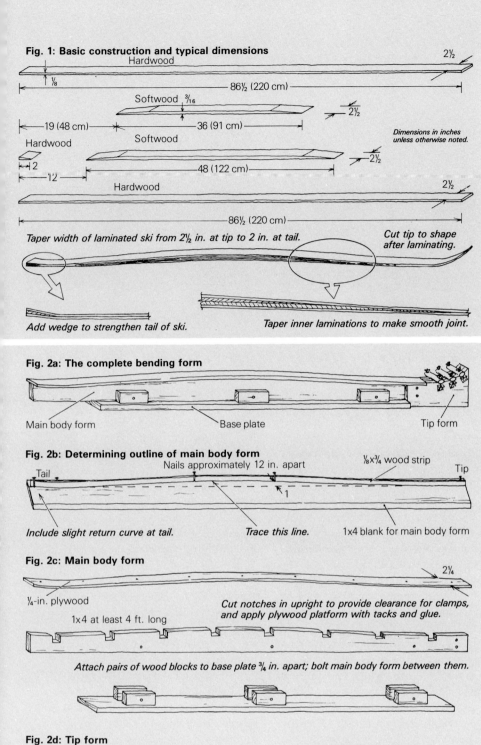

Fig. 1: Basic construction and typical dimensions

Hardwood

1/8

86½ (220 cm)

2½

Softwood 3/16

2½

19 (48 cm)

36 (91 cm)

Dimensions in inches unless otherwise noted.

Hardwood

Softwood

2½

2

12

48 (122 cm)

Hardwood

2½

86½ (220 cm)

Taper width of laminated ski from 2½ in. at tip to 2 in. at tail.

Cut tip to shape after laminating.

Add wedge to strengthen tail of ski.

Taper inner laminations to make smooth joint.

Fig. 2a: The complete bending form

Main body form

Base plate

Tip form

Fig. 2b: Determining outline of main body form

Nails approximately 12 in. apart

1/8 x 3/4 wood strip

Tail

Tip

1

Include slight return curve at tail.

Trace this line.

1x4 blank for main body form

Fig. 2c: Main body form

2¼

¼-in. plywood

1x4 at least 4 ft. long

Cut notches in upright to provide clearance for clamps, and apply plywood platform with tacks and glue.

Attach pairs of wood blocks to base plate ¾ in. apart; bolt main body form between them.

Fig. 2d: Tip form

¼

2½

¾-in. solid wood or plywood

8

¼-in. offset allows tip form to be bolted to main body form

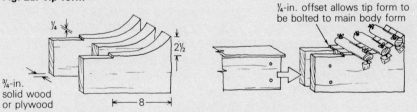

Fig. 3: Homemade clamps

Clamp for main body form

Tip-form clamp

¼-in. bolt

½-in. plywood

Wooden wedges

Attach angle iron to the tip form with wood screws.

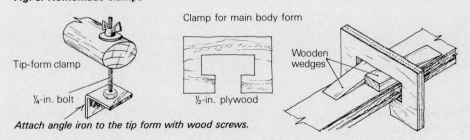

Drawings: Christopher Clapp

amount of side cut; the ski should be about ½-in. narrower at the tail than at the forward end, and the outline should be gently concave. Also relieve the bottom surface of the tail to produce a slight upswing that will enhance maneuverability. Perform whatever final sanding is necessary to remove tool marks or surface blemishes, then apply two or three coats of clear gloss varnish, sanding lightly between coats. Do not varnish the bottom surface of the ski, since this would prevent proper adhesion of ski wax. Instead, treat the bottom with a commercial base preparation such as pine tar.

Alternately, waxless skis can be made by routing the soles for mohair strips or multistep plastic bases. Both these materials are available from ski shops or the manufacturer—Rossignol, Industrial Ave., Williston, Vt. 05455.

To mount bindings, first locate the balance point of the ski by placing it across the edge of a thin wood strip. Pin bindings should be mounted so the leading edge of the binding is about 1 in. in front of the balance point. Heavy cable bindings should be placed on the ski in approximate position before determining the balance point. Then move the bindings slightly forward. When bindings are properly placed the ski tip should point downward at about a 20° angle when the user lifts the boot.

Now that your skis are completed, you can easily check the performance—just take them skiing. But before you leave the house it's possible to determine how well the degree of camber matches your weight. Place the skis side by side on a smooth floor, inserting a piece of paper between the skis and the floor directly beneath where your feet will be placed. Now stand on the skis as if you were actually out on a trail. If the paper can still be slid sideways with only slight friction, the camber is perfect. If it's not, there's not much you can do about it, except make adjustments in length and thickness of laminations in your next pair. But try your skis out first. Most cross-country skiers can tell little difference in performance from slight variations in ski lengths or degrees of camber. A less-than-perfect fit need not limit your fun. □

George Mustoe is a part-time geology technician and woodworker who lives in Bellingham, Wash.

Cross-Country Skis, Norwegian Style

by Richard Starr

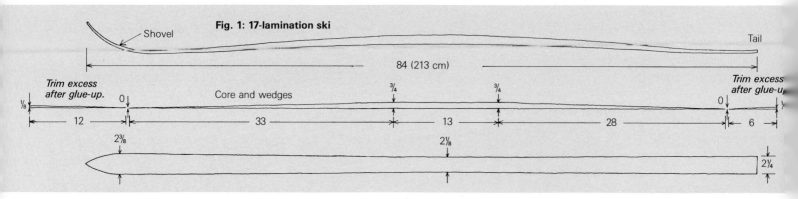

Fig. 1: 17-lamination ski

Shovel

Tail

84 (213 cm)

Trim excess after glue-up.

0

Core and wedges

¾

¾

0

Trim excess after glue-up

⅛

12

33

13

28

6

2⅜

2⅛

2¼

Walker Weed of Etna, N.H., has been making his family's cross-country skis since he learned the method in Norway some years ago. He taught the method at Dartmouth College where, until his recent retirement, he was director of the craft shops.

In the old days, when skis were of solid wood steambent to shape, you could stiffen your ski by rebending it to a deeper camber. Laminated skis hold their shape much longer than solid skis, but no adjustment is possible once the ski is glued together. The degree of stiffness must be accounted for during construction, and depends not only on camber but also on laminate thickness, type of wood and character of the particular pieces you use. There is an element of trial and error in learning to make well-tuned wooden skis. Modern skis, usually a combination of plastics or wood and plastics, perform better and require much less maintenance than those made of wood. You can buy a better ski than you can make, though high-quality skis are expensive. You'll save money and get extra satisfaction from running trails if you make the skis yourself.

Weed's method is a little more complex than Mustoe's (p. 152), but it produces stronger, lighter skis in pairs that will match more closely in balance and flexibility. This is achieved by laminating the ski across its width as well as across its thickness, and by systematic placement of matching laminations (figure 1). Also, the tips are reinforced with an extra lamination, and the sides of the softwood core are protected with strips of hardwood.

Weed uses hickory soles for toughness and birch tops to save weight. If you were to make both surfaces of the same wood, you could saw all four pieces for a pair of skis from a single piece of laminated stock. If you use different woods you must glue up separate pieces for tops and soles.

To make a 210-cm ski, the average size for adults, begin with a piece of straight-grained hardwood at least 86 in. long, 3½ in. wide, and an inch or so in thickness, depending on the thickness of your sawblade and on how many parts you will need from the lamination. Witness-mark the face of the board (figure 2), then rip it into six strips slightly more than ½ in. wide so that jointing or thickness-planing the sawn surfaces will yield ½-in. wide stock. Lay the strips in their original relationship according to the witness mark, then turn alternate strips end for end and upside down. By doing this you will distribute variations in grain and density through the lamination, resulting in a stronger ski. Glue the strips with Weldwood plastic resin or Cascamite (Elmer's plastic resin).

When the glue has dried, you have a lamination 3 in. wide and an inch or so in thickness. Witness-mark a side and an end of the lamination, then joint one face and thickness-plane its opposite face. Saw a strip 3/16 in. thick from one face, plane the newly exposed face of the lamination and saw off the next strip. If you are using a single laminated blank for soles and tops, number the strips as they come off and use adjacent pieces in matching positions in each ski. Plane each strip ⅛ in. thick, backing it with a piece of plywood while planing.

The stock for the core is 76 in. long, 3 in. wide and 2 in. thick, laminated across the 3-in. width. Out of this will come two blanks ¾ in. thick. The center is three ½-in. wide softwood strips (spruce is best), with outer layers of ¾-in. wide hardwood. You make this lamination from scraps, but for maximum strength and match, flip the central softwood strip end for end, as in the procedure described above, and use hardwood cut from the same board and arranged as shown in figure 3. After gluing, saw the lamination across the gluelines and plane the two pieces to ¾ in. by 3 in. by 74 in.

Cut the wedges and cores from these strips using the dimensions in figure 1. Supported on a wedge made from scrap, Weed puts these pieces through a thickness planer to get a perfect taper feathered down to zero thickness. (See "Tapered Laminations" by Jere Osgood, *FWW* #14, Jan. '79, pp. 48-51).

Weed's bending form (figure 4) is simpler than Mustoe's, though it requires more material and larger clamps. Laminate a block of solid or fir plywood 3 in. by 7½ in. by 90 in. Square it up, then scribe the shape of a good ski on the wide face. After bandsawing, smooth the curved surfaces, checking across the curve for squareness to the sides. Cut a series of steps on the front end as clamp seats, screw five or six aligning blocks along each side and wax everything likely to come in contact with glue. To clear the clamp ends, rest the form on horses or support it off the workbench on blocks. Weed suggests using a clamp every 3 in. or closer. If you run short, make clamps from hardwood strips and carriage bolts as shown in figure 4. From ¼-in. plywood scraps, cut 3-in. wide strips and butt them up against one another to cover the length of the ski and protect it from clamp damage.

When using Cascamite or Weldwood plastic resin, always dampen the wood with a rag to avoid dehydrating the glue. Apply adhesive to both surfaces with a brush and be sure to leave no dry spots. Clamp the ski from one end to the other or from the middle toward the ends, but never at random. Be sure the witness marks (top and edge) of corresponding pieces are in the same positions when gluing up the second ski.

Rather than scraping and chipping off dried glue, Weed saves time by belt-sanding it off, since these glues don't clog sandpaper. With the cleaned edge bearing on the fence of the table saw, he trims the other edge straight, using a carbide-tipped blade. Then, reversing the ski and setting the fence in a little, the sanded edge is sawn clean and straight. The ski now has parallel edges.

To cut the round-bottom groove in the bottom surface to help the ski track straight, Weed uses a molding head on a table saw (figure 5). The groove must be less than ⅛ in. deep to avoid cutting through the bottom lamination, and should be about ½ in. wide; a cutter whose radius is ½ in. will do the trick. Clamp a board about 8 in. wide to the saw as shown in figure 5, and raise the running cutter up through it; the board functions as a short table to accommodate the ski's camber. Set the fence so the groove is centered on the ski, and check the depth setting on a piece of scrap. The ski's groove starts just behind the shovel and ends just before the tail; mark these positions on the ski's top. By matching these marks with lines on the saw fence indicating the position of the cutter, you can start and end the groove quite accurately.

Relieving the sides to produce a concave contour in plan gives better edge bite in the snow and assures that the track cut by the shovel is wider than the rest of the ski. It is usually a gentle curve rather than a straight taper. You can take three width dimensions from an old ski, at the shovel, foot and tail, or use measurements given in figure 1. Be sure that the side camber is centered on the groove, and use a long, flexible batten through the three points to get a smooth curve. Bandsaw the sides, cut the tip shape, and smooth all edges with spokeshave and sandpaper. Chamfer the top corners but leave the bottom corners square. □

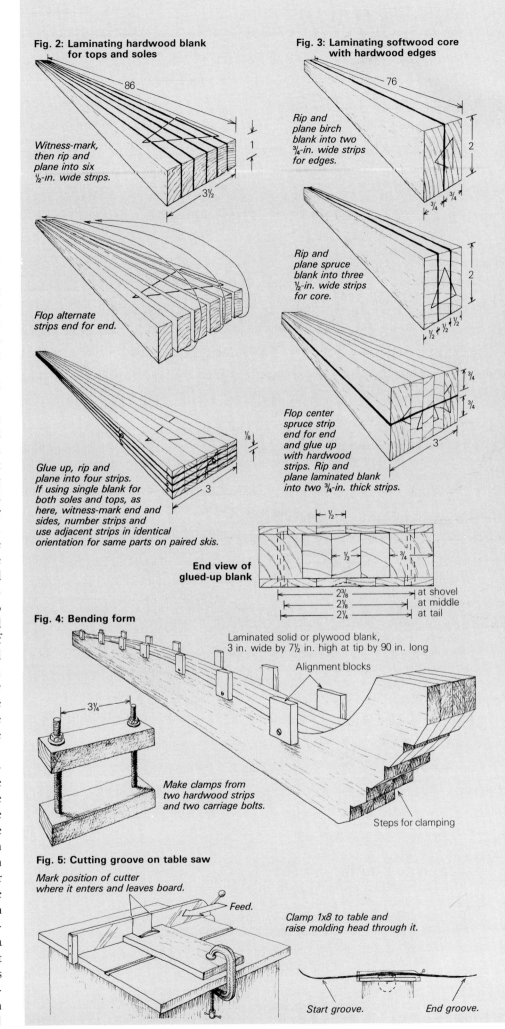

Fig. 2: Laminating hardwood blank for tops and soles

Witness-mark, then rip and plane into six ½-in. wide strips.

Flop alternate strips end for end.

Glue up, rip and plane into four strips. If using single blank for both soles and tops, as here, witness-mark end and sides, number strips and use adjacent strips in identical orientation for same parts on paired skis.

Fig. 3: Laminating softwood core with hardwood edges

Rip and plane birch blank into two ¾-in. wide strips for edges.

Rip and plane spruce blank into three ½-in. wide strips for core.

Flop center spruce strip end for end and glue up with hardwood strips. Rip and plane laminated blank into two ¾-in. thick strips.

End view of glued-up blank

2⅜ at shovel
2⅛ at middle
2¼ at tail

Fig. 4: Bending form

Laminated solid or plywood blank, 3 in. wide by 7½ in. high at tip by 90 in. long

Alignment blocks

Make clamps from two hardwood strips and two carriage bolts.

Steps for clamping

Fig. 5: Cutting groove on table saw

Mark position of cutter where it enters and leaves board.

Feed.

Clamp 1x8 to table and raise molding head through it.

Start groove.   End groove.

Methods of Work

Expanding-action bracelet mandrel

Here is an effective mandrel for turning the outside contours of bracelets. You'll need an arbor (made for using buffing and grinding wheels on the lathe), a rubber stopper and a small piece of ¼-in. thick plywood. Turn the rubber stopper to a ⁵⁄₁₆-in. thick, 2⅝-in. wide disc. This diameter works well for bracelets, which usually range from 2⅝ in. to 2¾ in. in inside diameter. Turn also two ¼-in. plywood discs—one to a diameter of 3 in., the other to 2½ in. Assemble the mandrel with the arbor's steel washers to the outside and the rubber disc sandwiched between the plywood discs as shown.

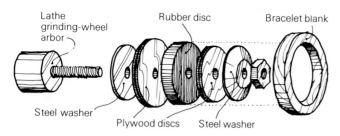

Lathe grinding-wheel arbor · Rubber disc · Bracelet blank · Steel washer · Plywood discs · Steel washer

To use the mandrel, cut the inside of the bracelet blank with a circle cutter, bandsaw the outside to rough shape and slip the blank over the rubber disc. Now tighten the nut. The rubber will expand uniformly to exert enough pressure to hold the bracelet. Turn one side of the outside contour, then reverse the blank and turn the other face.

This method could be adapted to napkin rings and other ring-shaped objects by sizing the rubber and plywood discs to the project. —Max M. Kline, Saluda, N.C.

Approximating angles

Here's a surprisingly accurate procedure to estimate angles using only a rule and a compass. First, draw a circle with a radius of 5¾ in. Now say you want a 10° angle. Mark off two points one inch (a 1-in. chord) on the circumference. Join the two points with the center of the circle, and the resulting angle is almost exactly 10°. If you want 20°, just lay out two 1-in. chords (not one 2-in. chord). Use fractions of an inch or just split the distance by eye for angles less than 10°. For large angles lay out multiples of 60° (using the compass to set the circle's radius), then add or subtract 1-in. (10°) slices to get the angle you want. —Jules Paquin, Laval, Quebec

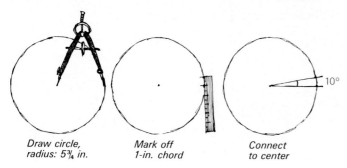

Draw circle, radius: 5¾ in. · Mark off 1-in. chord · Connect to center · 10°

Laminated leather hinge

This hardware-free leather hinge is laminated into the wood to be revealed later by routing. Faced with designing some wooden book covers, I decided to use thin, home-laminated plywood for strength. To allow the covers to flex when the book opened, I embedded a 1-in. wide strip of thin leather in the center of the 5-ply veneer stack. After the plywood glue cured, I used a ⅛-in. straight router bit to rout away the two plies of wood on the top and on the bottom of the leather hinge. To achieve precise depth control I used paper shims between router base and book cover, removing one sheet at a

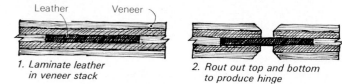

Leather · Veneer

1. Laminate leather in veneer stack

2. Rout out top and bottom to produce hinge

time until the depth was exactly right. Although I chamfered the edges of the routed groove by hand, it is possible to chamfer with a V-groove bit. The width of the routed groove depends on the thickness of the plies and the required travel of the flexing pieces.

I would not use this hinge for a vertical cabinet door but it would work fine in many horizontal applications such as the top of a lap desk. There is no crack for dust to get through. The general principle might be useful in making tambours as well. Just keep in mind that the leather hinge must be routed out of the surrounding stock if it ever wears out.

—James. D. Thomson, Toronto, Ontario

Chest lid stop

Here is a sketch of a chest lid stop that has worked well for me. It is simple to make and is completely out of the way when the lid is closed. The stop consists of two brass or aluminum plates, a short length of ball chain and a 30-caliber hollow-point bullet for weight. Drill a hole for the bullet in the side of the box and inlet the two plates to complete the construction. Be sure to position the top plate right over the bottom plate. Other construction details are shown in the sketch. —John Warren, Eastham, Mass.

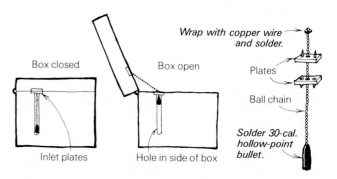

Box closed · Box open · Wrap with copper wire and solder. · Plates · Ball chain · Solder 30-cal. hollow-point bullet. · Inlet plates · Hole in side of box

Adjustable table feet

If the floor is not even, a small table will rock despite your efforts to have cut all four legs to the same length. These adjustable feet solve the problem better than cardboard or wooden shims, the usual solution. To make the feet, tap the head of a #10 or #12 wood screw to accept a #4-40 machine screw. Drill ½-in. holes in each table leg, then assemble the dowel-plug feet as shown below. Loosen or tighten the screw to adjust the foot.

—J.A. Hiltebeitel, S. Burlington, Vt.

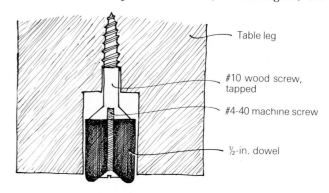

Table leg · #10 wood screw, tapped · #4-40 machine screw · ½-in. dowel

Making wooden checkers

Here's my method for making wooden checkers on the drill press. First grind the point off a 1½-in. spade bit. Only one side of the bit cuts, so grind it to the shape shown in the sketch (below) and sharpen. Grind the other side of the bit back so it won't touch. Next, make a wooden jig with a ¼-in. deep, 2½-wide channel as shown. Install a ¼-in. dowel near one edge. Clamp the jig to the drill-press table, aligning the dowel with the centerline of the chuck.

Use 2½-in. wide, 5/16-in. thick material for the checker blank (I use walnut and maple). Drill ¼-in. registration holes along one of the checker blanks, making sure the holes are the same distance from the edge as the ¼-in. dowel is from the edge of the jig. Place the blank in the jig with a hole over the dowel. Set the drill press at its fastest speed and lower the bit ⅛ in. or so into the blank. You may have to experiment with the depth to get the checkers to stack right. After shaping the top sides of all the checkers with the spade bit, use a fly cutter to cut almost through the blank. Grind another fly

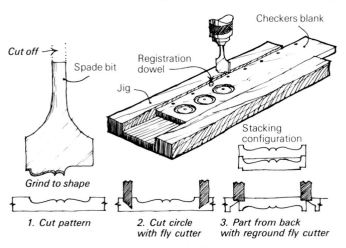

Cut off →

Spade bit

Grind to shape

Checkers blank

Registration dowel

Jig

Stacking configuration

1. Cut pattern

2. Cut circle with fly cutter

3. Part from back with reground fly cutter

cutter so it will cut square, turn the blanks over and part the checkers with a shoulder as shown above. The shoulder of one checker should mate with the shaped cavity in the top of another for stacking.   —*Larry W. Brewer, Roanoke, Va.*

Making toy wheels

Hardwood wheels for toys are expensive, not well sanded and do not come in many varieties of wood. I tried making my own, but the work was prohibitively time-consuming until I came up with the modified screw center I now use. With it I can turn out a wheel every four minutes on production runs.

I started with a standard morse-taper screw center (Sears) that I modified in two ways. First, I drilled and tapped the tail of the screw center to accept a ¼-in. drawbolt which holds the tapered shaft tight from the back of the headstock through the spindle. The drawbolt is simply a length of threaded rod with a washer and wing nut. The second modification was to remove the screw center. This leaves a ¼-20 threaded hole for attaching the work.

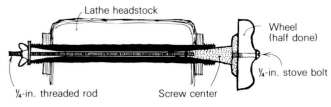

Lathe headstock

Wheel (half done)

¼-in. threaded rod

Screw center

¼-in. stove bolt

I cut the wheel blanks from scrap using a hole saw with a ¼-in. pilot bit. Then I mount a blank on the modified center with an ordinary stove bolt. It takes about a minute to shape

and sand each side. I try to completely finish one side before I turn the wheel around. While shaping, make sure the hub area is slightly thicker than the wheel rim for clearance.

For axles on toys, I use ¼-in. stove bolts screwed into a hidden nut mortised and epoxied in the vehicle's side. This is stronger and longer-lasting than wooden axles and allows the owner to take apart the toy and put it back together.
     —*George Pilling, Springville, Calif.*

Fluting jig

This jig routs accurate and consistent flutes on tapered turned legs. The jig is a U-shaped plywood channel as wide as your router base, mounted to the lathe bed. Dimensions will vary according to your router base and the peculiarities of your lathe bed. Attach two router-support strips to the inside of the jig with bolts and wing nuts through slotted holes so the strips can be angled parallel with the tapered leg.

To use the jig, first turn all legs to shape, then mount the jig to the lathe bed. Chuck one leg between centers, locking it into position with the index head. Now set the router-support strips parallel with the turned workpiece. To do this, simply set a board (as wide as the interior of the jig) on the work and tighten the support strip's wing nuts with the strips resting on the board. Remove this adjustment board and fasten stops to the support strips so each flute will be the same length. Now you're ready to rout the flute. Use the holes in the lathe's indexing head for accurate spacing of the flutes around the leg.   —*John Sanford, Camden, Maine*

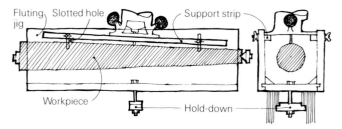

Fluting jig

Slotted hole

Support strip

Workpiece

Hold-down

Cutting corner bridle joints

This procedure eliminates the tedious fence adjustments and frustrating 1/32-in. errors that go with cutting open mortise-and-tenon joints on the table saw. It is based on a thin auxiliary fence or shim that's exactly as thick as the saw kerf of the blade you're using. The shim stock, made of thin plywood (door skin) or surfaced from solid stock, should be as wide as your fence is tall, and should be long enough to clamp to your fence—say 8 in. by 16 in.

To use, set up the saw to cut the open mortise. Saw the mortise as usual by passing both cheeks of the stock over the blade. Do not adjust the fence to saw the tenon. Simply clamp the shim to the fence and saw out the tenon—first one face, then the other. The shim repositions the tenon stock just to the other side of the cut line. The joint will be just right.
     —*John F. Anderson, Bottineau, N.D.*
     and Ivan Hentschel, Kingston, N.J

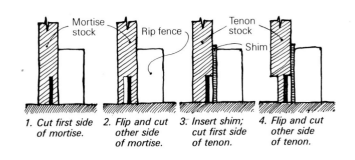

Mortise stock

Rip fence

Tenon stock

Shim

1. Cut first side of mortise.

2. Flip and cut other side of mortise.

3. Insert shim; cut first side of tenon.

4. Flip and cut other side of tenon.

SPECIALTIES

Making It Big
Constructing and carving large sculptures

by Federico Armijo

Quite by chance in 1972, after completing a commission to design and make sculptured door handles and benches for a shopping mall in Phoenix, Ariz., I got a phone call from the developer asking if I would be interested in creating a large-scale sculpture for the Sears Court in the same mall. I was elated. I'd always wanted to do a large-scale piece, and here was my opportunity. Two months later my studio completed the 20-ft. high oak sculpture. It

Large-scale sculpture demands careful planning and close cooperation between builder, client, structural engineer and installation crew. Above, Armijo's oak sculpture for the Sears Court in Phoenix is 20 ft. high and weighs close to six tons. Right, 30-ft. sculpture of laminated 8/4 Philippine mahogany at the Broadway Court Mall in Phoenix leans 5° and is supported by an I-beam that runs through the central spine and is anchored in a concrete footing below. The cement base was poured after the sculpture was installed.

weighed six tons and required a crew of seven people to build.

Though the following is a description of how I planned and built another of my commissioned pieces, the sculpture for the Broadway Court in Phoenix, the basic design and construction techniques I'll talk about can be adapted to handle almost any large-scale project requiring long, heavy laminations. For example, variations of the clamping form I'll describe later could be used to make laminated beams for curvilinear roof structures or other architectural components. A good source of general information about large laminated beams is Chapter 10 of the *Wood Handbook,* published by Forest Products Laboratory, U.S. Dept. of Agriculture. Write to the U.S. Government Printing Office, Washington, D.C. 20402, and ask for stock #0100-03200.

The Broadway Court sculpture is 30 ft. high, weighs two tons and is made of Philippine mahogany. Its design began with several meetings with the developer and the architect; the conversations centered around aesthetics, materials, costs and scheduling. Then I visited the site. Architectural drawings are helpful, but if you're going to comprehend the possibilities of the space, there's no substitute for seeing where the sculpture is supposed to go.

Designing a large-scale sculpture demands care and continual sensitivity to the relationship between the materials used and the composition of the piece. One mistake in judgment or planning, given the huge size and weight of such a sculpture, can turn into a serious financial loss or, even worse, injury to a workman or a bystander. Many things therefore must be considered—milling and fabricating the laminations, mobility of component pieces, transportation and setup of machinery, insurance and costing. And all of these factors must be kept in mind while you are still designing the piece.

The first step in the actual design is to construct a scale model from a series of

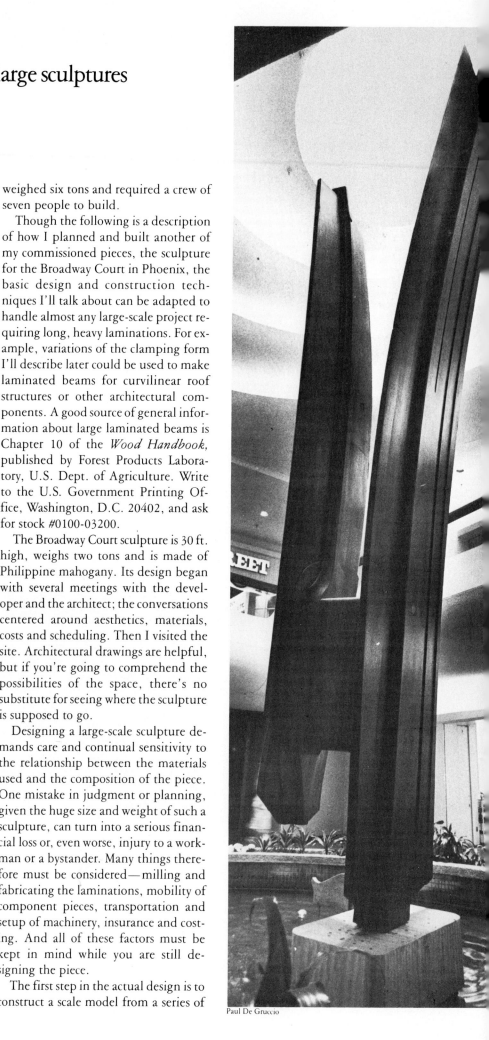

Paul De Gruccio

sketches. Sometimes, if the original idea is strong enough, I bypass the sketching process and compose directly on the band saw, working with suitable-sized scraps of wood. The modelmaking phase is slow, often taking a week or more to fully develop a pleasing design. Experience has shown me that for a formal presentation to a prospective client, it's best to have prepared two or three different models.

Because selling a design to a client involves a lot of subjective considerations on both sides of the bargaining table, you should have several "design packages" in your presentation, each of them within a different price range. Don't underestimate the importance of your presentation, and try to have a ready answer for every question you might be asked about design, materials costs and time schedules. Winning your client's confidence is necessary to getting his contract.

Once I'd gotten the contract for the Broadway Court sculpture and the model had been approved, I hired a structural engineer to study the model and to determine the minimal required sectional properties for static and dynamic stresses. His job was made more complicated because the sculpture leans 5° from vertical in one direction. On completing his assignment, he handed me 10 pages of computations, and I was legally bound to follow his specifica-tions in every detail. After purchasing several thousand board feet of 8/4 Philippine mahogany, we began to laminate the stock for one of the sculpture's 30-ft. long central beams and its adjoining wings or fans. Fortunately the design allowed for uniformly dimensioned plies throughout, though the length and thicknesses of the different lamina-tions varied. So our initial step was to glue up the stock for the plies by edge-joining 4½-in. widths of the 8/4 stock, which we cut alternately into 14-ft. and 16-ft. lengths. The boards were clamped so that the end-grain joints were stag-gered, and we reinforced these with dowels for added strength. When glu-ing was complete (we used Titebond throughout), we surfaced each ply to a finished thickness of 1½ in., having oriented the grain during assembly to minimize tear-out as the laminated boards were fed through the planer.

While one part of the crew was mak-ing the plies, another group was busy preparing the forms for laminating the curved beams, which when glued to-gether would form the basic shape of the sculpture. We began by making the base of the form from a number of wood py-lons (figure 1, detail A). We spaced these 2 ft. apart, then aligned them with a level/transit and bolted them to the concrete floor. Next we bridged the pylons with lengths of 6/4 fir planks, which we bolted onto the tops of the pylons (figure 1). We double-checked with the transit to make certain the base was absolutely level and perfectly straight. Wedges driven between the floor and pylons let us bring the whole length of the base into a single plane. This required a lot of tedious work, but to build an accurate, workable form re-quires a true base, else you'll end up with twisted laminations.

With the base complete we built the curved superstructure that would deter-mine the arc of the lamination (figure 2). Fir uprights (2x8s) were cut to appropri-ate length, depending on the part of the arc they supported, and then nailed to the ends of the pylons and cross-braced with short lengths of 2x4s. On the back side of the form, every other upright was cut to extend 12 in. above the surface of the form. Their purpose was to align the stacked laminations and to provide ver-tical clamping surfaces. The bed of the form we made from 6/4 fir planks sheathed with ¾-in. plywood to smooth out the junctures and add strength to the curved platform. Figure 2, detail B shows an end elevation of a typical pylon assembly. To finish the form, we covered it with plastic film so that glue squeeze-out from the laminations would not foul its surfaces.

First we laminated the two halves of the central supporting beam, each half consisting of six plies 1½ in. thick, 9 in. wide and 30 ft. long. Each board was

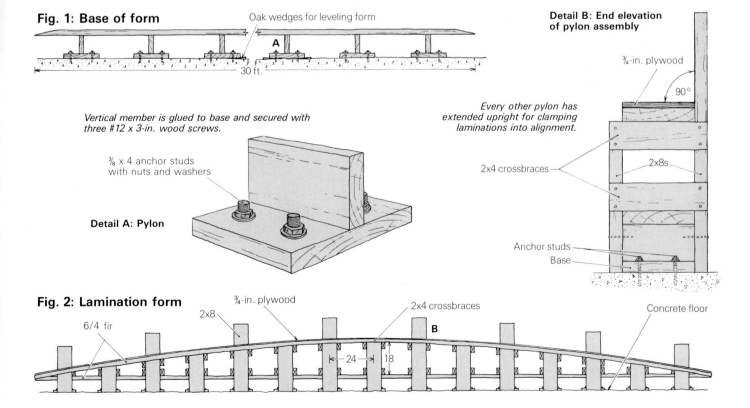

Fig. 1: Base of form

Oak wedges for leveling form

A

30 ft.

Vertical member is glued to base and secured with three #12 x 3-in. wood screws.

⅜ x 4 anchor studs with nuts and washers

Detail A: Pylon

Detail B: End elevation of pylon assembly

¾-in. plywood

90°

Every other pylon has extended upright for clamping laminations into alignment.

2x4 crossbraces

2x8s

Anchor studs

Base

Fig. 2: Lamination form

¾-in. plywood

2x8

2x4 crossbraces

B

6/4 fir

24   18

Concrete floor

scraped free of mill marks left by the planer, which was carefully tuned and adjusted to produce no snipes that would interfere with the strength of the glue lines. Making sure that all gluing surfaces were clean, we oriented the grain the most advantageous way, staggered the butt joints in the plies and stacked the boards on sawhorses in their proper sequence so the first one on would be the last one off.

Gluing up a beam of this size required close cooperation among the three team members to eliminate unnecessary, time-wasting movements and foul-ups that might ruin the lamination. Gallon glue bottles were prepared, and 100 bar clamps were adjusted and placed into positions along the form where they could be gotten to quickly, and the whole procedure was rehearsed to ensure that everyone understood what to do and when to do it. To keep the glue from setting too quickly, we stopped the airflow through the shop. One person poured a substantial bead of glue down the center of each ply, while another spread it evenly. Then all three men placed the ply on the form. Spreading the glue and stacking the plies was done as rapidly as possible, and when all six plies were stacked, we clamped them to the extended uprights (figure 3) using battens to align them before we clamped them down to the curved surface of the form. The clamps holding the plies in alignment against the uprights weren't so tight as to make clamping downward difficult. We also used battens across the width of the plies to provide even clamping pressure. To avoid bubbles and ensure uniform distribution of the glue, we began clamping the beam in the center and proceeded outward to the ends.

The next day we removed all of the clamps and scraped off the excess hardened glue. Then with the help of roller tables to support the curved beam, we ran it through the thickness planer to joint the edges. The second half of the main beam was made in exactly the same way, and when it too was jointed with the planer, the two surfaces mated perfectly. Before gluing the two halves of the main beam together, we slotted the bottom portion of it to receive an I-beam, which became the supporting member of the sculpture.

After bolting it in place we glued the two halves together. Then the six curved laminations for the wings, each two plies thick, were glued to the main beam, three on each side, and staggered to form blanks for curved surfaces. The other half of the sculpture was fabricated in the same way, only it was not as long. These two halves were not to be joined until the entire piece was installed at the site, where they would be connected by a central mass of shaped wood and four 1-in. tempered steel bolts (figure 5).

Being interested in making the wings graceful, slightly concave and convex forms along the length of the sculpture, I devised a sliding jig for my portable circular saw and router (figure 4). Ingenious variations of this basic jig can produce more complex forms, but the simple one I made slid along the length of

Fig. 3: Laminating the beams

Align plies by clamping them with battens against the uprights with light pressure; then, working from the center out, clamp the plies to the form using battens across the top, one for each pair of clamps.

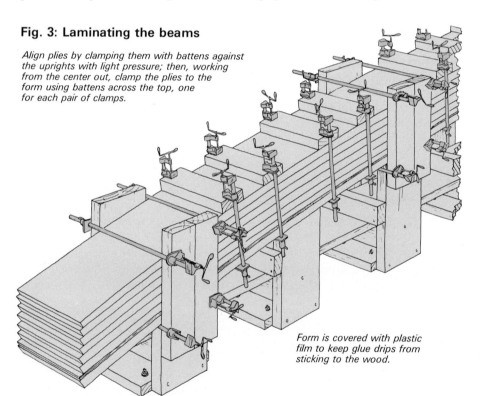

Form is covered with plastic film to keep glue drips from sticking to the wood.

Fig. 4: Jig for saw and router

First, mount circular saw in jig to waste most of the stock by cutting kerfs ⅛ in. apart. After removing ridges with hammer, level the resulting surface with router mounted in the same jig.

Use 3¾-in. long bit with ½-in. shank for clean, chatter-free cutting.

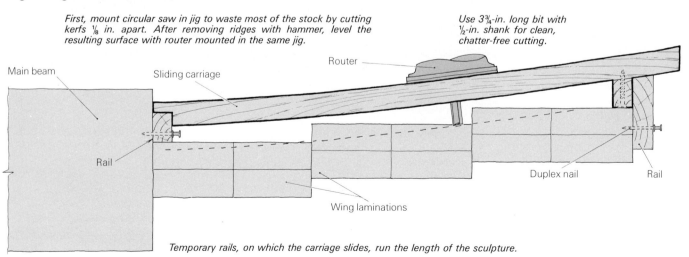

Main beam

Sliding carriage

Router

Rail

Wing laminations

Duplex nail

Rail

Temporary rails, on which the carriage slides, run the length of the sculpture.

the sculpture's wings and allowed me to cut a series of kerfs across the grain with the circular saw. Spacing the kerfs about ⅛ in. apart, it was easy to remove the rest of the wood by striking along the grain with a hammer. Next I mounted the router in the jig and leveled the surface using a ½-in. straight-face bit with a ½-in. shank. All four wings of the sculpture were treated in this manner, and we simply turned the jig over to produce the convex surfaces.

Turning the sculpture over was not an easy matter so we finished one side of each half before attempting to invert it. This was done with the use of an overhead chain hoist. To sand the surfaces, we used pneumatic sanders with foam-backed discs, which minimize swirl marks and gouges. In appropriate places we used vibrating sanders, and where necessary we sanded by hand. We started with 80-grit silicon-carbide abrasive and then finished the surfaces with 120-grit paper. Given the size of the piece and the fact that I was going to lacquer it, further sanding and smoothing seemed a waste of time.

First we stained it with Watco "decorator red." Then we stained with "black Danish oil" to get the look of vermilion (padauk), followed by a coat of Thompson water seal. Next came a coat of sanding sealer, followed by two coats of Sherwin-Williams moisture-resistant lacquer, rubbing between the sprayed coats with 400-grit wet/dry paper. With a wool wheel charged with buffing compound, we burnished the entire piece, then applied a final coat of natural Watco oil wiped off with a soft cloth. The sculpture glowed with a subdued luster.

We loaded the sculpture on a flatbed truck with a forklift in the middle of a blizzard. It was no fun at all. But the next day, sculpture and crew arrived intact in Phoenix.

We rolled the two halves of the sculpture into the mall on heavy-duty dollies where the crane operator could pick them up and hoist them into position—using a 12,000-lb. test nylon strap. Since cranes and their operators charge by the hour, I had met earlier with the operator, and we had rehearsed the whole installation process using a model of the sculpture. So the actual installation went quite smoothly. Figure 5 shows how the sculpture was mounted on its concrete footing.

For a project like this, I can't overemphasize the importance of communication and collaboration. It took the combined efforts of more than 50 people to see it through to the end. And from beginning to end, every aspect of the project was insured. Workmen's compensation protected the craftsmen in the shop from accidental injury; a general liability policy covered non-employees in the shop on business, and a product liability policy protected me against possible loss from an injury caused by a defect in the sculpture. I also required certificates of liability from the transportation company and from the crane company, and all of these policies and certificates became part of the contract file. If you decide to build a large-scale sculpture, be prepared to spend as much time in your office pushing paper as you do in your shop working wood. □

Federico Armijo, 34, of Albuquerque, N. Mex., makes sculpture, furniture and doors in wood, metal and stone.

Fig. 5: Sectional elevation of sculpture

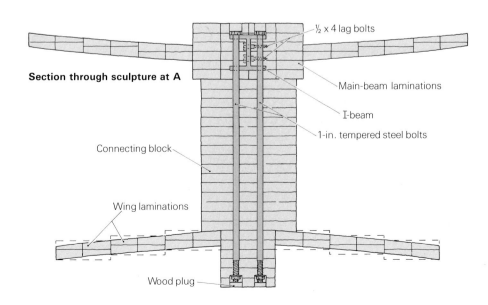

Section through sculpture at A

163

Small-Scale Cabinetmaking
With measured drawings for a roll-top desk

by James H. Dorsett

Four years ago I built a scale model of the Stanley-Whitman house in Farmington, Conn. It's a post-and-beam structure with a framed overhang, built in 1660. While I could have built a believable model using the plywood shell that is standard in miniature house construction, I chose instead to research and to replicate the framing of the original—stick by stick, joint by joint, from the sills up to the ridge pole.

Miniatures such as this have universal human appeal. As children, we don't have to be taught to enjoy dollhouses or model trains, and as adults only the most prosaic of us have outgrown a fascination with toys. We just develop more sophisticated tastes, appreciating greater realism in the objects we fancy. The more faithfully a model follows its full-scale original, the greater our wonder in beholding it. It is, after all, the contrast with the real world, pronounced in a miniature's detail, that captures the eye and stirs the imagination. And it is the execution of these minute details that most challenges the craftsman and rewards his efforts.

Scale cabinetmaking has become more than an increasingly popular hobby. The greater demand from collectors, and with it the higher prices they are willing to pay for commissioned pieces, have made modelmaking more attractive to serious woodworkers. Encountering the craft of making miniatures for the first time, the full-scale cabinetmaker will recognize similarities as well as differences between working full size and working to scale. To illustrate the shared and unique elements of miniature cabinetmaking, I will describe the construction of the ¹⁄₁₂-scale roll-top desk shown below, including

plans that could serve to help reproduce the original, down to the carving on the drawer pulls. This example will show how the scale modeler selects materials, buys, adapts and improvises tools, and devises special techniques to produce precisely detailed replicas in miniature. But first some discussion of the scale modeler's ethos is necessary.

In the past a dollhouse or a piece of doll furniture was judged for its visual impact, not for its structural integrity or its replicative accuracy. During the past ten years, as interest and sophistication in the craft have grown, there has been more attention to the fidelity of the replication to the original. Yet there are all kinds of miniatures being built, and a useful distinction can be made between *simulations*, essentially furniture for dollhouses, and *replications*, miniatures that conform to a particular scale and to the standards of construction and design of particular periods and prototypes. While various scales are currently used, ranging upward from ½ in.:1 ft., the de facto standard has become 1 in.:1 ft. This ¹⁄₁₂ scale, like HO scale in model railroading, combines the advantages of a reasonable level of achievable detail with an economy of space and material costs.

Though the movement has been toward more accurate replication, the other pole—simulation for affective impact—continues to help define the range of approaches the craftsman may take in designing and constructing a miniature piece. Simulation creates in the viewer the belief that the miniature is real, for if it is successful, he will perceive all of the form and detail that exist in the original, whether or not they are actually built in the miniature. The viewer will believe that joinery systems undergird the surface of the piece, that doors swing and that drawers may be opened.

On the other hand, replication's primary appeal is for the craftsman himself. Alone in his shop, he feels challenged to incorporate in the miniature details of cabinetry that may never be seen. He takes pride in the quiet integrity of his piece, and can, with an audience, show that his piece works.

Every miniature combines simulation and replication. In the best pieces there is a sensitive balance between the two. It is not only that materials reach a point of intractability, but also that the degree of perceived detail reaches a point of diminishing returns. Even if techniques, tools and materials allow the craftsman to model the detail of a shell or

This desk may look like the real thing, but it is only 4 in. high and 5 in. long. Built to ¹⁄₁₂ scale, it exactly replicates the full-size original, incorporating all its structural and decorative details. The measured drawings beginning on p. 166 show how to construct the miniature, or they can help in reproducing the original desk at full scale.

foliated carving, the viewer's eye need see only the primary and some secondary motifs to be convinced of the carving's quality and authenticity. To do more would look cluttered. Also, the scale cabinetmaker may deviate from exact replication in order to maintain the sense of proportion in the original piece. The heavy cabriole leg of a Chippendale chair, for instance, may be carved undersize on the miniature because the bulk of the precisely proportioned leg might overwhelm the visual balance of the miniature. Thus the aesthetic sense of the craftsman is the final arbiter between simulation and replication.

The tension between simulation and replication is not essentially a difference between greater or lesser levels of craftsmanship. Considerable skill, though often of different sorts, is required to do each well. Compare the dioramist—an architectural scale modeler who uses multiple vanishing points and other modes of artifice—with the tool-and-die maker, who must work to close tolerances. Both sets of skills mingle in the work of the experienced miniaturist.

The selection of materials for a miniature is critical to the success of the project, and points to the necessity of balancing replication with simulation. No matter how painstakingly accurate the planning and the execution of the construction of a piece may be, improperly chosen materials can ruin its effect. And the reason is plain. While dimensions lend themselves to scale reduction, texture often does not. Two materials that can quickly destroy the illusion created by the miniature are wood and fabric. Wood grain in particular is inherently resistant to scale reduction. Exactly replicating the materials of the original piece does not yield a successful miniature.

A successful miniature begins with a complete understanding of the original to be copied. In this respect the scale cabinetmaker is like his full-scale counterpart. The poorly designed and poorly made miniature typically reveals the builder's inadequate knowledge of full-sized furniture. Only beyond this common starting point do the differences between the scale modeler and full-scale cabinetmaker become apparent. The differences include design decisions, material selection, tool choice and use, and special techniques for achieving effects comparable to those in the full-scale craft.

I constructed the $\frac{1}{12}$-scale roll-top desk illustrated here as the design model for an article that appeared in *The Scale Cabinetmaker* 3:4 (Summer 1979, pp. 23-28). The structure and detail of the original were no mystery to me; it is my own office desk at which I have worked for years. I rescued it from the attic of a Kansas lumberyard and rebuilt it entirely. The design of the miniature began with a set of sketches and measurements of the original—useful in building either a full-size duplicate or a scale model. For several reasons, I chose to replicate the original as closely as tools and skills would allow. First, I wanted to see if a tambour curtain could be designed and built in scale that would articulate over the S-curves of the desk sides in the same way and with the same look as in the original. Second, I wanted to illustrate the use of machinist's slotting saws for cutting the mortise-and-tenon joints in the desk's rail-and-stile base and top panels.

Having decided to reproduce the frame joinery of the original, I decided to match the other joints as well—the dovetails in the drawers and the tongues and grooves in the pull-out writing boards. Actually, I excluded from the model only one feature of the original—the spring-loaded latching bars that lock the drawers shut when the tambour curtain is lowered. Originally I intended to make this hardware item as well, but in the end I let the challenge pass.

The original roll-top desk has quartersawn oak in its framing members and drawer fronts and plainsawn oak in the panels. But for use in the miniature, oak with its open pores and flaring grain is inappropriate. Miniatures require a medium-hard, close-grained, finely textured wood. For that reason, many miniaturists use satinwood, pearwood, holly, boxwood and cherry. Walnut, while widely used, varies considerably as a satisfactory material, according to its growth rate. Walnut from semi-arid regions is more likely to yield usable material for models than are faster-growing eastern varieties. Basswood is probably the most widely used material for miniatures because of its availability and low price. It is easily worked and offers the appearance of a wide range of full-scale grains from bird's-eye maple to quartersawn oak. However, while it serves as a ground for simulating a variety of wood grains, its short fiber and surface fuzz make tight joint lines and surface preparation a serious problem.

The scale cabinetmaker has the same jealous regard of his materials as does the full-scale woodworker, squirreling away select stuff against future need: pieces of crotch and burl, or boards with special grain. From such a pile I chose some quartersawn cherry for the desk. It was cut from a heavy branch rather than from a trunk section, where annual rings produce too broad a grain. The ray fleck in the cherry provides a believable substitute for the distinctive look of quartered oak. Lighter-colored boards I set aside for the pigeonhole unit; darker wood I used in framing the main carcase, and boards with a more pronounced figure I ticketed for panels.

I might have used commercially produced hardwood boards. However, such material is typically flatsawn, and therefore yields too few boards with useful figure. And it is commonly supplied in fractional rather than in scale thicknesses. If in a $\frac{1}{12}$-scale project the modeler wishes a board that is a scale 1 in. thick, commercial material offers him either $\frac{5}{64}$ in. or $\frac{3}{32}$ in. thick. Since in $\frac{1}{12}$th scale, one inch is 0.0833 in., the commercial stock is either 0.011 in. too thick or 0.005 in. too thin. So the scale cabinetmaker is better off ripping and sizing his own stock. The materials in the desk are precisely scaled to the materials in the prototype with one exception: the entire cubby unit was built of scale $\frac{1}{4}$-in. thick material even though some of the vertical and horizontal dividers in the prototype are $\frac{1}{8}$ in. thick. With scale lumber, a piece that is 0.0104 in. thick simply has no structural stability, and could not be used.

Tools and workbench techniques also change as scale reduction takes place. Some full-size shop tools are useful in preparing materials—table saw, bandsaw, jigsaw, jointer and thickness planer. However, beyond the useful limits of these tools, the maker of miniatures is forced by the inadequacies of the marketplace to become inventive in his search for functional precision tools. While it is possible to build an excellent miniature with a jackknife, as one outstanding craftsman indeed does, precision tools of high quality do increase the chances of achieving good results. The hobby industry produces some good-quality hand and power tools—knives, handsaws, clamps, power hand grinders, belt and disc sanders, and jigsaws. However, many hobby tools are either overengineered toys or underengineered tools. For example, small (4-in.) table saws with tilting arbors appear to incorporate all the features of a full-sized shop machine, but their

(text continued on p. 170)

Roll-top desk: front elevation

Plans are 1½ times the size of the miniature.

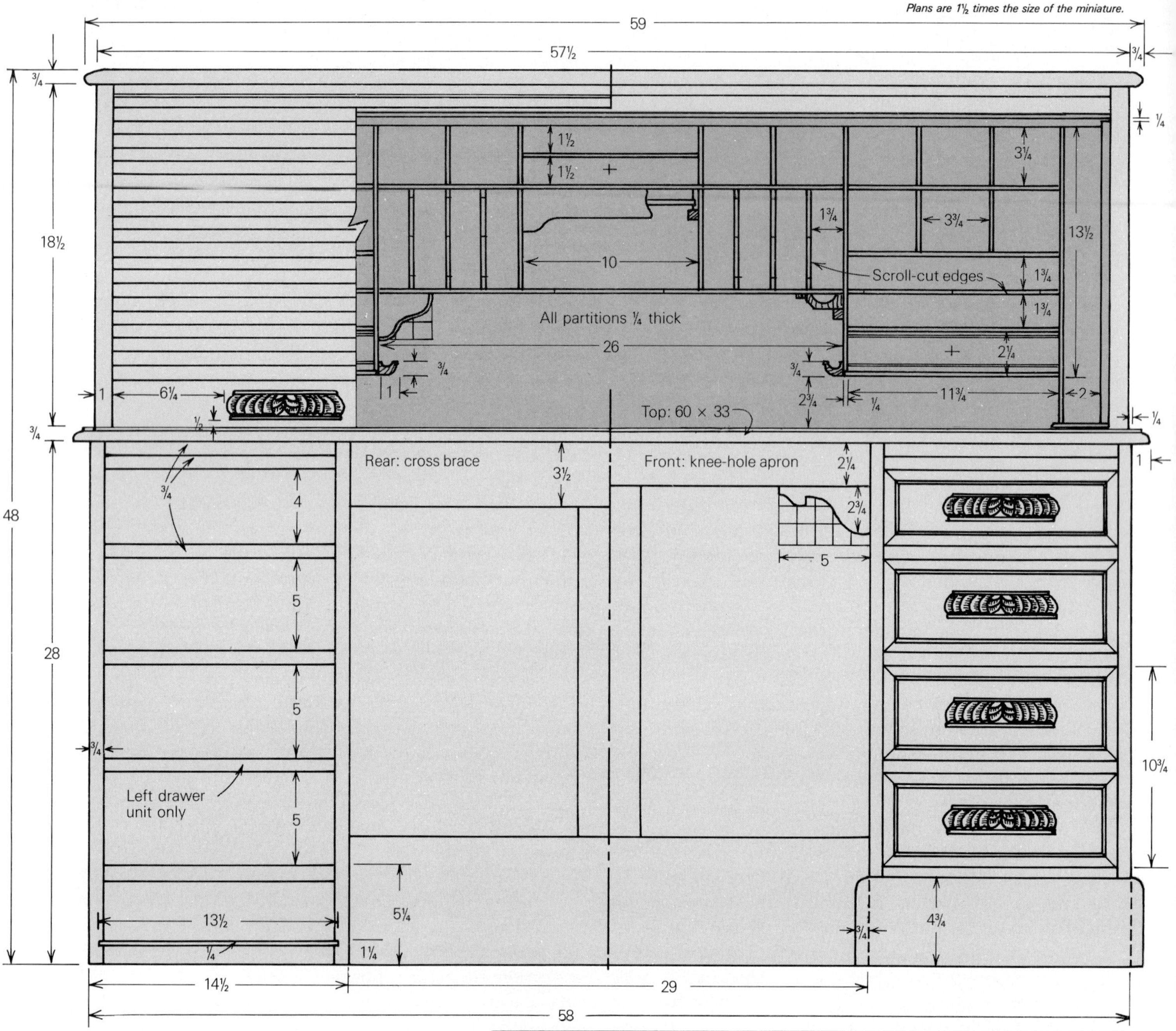
59
57½
¾
18½
48
28
1½
1½
10
1¾
3¼
3¾
13½
Scroll-cut edges
1¾
1¾
All partitions ¼ thick
26
2¼
¾
¾
1
6¼
2¾
¼
11¾
2
Top: 60 × 33
½
Rear: cross brace
3½
Front: knee-hole apron
2¼
2¾
5
4
5
5
5
Left drawer
unit only
10¾
13½
¼
5¼
1¼
4¾
14½
29
58

Typical of early 20th-century factory-made office furniture, the original desk was designed for machine production. If you use these drawings to make the piece full size in your own shop, you might want to improve upon the existing joinery. The main vertical dividers in the pigeonhole unit could be dadoed or routed for dovetail housings to receive the shelves. Likewise, the main shelves could be routed to receive the minor dividers. To secure the writing surface (desk top) to the drawer units, cut square, wedged tenons on the stiles at the four corners, and mortise the desk top to receive them.

Scroll profiles

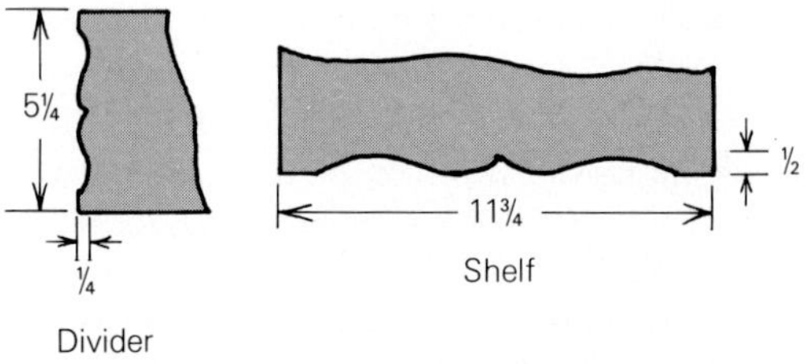
5¼
¼
Divider
11¾
½
Shelf

Plan of central shelf

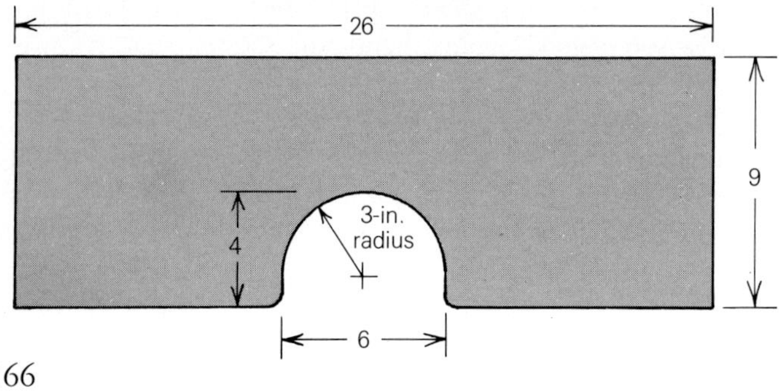
26
9
4
3-in.
radius
6

Drawer-pull detail

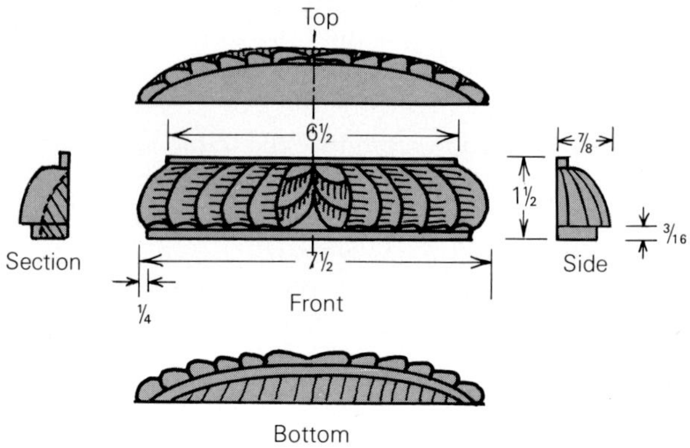
Top
6½
1½
⅞
3/16
Section
7½
Side
¼
Front
Bottom

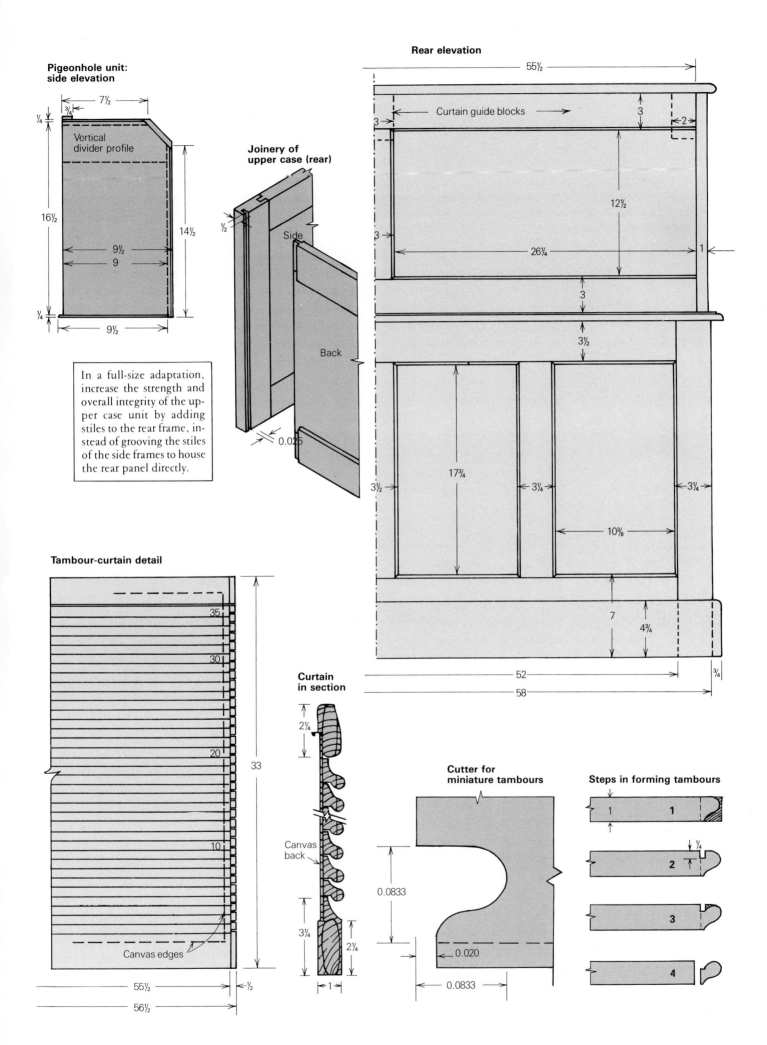

Pigeonhole unit: side elevation

7½
¾
¼
Vertical divider profile
16½
14½
9½
9
¼
9½

In a full-size adaptation, increase the strength and overall integrity of the upper case unit by adding stiles to the rear frame, instead of grooving the stiles of the side frames to house the rear panel directly.

Joinery of upper case (rear)

½
Side
Back
0.025

Rear elevation

55½
Curtain guide blocks
3
2
3
12½
3
26¼
1
3
3½
3½
17¾
3¼
3¼
10⅜
7
4¾
52
58
¾

Tambour-curtain detail

35
30
20
10
33
Canvas edges
55½
½
56½

Curtain in section

2¼
Canvas back
3¼
2¼
1

Cutter for miniature tambours

0.0833
0.020
0.0833

Steps in forming tambours

1
1
¼
2
3
4

Case assembly for left-hand drawer unit

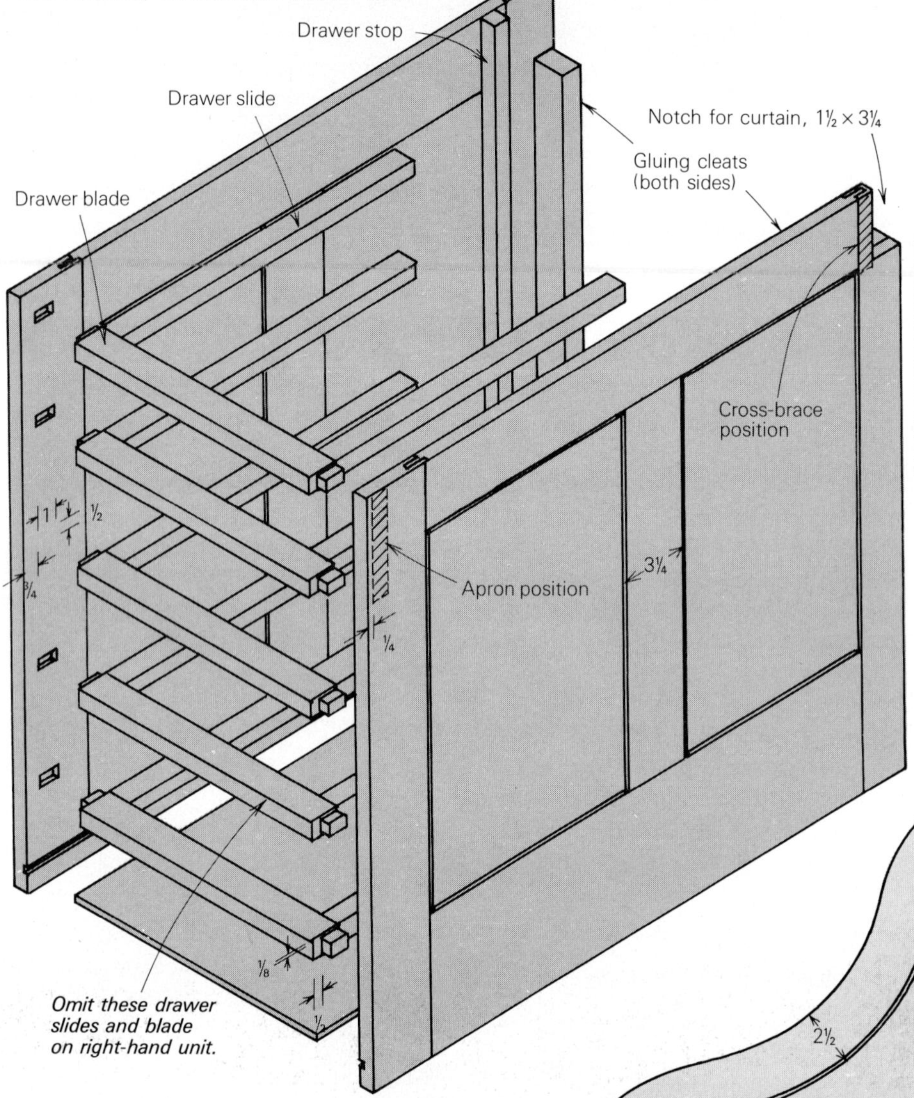
Drawer stop
Drawer slide
Drawer blade
Notch for curtain, 1½ × 3¼
Gluing cleats (both sides)
Cross-brace position
Apron position
3¼
1
½
¾
¼
⅛
½
Omit these drawer slides and blade on right-hand unit.

You can improve the case joinery of the original by increasing the length of the tenons on the frame rails and muntins. Double tenons on the drawer blades will make the drawer units stronger. In finding means for attaching the drawer guides to the inside of the case, be sure to take wood movement into account.

Side elevation

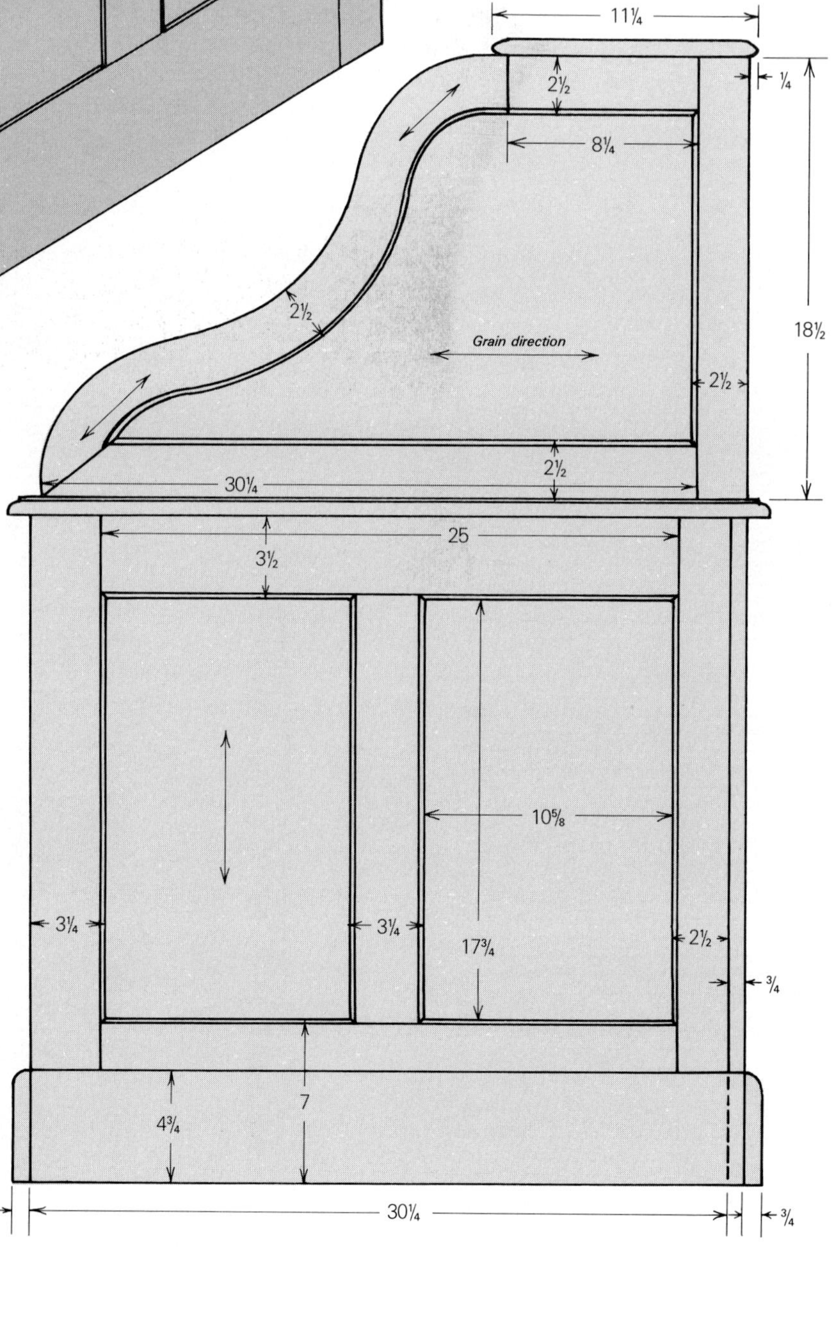
11¼
2½
¼
8¼
2½
Grain direction
18½
2½
2½
30¼
25
3½
10⅝
3¼
3¼
17¾
2½
¾
7
4¾
¾
30¼
¾

Frame assembly for drawer unit

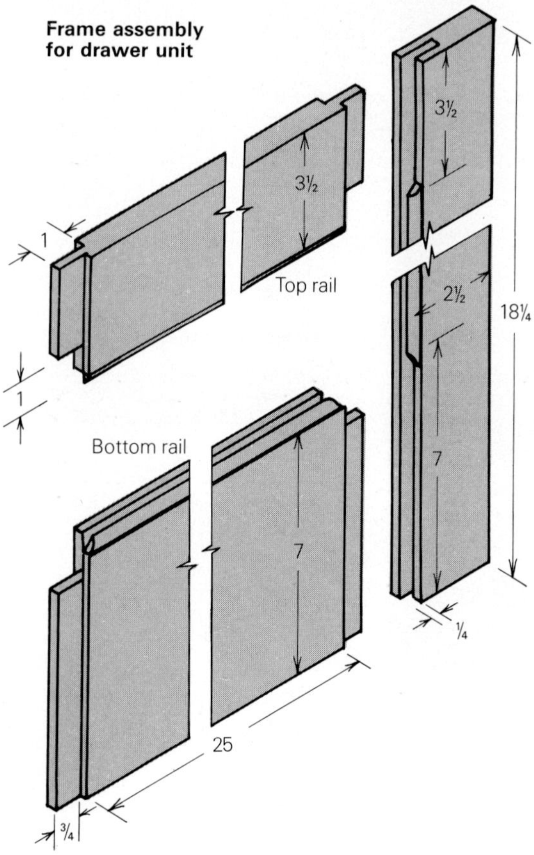
1
3½
Top rail
1
3½
2½
18¼
Bottom rail
7
7
25
¼
¾

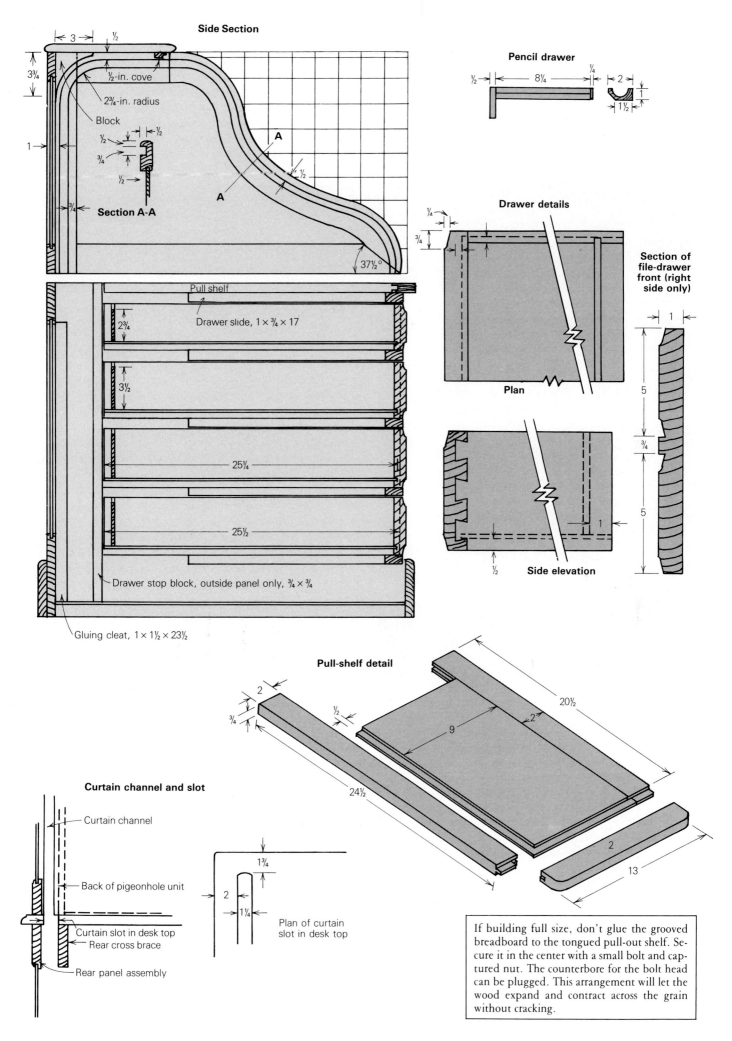

Side Section

3
½
3¾
½-in. cove
2¾-in. radius
Block
1
½
½
¾
½
Section A-A
A
A
½
37½°

Pull shelf
Drawer slide, 1 × ¾ × 17
2¾
3½
25¼
25½
Drawer stop block, outside panel only, ¾ × ¾
Gluing cleat, 1 × 1½ × 23½

Pencil drawer
½   8¼   ¼   2
1½

Drawer details
¼
¾
Plan

Side elevation
½
1

Section of file-drawer front (right side only)
1
5
¾
5

Pull-shelf detail
2
¾
½
2
9
20½
24½
2
13

Curtain channel and slot
Curtain channel
Back of pigeonhole unit
Curtain slot in desk top
Rear cross brace
Rear panel assembly
1¾
2
1¼
Plan of curtain slot in desk top

If building full size, don't glue the grooved breadboard to the tongued pull-out shelf. Secure it in the center with a small bolt and captured nut. The counterbore for the bolt head can be plugged. This arrangement will let the wood expand and contract across the grain without cracking.

169

To thickness his stock to precise dimensions, the author first sands to rough thickness using a drum sander mounted in his radial-arm saw and feeding the boards between the rotating drum and the fence.

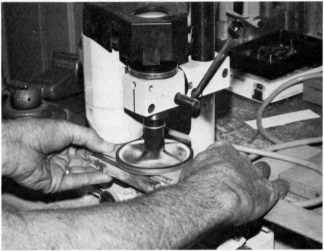

For final finishing, he chucks a sanding disc in his Unimat drill press and draws the stock between the disc and the milling table beneath.

A better method for thicknessing stock employs a tapered sanding disc mounted on a direct-drive mandrel opposite an adjustable fence. This device will give accurate results, thicknessing 1½-in. wide planks to tolerances of 0.003 in. edge to edge.

blades, bearings, fences, work surfaces and power lack the degree of precision and durability that is desirable.

Probably the most adequate and widely used power tools produced for the scale modeler are small machine lathes (Unimat, Sherline, Taig, Machinex). Yet even here the tools were not designed for the woodworking miniaturist. They are essentially down-sized versions of full-sized machine lathes, useful in metalturning. Still, offering such auxiliary capabilities as drill press, table saw, milling machine and disc sander, the small machine lathe is affordable, and essential.

Beyond the limits of available, useful hand tools, improvisation must be practiced at the miniaturist's workbench. Dental burrs and chisels become molding cutters and wood chisels. Jewelry-supply houses are another source of precision hand tools, from pliers to gravers. Small mills from tool-and-die supply houses become routing bits, and a machinist's depth gauge serves as a try square.

Measuring instruments vary with the degree of precision required by the project. Several high-quality 1-in. scale steel rules are available, marked off in scale increments of ¼ in., similar in function to the 1-in. architect's scale. Where finer measuring increments are required, scale dimensions are translated into decimal inches, and a machinist's 100th rule, dial caliper and micrometer are used. Unless your favorite form of masochism is the division of fractions, avoid the use of 1/16 scale in building miniatures. Given a scale dimension of 23½ in., for instance, it is much simpler to mark off the scale distance with a 1-in. scale instrument than to contend with a distance that is almost, but not exactly, 1⁶¹/₆₄ in. on a 1/16-in. rule. If greater precision is needed, the measured distance with a dial caliper is 1.9583 in.

Several tools required in the desk project illustrate the miniaturist's need to improvise. The basic problem in miniature projects is the need for precisely sized and thicknessed lumber. This desk called for scale lumber in the following sizes: ¼ in. (0.0208 in.), 5/16 in. (slightly undersize at 0.024 in. to fit the groove made with a 0.025 in. slotting saw), ½ in. (0.0416 in.), ¾ in. (0.0625 in.) and 1 in. (0.0833 in.). Short of investing in a planer that will work to these thicknesses, there are two alternative approaches. The more tedious and less satisfactory approach involves rough-sanding the lumber down to approximate thickness with a drum sander mounted against a 90° fence of a radial-arm saw. The semi-finished boards are then sanded down to final thickness with a flat disc mounted over a milling table in a Unimat drill press.

A better solution employs a thicknessing sander, as made by Jim Jedlicka (*The Scale Cabinetmaker* 4:4, Summer 1980). This tool, designed with the scale cabinetmaker in mind, employs an 8-in. tapered (2°) disc and is powered by a flea-market motor. In thicknessing 1½-in. wide boards, it is accurate to within 0.003 in. (edge to edge). In contrast with the chipping and splintering that often result with jointer knives on uneven or knotted grain, the disc grinds off the surface of thin stock without marring or chipping.

A second problem—cutting the system of tenons and grooves in the panel framing—I solved by using machinist's slotting saws. A 1½-in. dia. by 0.025-in. blade on a mandrel with a ⅜-in. arbor was mounted in a Unimat drill press over a table, which was in turn mounted to the lathe's cross slide. With a hardwood fence covering the blade, the height of the blade above the table could be controlled with the drill press and the depth of the cut with the longitudinal feed screw of the lathe. The setup produces joints that are crisp and precise. Blades are typically available in diameters ranging upward from ¾ in. and in thicknesses from 0.010 in. to 0.030 in.

The tambour curtain posed yet another problem. Because there is no commercial source for scale molding cutters, I had several options when special molding faces were required, as found on the beaded edges of the desk's stiles and rails or the S-profile of the tambours. Although some commercial moldings are available and can be adapted to a range of needs, these are typically supplied in basswood only. The desk moldings could have been cut with ball-and-cone dental burrs (as indeed the pencil shelves and drawers in the cubby unit were made), but hand-shaping of the finished profiles would have been required, destroying some of the crisp uniformity I wanted. So I chose another method. The needed molding profile is lathe-turned in mild steel. Flutes are milled on the end of the turned steel and dressed with pattern files, and then it is case-hardened. The resulting tool is not meant for production runs, but it does provide an adequate solution to a recurring problem in the craft.

Assembly always poses a variety of jigging and clamping difficulties, most of which are familiar to the full-scale woodworker. Sometimes the solution is unique to the particular piece being assembled. For that reason most miniaturists keep on hand an array of clamping tools—rubber bands, bulldog and alligator clips, C-clamps, spring clamps, handscrews, jeweler's ring clamps, clothespins and others. In assembling the desk base unit, for example, I often used two kinds of clamps—flat, magnetic holding jigs for clamping the flat panel sections, and violinmaker's clamps for holding the assembled pedestal. The jig consists of a flat, steel plate with pieces of 90° aluminum angle along two sides. Clamping is done with a number of small, square magnets, which hold the glued assembly in place. Violinmaker's clamps with their screw-tightened, cork-faced blocks provide a firm, but gentle, means of holding a carcase assembly during gluing.

The majority of miniaturists use either polyvinyl (white) or aliphatic resin (yellow) glue in assembly. Some of the high-viscosity, slow-set cyanoacrylates offer promise as general-purpose glues in modeling but are still relatively new. Regardless of the type of adhesive used, the woodworker's typical problem of pre-finish glue spotting is compounded in miniature cabinetry by the size of the workpiece. Pre-assembly sealing of the wood is a common solution, and excess glue is avoided. The desk was assembled with white glue, but a flexible polyvinyl fabric glue was used to attach the tambours to the linen back. The finish consists of a light wash of cherry stain and several light, rubbed coats of satin spray lacquer. Because the cherry will darken with age, the stain was optional. An equally desirable sealer might have been several coats of cut shellac (rubbed in). Sealer is used on a miniature to provide a finish without the type of surface buildup that will obscure the crispness of detail (or what one craftsman has called the appearance of "having been dipped in black molasses and drip-dried during a monsoon").

Had the function of the desk been only to fill out the illusion of an entire miniature setting, other design options could have been considered. The effect of the raised desk curtain could have been simulated with the application of only a few slats across the top of the open desk front. The structure of the pedestals could have been simulated through a system of flat, butt-joined boards to which fascia "rails" and "stiles"

Dovetail jig, patterned after its full-size counterpart and used in conjunction with a Dremel drill press and small tapered mills, cuts the joints for the drawers.

To cut moldings for limited runs, Dorsett equips his Dremel drill press with a shop-made cutter, left. To make a cutter, he turns the desired profile on a small bar of mild steel and then mills flutes in the sides. Once dressed and sharpened, the cutter is case-hardened.

For producing crisp and precise mortises, grooves and tenons, Dorsett uses a machinist's slotting saw mounted on a mandrel and driven by a horizontal miller. Fence and table register the stock.

would be glued. If carefully assembled and finished in this way, the joint lines could be made invisible and the appearance of the piece would be identical to that of the miniature employing mortises and tenons. Assuming that the miniature would never be subjected to the same stresses from use or changing humidity as would the full-sized desk, the simulated model should have proven quite durable and quite convincing. But I would have known the difference. □

Jim Dorsett, 51, of Pembroke, Va., is editor and publisher of The Scale Cabinetmaker, *a quarterly journal for miniaturists ($15 a year from Dorsett Publications, Inc., Box 87, Pembroke, Va. 24136).*

Carved Signs

Freehand lettering with the Murphy knife

by Roger Schroeder

Close to 200 of Paul McCarthy's signs adorn homes and proclaim businesses in the seaside town of Scituate, Mass. A 3-ft. wide carved clamshell hangs in front of a custom-framing shop; a jewelry store's sign features a wooden, in-the-round black pot overflowing with carved gems, and quarterboards with incised gold-leaf lettering are everywhere. Though originally mounted on a ship's transom beneath the quarterdeck, quarterboards have become popular on land, where they are most often applied directly to the side of a building, usually above a door. Apart from being a prolific carver (his shop produces about 40 hand-carved signs in a week), McCarthy is a teacher and conducts four classes a week, with 15 or 20 students in each.

McCarthy's lettering is done without templates or patterns, and also without a lot of carving tools. His primary tool, aside from a fishtail gouge, is the Murphy knife, named after the manufacturer in Ayer, Mass. This tool consists of a handle through which slides a high-carbon, chrome-vanadium steel blade. The blade itself ends not in a point, but a double-beveled skew. A setscrew allows for a variety of blade-length adjustments, and the cutting tip can be ground to different shapes. Whereas incised lettering has traditionally been carved using a variety of tools *(FWW #14, Jan. '79, p. 66)*, including straight chisels, gouges and V-tools, McCarthy uses only this knife. "Most books tell you to get a tool that fits each curve," he points out. "Well, if I had to have a tool that fit each curve in an italic S with serifs, I'd have to use five different tools." Many other sign carvers use a router, which, McCarthy says, he can beat if you include the time spent setting up the templates. In a matter of minutes he will freehand the letters to be carved using only parallel lines and a homemade bevel (two 1x1s joined with a wing nut). He can carve an eight-letter quarterboard in 20 minutes or less, whether the letters are Roman or italic.

McCarthy cuts into the letter using the point, not the flat, of the knife. Practice is needed, he will tell you, to establish the angle and depth of the cut. Starting inside the outline of the letter, especially if more than one pass is needed, as with large letters, he draws his entire arm down, with the back of his hand resting on the board. He advises choking up on the

knife, avoiding excessive pressure on the back of the hand. To cut the opposite side of a curve or straight line, he turns his hand over and follows the same procedure. For a large letter, the first incisions will take out waste wood in the center. The serifs require no other tool, for the Murphy knife naturally follows the tightest curves.

The advantages of the knife are clear. Not only can it adapt to any kind of lettering style, but it also slices wood as opposed to crushing or splintering it. The problem with the V-parting tool, often used for cutting the channel in a letter, is that it has two cutting edges. While one may go with the grain, the other will go against it. Aware of this, McCarthy deals with wood grain as though it were the wind, and he follows it to get around curves.

As a boy, McCarthy loved whittling and he liked nautical art. All this led to his profession, which has now spanned over a decade. In that time McCarthy has taught some thousand students and has carved an estimated 16,000 pieces that include birds, quarterboards and elaborate signs. Aside from making what is probably the largest quarterboard in the country, for the U.S.S. Constitution Museum in Boston, he has carved an American eagle that stands 8 ft. high and has a wingspan of 13 ft. It is styled after the figurehead made by New England shipcarver John Bellamy in 1880 for the U.S.S. Lancaster. McCarthy's eagle lives in his shop.

Calls for his work come from all over the country, and a personalized sign that may have relief or in-the-round carving is his specialty. "I'm not a supreme artist," he says, "I want people to participate in the designs." So he is careful to get as much input from a customer as he can. First he might ask where the sign is to be hung. Then he will inquire about the kind of house the customer owns, its color, its landscaping. He will refuse a commission if he thinks a carved piece is inappropriate to its surroundings.

Sketching in front of a customer, McCarthy looks for what he calls a glint of satisfaction. Once found, he elaborates on the design. His interest in the customer's approval extends beyond the date of delivery, and he will repair signs that might get damaged. "It's always my sign, no matter how much a customer spends," he says. And he gets a lot of repeat business, especially from people who give his signs as gifts. Most people want quarterboards, which McCarthy believes to be "visible and in good taste, without being showy." Some

---

Roger Schroeder of Amityville, N.Y., is a frequent contributor to this magazine.

Quarterboards like this one are everywhere in Scituate.

Originally meant for ships, they now adorn buildings.

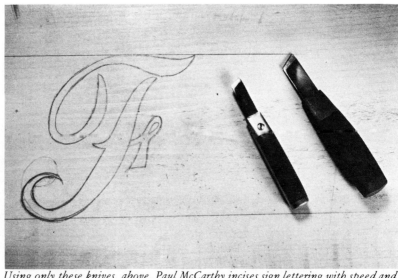

Using only these knives, above, Paul McCarthy incises sign lettering with speed and accuracy. The tips of both knives are ground to about 45° and have a bevel on both sides. The finished letter, left, shows none of the transition marks caused by using several different gouges for different parts of the curve. For results like this, the knife must be kept razor-sharp with frequent honings.

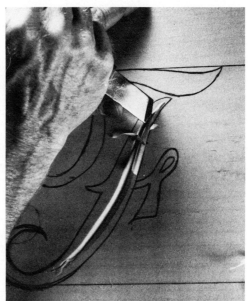

Carving begins (photo, left) by making a narrow V-trough down the stem of the letter. Back of right hand rests on work for downward strokes; thumb of left hand helps guide and power the cut. For upward strokes (photo, right), right hand is held off the work surface; thumb of left hand still provides guidance and force at the back of the blade.

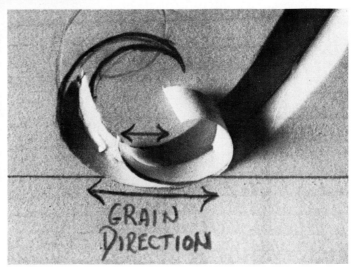

The trough is gradually enlarged with successive cuts, each taking a thin shaving, to keep the knife from digging in. Above, a final cut forms the finished wall of the mid-section of the stem. In tight curves (photo, right), direction of cut must be changed often to avoid going against the grain and tearing the wood. This is what McCarthy means by "following the grain like the wind."

Made for a Scituate restaurant, sign at right sports a carved lobster and clams in-the-round. The incised lettering and little shell at top are gold-leafed. Sign at left was made for the same restaurant.

customers like double-sided signs. One he made for a liquor store in Scituate Harbor has a wine cask with the merchant's name on either side. To save a customer's money, he suggests that one side should be elaborate, the opposite side simple, perhaps with only a monogram.

Once a design is settled on, whether a simple quarterboard or a relief of a lowboy, the wood is cut to shape and assembled with resorcinol glue. His large signs are almost always made from 8/4 Eastern white pine, while quarterboards are 4/4 pine. He doesn't use rods or dowels for the big signs, which are usually steel-banded by a local blacksmith.

McCarthy's signs get two primer coats and three coats of color. He finds lead-base paints the best. "They cover well, they are durable, they don't lose their color and they stay bright," he notes. But the most outstanding aspect of his signs is his gold-leafing. Gold leaf not only gives brilliance to lettering or carving, but it also lasts some thirty years out-of-doors. A gold-leaf sizing, which is an adhesive base, is applied after the primer and color are painted onto a smooth surface. He uses a sizing that has a slow drying time, and he will wait as long as 24 hours before applying gold leaf, depending on humidity and temperature. "If the sizing is too

EDITOR'S NOTE: You can purchase gold leaf from well-stocked artist-supply stores or from Constantine's, 2050 Eastchester Rd., Bronx, N.Y. 10461. Murphy knives, also called general-purpose knives or mill knives, are available from most mail-order tool-supply stores.

wet, the gold leaf will dissolve. If it's too dry, it won't stick." So he listens for a squeaky tackiness as he rubs a finger over the sizing, and then he applies a sheet of gold leaf over the area and tamps it with a sign-writer's quill.

Some of his signs are entirely gold-leafed. The shell for the custom-framing shop is done in gold leaf, as are the scales of justice he made for a local lawyer. When asked why he doesn't use gold paint, McCarthy says that even the best will tarnish out-of-doors or turn brown. The only problem with gilded signs is that they do accumulate dirt and road pitch, especially if near a highway. McCarthy suggests cleaning dirty gold leaf with muriatic acid. He warns that varnish should not be applied over gold leaf as it will, owing to the degrading effects of sunlight, lift the gold from the sign.

When not carving, McCarthy is teaching. His youngest student is eleven years old. But regardless of age, they all start with quarterboards. Given blanks, students are taught immediately to use the Murphy knife, beginning with straight lines. McCarthy says quarterboards are easy to master and don't take up much room. After quarterboards, students have their choice of projects. At one class, students were doing signs, relief carving, gunstocks, caricatures, mantelpiece ships, animals and birds.

Some of McCarthy's students have gone off to start their own sign-carving businesses. Of competition he says, "I'm not afraid of it. It's a way of keeping woodcarving going." □

A Not-So-Classic Rosette for Classical Guitars

by Al Ching

Classical guitar construction is so steeped in tradition, the luthier has relatively few opportunities to exhibit his originality. The profile of the peghead and the design of the rosette are two prominent features available for a signature. Historically, the rosette, the decorative border around the soundhole, is a mosaic comprised of tiles made from the end grain of tiny sticks. I have always admired the end-grain pattern of whole logs. A rosette made from a single piece of end grain became a logical departure for the classical guitar I am building.

My rosette was made in four steps: First I took a slab from a small log. Then I used an adjustable circle cutter in the drill press to outline the rosette. (A circle cutter can be a nasty tool—keep your hands clear of it, use it at the lowest possible RPM, feeding lightly, and be sure to secure the work.) Next I cut the slab to the required thickness. I then finished off the resulting "doughnut" with contrasting strips of wood, bordering the inner and outer circumferences. At this point the rosette was complete and ready for inlay into the soundboard. □

Al Ching is professor of art at California State University, Fullerton. For more on guitar embellishment, see p. 176.

2. *Adjustable circle cutter defines inner circumference of rosette; outer circumference has already been cut. If either one of these cuts produces tear-out, try regrinding the cutter to the opposite angle. Slab has been glued to a large, square beam and is thick enough for two rosettes, about the depth limit of the circle cutter.*

3. *A first pass through the table saw cuts more than halfway through the rosette. Beam is flipped, end for end, and a length of string is looped through the part of the rosette already cut. The other end of the string is held lightly between thumb and forefinger (not wrapped around the latter) as the second and final pass, above, is made through the saw. For a truer rosette and safer operation, this final cut should be made with one person holding the string and another doing the sawing. To save the center/waste portion of the rosette to use as inlay material on other parts of the guitar, tape it to the rosette in about four places. Instead of being 'swallowed' by the saw, the rosette and center portion will be lifted as a unit with the string.*

1. *A spacer block and pencil are used to mark the thickness of the slab to be bandsawn from the log. Log end has already been faced by an initial cut and flattened on the side parallel to the longest axis of the end grain. This makes for a steadier and safer workpiece when put through the band saw. The flat was produced with an adze, jointer plane and winding sticks.*

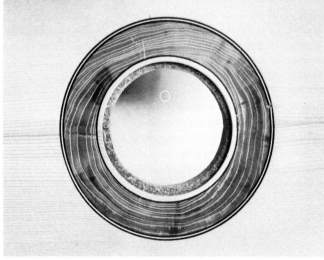

4. *Rosette inlaid in spruce soundboard. The rosette is California live oak banded with Macassar ebony and birch. The soundboard is clamped to a particleboard work board, a portion of which can be seen below the soundhole. Photos: Al Ching.*

Guitar Binding and Purfling
Decorating edges with thin wood

by William R. Cumpiano and Jonathan D. Natelson

Broadly speaking, purfling (from the Latin *profilum*, threading forth) means finishing or decorating the border or edge of a piece of woodwork with thin bands of contrasting material. Although the technique of purfling has been almost forgotten to modern woodworking, it is very much current in the luthier's art. The same basic techniques described here for guitars can be used to decorate tabletops and drawer fronts or to refine boxes.

Binding the body of the guitar closes those unfinished seams that will not be concealed by other parts of the instrument. It is as well an opportunity to refine the appearance of the instrument and to display the taste and workmanship of the artisan. Many guitarmakers feel the addition of purfling also enhances the acoustics of the guitar by thinning the section where the top joins the sides to make the top more a hinged rather than a clamped membrane.

The perimeter of a guitar's sound box consists of a purfling strip and a corner strip called the binding. The guitar sides may also be purfled where they meet the binding. The purfling can be made up of contrasting lines, marquetry or shell inlay. The binding strips are commonly maple, rosewood or plastic. "To bind" generally means to apply the binding and purfling strips in rabbets cut into the edge of the guitar box or headstock. Sometimes steel-string-guitar fingerboards are also bound.

Aesthetic considerations—When Antonio de Torres (1817-1892) first laid out the scheme for what would later be called the modern classical guitar, he broke with tradition by building a larger, louder, acoustically improved instrument of spare, refined appearance. Torres banished the floral carvings, pearl incrustations and harlequin stripes that were popular in the mid-19th century and replaced them with a careful linear motif that simply framed all the plates of the instrument, eliminating distraction from the inherent beauty of the material. He used color sparingly. His preferences are basic to modern design, and any radical departure by a modern classical guitarmaker seems arbitrary and presumptuous.

Materials—The stock for wooden binding should be straight-grained and uniform in color. The cross section of the binding strips on steel-string guitars is commonly $\frac{3}{32}$ in by $\frac{3}{16}$ in. (slightly smaller on classical guitars) with the grain quartersawn. If the pieces are wavy-grained or flatsawn, they are likely to twist or break during bending.

To cut your own binding and purfling strips, you'll need a good table saw with smoothly operating adjustments, a couple of small-diameter, fine-toothed blades with little or no set and a measuring caliper or micrometer for testing uniformity. If you don't have a veneer sawblade, a small portable circular sawblade can be rim-ground to a no-set $\frac{1}{16}$-in. kerf. To keep the strips from falling into the saw, clamp a piece of $\frac{1}{8}$-in. or

$\frac{1}{4}$-in. plywood onto the saw table and crank the blade up while running so that it protrudes through the plywood, leaving no gap. A straight board can be clamped parallel to the blade to serve as a fence. Alternately, a replacement table insert can be fashioned out of thin wooden scrap through which the fine-kerf blade can protrude. The regular saw fence can then be used.

Binding strips can be mass produced by resawing a billet into sheets, which are then milled with an abrasive thicknesser to a consistent $\frac{3}{16}$-in. thickness. The $\frac{3}{32}$-in. (or vice versa, depending on grain direction) slices are then cut with thin-kerf sawblades singly or ganged.

Purfling lines can be mass produced by sandwiching many $\frac{1}{40}$-in. veneers (without glue) between two thicker pieces of wood. Tape the edges to prevent shifting and pass the entire assembly through the saw. The resulting lines can be retrieved and the few larger pieces sorted out as scrap. If only a few are needed, the strips can be sawn individually or sliced with a straightedge and razor knife. Typical line widths are $\frac{3}{32}$ in. for side purflings and $\frac{1}{16}$ in. for face purfling.

Very fine black or white purfling lines are made from closed-grain woods such as holly or maple. They can then be dyed black or any color by soaking in aniline-dye solution, non-grain-raising stains or leather dyes.

The ideal tool for all purfling and binding manufacture is a wide-belt abrasive planer such as described in *FWW* #23, July '80. Strips of consistent thickness down to 0.005 in. in any material are possible, and these extra-fine lines can greatly improve the appearance of the binding. The builder with more modest resources must rely on the $\frac{1}{40}$-in. white or black veneer sheets available commercially.

Bending—At first, bending your purfling and binding strips over a hot pipe may seem tricky and frustrating. Even under the best of circumstances, strips can break, so it is best to prepare a few extras. Though purfling lines to be used on the face or back of the guitar rarely need pre-bending, lines on the sides always do, since they will almost certainly buckle or break when bent around a curved

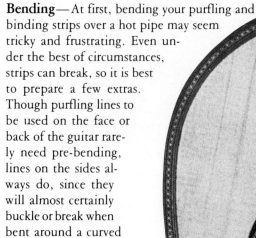

Purfling and binding of a a guitar made in 1863 by Antonio de Torres and restored by Bill Cumpiano. A close view is shown above.

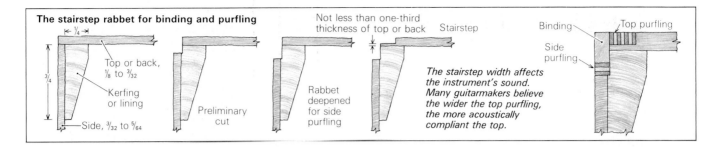

The stairstep rabbet for binding and purfling

Top or back, ⅛ to ³/₃₂

Kerfing or lining

Side, ³/₃₂ to ⁵/₆₄

¾, ¼

Preliminary cut

Not less than one-third thickness of top or back

Rabbet deepened for side purfling

Stairstep

Binding

Side purfling

Top purfling

The stairstep width affects the instrument's sound. Many guitarmakers believe the wider the top purfling, the more acoustically compliant the top.

ledge. The strips must therefore be supported by heftier strips of wood, such as scrap or the binding strips themselves. If you use the binding strips, glue them first to the purfling lines in the sequence that will appear on the finished guitar side. Apply thin, white, fast-setting glue to each member and press the entire combination together briefly between two long, straight boards. Alternately, you can glue up a larger sandwich of the binding and purfling material in sheet form and then resaw the package into finished, composite binding/purfling strips ready for bending.

It is best to tape several of these composite strips tightly together, with the thinnest lines facing inward, in order to prevent delamination and buckling. General bending procedures and a typical hot-pipe bending iron are discussed in *FWW #10*, Spring '78. The important differences that apply only to binding/purfling strips are that water is used sparingly (the strips should be dipped only momentarily), the pipe should be very hot and pressure should be light. Because the purfling and binding material is naturally flexible, it need match the template only along the tighter curves. For small-radius bends, use a small-diameter pipe with a torch trained on it and use strips that are less than ³/₃₂ in. thick. With patience and an eye (or nose) for excessive heat, you can make the strip turn on a dime. Consistent breakage probably means bad materials, a cross-sectional thickness greater than ³/₃₂ in. or the failure to apply your concentration over an extended period of time.

Cutting the ledge with a router—A handtool called a purfling cutter is traditionally used for cutting the ledge into which the binding and purfling is laid. The instrument looks like a marking gauge, except that an adjustable cutter takes the place of the marking pin. If the cutter is sharp beyond question and you have plenty of time, a flawless job can result. Otherwise the tool can mangle your guitar.

The same flawless job can be consistently and quickly done using a router with a laminate-trimming attachment. Every major router manufacturer offers such a device, which consists of a pilot wheel that adjusts closer or farther away from the bit. (For another design, see Methods of Work, *FWW #21*, March '80.) Because the wheel is offset, the bit can pivot around it and cut a narrower slot than desired. It is therefore necessary to keep the pilot wheel pressed against the side of the guitar, and to keep the line between it and the bit perpendicular to the tangent of the curve.

When cutting the ledge on the back near the neck and just behind the waist, because the back is arched, the router base will tip slightly relative to the guitar side, causing the bit to cut shy. Correct this with the purfling cutter. If you are uneasy about using the cutter to remove material, use it as a marking gauge to determine the limit of the rabbet and then chisel away the waste.

Binding the guitar—A guitar can be assembled with the neck as an integral part of the body (Spanish method) or with the neck and body as separate components (see *FWW #5*, Winter '76). In either case, the binding process begins when the box has been assembled, that is, when the soundboard, sides and back form an enclosed cavity. Before binding the edges, the seam at the bottom end of the guitar, where the two sides meet, must be finished. This is accomplished by means of a bottom inlay (or end graft).

To work on the bottom inlay, the guitar top and back, which overlap the sides from assembly, must first be trimmed. Start by cutting the edges adjacent to either end of the seam back to the depth of the binding strip. Make this preliminary cut with your router and laminate-trimmer depth set to the dimensions of the binding strip minus all purfling. But before using the router, trim with a chisel the back and top overlap to within ⅛ in. of the sides. Cutting a greater overlap with a router is dangerous, as the bit may snag and rip out stock, especially spruce. Note also that the unfinished seam of the sides at the end graft will present a "pothole" to the pilot wheel, and must be skirted during the cut. Pare down with a chisel what the router misses.

Now stand the guitar on end and clamp the box to the edge of the workbench, as shown in photo A on the next page. The end-graft slot may be cut with parallel or tapered sides. A parallel slot requires an inlay that is trimmed to fit perfectly. A slightly tapered slot allows greater leeway and ultimately a tighter pressure-fit. To cut the slot, draft the boundaries of the graft, plus the bordering purfling lines, at either side of the guitar centerline. This should be done with several light passes of a sharp razor knife pressed against a metal straightedge. You may saw along these lines down to the tail glueblock with a fine backsaw and remove the waste with a narrow chisel. Or you can scribe with the knife and clean out with a chisel. Take care that the walls do not creep out of square. If you have many to do, the slot may also be routed using a jig.

The end graft itself is made of thin stock that matches the binding and must be tapered with a block plane. Starting with an overlong, overwide blank, plane until the tapers match perfectly, testing the piece in the slot. If you are using line or marquetry strips, they can be bunched on one side while fitting. When the fit is perfect, remove all the pieces and cover the bottom of the slot thinly with glue. Position the decorative lines, working glue between all adjacent surfaces. Now slide the graft in while holding the lines in place. Once the graft is tight, secure it with a couple of gentle taps on the wide end (photo B, next page). When the glue is dry, scrape the excess until the inlay is flush. Cut the overhang of the graft with a fine backsaw and then trim with the router, using the original setting.

Next, increase the existing vertical depth of cut by the

A

B

C

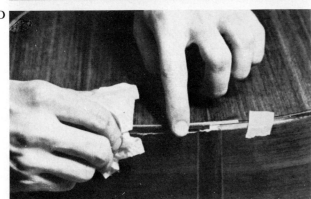

D

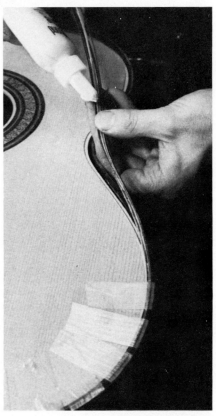

E

Binding a guitar: A preliminary cut of the stairstep rabbet (drawing, previous page) is made near the end graft. Then the guitar is clamped to the workbench, butt end up (A). The tapered end graft (B) is tapped into a tapered slot that has been sawn or knifed and chiseled in the end of the guitar. The end graft is sawn to length and the stairstep routed almost to the end-graft purfling (C). The nub of wood remaining will be removed with a chisel and the end-graft purfling mitered to receive the side purfling. Begin gluing the binding with purfling to one edge of the bottom (D), by first loosely taping the strips in place. Once the miter at the end graft is fit, you can continue around to the heel—gluing, pressing in and taping down the strips. For the top, where there are usually more purfling strips, glue the strips themselves (E), as you work around, pressing them into the stairstep. The finished end of the guitar (F) displays the results of precise work.

F

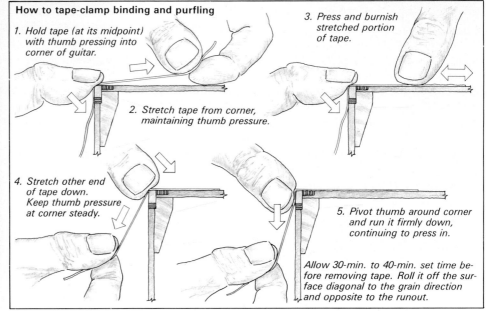

How to tape-clamp binding and purfling

1. Hold tape (at its midpoint) with thumb pressing into corner of guitar.

2. Stretch tape from corner, maintaining thumb pressure.

3. Press and burnish stretched portion of tape.

4. Stretch other end of tape down. Keep thumb pressure at corner steady.

5. Pivot thumb around corner and run it firmly down, continuing to press in.

Allow 30-min. to 40-min. set time before removing tape. Roll it off the surface diagonal to the grain direction and opposite to the runout.

thickness of the side purfling you plan to use. Cut all the way around the contour of the soundbox, stopping short of the end-graft purflings on either side of the end graft (photo C). If your guitar has an integral neck, your cuts will be blocked by the neck. If the box and neck are separate, you will be able to rout the top unhindered. The back, however, must be skirted at the mortise (or dovetail) where the heel will eventually sit, as there is no surface for the pilot to follow.

Adjust the router for the shallow stairstep cut into which you will lay the purfling lines on the back, inboard of the binding strips. Follow the contour of the sides again, stopping at the neck or skirting its mortise. If necessary, reset the router for the stairstep cut on the top. Stairstep cuts should be no deeper than two-thirds of the thickness of the top or back plates; otherwise you weaken the corner of the instrument.

Complete the stairstep with a chisel; trim the nub of wood remaining at each corner of the end graft and miter the end-graft purfling at 45° to receive the side purfling. In the Spanish assembly, the stairstep at the neck must also be cut by hand, with chisels and a saw.

Gluing the binding and purfling—There are two ways to apply pressure to the binding and purfling strips while gluing them into the stairstep around the guitar. One is to wrap a long strip of sturdy fabric, such as upholsterer's canvas tape, tightly around the guitar, forcing the binding into the groove. Glue is applied to the ledge and to the individual strips as the binding progresses. We prefer a method using short, doubled-up strips of masking tape (or single strips of nylon-reinforced strapping tape) cut to 4-in. or 5-in. lengths ahead of time or pulled from a fixed or heavy tape dispenser.

Start with the back of the guitar. Take the bent binding/side-purfling strip and slip it back and forth in the ledge to find the point where the waist of the guitar best matches the waist of the bent strip. Tape it securely in place. Run your finger along the strip toward the tail of the guitar, pressing the binding strip into the ledge as it will be when glued. Mark where it intersects the centerline of the guitar with a razor saw. Repeat the operation with the upper bout (above the waist), marking at the heel. Remove the strip and saw it through slightly beyond each mark. With a wide chisel held upright, trim back the bottom end smooth and square. Leave the top end untrimmed. Place the strip back on the ledge, lining up the centerline with the trimmed end. Mark where the side purfling will meet the end-graft purfling. Carefully shave the side-purfling lines back to that point, leaving them mitered at 45°. If the miters do not meet perfectly, pare the side lines (not the end-graft lines) until they do. Your margin is less than ⅛ in.; shifting the strips more than that will create excessive tension on the bends. Once you have a proper fit at the end-graft miter (the purfling on the back face can overhang), loosely tape the strip to keep it from dangling.

Now remove the tape near the end graft, lift the binding strip and apply glue to the stairstep here. Press the strip into place and wipe off the initial glue squeeze-out (photo D). Make sure that the fit is snug and that the miters still meet. Place the first piece of tape an inch or so from the end graft and secure it as shown in the drawing at left. This is your last opportunity to check your miter. Tape directly over the centerline and the miter. Continue the taping around to the heel, working glue in a few inches at a time. When you get to the widest part of the upper bout, press the remainder of the

strip into place without glue and check where it ends in relation to the centerline. If necessary, shave it back with a chisel before gluing the final few inches.

While waiting for the glue to dry on this first bottom strip, you can begin binding the top side diagonally opposite from the one just done. The operation is the same as on the back except that you may have to deal with a larger number of lines. The guitar in the photographs has seven lines on the top. In this case, you must apply glue to the lines as a separate operation. Once everything else is fitted, take the band of top purfling lines and apply glue to the first few inches. Fan the lines and work glue between them as shown (photo E). Apply glue to the first few inches of the stairstep, place the wide band in its slot (overlapping the centerline slightly) and position and tape the miter as on the back. As you progress around the guitar, repeat the fanning operation each time you apply glue to the stairstep. All the lines must touch the bottom of the rabbet. Break off the purfling strips at the neck; precision is unnecessary, since the fingerboard covers the whole area.

When the glue is dry, return to the back and remove the first couple of tape strips. Trim the excess purfling to the end of the binding at both tail and heel. The positioning operation is more complex now, because you must mate the two binding ends as well as the miter. Leave at least 1/16-in. excess when initially trimming the binding strip so that you can shave the binding strip and purfling lines bit by bit until you have both a perfect miter and mated ends without distortion at the waist. Once this is accomplished, mate the back purfling strips. Glue the same as before, starting the tape an inch away from the end to allow one final check. When you reach the heel, you will have to trim both binding and purfling to mate with the other side. This time, when you press the remainder of the strip in without glue, mark the purfling strip and then the binding strip where the excess must be removed. Place veneer over the heel to protect the soft mahogany, and trim each strip with a chisel held vertically. You want to avoid a gap here, but no buckling of the binding is permissible. Better to have a slight cosmetic defect than a weak glue joint. Getting it exactly right takes practice, so getting it close is good for the first try.

To finish binding the top you have essentially the same operation. However, because the top is spruce and the band of purfling may be wider than on the back, you should cut almost through with a razor saw on a diagonal. Finish trimming and clean the stairstep with a sharp chisel. Leave a clean, square edge, but avoid increasing the stairstep width, for this will make the purfling lines appear staggered where they mate. Fit the binding strip as on the back, and check the top purfling lines for fit. To achieve the appearance of a continuous band, you may have to vary the horizontal pressure when taping. After the glue is dry, remove the tape and scrape the excess wood and glue flush. But scrape minimally—you are working with fine, brittle strips and very thin plates. □

Luthiers Bill Cumpiano and Jon Natelson work in North Adams, Mass. Their shop recently completed the interior work on a silver desk-top accessory box, a gift to President Reagan from his political friends and associates. The box, lined with rosewood, contains a removable pencil tray and a concealed Swiss musical movement that plays "Hail to the Chief" when the lid is opened.

How Inlay is Made
Commercial techniques for marquetry inserts and banding

by Rick Mastelli

Traditional designs for marquetry inserts include fans, sunbursts, shells, urns, American eagles and floral patterns. They are often round or oval in perimeter, bordered by a thin strip bent around and joined, or by a thin ring cut whole from a sheet of veneer. Within the border can be any number of individually sawn pieces set into a figured background veneer of the same standard thickness. The pieces are often shaded by scorching in hot sand to give the picture the illusion of depth. Once assembled, the marquetry insert can become part of a veneered surface or be let into the solid surface of a box or piece of furniture by routing a recess slightly shallower than the thickness of the insert (for how to do this, see *FWW* #17, July '79, pp. 68-69). The other sort of commercially available inlay is banding, used to decorate the borders of drawers, doors, panels and tabletops. Also 1/20 in.

Marquetry inserts at Dover Inlay like the sunburst, top, are assembled on a light-tack tape. Above, an American eagle in all its parts.

to 1/28 in. thick, it's typically patterned in repetitive geometric shapes and sold in 36-in. lengths of various widths.

There used to be many manufacturers of banding and marquetry inserts, but few survived the Depression and War years. Now there are only Danker Marquetry in Traverse City, Mich., Inlaid Woodcraft in Kirkland, Ill., Dover Inlay in Mineola, N.Y., and Jason French in West Chelmsford, Mass. Together these four supply the period-furniture industry, the mail-order woodworking supply houses, the individual craftsman, and the reproduction and restoration specialists with traditional and custom-made inlay. I visited Jason French and Dover Inlay, and I discovered that both shops make inlay today pretty much the same way it's been made for more than a hundred years. They still use a perforated paper master to make multiple pounce patterns, which they cut into the individual elements of each design. They glue these pattern elements to stacks of up to 30 veneers, and jigsaw the whole stack at once. The pieces that require shading are scorched in frying pans of hot sand, and the inserts are assembled by hand, one at a time. There's nothing sophisticated about the equipment (except at Inlaid Woodcraft, which has recently introduced a woodcutting laser). Inlay still comes from an artistic eye and a patient hand. These firms have the experience and the panache to execute traditional designs in quantity, but their methods are straightforward—you can apply them to any sort of design, in any quantity.

Jason French, 63, has done marquetry since he was a boy. His father, upon graduating from high school, went to New York City to learn cabinetmaking, whereupon he discovered inlay. He returned to Cambridge, Mass., in 1905 and opened his own shop, soon specializing in inlay. Jason has been a watchmaker and modelmaker, but he always worked nights and weekends in his father's shop. In 1968, Jason took over the business; he's not been without work since. He works with his wife, Violet, who does most of the assembly and the shading, while he designs and saws. It's very much a cottage industry on the second floor of their backyard garage. Their simple machinery consists of a Rockwell jigsaw, a Powermatic 10-in. table saw (fit with a thin-rim veneer blade), a Delta drill press and a Craftsman 12-in. bandsaw. French's pride is a 4-ft. by 13-in., 5-screw veneer press, and the thousands of feet of various woods he has squirreled away, "everything from aspen to zebrawood," he tells me.

Dover is a larger operation, though it is also a couple of generations old (established in 1919) and still works in traditional ways. It's owned and operated by Paul and Don Boege, father and son. They've experimented with various alternatives to jigsawing, the most skill-demanding part of making inlay, but die cutting, they found, leaves a beveled edge on the parts, visible as a gap in the finished design, and the laser wasn't cost-effective for the scale of their operation. They employ three people on jigsaws, including Don Boege, and at

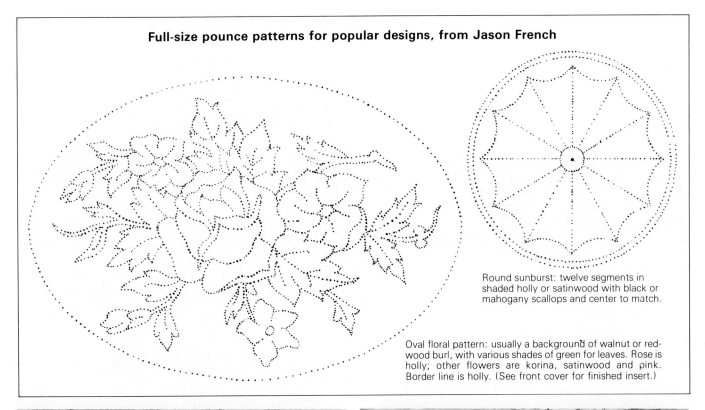

Full-size pounce patterns for popular designs, from Jason French

Round sunburst: twelve segments in shaded holly or satinwood with black or mahogany scallops and center to match.

Oval floral pattern: usually a background of walnut or red-wood burl, with various shades of green for leaves. Rose is holly; other flowers are korina, satinwood and pink. Border line is holly. (See front cover for finished insert.)

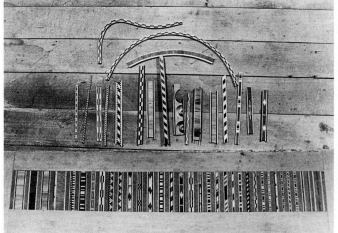

Jason French's work includes banding, left, and face veneers for square-tapered legs, right. Note that these are samples and that the leg veneers would run the entire length of the leg, including the border line, which is sawn.

least four people at the assembly bench. One-third of their 6,000-sq. ft. shop is devoted to storage, mainly 1/28-in. veneers, though there's also lumber for making into banding. Their machinery is only slightly more sophisticated than French's. Table-saw tops hinge up so blades can be changed without affecting arbor or fence adjustments, and their jigsaws are large, wooden-frame designs able to cut accurately a stack of 30 veneers at a time. The saws incorporate a clutch that saves turning off and on the motor to thread the blade through drilled holes for interior cuts. One jigsaw (shown on the next page) has an almost infinite throat, limited only by the walls of the shop, for instead of an arm from the base supporting the upper end of the blade, a post mounted and guyed to the ceiling extends down to within 12 in. of the table top. The blade, powered from below, is attached at its upper end to a spring in the post. They use this saw for cutting out bell flowers and borders in face veneers for square-tapered legs and other large assemblages.

At both the French and Dover shops, a marquetry insert begins with a pattern drawn on thin, 100% rag paper from which copies must be made; the number of copies depends on the intricacy of the design (adjacent parts require separate patterns cut from separate copies) and on the number of stacks of veneer to be sawn. The pattern must realistically anticipate the fineness and curvature of the cut their saws and sawyers can manage, and notations on it indicate what kind of wood each piece will be. This is a pre-zerox method that has the advantage of a durable master from which thousands of exact copies can be made (photocopies are usually a slightly different size from the original). If the pattern is symmetrical, the paper is folded and only half the pattern is drawn. Then the paper is perforated along the pattern lines with tiny holes, spaced as close together as possible. French uses a pin and pin vise, backing the paper with an even-grained, medium-density hardwood. Dover uses a fine needle stuck in a wooden handle. To make a copy, the perforated master is placed on the copy paper, and pounce, a fine asphaltum powder (French uses pulverized gilsonite from the American Gilsonite Co., 1150 Kennecott Bldg., 10 E. South Temple St., Salt Lake City, Utah 84133) is daubed up with a felt pad and

Jason French saws a sandwich of 16 veneers for fan inlay parts. The dotted line is pounce, a powdered asphaltum applied through perforations in the master pattern.

Left and above, Don Boege saws a bell-flower pattern in a stack of 30 face veneers for square-tapered legs. The jigsaw has an almost limitless throat because the top of the blade is attached to a spring in the ceiling-suspended post.

rubbed through the perforations. The copy is then carefully moved over a heating element (French uses an electric hot plate), which fixes the powder to the paper so it can't smear or blow off. The copy is then scissored into its individual parts, well outside the dotted line, and the parts are sorted according to what species of wood each will be sawn from.

French saws from 6 to 20 units at a time, depending on the run he is producing and on the delicacy of the cut—details will be cleaner from a smaller stack. He sandwiches the veneers between two pieces of plywood (¼-in. on top, ⅛-in. on the bottom) to prevent tear-out. The sandwich has to accommodate all the parts of the pattern to be cut from that type of wood. French hide-glues the pattern parts to the top of the sandwich and holds it together by driving brads through the waste areas, clinching them on the bottom side. Sawing is then a matter of care and skill. French tries to split the dotted line on both the individual parts and the background veneer to produce a good, snug fit. For most cuts he uses a Trojan #2 coarse blade, 0.085 in. by 0.020 in., 15 teeth per inch. "It says it's filed and set when you get it," he says, "but you can't believe that. I sharpen each blade before I use it, filing straight across. It takes me about two days to saw out all the pieces for a complex pattern in a run of 30, my usual number. The hardest cut in the book, though, is a long, straight line into a square corner, like on table legs."

Pieces that need shading are brought over to a sand-filled frying pan on an electric hot plate. The pieces are held in handmade wooden tweezers, two at a time, show-face out, and dipped into the sand for scorching. The edge is made darkest, fading gradually toward the interior.

The piles of identical parts are then organized on the assembly bench around a sheet of newspaper. First the background veneer is tacked down with brads, show-face up. Then the point of a razor-knife spears each tiny piece, and a dab of hot hide glue on the newspaper holds it in place in the background. It's like assembling a jigsaw puzzle, tack-gluing each piece as the puzzle proceeds. When all the pieces are in place, French coats a piece of heavy brown paper with hide glue and lays it over the top. He presses the assemblages immediately with a wool rug for about an hour to make up for any unevenness. When the glue has set, the newspaper (under) side of each picture is moistened and scraped clean. A mixture of hide glue, water and mahogany dust is rubbed into the spaces between the pieces and into the sawn lines that represent detailing on the larger pieces. French uses the edge of a Teflon block to squeegee off the excess filler. The remainder is left to set while the pictures are kept flat under a heavy board. A finished insert will retail for anywhere from $2.50 to $20. If he did little else, French figures he could produce 50 to 75 inserts in a week.

Dover Inlay can produce hundreds. Besides its larger staff, the firm has streamlined assembly by using, instead of hot hide glue, two kinds of tape. Individual pieces are still speared, show-face up, and positioned with the point of a razor-knife, but instead of newspaper and glue, a ground of light-tack tape holds them in place. When assembly is complete, a gummed tape, similar to packaging tape, is placed over the show-face. The light-tack tape is removed from the back and a filler of water-soluble glue, water and mahogany dust is pressed in. With this method you don't have to tend the glue pot or contend with the wood curling from moisture taken on from the backing glue, and you don't have to clamp.

Banding is made entirely differently. Instead of tiny pieces assembled into finished units one at a time, a 36-in. long, 6-in. or 8-in. wide "trunk" pattern is assembled, and ⅟₂₈-in. strips are cut from it on the table saw, like slicing pastrami. Often what appears in the finished banding as tiny components is the result of an earlier generation of assembling and slicing larger pieces of wood or sheets of veneer. A typical design will begin with two or three pieces of contrasting veneer, 36 in. by 6 in., laid down with glue between. French prefers traditional hot hide glue because of its long assembly time; hot cauls applied to the assembly before it goes in the press reliquefy the glue. Dover Inlay uses Cascamite, and Danker Marquetry, the other large producer of banding, has switched to a slow-set Titebond. Next a series of 6-in. long sticks of complementary section, or a series of 6-in. long assemblages from an earlier gluing and slicing (parallelograms, say, from 45° cuts) are glued together and onto the veneer. Another two or three layers of veneer on top complete the sandwich, and the whole thing goes in the press for a day. When the assemblage is removed and sliced, the components will appear as arrowhead banding, bordered by thin lines, as in the drawing at right. With a veneer blade producing a ⅟₃₂-in. kerf, about ninety 36-in. long strips can be gotten from a 6-in. wide lamination. These sell for anywhere from 70ᶜ to $7 a yard. Hundreds of patterns are currently produced. "There's no end to inlay," says French, "because there's always someone coming up with some new challenge."

Both French and Dover have found that the demand for their products has increased in the last two years. This popularity seems to be part of a cycle that has gone on for as long as woodworking itself. Interest in decorating furniture alternates with the primary interest in constructing it. Medieval joiners, for instance, when they had satisfied the demands of their time for building in solid wood, devoted more and more of their energies to decoration. Carved designs (FWW #19, Nov. '79, pp. 80-82 and #22, May '80, pp. 48-50) were the most popular, but straight-walled recesses were also cut into solid wood surfaces, using a shoulder knife, and thin pieces of wood let in to describe floral patterns and religious pictures. This was the beginning of marquetry in the West. In some monastic orders, marquetry became an art in its own right, not wed to furniture as decoration, and wooden pictures came to rival oil paintings for their detail and realism. The invention of the fretsaw in 1562 took marquetry out of the domain of the artist and gave it over to the craftsman, who could follow designs prepared by more artistic hands than his own. The result was a decline in the quality of the pictorial images and an increase in their use as decoration. Throughout the ensuing era of the cabinetmaker, there can be traced an ebb and flow in the taste for decorating furniture with thin wood. At least part of the reason lies with the makers themselves. Newly challenged by the construc-

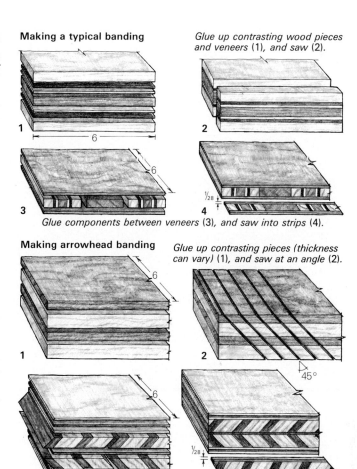

Making a typical banding

Glue up contrasting wood pieces and veneers (1), and saw (2).

Glue components between veneers (3), and saw into strips (4).

Making arrowhead banding

Glue up contrasting pieces (thickness can vary) (1), and saw at an angle (2).

Glue components between veneers (3), and saw into strips (4).

tional demands of a compound-curved surface, say, or a tambour door, the cabinetmaker is absorbed. After mastering the difficulties, he looks for more; he decorates, often by inlaying.

Contemporary woodworking seems not immune to this cycle. Since the end of World War II, when Danish designs became aligned with modern tastes, many people have appreciated solid, unembellished wood, and have been absorbed in constructing with it. Even in the period-furniture trade, Queen Anne and Chippendale have been far more popular than decoratively veneered Hepplewhite, Sheraton and Louis XV or XVI. Until recently, that is. Period-furniture manufacturers are now responding to increased interest in Federal furniture, typically decorated with banding and marquetry inserts. The mail-order companies that sell inlays (Constantine, 2050 Eastchester Rd., Bronx, N.Y. 10461; Craftsman, 1735 West Cortland Ct., Addison, Ill., 60101; and The Woodworkers' Store, 21801 Industrial Blvd., Rogers, Minn. 55374) are selling more these days. And recent gallery shows have included more inlaid work, reflecting the greater sophistication of contemporary woodworkers who have been in the trade long enough to have outgrown their image as the first wave of a resurgence in crafts. □

EDITOR'S NOTE: For more about marquetry and inlay, see FWW #1, Winter '75, pp. 33-36; #5, Winter '76, pp. 38-40; and #22, May '79, p. 76. The Marquetry Society of America publishes a monthly newsletter (940 N. Hamilton Ave., Lindenhurst, N.Y. 11757). Books on the subject include *The Art and Practice of Marquetry* by William Alexander Lincoln (London: Thames and Hudson, 1971), $5.95; *Modern Marquetry Handbook* ed. Harry Hobbs and Alan Fitchett (New York: Constantine, 1978), $7.95; and *Veneering Simplified* by Harry Hobbs (New York: Constantine, 1978), $6.95. All three are available from Constantine, 2050 Eastchester Rd., Bronx, N.Y. 10461.

Inlaying Mother-of-Pearl
Watching one banjo maker cut and fit a delicate design

by John Lively

Though most often found as decoration on musical instruments, mother-of-pearl inlays traditionally have graced a diversity of articles—furniture large and small, gunstocks and knife handles, walking sticks and billiard cues. Mother-of-pearl and its more colorful cousin, abalone shell, are sold in small, thin pieces (the box below lists some suppliers), that are quite abrasive, hence hard on tools, and extremely brittle. You can't just saw it as though it were maple veneer. A highly developed craft practiced by the Chinese as early as the 14th century, mother-of-pearl inlay was very popular among the 18th-century *ébénistes*, and it distinguishes the work of such

20th-century inheritors of that tradition as Louis Suë and André Mare.

To learn how to cut and inlay mother-of-pearl, I visited Richard Newman (whose banjo appeard in *FWW* #1, Winter '75) at his shop in Rochester, N.Y. He demonstrated the technique by cutting a stylized Georgian dolphin in pearl, then inlaying it into a piece of scrap ebony. Here's how he did it:

From his stash of mother-of-pearl chips, Newman selected one and pasted a paper cartoon of the sea beast on top of it. Next, he clamped his bird's mouth (a rectangular block with

Sources of supply for mother-of-pearl and abalone

Mother-of-pearl does not come from the oyster that produces seed pearls, but from various bivalve mollusks, some of which grow as large as 2 ft. in diameter. Most pearl shell is imported from the western Pacific; the cold waters of Australia produce the finest shells, less likely to be damaged by sea worms, barnacles or other parasites. Colors range from white and grey to pink and deep gold; gold pearl, from the lip of the shell, is the most expensive cut. Some pieces of pearl are preferred for their evenness of color; others are irridescent and highly figured, sometimes desig-

Arthur Sweeney is a professional stringed-instrument maker. He lives in Napa, Calif.

nated wavy or fiddleback after the wood figures they resemble.

Abalone is cut from the shell of a monovalve mollusk native to southern Californian and Mexican waters. It is generally more spectacular than pearl, with black fracture lines along twisting planes of bright colors that blend and shift under changing light. There is green abalone, which has become rare, and there is larger, less expensive red abalone. The central portion of the shell, where the muscle attaches, is called the heart and is most prized. It looks something like crinkled tinfoil, sparkling with green, blue and red.

Suppliers cut mother-of-pearl and abalone with a lapidary saw, attending to the figure and curvature of the shell. The

pieces are irregularly shaped, usually about 1 in. square (a 3-in. piece is considered large). Then they're ground to thicknesses ranging from 0.035 in. to 0.060 in. The thicker stock is best for curved surfaces, like fretboards, and for fine lines and sharp curves. Some suppliers grade their stock "select" (for exceptional figure and size), "#1" (good and clear), and "#2" (some parasite damage). Cost is figured by the ounce, $15 to $25 an ounce being typical. Some suppliers, as indicated below, will custom-cut designs; some provide precut blanks in a limited number of designs.　　　*—Arthur Sweeney*

Suppliers:

Erika, 12731 Loma Rica Dr., Suite G, Grass Valley, Calif. 95945. Mother-of-pearl and abalone blanks.

Handy Trading Co., 8560 Venice Blvd., Los Angeles, Calif. 90034. Mother-of-pearl and abalone in bulk.

Pearl Works, Larry Sifel, Rt. 3, Box 98B, Mechanicsville, Md. 20659. Mother-of-pearl and abalone blanks; precut designs; will custom-cut designs.

Vitali Imports, 5944 Atlantic Boulevard, Maywood, Calif. 90270. Mother-of-pearl blanks.

David Russell Young, 7134 Balboa Boulevard, Van Nuys, Calif. 91406. Mother-of-pearl and abalone blanks.

Zaharoff Industries, 26 Max Ave., Hicksville, N.Y. 11801. Mother-of-pearl and abalone blanks; will custom-cut designs. □

Chinese k'ang (a type of bed) from the Ming dynasty (1368-1644) exemplifies the sophistication of mother-of-pearl inlay work before it became popular in Europe. Metropolitan Museum of Art, gift of Mrs. Jean Mayzé, 1961.

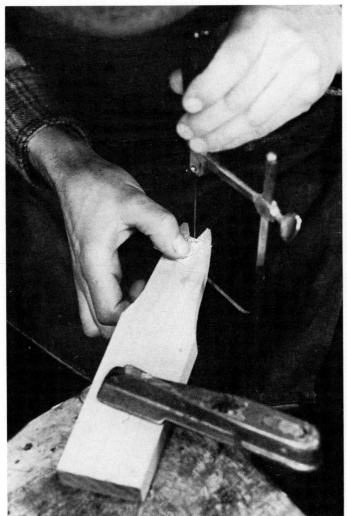

Very fragile and brittle, pearl must be sawn with a studied technique and special care. Left, with jeweler's saw and bird's mouth (the V-notched board clamped to his bench), Newman cuts a mythical sea beast from a mother-of-pearl chip. Top right, Dremel equipped with a tiny end mill routs the recess for the pearl inlay. It must fit easily, but with no gaps. Center, Newman uses an engraver's block to hold the stock when incising detail into the pearl. Engraver's blocks are necessary for good results, since engraving requires moving the work into the tool rather than the other way around, as is the case with carving wood. Engraved gouges filled with epoxy/aniline dye mixture delineate details and add depth to the finished dolphin (about twice actual size), right. Newman used black dye, but other colors would work as well.

a V-notch cut in one end) to his bench. With jeweler's saw in hand, handle up, teeth down, he proceeded to cut around the shape of the beast, using a #3 jeweler's blade (photo, above left). Sometimes moving the pearl into the blade and sometimes moving the blade into the pearl, his easy sawing rhythm kept the blade from binding, which, had it occurred, would have fractured the pearl. Rhythm, he told me, is especially important when sawing tight curves, because interrupting the up-and-down motion can snag the blade, chip the pearl and ruin the whole job.

While sawing away, Newman pointed out that pearl dust is toxic and said you should blow the dust away from your face. He uses a respirator when sawing it for extended periods, and warns that lung damage can result from inhaling too much of the powder. To saw the sharp points on the tail and pectoral fins, he always cut from the outside in, sawing out little loops in the waste part of the pearl to make space for a new angle of attack. This part of the job was slow-going, but the tedium paid off. The finished dolphin required only a few deft touches with a needle file to make its profile precisely right.

To prepare the ebony for inletting, he glued the pearl dolphin on the surface with Duco quick-dry cement. Then,

carefully, he traced around the figure with a sharp machinist's scribe, deepening the scratch a little at a time until the outline was clearly visible. Tracing complete, he slid a razor blade under the pearl and popped it free, leaving its silhouette behind. For routing out the area for inletting, Newman used a 2-flute, single-end micro-miniature end mill with a ⅛-in. shank (available from the Woodson Tool Co., 544 W. 132nd St., Gardena, Calif. 90248). The bit was mounted in a Dremel Moto-Tool equipped with a router base (photo, top right). Newman set the depth of cut slightly shallower than the thickness of the pearl. This end mill will cut a channel as narrow as ⅟₃₂ in., thus minimizing the areas that will need to be filled in later at sharp corners.

It took a little trial fitting and re-routing to make the pearl drop neatly into place. Next, Newman applied silver leaf to the back of the inlay, and then he mixed a pinch of ebony sanding dust into a batch of five-minute epoxy (full-cure epoxy is better), smeared some into the recess and inserted the dolphin, pushing down gently and letting the epoxy/dust mixture ooze out slowly. He covered the inlay with plastic wrap and clamped a block on top of it. After 30 minutes drying (the epoxy has to set hard), he removed the block and

Newman saws mother-of-pearl the traditional way.

filed, scraped and sanded the whole business flush with the surface of the wood. Whatever gaps there were between the pearl and the wood (I saw only a speck or two) had been neatly filled with the dust/epoxy mixture.

Sanding, of course, made powder of the original cartoon. But he had lots of them on hand (they're photocopies of his original drawing) and got another out to use as a guide for penciling on the blank form all of its details—eye, scales and frilly gill. To engrave these little details into the beast's surface, Newman secured the wood in an engraver's block (photo, previous page, center). Unlike carving wood, where one moves the tool into the work, engraving calls for moving the work into the tool, which is held almost stationary. The engraver's block, with its heavy hemispherical base, is designed for this. You can order one from Brownell's Inc., Rt. 2, Box 1, Montezuma, Iowa 50171, or from Paul H. Gesswein Co., 235 Park Ave. South, New York, N.Y. 10003. With a square high-speed steel graver, Newman incised the details into the pearl. You can engrave pearl without an engraver's block, but it's not easy. You'll have to clamp and reclamp the stock to your bench because you will need both hands to control the tool, and your avenues of approaching the work will be limited, since you must lock your arms to your sides and move your whole body into the cut.

With the engraving done, Newman made another epoxy puddle, mixed in powdered black aniline dye and spread the inky stuff over the entire surface of the pearl, filling in the engraved areas. When the mess had dried, he sanded it down flush with the surface of the wood. Upon lifting the sanding block and wiping the dust away, some three hours after taking saw in hand, there lay the finished dolphin, its incised features boldly alive and vividly defined. □

Follow-up on how to saw pearl

On page 185 and above, Richard Newman is pictured sawing "...mother-of-pearl the traditional way." No he is not. He is using the saw upside down.

The jeweler's saw was developed centuries ago and is used with the handle below the V-notch supporting the work. The teeth of the blade point toward the handle. These teeth, as a rule, have no set and the blade fits snugly in the slot it cuts. One end of the blade is clamped in what is a direct extension of the handle, and the frame of the saw is adjusted so it holds tension on the other end of the blade. The reason for all of this is that as the power cut is made, the work is held firmly against the notch by the pressure of the cut, and the pull of the blade is taken directly by the handle. The spring of the frame holds that part of the blade above the work under constant tension, and so straight.

When the saw is used upside down, as Newman is using it, the teeth of the blade point toward the end of the arm. As the power cut is made, the work is held against the V-notch and the blade below the work is pulled on by the end of the frame. In pulling on the blade, the frame springs, the blade above the work, no longer under tension, arcs, binds in the cut and breaks....Also, with his hand holding the saw below the work where it belongs, Newman would no longer have to cock and cant his head in order to keep the cut in view.
—*Robert M. Rose, Metairie, La.*

Robert M. Rose's letter about how I saw mother-of-pearl deserves some response. His elucidation of the theory behind the jeweler's saw is sensible and no doubt correct. However, the fact remains that after years of sawing the orthodox way, with the saw's handle below the work, I have found that I prefer doing it wrong.

I tried turning the saw upside down at the suggestion of Chuck Erickson of Erika Banjos. We discussed mechanized methods of sawing pearl to make this tedious job go faster. He described attempts at using tiny, diamond-coated bandsaws and lasers, but each of these proved unsuitable. He had concluded that the fastest and most accurate way was the good old hand saw, used upside down. After some practice I found I had more control, the fingers being far more sensitive than the wrist. I break fewer blades, actually they become dull and break only if one continues to push them through the cut. As to my vision, the saw is just not in my way.

The real point is that one should never be afraid to try something unorthodox, as this is often how important discoveries are made. I am neither pedant nor academician, just a craftsman seeking the best and fastest way to achieve my goals. If it works, I'll use it.
—*Richard Newman, Rochester, N.Y.*

Cutting a dutchman

"Dutchman" is the name given to an irregularly shaped inlay that's used to repair a blemish (such as a cigarette burn) in woodwork. Typically the woodworker cuts the inlay first, traces its outline on the stock and cuts the shallow mortise to fit. Here's an alternate approach that allows you to cut the mortise first or match an existing mortise. I'm sure the technique could be applied to marquetry work as well.

Lay a piece of paper over the mortise and shade the area around the mortise with the flat of a pencil (sketch, below). The edges of the mortise will stand out sharply. Tape the paper to the dutchman stock and transfer the pattern to the stock with a chisel and mallet. Remove the paper, cut out the dutchman and you should have a perfectly fitting inlay.

—Donald M. Stevens, Mansfield Center, Conn.

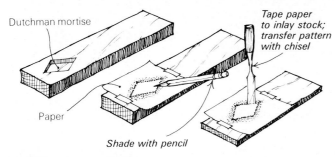

Dutchman mortise

Tape paper to inlay stock; transfer pattern with chisel

Paper

Shade with pencil

Folding saw-dolly

I have to share my shop space with an automobile and other "foreign objects" so from time to time I have to move my

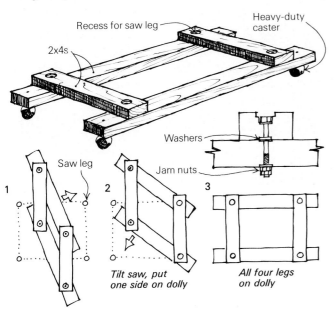

Recess for saw leg

Heavy-duty caster

2x4s

Washers

Jam nuts

Saw leg

1 2 3

Tilt saw, put one side on dolly

All four legs on dolly

table saw, which is on a four-legged, sheet-metal stand. To avoid having to drag the saw across the floor, I made a dolly that collapses like a pantograph. The folding action allows me to load the saw on the dolly one side at a time as shown in the sequence above. *—Robert E. Warren, Camarillo, Calif.*

Chair-rung chuck

In the Southern Appalachian mountains we turn dowels and rungs from stock that's been riven with a froe, then cleaned up with a hatchet or drawknife. With the device sketched below, you can quickly chuck the rough stock in the lathe.

To make the chuck, screw a 1½-in. thick hardwood block to a small faceplate. Turn the block to a 3-in. cylinder with a cone-shaped depression in the face, as shown in the sketch. Stop the lathe and with a V-parting chisel cut four ⅛-in. deep

grooves in the walls of the cone 90° apart to grab the corners of square stock.

Prepare the stock to be turned by giving it four quick licks with a hatchet to cut a short, square section on one end. With the square end of the stock in the cone, tighten the lathe's tailstock on the other end and you're ready to turn.

—W.W. Kelly, Clinton, Tenn.

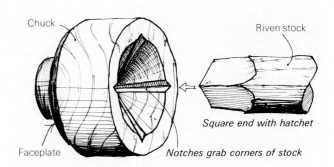

Chuck

Riven stock

Faceplate

Square end with hatchet

Notches grab corners of stock

Removing broken screws

To remove a broken screw, drill a small hole in the shank. Insert a copper wire in the hole to conduct heat, then heat the wire with a torch until the wood around the screw bubbles and smokes a bit. Quickly tap a tapered, square punch into

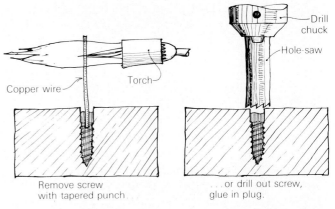

Drill chuck

Hole-saw

Copper wire

Torch

Remove screw with tapered punch . . .

. . . or drill out screw, glue in plug.

the hole and back out the screw. The heat liquefies resins in the wood and makes removal easier. Properly done, the procedure does not damage the hole, and another screw the same size may be used.

If the heat procedure doesn't work, drill out the broken screw with a tubular hole-saw just large enough to slip over the screw shank. Make the hole-saw by filing several coarse teeth in the end of a short section of thin steel tube. Drill out the broken screw, then glue in a plug to fill the hole.

—Jerry C. Blanchard, Carmel, Calif.

Adjustable miter-gauge stop

Here is a jig that's easy and fast to make and to use. It's basically a stick with a dowel through it, clamped to the table-saw miter gauge to give precise production-run cutoffs. It works at any angle. *—Alan Miller, Lakewood, Colo.*

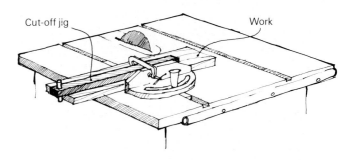

Cut-off jig

Work

Fixtures for Steambending
Adjustable end-stop and versatile table control breakage, springback

by Michael C. Fortune

Steambending allows me to work with simply curved pieces of wood that I can shape and blend together. Most of the curves I bend happen in one plane and are not exercises in pushing the limits of the process; most of my jobs are multiples, like sets of dining chairs. The trouble with steambending is the inconsistent and unpredictable results—breakage during the bending and springback afterward.

Since I cannot afford to cut extra blanks in anticipation of rejects, I've had to devise techniques that will ensure uniform results. I also required a high degree of design flexibility, a reasonable rate of productivity, quick set-up time and easy operation by one person, and low capital investment. The system I'll describe is based upon an adjustable end-stop that's attached to the usual steel back-up strap, and a special clamping table to which I can bolt a variety of bending forms.

When I've worked out a design, an integral part of my sequence for building the object is making a complete technical drawing. For steambending, this provides the length of the blanks to be bent, their cross-sectional dimensions so that I am sure of having enough material to shape and carve around joints, the joinery details and index points for the machine jigs I use, and the size and shape of the bending form itself. The way I work, it is not practical to guess about springback, nor to accommodate each part individually, nor to discard parts that do not match. In some cases, the grain in a bending blank is part of a visual composition and could not be substituted without sacrificing other components as well.

Immersing a straight piece of wood in hot steam plasticizes its fibers. When the steamed wood is bent, the fibers on the inside of the curve are compressed while those on the outside must stretch. Since the wood is much stronger in compression than in tension, a steel back-up strap with fixed end-stops is commonly used to restrain the length of the blank, thus shifting most of the stress into compression. If the strap is too loose, tension failure is the likely result—the wood fibers on the convex side of the bend stretch until they break. If the strap is too tight, the fibers on the inside of the curve may wrinkle and buckle, called compression failure.

In my early experiments, using fixed end-stops on the back-up strap, I got a few pieces of furniture and a large pile of rejected parts. Although I had machined all the blanks to the same length, some of the rejects failed in compression, while others failed in tension. I attributed these inconsistent results to the strap's having stretched during repeated use, and to my having used kiln-dried wood, which could have had such baked-in defects as casehardening or surface checking. The steaming time was also marginally inconsistent, since I put several pieces into the steam box at once, then used them one at a time. Eccentricities that grow into most

Michael Fortune, 29, designs and makes furniture in Toronto, Ont. He has also taught at Sheridan College.

pieces of wood also contributed to these inconsistent results.

To control these variables, I discarded the fixed end-stops for an adjustable end-fixture that could respond to each blank as the bend progressed. Also, I now use only air-dried wood, which in Ontario ranges in moisture content from 12% to 20% out-of-doors. Since severe bends may require more moisture, say 25% M.C., I may pre-steam the blank for an hour and let it sit in the steam box for a day before bending. I've successfully bent white oak, black walnut, cherry, ash and red oak, but the bending stock must be high quality, straight and free of defects.

Adjustable end-stop—The end-stops on the steel strap are subjected to considerable force as they compress the wood fibers around the bend. The end-stop must accommodate this force. The ones I am now using are shown in figure 1, on the next page, and an earlier version of the adjustable end-stop is shown in the photo. The principal material in both is ¼-in. and ⅜-in. by 2-in. bars of hot-rolled mild steel. My current version is welded from three thicknesses of bar. The adjustable end-stop fixture is not welded to the strap, but is detachable, so it can be mounted on straps that range from 1 in. to 6 in. wide according to the stock to be bent. The bottom of the fixture includes a 45° step that interlocks with a 45° step on the bending strap. A machine screw holds the fixture in place but does not receive any lateral force; if it did, it would quickly shear off. The adjusting thread is ⅜-11 N.C. running through a coupling nut about 2 in. long. The end-stop itself is made of ¼-in. or ⅜-in. angle iron with a short length of black iron pipe welded onto it. The pipe both locates the stop on the threaded rod and reinforces the angle iron. I generally make the stop 2 in. wide, but I add a steel reinforcing plate to the working face of the angle to make it larger than the end of the stock I am bending.

The strap is ¹⁄₁₆-in. steel, wide or wider than the stock, and able to take a bend without kinking. Holes are drilled ⅜ in. or ½ in. in diameter on 4-in. centers down the length of the strap, so its overall length can be grossly adjusted by the location of the fixed, hardwood end-stop, which is bolted on. Two holes are drilled through the end-stop for this purpose, with about 1½ in. overhanging on the end that faces the stock and 3 in. on the other end.

Bending table—I used to bend steamed wood around a form clamped to my workbench. To gain mechanical advantage, I attached levers to the end-stop and back-up strap assembly. My body weight was the main force, plus anyone willing to hang on for 15 minutes until the bent part could be removed and clamped to a drying jig. I needed a better way.

The versatile cast-iron table with square holes that welders use seemed appropriate. With this in mind, I fabricated a plywood table 4 ft. by 5 ft. by 3 in. thick to which I could

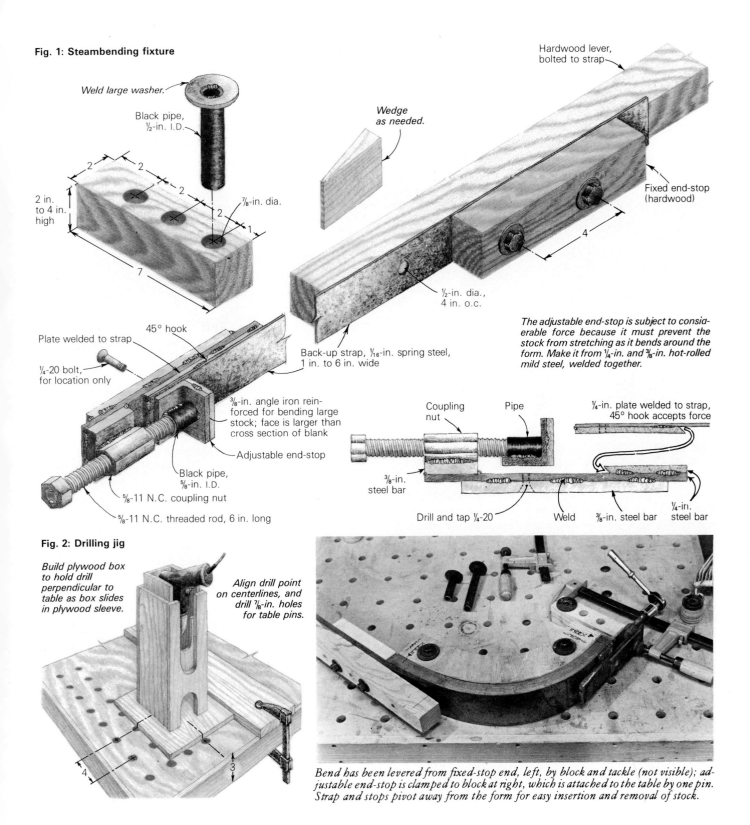

Fig. 1: Steambending fixture

Weld large washer.

Black pipe, ½-in. I.D.

⅞-in. dia.

2 in. to 4 in. high

2
2
2
2
1
7

Wedge as needed.

Hardwood lever, bolted to strap

Fixed end-stop (hardwood)

4

½-in. dia., 4 in. o.c.

The adjustable end-stop is subject to consid-erable force because it must prevent the stock from stretching as it bends around the form. Make it from ¼-in. and ⅜-in. hot-rolled mild steel, welded together.

45° hook

Plate welded to strap

¼-20 bolt, for location only

⅜-in. angle iron rein-forced for bending large stock; face is larger than cross section of blank

Adjustable end-stop

Back-up strap, ¹⁄₁₆-in. spring steel, 1 in. to 6 in. wide

Black pipe, ⅝-in. I.D.

⅝-11 N.C. coupling nut

⅝-11 N.C. threaded rod, 6 in. long

Coupling nut

Pipe

¼-in. plate welded to strap, 45° hook accepts force

⅜-in. steel bar

Drill and tap ¼-20

Weld

⅜-in. steel bar

¼-in. steel bar

Fig. 2: Drilling jig

Build plywood box to hold drill perpendicular to table as box slides in plywood sleeve.

Align drill point on centerlines, and drill ⅞-in. holes for table pins.

4

3

Bend has been levered from fixed-stop end, left, by block and tackle (not visible); ad-justable end-stop is clamped to block at right, which is attached to the table by one pin. Strap and stops pivot away from the form for easy insertion and removal of stock.

fasten bending forms. My table was laminated from four sheets of ¾-in. plywood, hardwood ply for the faces and floor sheathing for the core. Not having a veneer press, I laminated the sheets one at a time, using wood screws to provide clamp-ing pressure. I removed the screws before adding the next layer, so I could drill holes anywhere in the table without hit-ting embedded hardware. For design flexibility, I drilled a regular pattern of ⅞-in. holes through the table, and holes in my bending forms and adjustable end-stop fixture. These ac-commodate short lengths of iron pipe, ½-in. I.D., which act as locating pins. They can handle the substantial shear forces of the bending process and have a large washer welded to the top for easy insertion and removal. Half-inch bolts pass

through the table pins to secure the bending forms and ad-justable end-stop fixture to the table.

To drill perfectly perpendicular ⅞-in. holes through the large table, I constructed a tight-fitting box around a ½-in. hand drill. It slips into a sleeve mounted on a square of plywood, as shown in figure 2.

The pattern of holes eliminates the need for large, rein-forced bending forms, because most forms can be bolted to the table at several points. I prefer plywood forms, as the less dense core of particleboard will crush after repeated use. I cut the inside shape of the form parallel to its face so that clamps can be applied wherever they might be required.

The photo, above, shows how I mount the assembly. Note

Above, Fortune begins to pull in the block and tackle for the first bend of a chair seat. The stock is first steamed in the plywood box in the background; steam is generated by a salvaged boiler containing a 4.5-kilowatt immersion heater. Below, with the first corner turned, Fortune slackens off the adjustable end-stop before levering the wood around the second bend.

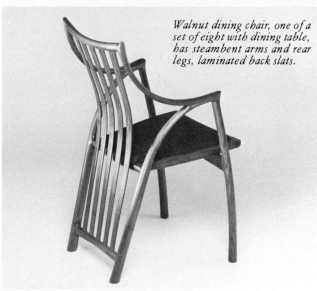

Walnut dining chair, one of a set of eight with dining table, has steambent arms and rear legs, laminated back slats.

David Allen

that the adjustable end-stop is at the starting point of the bend, and the fixed stop is at the free end of the blank. The adjustable end-stop is clamped to a wooden block, which in turn is located on the table by a table pin and a bolt. This arrangement allows the strap with both end-stops to pivot away from the form for quick installation of the heated blank, and easy removal of the bent piece. Index marks can be made on the form and transferred to the bent piece for later reference when machining joints. A dozen wooden clamping blocks, drilled with ⅞-in. holes, will come in handy, as they can be bolted down anywhere and wedged against the bent blank.

The final piece of the assembly is a lever bolted to the back of the bending strap at the wooden fixed-stop end. It provides mechanical advantage and supports the blank, which otherwise might compress locally or overturn off the strap. The lever reaches several inches beyond the stop toward the blank (see figure 1). It can be clamped to the blank here if trouble starts to develop, then the clamp removed when the blank is bent close to the form. A block and tackle can be attached to the lever at its far end, for additional leverage. This can be tied off in mid-bend, freeing the operator to adjust the end-fixture or to place clamps. A marine hardware spring-loaded cinch would be useful here too.

The bending process—Before bending, make sure that all forms, fixtures and clamps are in place. Set the steamed blank (steam an hour for every 1 in. of thickness) in the strap, making sure it's in line with the strap and with both end-stops. Tighten the threaded rod on the adjustable end-fixture. I use a ratchet, tightening until it's secure, then giving it another half-turn. This should flatten any kinks out of the strap.

The photos at left show a U-shaped bend around a chair-seat form. The first curve and first corner can be bent without backing off the adjustable fixture. However, upon approaching the second corner, the straight portion of the blank will start to arch away from the strap or to deform in an S-shape. I loosen the fixture just enough to relieve the excessive compression forces that have built up. The second bend can then be made.

I've found that springback can be minimized by leaving the bent part to cool on the form for 15 minutes, bathed in a slow stream of compressed air. Then it's quickly transferred to a setting jig of the same shape as the form before it has time to spring back. It is clamped there, and left for a week or preferably two weeks. The setting jig should be wide enough to accommodate all the parts being bent; clamps spanning the bend will maintain the distance between the ends of the blanks but do not help to maintain the shape. I accommodate the setting time by proceeding with other parts of the job according to my drawings.

It's important to allow the bent fibers to relax, and the wood to reach moisture equilibrium with the atmosphere. Since pieces may come out of the strap at 20% moisture content or higher (for severe bends), they must dry slowly, else they'll check. This problem is acute when bending red and white oak. I cover the setting jig with a blanket to restrict air flow for a few days, and this seems to control the problem. ☐

Further Reading
"Steam Bending," W.A. Keyser, *FWW* #8, Fall '77, pp. 40-45.
"Michael Thonet," John Dunnigan, *FWW* #21, Jan. '80, pp. 38-45.
Wood Bending Handbook, W.C. Stevens and N. Turner. Woodcraft Supply, 313 Montvale Ave., Woburn, Mass. 01888, $9.35, 110 pp.

Bending with Ammonia

by Bill Keenan

Consider the possibilities if wood were as pliable as leather. Form could be added to the beauty of wood without having to use subtractive methods of shaping. With this in mind, Huff Wesler, at the University of Wisconsin's Art Department, has experimented with wood that is plasticized by immersion in gaseous anhydrous ammonia. After exposure to the ammonia, wood can readily be coaxed into fantastic forms.

The underlying principle of this process is not hard to understand. A solvent applied to the wood diffuses into the cell-wall structure. The bonds that clamp the wood's microscopic components together are disassembled. The wood becomes flexible, and when bending force is applied the components are physically displaced. As the solvent diffuses out of the wood, these microscopic cell components bond together in their new positions. The piece regains its rigidity in the new shape, like hair after a permanent-wave treatment.

Steam has traditionally been used to soften wood, but ammonia plasticizes the fibers more quickly and more completely; yet ammonia is not so strong that it will dissolve cell tissue as might a stronger solvent. Only the cell components are separated, allowing movement with minimal bending stresses.

The process Wesler uses derives from research conducted over the past 15 years at Syracuse University, and commercial applications of it are covered by a number of U.S. patents. It's important to note that anhydrous ammonia (anhydrous means without water) is chemically pure NH_3, whereas household ammonia is a dilute solution of ammonia gas in water. Experiments with household ammonia will not bend wood.

Ammonia vapors are extremely dangerous to the eyes and lungs, and this process releases quantities of these noxious fumes. A fume hood and goggles are essential parts of the apparatus. The original Syracuse experiments were conducted atop a tall building, where strong winds carried the fumes away. Despite the awful vapors, Wesler believes the process holds real potential for the craftsman and sculptor.

He built a treatment chamber (see drawing at right) for introducing ammonia into wood; using parts acquired from ordinary plumbing suppliers and stainless-steel fittings from dairy suppliers, he spent under $1,000. The unit was welded together to withstand a pressure of 800 PSI as a safety measure. Pure, anhydrous ammonia at room temperature and at approximately 130 PSI pressure is used in the chamber.

The first step in treatment is selecting the right piece of wood. In general, woods good for steambending are also good for ammonia bending. Certain species work better than others; oak works well whereas maple does not. Bending stock should be straight-grained and flatsawn. Surface irregularities and such defects as knots should be avoided, because they tend to concentrate stress. Moisture content of the wood is also important. Wesler prepares his bending stock in a plastic enclosure into which moist heat is fed, like a steam room. The stock stays there for about a month, until its moisture content is raised to an optimal 20%.

The rest is simple. In a demonstration, Wesler places a ¼-in. thick hickory board in the treatment chamber and exposes it to the gaseous ammonia for about 45 minutes. Exposure time varies according to thickness and species of wood. Generally, an hour per ¼-in. thickness is adequate. When he

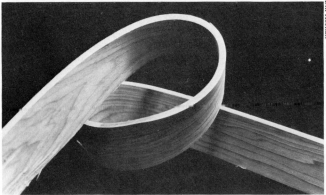

After plasticizing in anhydrous ammonia, the ¼-in. stock above was easily bent into a pretzel shape.

Anhydrous-ammonia treatment apparatus

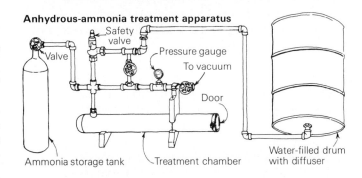

removes the piece, it's soft and ready to be shaped. Watching the piece being twisted into a pretzel shape reminds me of the delight I got as a child from watching a chicken bone that had been rubberized in a pressure cooker and was being flexed back and forth.

The bending rate can mean the difference between success and failure. If the piece crumples or kinks along its concave face, bending should be halted for about 30 seconds to allow the wood to flow. But there is also a time constraint, as the wood will begin to stiffen in about 15 minutes.

Ammonia-treated wood requires significantly less force to bend than steam-treated wood. Pieces ¼ in. thick can be bent by hand and then restrained by taping or clamping. There are other methods of bending, such as form bending, for which a mold is required. A pipe makes an excellent form for a helix or circle. Thicker pieces require a bending strap.

Once the bending is completed, the piece is dried until it reaches equilibrium with surrounding humidity conditions. A temperature and humidity-controlled drying room is best, but air-drying works well too. Warping and distortion can be controlled by leaving restraints on the piece until it is dry. This may take from hours to weeks, depending on the size and type of wood, and on the drying conditions.

Following exposure to ammonia, wood is changed in several ways. It is often denser and harder than before, a condition you can augment by compressing the wood while it is still soft. The color of the wood usually darkens slightly, but this can be an asset, as some plain woods come to life. Color change can be prevented with a sulfur-dioxide pretreatment.

There are a lot of variables involved in plasticizing wood, but the results are worth the trouble. The ease with which ammonia-treated wood can be bent, molded, embossed, densified or any combination of these processes offers a new horizon for the wood craftsman.

Bill Keenan is a woodworker and forester in Milwaukee, Wisc.

191

Building Stairs
Harry Waldemar shows the old-time way to a custom job

An open staircase. The closed stringer fits against a wall, while the open stringer on the handrail side shows in the downstairs room.

When Harry Waldemar, of Ardsley, N.Y., began his four-year apprenticeship in 1925, the stairbuilding trade had already begun to decline. During the 19th century, New York stairbuilders were known all over the country, and were called in for the toughest jobs everywhere. This was chiefly because the typical New York brownstone house contained a difficult stair whose handrail required a hairpin twist. The stairs were built and assembled in the shop, then shipped to the site for installation.

In 1903, a new law required all stairs over three stories to be fireproof, so much new construction turned to metal stairs. Then in 1925, the year Waldemar started in the shop of Oscar Neilsen, stock parts for making treads, balusters and handrails came on the market. Still, the builder of custom stairs was able to compete against the production shop until after World War II, when the postwar demand for housing encouraged quicker techniques and cheaper construction. Production shops took the lead for all but the most complicated stairways. Fewer and fewer men entered the old trade; those who did were older than an apprentice ought to be, and new labor laws made training a man unprofitable. By the time Waldemar retired in 1976, the art of building stairs from scratch had just about died. The situation has improved a little in the last few years, with surging interest in restoring old houses and reviving traditional craft techniques. Waldemar, whose long career includes building and installing a three-story tapering spiral stairway in the Rockefeller house at Seal Harbor, Me., increasingly found himself invited to conduct workshops for young carpenters.

An uneasy lecturer, Waldemar decided to record what he knew in the form of precisely detailed knock-down models, at one-half and one-quarter scale, of the various forms a good stair can take. But no matter how tricky the stair, the basic methods and standards of the craft remain the same. Waldemar demonstrates these on the following pages using his model of an open stair, where one stringer is fastened to the wall and the other is open to view in the downstairs room. This and his other models will be on display at the New York State Museum in Albany. Waldemar is also working on a book about stairbuilding.

—*Deborah Fillion*

Brownstone stairs, at one-quarter scale.

Waldemar disassembles the half-scale model.

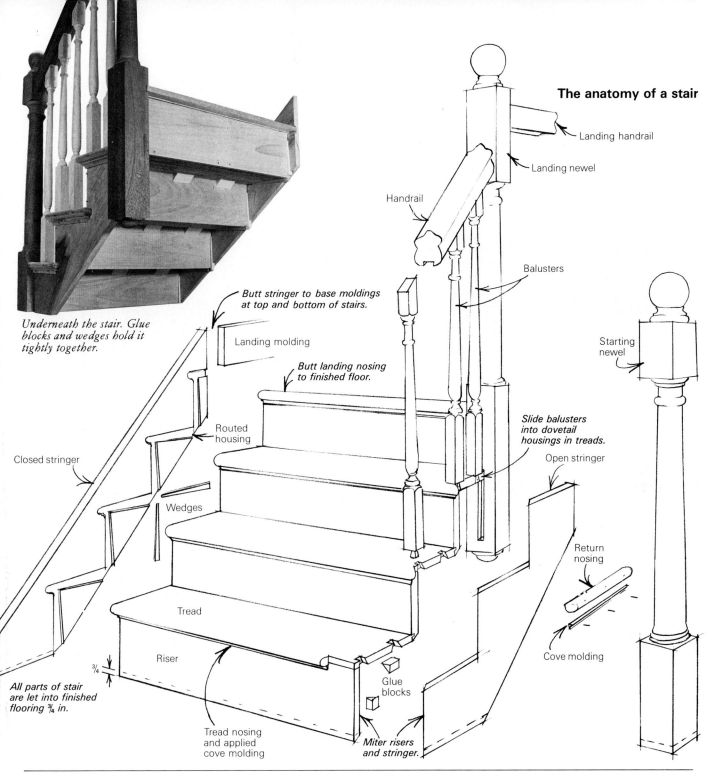

Underneath the stair. Glue blocks and wedges hold it tightly together.

The anatomy of a stair

Landing handrail

Landing newel

Handrail

Balusters

Butt stringer to base moldings at top and bottom of stairs.

Landing molding

Butt landing nosing to finished floor.

Starting newel

Routed housing

Slide balusters into dovetail housings in treads.

Closed stringer

Open stringer

Wedges

Return nosing

Tread

Riser

3/4

Glue blocks

Cove molding

All parts of stair are let into finished flooring 3/4 in.

Tread nosing and applied cove molding

Miter risers and stringer.

At the job site—A staircase consists of a stack of steps, and a step consists of one riser (the vertical board) and one tread (where you walk). The work begins by accurately measuring at the site; the drawing at right shows a typical flight, although the models that follow contain only four steps. The first measurement is the total rise from finished floor to finished floor. Always verify that the lower floor is level. If it's not, measure the variation at A' and allow for it. Since an average flight contains 14 risers, divide the rise by 14 to obtain the height of one riser. This dimension can vary from one stairway to another, but must be uniform within a flight, or else people will stumble. Risers are usually about 7¾ in. high.

There's always one fewer tread than riser, and an average run is 9 in. Thus 13 treads times 9 in. gives the total run of the flight, providing this run will permit headroom of 6½ ft., as drawn. Tread and riser dimensions can be adjusted, but this rule of thumb should always be observed: Two times the rise plus once the run should total between 24 in. and 25 in.

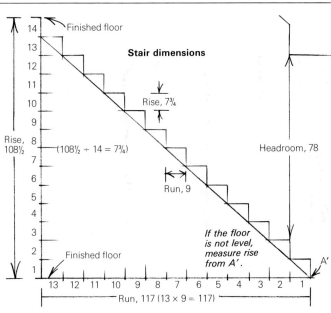

Finished floor

Stair dimensions

Rise, 7¾

Rise, 108½

(108½ ÷ 14 = 7¾)

Headroom, 78

Run, 9

If the floor is not level, measure rise from A'.

Finished floor

A'

Run, 117 (13 × 9 = 117)

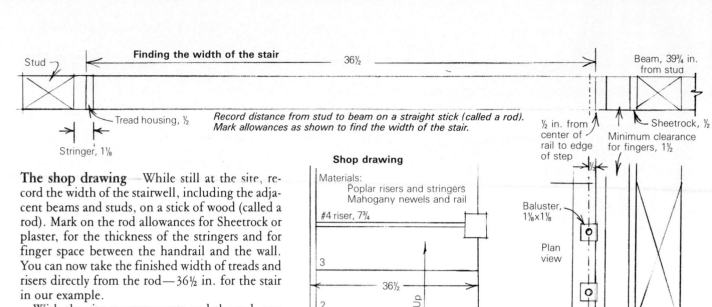

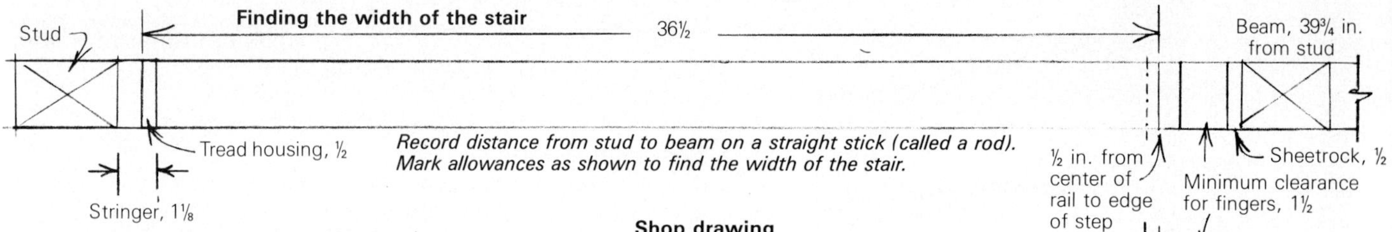
Finding the width of the stair
Stud
36½
Beam, 39¾ in. from stud
Tread housing, ½
Stringer, 1⅛
Record distance from stud to beam on a straight stick (called a rod). Mark allowances as shown to find the width of the stair.
½ in. from center of rail to edge of step
Sheetrock, ½
Minimum clearance for fingers, 1½

The shop drawing—While still at the site, record the width of the stairwell, including the adjacent beams and studs, on a stick of wood (called a rod). Mark on the rod allowances for Sheetrock or plaster, for the thickness of the stringers and for finger space between the handrail and the wall. You can now take the finished width of treads and risers directly from the rod—36½ in. for the stair in our example.

With the site measurements and the rod, you know enough to make a working drawing of the flight, in plan view (right). This drawing contains the information you'll need back at the shop to make and assemble all the parts of the stair.

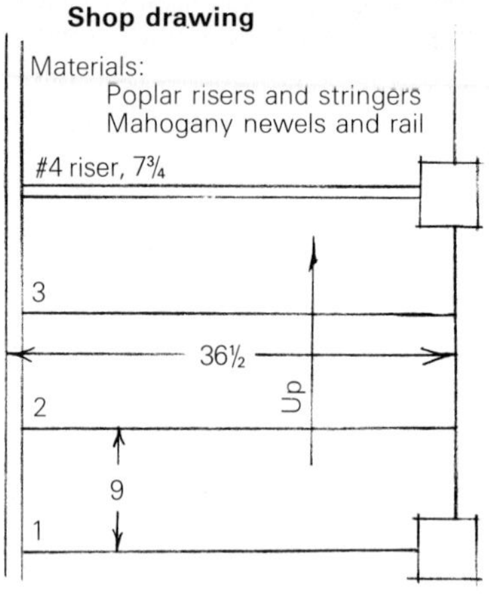
Shop drawing
Materials:
Poplar risers and stringers
Mahogany newels and rail
#4 riser, 7¾
3
36½
Up
2
9
1

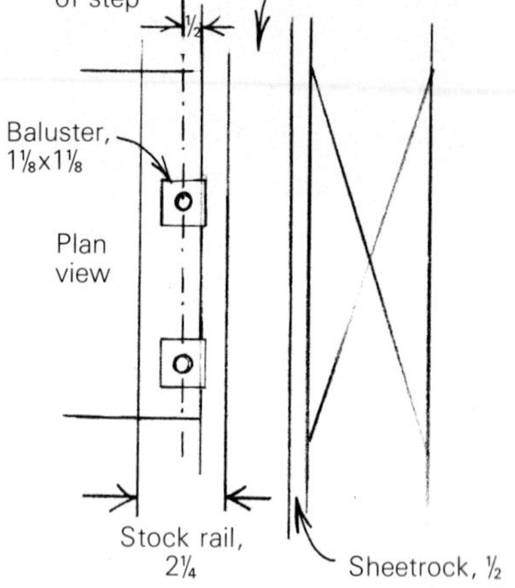
½
Baluster, 1⅛x1⅛
Plan view
Stock rail, 2¼
Sheetrock, ½

The pitch board—Back at the shop, the first things to make are a pitch board and two stair gauges. The pitch board is a right-angled triangle sawn from plywood, whose sides are the rise of one riser and the run of one tread. The stair gauges, one for the closed stringer and one for the open stringer, are used to position the pitch board when laying out the stringers, as shown below. You'll refer to the pitch board throughout the job, so make sure it's accurate.

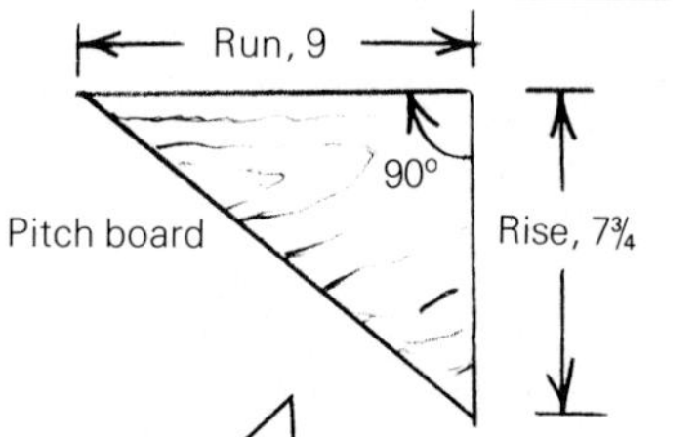
Run, 9
90°
Pitch board
Rise, 7¾

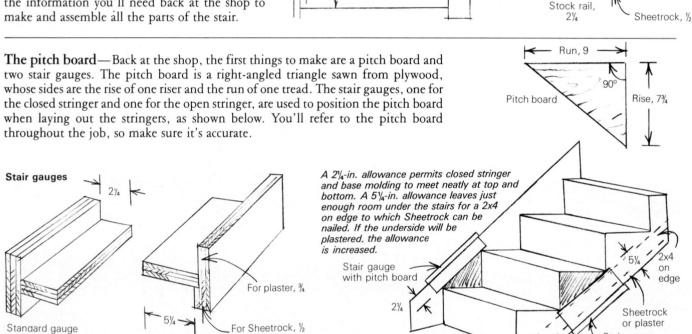

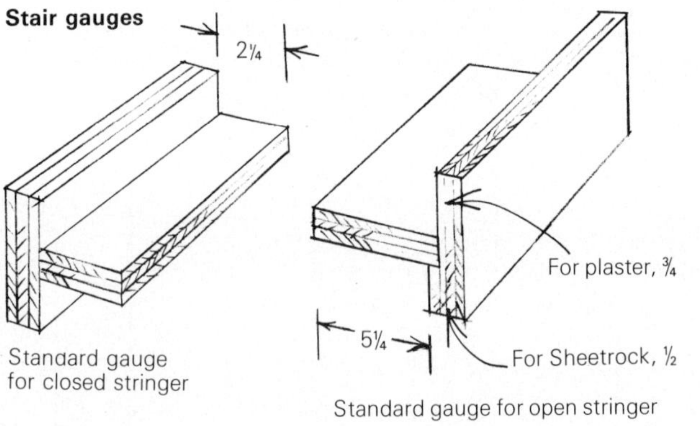
Stair gauges
2¼
For plaster, ¾
5¼
For Sheetrock, ½
Standard gauge for closed stringer
Standard gauge for open stringer

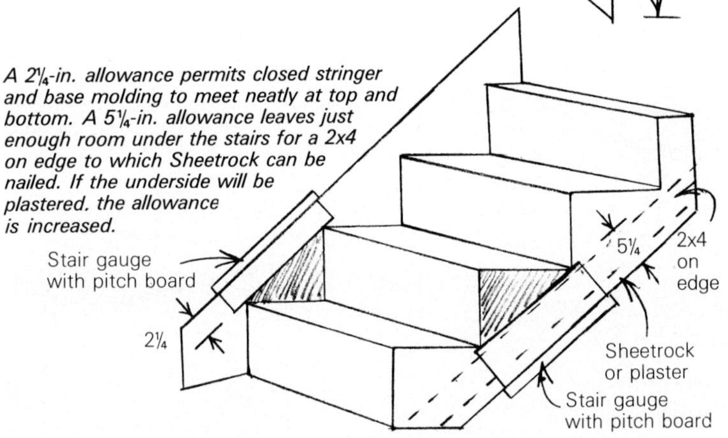
A 2¼-in. allowance permits closed stringer and base molding to meet neatly at top and bottom. A 5¼-in. allowance leaves just enough room under the stairs for a 2x4 on edge to which Sheetrock can be nailed. If the underside will be plastered, the allowance is increased.
Stair gauge with pitch board
2¼
5¼
2x4 on edge
Sheetrock or plaster
Stair gauge with pitch board

The closed stringer—The closed stringer, also called the housed stringer, anchors one side of the stair to the stairwell wall. It starts out as a 5/4x10 board (1⅛x9¼) of pine or poplar. To find its rough length, measure the long side of the pitch board (12 in. in our example) and multiply by the number of steps, then add a foot or two for waste. Normally, for 14 risers, you'll need a 16-ft. board.

Layout begins at the top, using the pitch board and the closed-stringer gauge to establish a line that will be the vertical end of the stringer in the finished stair. Next, shift the pitch board 3 in. to allow for the landing nosing, then trace around the pitch board to locate the outside faces of the first riser and tread. Proceed down the board. At the bottom, add the thickness of the finished floor (usually ¾ in.) to the height of the last riser. Good stairs rest on the subfloor, with the finished floor fit around the bottom step and newel post. Thus the floor holds the stairs in place. If the floor's already installed, you must chop it out to fit.

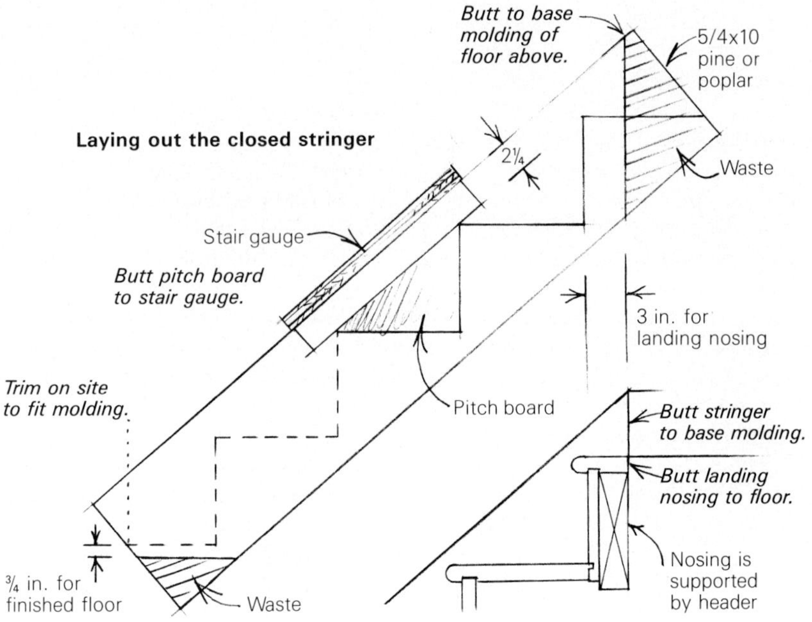
Laying out the closed stringer
Butt to base molding of floor above.
5/4x10 pine or poplar
2¼
Waste
Stair gauge
Butt pitch board to stair gauge.
3 in. for landing nosing
Trim on site to fit molding.
Pitch board
Butt stringer to base molding.
Butt landing nosing to floor.
Nosing is supported by header
¾ in. for finished floor
Waste

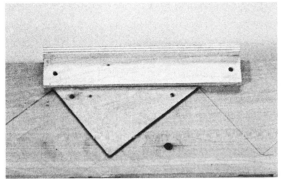

After laying out the closed stringer with pitch board and stair gauge, above, the router template, right (oversize for various size stairs), is used to rout the step housings.

Routing the closed stringer—The zig-zag housing is routed ½ in. deep into the closed stringer, to accept the ends of the treads and risers, plus the wedges that lock them in place. You can make a router template for use with a guide bushing (photo, top right), or you can develop the housing layout from the pitch-block lines and excavate the waste with saw, chisel and router plane. Routing done, finish up by chopping small recesses to receive the end of the cove molding that covers the joint between the tread nosing and the riser below. Production shops merely butt this molding against the stringer.

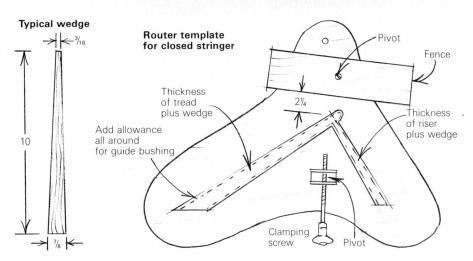

The open stringer—The open stringer supports the other side of the stair; treads rest on it and risers meet it in a neat miter. At the bottom it rests on the subfloor, at the top it is housed in the landing newel. Thus it is shorter than the housed stringer by the amount of the top riser and the 3-in. nosing allowance. It's also wider, being cut from a 5/4x12 board of pine or poplar. Use the pitch board and the 5¼-in. gauge to lay it out as shown, starting with a full tread at the top and allowing for the finished floor at the bottom. It can be cut out on the table saw and bandsaw, but not easily. Stairbuilders saw it by hand at the bench, using a leg vise that rises several inches above the bench surface. First make a relief cut above the line of each tread, then saw all the treads, then saw the miters for the risers. The miters should be accurate, although they can be undercut by about the thickness of a pencil line to make a neat fit certain.

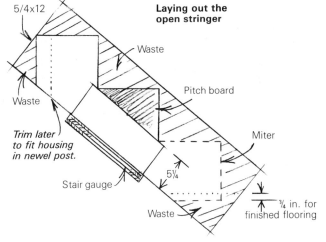

The completed stringers, below.

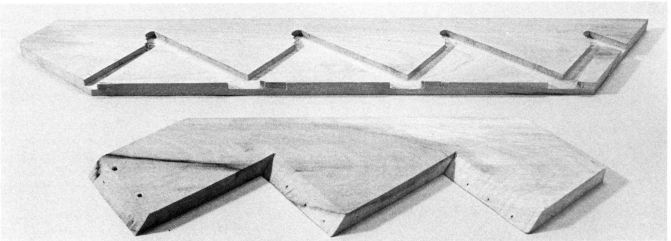

195

Treads—It's usual to buy pre-milled tread stock of white or red oak, 12 in. wide and 36 in. or 42 in. long, planed to 1 in. thick, with the nosing molded on one edge. The tread depth in our example is the 9-in. run, plus 1¼ in. for the nosing, plus ¼ in. for the tongue, a total of 10½ in. Rip the stock to this width.

The measuring stick gives us the length of each tread, 36½ in. This includes the half-inch that's housed inside the closed stringer, but you must still add 1¼ in. for the miter that meets the return nosing on the open side, plus ⅛ in. in order to have a place to start sawing this miter. Thus the treads must be crosscut to 37⅞ in. long; this requires purchasing 42-in. stock. Using the table saw, router or shaper, make the ¼-in. tongue on the back edge of each tread, and the ¾-in. groove on the underside where the riser fits. The spindle shaper is the right machine for these operations, and is essential in the small stair shop because it will also produce moldings, nosings and handrails.

Lay out the nosing miter. On the table saw, crosscut to within 2 in. of the miter, cut the miter itself, then remove the waste.

Section through step

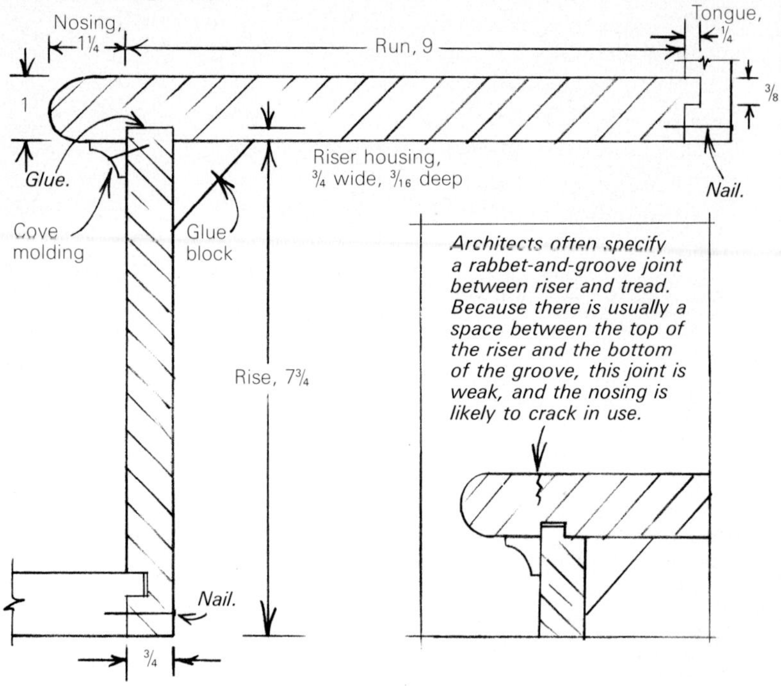

Nosing, 1¼
Run, 9
Tongue, ¼
1
⅜
Glue.
Nail.
Riser housing, ¾ wide, ³⁄₁₆ deep
Cove molding
Glue block
Rise, 7¾
Nail.
¾
Architects often specify a rabbet-and-groove joint between riser and tread. Because there is usually a space between the top of the riser and the bottom of the groove, this joint is weak, and the nosing is likely to crack in use.

Plan of tread

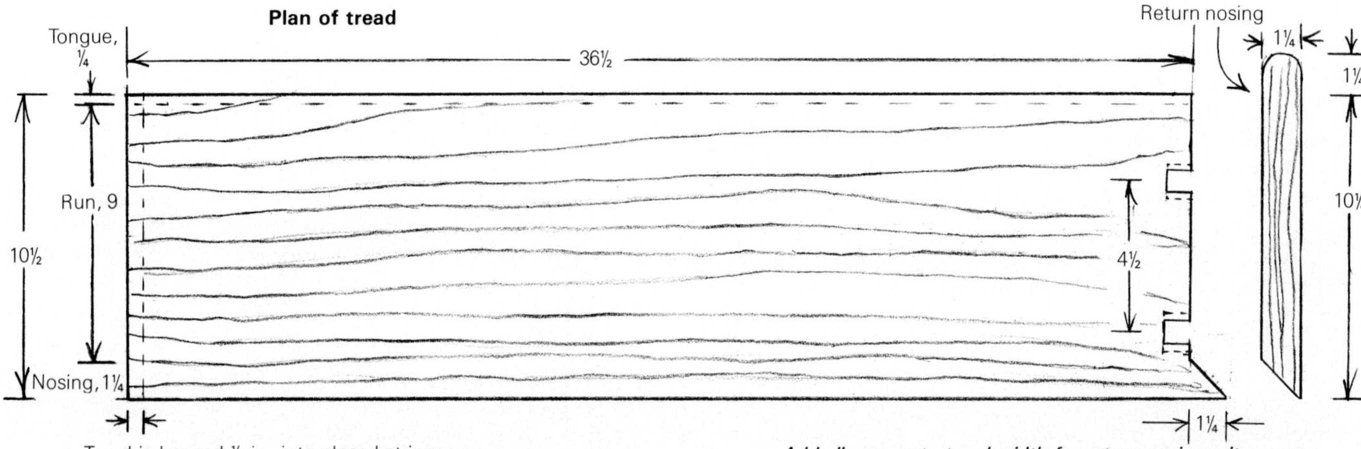

Tongue, ¼
36½
Return nosing
1¼
Run, 9
10½
4½
10¼
Nosing, 1¼
1¼

Tread is housed ½ in. into closed stringer

Add allowance to tread width for return-nosing miter.

Baluster housings—If you turn your own balusters, you'll be able to make the traditional dovetail on their bottoms, which allows you to mount the balusters from the stair's open side after the handrail is in place. Besides finishing the end of the tread, the return nosing then traps the balusters. You'll need to cut a pair of dovetail housings in the open end of each tread. Position the front housing so the front edge of the baluster is directly over the face of the riser below. The housing is normally ¾ in. wide on the top surface of the tread, spreading to 1¼ in. at the bottom, and a uniform ¾ in. deep.

If you are buying stock balusters, they'll come with a round pin instead of a dovetail. Drill for the pin so that the shoulder of the baluster covers the joint between the tread and the return nosing by ¹⁄₁₆ in. Then saw a slot so the baluster can still be slipped in from the open side. Whether the pin is round or dovetailed, a single nail locks it in place.

Return nosing—The return nosing completes the tread. You can buy it by the running foot, leaving you to shape the back end like the nosing profile and miter the front end to length. Or, you can shape and saw it from tread scrap, starting with pieces 12 in. wide and 14 in. or so long. The strategy is to shape all four edges of the scrap, rip a nosing 1¼ in. wide from each long edge, reshape the cut edges and rip again. Then miter each nosing to an overall length of 11½ in.—the 9-in. run plus 1¼ in. at both ends, as shown below, at right.

Two types of baluster housings

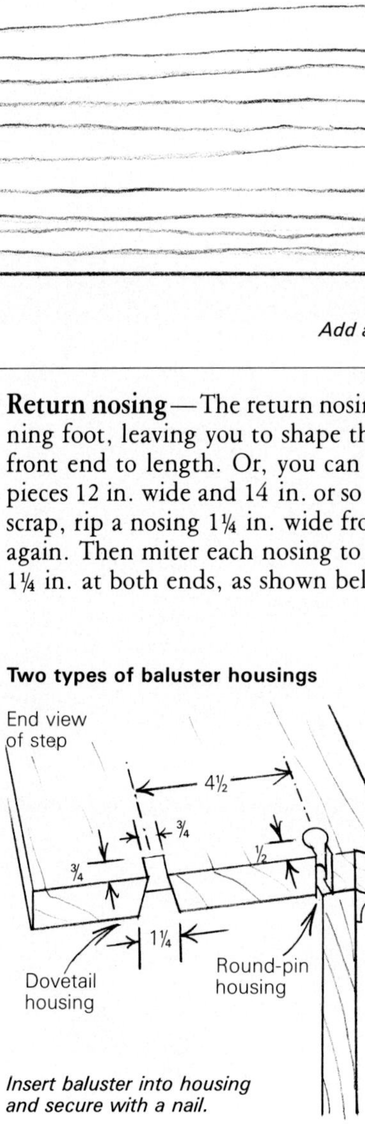

End view of step
4½
¾
¾
½
1¼
Dovetail housing
Round-pin housing

Insert baluster into housing and secure with a nail.

Shaping return nosing

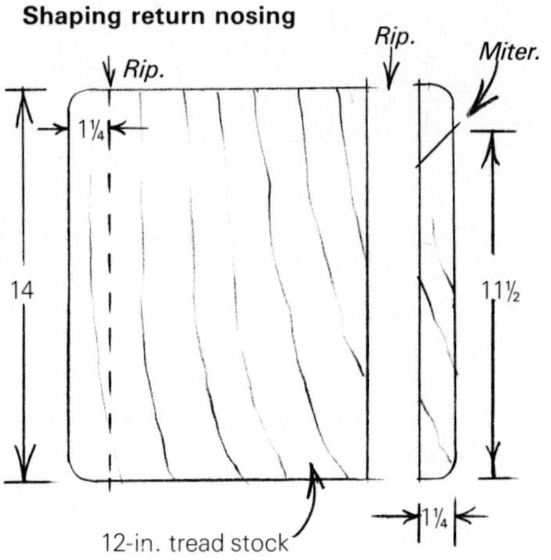

Rip.
Rip.
Miter.
1¼
14
11½
1¼
12-in. tread stock

Here's how all the pieces of a finished step come together at the housed side (left) and the open-stringer side (right). You can see the fine points that make the difference between custom and production stairs. In custom stairs the riser is fully housed in the bottom of the tread, rather than being nailed or rabbeted, as in production stairs. The coved molding at this joint is let into the closed stringer in custom stairs, cut

short to abutt it in production stairs. Production builders also often skip the tongue and groove at the back of the treads and lower face of the risers, relying on a few nails here instead. They usually do without glue blocks underneath too. Not much holds such stairs together, and that's why they squeak. Once the stair is installed, there's no way to get in and reinforce it, so it's best to do the job right in the first place.

Risers—Risers can be pine, but if they are to be painted, poplar is better. Buy 10-in. stock planed to ¾ in. thick, then rip it to 7¹⁵⁄₁₆ in. wide—that is, the rise of 7¾ in. plus ³⁄₁₆ in. which will be housed in the groove of the tread above. The waste ripped off can be shaped or routed into cove molding. Miter one end of the riser where it will meet the open stringer, then cut to finished length, 36½ in. in our example, taken from the measuring rod. It's best to cut the groove near the bottom edge of each riser after gluing, or else the steps could come out crooked.

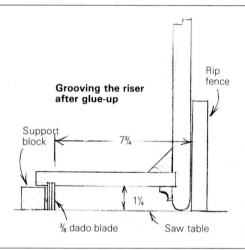

Grooving the riser after glue-up

Support block

Rip fence

7¾

1¼

³⁄₈ dado blade

Saw table

Gluing up—One step consists of a tread and the riser below it. Glue each riser into the groove milled on the bottom side of its tread, add glue blocks to the back, then glue and nail the cove molding to conceal the joint. When the glue has set, arrange the table saw as shown and cut the groove into the face of the riser ³⁄₈ in. wide and ¼ in. deep. The top of the groove will be parallel with and exactly 7¾ in. from the face of the tread. Tack the return nosing in place, using 6d finishing nails—you'll remove them later to insert the balusters. Sand the steps before assembly.

Assembling the flight—Stairs are usually assembled and glued up at the shop, then shipped to the job site in complete flights, although without handrail and balusters. Start at the top, with the first complete step (not the top riser and landing nosing). Lay the closed stringer flat on the floor, insert the step and tap in the wedges that lock it in place. Wedging the top step tight will be enough to square off the flight, so now drop the remaining steps into their housings, wedging loosely as needed. Add the open stringer, nailing through the miter into the end grain of the risers. Three nails per riser will hold it. Next, wedge the closed side, gluing in the riser wedges first and trimming them flush to allow clearance for the tread wedges to be glued in tightly. Then back-nail the bottom of the risers to the treads, spacing the nails 8 in. to 10 in. apart under the tongue. Add glue blocks to the open stringer, one block under each tread and one behind each riser. Like the wedges on the closed side of the staircase, these glue blocks will keep the stairs tight and free of squeaks. Tack the cove molding under the return nosings. Notice that nails are never driven into the face of the treads. Now you're ready to fit the newel posts, top riser and landing nosing, all of which must be done before installation because the finished floor will have to be fit and laid around them.

Open stringer will be glued and nailed to the partially assembled flight.

Starting newel—The starting newel, at the foot of the stair, has a large housing chopped in it to fit around the outside corner of the bottom step. The newel should be laid out before it is turned, usually from a blank 4 in. square by 4 ft. long. Start the layout by scribing a centerline on two adjacent faces of the blank, then locate the shoulders that separate the turned shaft and cap from the sections left square (right). Begin at the top of the post; the important dimension is from the crest of the handrail to the top of the first tread, 30 in. Since the handrail enters at the pitch angle, use the pitch board to establish its vertical thickness. At the foot of the post, the stringer is let in ½ in. past the centerline, whereas the face of the bottom riser goes in right on the centerline. There's also a shallow housing for the tread nosing and its cove molding (trimmed to fit). The return nosing is cut off flush with the newel. Allow an extra ¾-in. to be let into the finished floor. After laying out the newel, turn it and cross-cut it to length, then saw and chisel the housings.

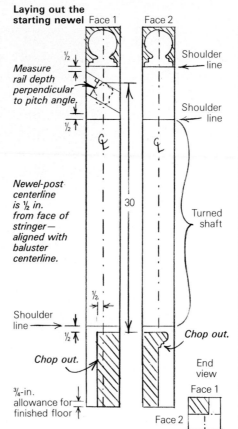

Laying out the starting newel

Face 1
Face 2

½

Measure rail depth perpendicular to pitch angle.

½

Shoulder line

Shoulder line

Newel-post centerline is ½ in. from face of stringer— aligned with baluster centerline.

Turned shaft

30

Shoulder line

½

Chop out.

½

Chop out.

End view

¾-in. allowance for finished floor

Face 1
Face 2

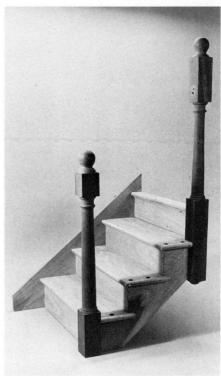

Screws from behind secure the newels. They are fitted to the flight before it's installed, so the floor can be laid around them.

The landing newel (top) and starting newel, with their housings. Note the difference in the lengths of the turned shaft and of the square sections.

The assembled flight, with newels removed. Portions of the top and bottom treads and their moldings must be sawn away to fit the newel housings.

The starting newel houses the tread nosing and its cove molding.

Landing newel—Because it accommodates a handrail on the landing, and also houses the top riser and the top of the open stringer, the landing newel is taller than the starting newel. A 5-ft. blank is usually long enough. The landing handrail runs straight out the back of the newel (face 1, right), so this newel must be laid out on three adjacent faces, beginning from centerlines and working down from the top. As before, the critical elevations to establish are the level of the landing itself, and of the shoulders that define the newel's turned portions. The crest of the landing rail is 34 in. above the landing nosing, and the crest of the pitched handrail is 30 in. above the landing, as it was on the starting newel. With these points established, you then scribe onto face 2 of the newel the profile of the nosing itself, of the top riser, and of the back end of the top tread, all of which should be cut back so they fit in what will be a ½-in. deep housing. The step profile and the end of the open stringer may then be scribed onto face 3. Leave 1¼ in. below the stringer before laying out the drop that completes the newel. Finally, scribe the housings for the landing rail. The pitched rail need not be housed. This layout is more difficult to describe and draw than to do; its logic is apparent when you have an assembled stair or a model that you can refer to.

Screws through stringer and riser, from beneath the stair, secure this type of newel in place. Newels are usually fitted to the flight before it leaves the shop, then removed for shipping. Make sure they're plumb, then measure between the newels to find the length of rail stock you need.

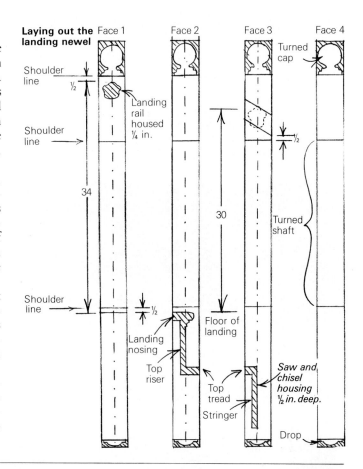

Handrailing—You can buy handrailing, or you can shape your own on the shaper. Either way, start by plowing a groove ¼ in. deep down the center of the underside of the rail, wide enough to fit the square section atop the balusters. Use the pitch board to miter the ends of the handrail, to the length you took by measuring between the newels. Butt the handrails to the newels and secure them with nails or screws.

Balusters—Each tread carries two balusters, one shorter than the other because of the handrail's pitch. They look best when the turned portion begins at the level of the top of the next tread, and ends at a uniform distance below the handrail. Thus the difference in length is accommodated in the central turning, not in the square sections at top and bottom. To lay them out, draw a full-size side elevation of one step. The turning must include stock for the dovetail pins that fit the housings in the ends of the treads. These dovetails can be sawn in the square baluster, but it's quicker to turn a cone-shape and trim it to fit. Leave the tops of the turnings overlong, and use the pitch board to trim them to length, not forgetting the extra ¼ in. that fits into the handrail. Two finishing nails into the handrail, and one through the dovetail, hold them in place. Replace the return nosing and its cove molding, gluing the mitered ends. Set the nails, drive a nail through the miter, and you're done. □

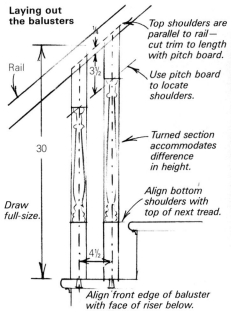

Two nails secure each baluster to the bottom of the handrail. The top of the baluster is sawn at the pitch angle.

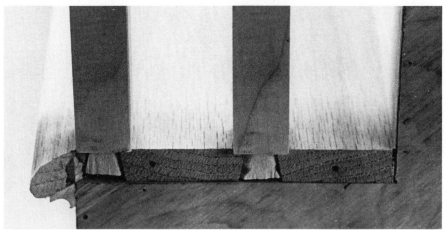

A single nail locks the bottom of the baluster to its tread.

WOOD, FINISHING

Man-Made Boards
Working with particleboard and fiberboard

by Simon Watts

Three man-made boards: left, waferboard, used only in construction; center, furniture-grade particleboard, showing characteristic layered structure (fine particles for the faces, coarse particles for the interior); and right, medium-density fiberboard, with uniformly dense edges. Photo: Forest Products Laboratory.

Howard solid wood is used to make furniture, its fibers, the actual strands of ligno-cellulose, remain arranged much as they were in the living tree. If the wood is sliced into sheets and then glued together so that the grain of adjacent layers runs at right angles to one another, we get plywood, a composite material with some of the properties of the original wood plus some new ones—it won't split easily and it's more stable. In spite of this, it is easily recognizable as wood, and the fibers in each veneer are still aligned almost as they were in the tree.

Instead of making plywood, suppose we grind the original piece of wood into flakes, chips or sawdust, coat the particles with glue and press the result into sheets. We have a new material—particleboard—with properties somewhat different from both plywood and solid wood. It is equally strong in both directions, for example. Although particleboard is barely recognizable as a wood product, if we inspect it under a hand lens we can see the individual elements still organized as they were in the tree.

We could go one step further and reduce the wood to its component fibers by steaming or with solvents. This technique opens up a new range of possibilities. Fibers can be mixed with water to form a slurry, which is deposited on moving, porous belts to make paper, or they can be dried, blown into forming machines and then pressed into fiberboard. Whatever the final result—tissue paper, cardboard, soft insulation board or hardboard—these products all have one thing in common. The arrangement of the individual fibers is now random, and has no relation to how they grew in the tree. Its fibers have been reorganized.

These processes of modifying the structure of wood do not end with fiberboard. The cellulose portion can be liquefied by solvents and used to make such new materials as rayon, cellulose lacquer and cellophane. But furniture-makers have not yet turned to cellophane, and plywood has been around long enough to be well understood. Particleboard and fiberboard, on the other hand, have developed so rapidly that the techniques of working with them and designing for them have not yet caught up.

It is time to take a fresh look at the new generation of sheet materials and to stop thinking of them as substitutes for solid wood. After manufacturing out of the tree all the irregularities that make it a unique material, it seems perverse to then reconstitute it to look like old barn boards or wormy chestnut. This practice only encourages people to think that man-made board and solid wood have a lot in common. Although they can be worked with the same tools, the fact is that they don't have much in common. Man-made board has large, smooth surfaces; although generally weaker, it is uniform and dimensionally stable, compared to solid wood, moving minimally and predictably in response to humidity changes.

Even woodworkers excited by these new materials have dif-

ficulty making the switch. This is because there is such a weight of accumulated experience where solid wood is concerned—much of which has to be discarded when working with man-made board. It is structurally incongruous, for instance, to use particleboard for frame-and-floating-panel construction, a design developed to allow for the seasonal movement of a solid-wood panel.

Solid wood, for practical reasons of weight and drying, has traditionally been worked in thicknesses under 2 in. But using man-made boards, it is possible to choose your own thickness by means other than lamination—hollow-core construction, for instance. The dimensional stability of man-made board makes it possible to organize the architecture of the piece—the interplay of solids and voids—in ways that are simply not possible in solid wood. Also, the large, smooth surfaces invite the use of color and texture in coverings that can produce a wide range of visual effects. These may have little or nothing to do with the underlying structure.

Particleboard, the oldest of the new man-made boards, first appeared in Europe after World War II. The forests had been depleted, and after the widespread destruction of the war there was a desperate need for building materials. Particleboard utilized low-grade raw materials—trees too small or crooked to be sawn into lumber, as well as sawdust and shavings. Particleboard panels were soon being produced in quantity, but America, with its vast timber resources, was slower to adopt its manufacture. In the past ten years this situation has changed dramatically—America produced 3.3 billion square feet in 1979, enough to cover 80,000 acres.

Particleboard can be made from almost any species of wood, hard or soft, from large trees or planer shavings. The wood does not have to be new, and even old railroad ties have been used experimentally. Starting with round logs, the first step is to remove the bark. The wood is then reduced to ¾-in. to 2-in. chips and fed into a ring-flaker, which yields thick shavings. It's then dried, graded by size and blown into large storage bins. As needed, the particles are sprayed with glue and shaped into mats in vacuum-forming machines where they are deposited, like snowflakes, on moving metal plates. These mats then enter a precompressor, which reduces them to a height of 10 in. or less. Next they are trimmed and sent to the main press for a 1,600-PSI squeeze.

After pressing, the panels must be immediately cooled or else the glue bond deteriorates. They are slowly pivoted on one edge, like the leaves of a giant book, trimmed again, then fed through a series of drum sanders to remove about 1/32 in. from each side, reducing them to uniform thickness.

Virtually all particleboard sold, both construction and furniture-grade, is made by pressing like this, but it can also be made by extrusion. Extruded particleboard begins with dry wood, which is splintered by grinding or hammer-milling and then sprayed with glue as before. The glue/particle mix is squeezed through a heated die and emerges as a continuous ribbon, like toothpaste. By changing the shape of the die, different sections can be made, and some experimenters have made 2x4s and even I-beams.

Extrusion is the cheaper process because no forming press is involved. But it cannot produce "layered boards" having a surface composition different from the interior. Particleboard intended for the furniture industry is different from construction-grade particleboard commonly sold in building-supply stores and used for sheathing and floor underlayment. It has this layered composition: fine particles on the surfaces and coarser ones in between. A board composed entirely of fine particles would be heavy and wasteful of glue; one made only of large particles would soon lose its smoothness as the surface absorbed moisture with changes in humidity. For this reason trying to cover construction-grade particleboard with wood veneer is a lost cause. The coarse surface particles will swell and soon show through the veneer until the surface has the texture of oatmeal.

Most furniture-grade particleboard goes directly, in large quantities, to furniture factories. It is therefore difficult to obtain at retail, though some of the larger outlets are beginning to stock it. It's easily recognized by its size: 4 ft. 1 in. by 8 ft. 1 in., instead of the standard 4x8 sheets used in the building trade. If your local lumber dealer doesn't carry it, ask him to order it for you from his wholesaler.

Fiberboard is not layered but still retains its smooth surface in spite of changes in humidity. The manufacturing process begins by softening and loosening the wood fibers. Raw sawmill wastes are first fed into large boilers, where they are subjected to intense steam pressure for several minutes. When the pressure is suddenly released, the particles explode into a pulpy mass. This thick batter is then forced through a ring-refiner where the shearing action between two rotating discs tears the particles to fibers. From here it goes to flash-tube driers where, in less than three seconds, its moisture content is reduced to 2% or 3%. Then it is sprayed with a fine mist of glue and stored in large bins until needed. The glue is activated under the heat and pressure of pressing.

This process is similar to making particleboard except that the fiberboard material is much fluffier, and a mat 23 in. high will squeeze down to make a 3/4-in. board. After pressing and cooling, boards are sanded and cut to order on a variety of computer-controlled equipment.

A typical fiberboard plant uses 300 tons of sawmill wastes—sawdust and shavings—each day, and 30 tons of

A knife-ring flaker reduces wood to chips on its way to becoming particleboard. Raw material enters the chute and is thrown against the rotating knives by centrifugal force. This machine is about 10 ft. high and contains 56 knives, each 2 ft. long. Photo: Pallmann Pulverizer Co.

A typical particleboard press. The largest of these presses, in Brazil, can produce 26 4x8 panels every six minutes—more than a million square feet per day. Photo: Washington Iron Works.

urea-formaldehyde glue. One of the striking features of such a plant is that it not only feeds on waste but also produces practically none itself. Offcuts prior to final pressing go back to the storage bins, subsequent trimmings fire the flash driers, and dust from the sanders is collected to heat the boilers.

Depending principally on the amount of pressure applied and the thickness of the original mat, the product of a fiberboard plant may be a lightweight insulation board, with a density of 15 lb. to 20 lb. per cubic foot; medium-density fiberboard (MDF) 44 lb. to 55 lb.; or a high-density fiberboard (HDF) weighing approximately 60 lb. per cubic foot. Known as hardboard or Masonite, high-density board can be toughened (tempered) and made weather resistant by hot-rolling with oil.

For making furniture, fiberboard is superior to particleboard in every respect except availability. It has a better surface quality that stays smooth regardless of changes in humidity, which makes it an excellent substrate for veneers. Its edges are tighter, making them easier to mill, mold and finish, and somewhat better able to hold fasteners. It is easier to glue because there are no voids. Its lower glue content makes it less abrasive to tools and, very likely, less of a health hazard to the woodworker. As its advantages become more

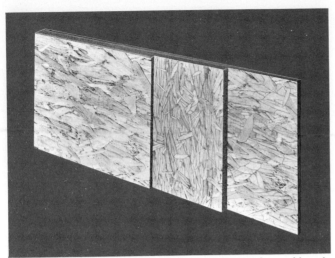

The newest type of man-made board is OSB (oriented-strand board), in which the face strands are aligned with the length of the board, while the interior strands run the width. Experiments are being conducted to produce boards with surfaces smooth enough to be used in furniture. Photo: Elmendorf Corp.

widely known, fiberboard could eventually supersede particleboard altogether. Again, the most likely way to obtain it at present is to ask your local retailer to order it for you from his wholesaler.

Oriented-strand board (OSB) has a layered construction, like furniture-grade particleboard, but the particles are not placed at random. It has a distinct "grain" because the fibers in the top and bottom surfaces are aligned lengthwise while the middle layer runs across the width of the board like plywood. Unlike plywood, however, it does not require scarce and expensive veneer logs but can be made from low-grade cordwood. The first U.S. manufacturer, Elmendorf Board Corp., has started production in Claremont, N.H.

Working with man-made boards—All these new sheet materials depend on glue, fiberboards less than particleboards because the interweaving of the fibers gives strength and also because the lignin remaining from the tree acts somewhat as a natural adhesive. The two common glues are urea and phenol formaldehyde, which release formaldehyde vapor both before and after manufacture.

When a Seattle research team exposed laboratory rats to this vapor at residual levels often found in mobile homes, whose interiors are sealed tight with man-made boards, the animals developed an abnormally high rate of nasal cancer. It is known also that with heat, as generated when machining man-made boards, these glues decompose, releasing formaldehyde. Without further research it is impossible to know what the health hazards of living and working with products made from these glues really are. The Federal Consumer Products Safety Commission has proposed a ban on urea-formaldehyde foam insulation (which also releases vapor), and industry is looking into alternative adhesives. In the meantime it seems prudent to work with these materials in well-ventilated areas, to wear a respirator with an organic-vapor cartridge when machining them, and to seal raw surfaces to reduce vapor emission in finished products.

Formaldehyde glues are highly abrasive and soon take the edge off even a high-quality steel blade. Particleboard is worse than fiberboard in this respect because of its higher glue content. Carbide-tipped sawblades are now used almost exclusively, and special tooth configurations have been developed (see *FWW* #23, July '80, p. 72). The features that everyone wants in a blade are long tool life, clean cutting and minimum tear-out. However, these requirements conflict, and no single tooth form or combination entirely satisfies them.

The common rip tooth (or flat-top) is not recommended for cutting particleboard because it takes such a big bite that

Structural properties of some man-made boards

This table compares the structural properties of ¾-in. particleboards and fiberboards typically used for furniture. As one would expect, the denser the material the stronger it is and the better able to hold fasteners. Expansion and contraction as a result of changes in humidity, although small, cannot always be disregarded. An 8-ft. panel of MDF, for example, would increase about ¼ in. in length as the relative humidity rose from 50% to 90%. Change in thickness due to changes in humidity depends too much on the species, size and geometry of the particles to be listed, but it is roughly ten times the linear expansion. Thickness movement is of little consequence, except that surface particles swell unevenly and produce an "orange peel" surface.

	Modulus of rupture (min. avg.) PSI	Modulus of elasticity (min. avg.) 10⁶ PSI	Internal bond (min. avg.) PSI	Linear expansion (max. avg.) Percent	Screw holding (min. avg.) lb. Face	Edge
¾-in. particleboard, interior grade						
Low density (37 lb./cu. ft. and under)	800	0.15	20	0.30	125	—
Medium density (37 to 50 lb./cu. ft.)	1,600	0.25	70	0.35	225	160
High density (50 lb./cu. ft. and over)	2,400	0.35	200	0.55	450	—
¾-in. fiberboard, medium density (48 lb./cu. ft.)	4,000	0.40	100	0.35	350	275
Eastern white pine (*Pinus strobus*)	8,600	1.24				
White oak (*Quercus alba*)	15,200	1.78				

Modulus of rupture: the load necessary to break a panel.
Modulus of elasticity: a measure of the resistance to deflection.
Internal bond: the force two faces of a panel will withstand before pulling apart.
Linear expansion: the change in length that occurs when relative humidity of surrounding air rises from 50% to 90%.
Screw holding: the force required to extract a 1-in. #10 type A or AB sheet-metal screw.

Data adapted from the National Bureau of Standards' Commercial Standard CS 236-66 and literature from the Plum Creek Lumber Co., Columbia Falls, Mont.

the large cutting pressures tear out the fibers at the point of exit. It also has a tendency to choke on its own waste, generating heat and requiring more power. The alternating-top-bevel tooth (ATB), often used for crosscutting, makes a smoother cut with minimum tear-out, but its sharp tips are vulnerable to shock loads and will wear quickly. If quality of cut is not crucial, the triple-chip design is the best to buy. But if you want a smooth cut and plan to use particleboard extensively, buy a blade specifically designed for man-made boards. Such blades usually combine an alternating face bevel with ATBs and sometimes beveled lead teeth as well. These are expensive blades—both to purchase and to maintain. (Winchester Carbide Saw, 2635 Papermill Rd., Winchester, Va. 22601 is one supplier.)

Other factors that affect the cutting of particleboard are hook angles, clearance angles, the thickness of the saw body and tooth approach angles. The first three of these are built into the saw but the last one can be changed by altering the height of the saw above the table, as shown at right.

With hard, abrasive materials like particleboard, cutting edges can dull quickly. For this reason a relatively large chip load, achieved by feeding the stock fast, is best. For the same reason, bandsaw blades for cutting 3/4-in. particleboard should not have more than three teeth per inch. Carbide-tipped router bits are more effective because high-speed steel bits soon dull, overheat and become useless.

Fiberboard has a tendency to flow back, which means that the material recovers slightly after its fibers are compressed by, say, a drilling or routing operation. This can result in a smaller hole than intended, sometimes an advantage when doweling or splining.

Joining man-made boards

Joining man-made boards—Man-made board is weaker than solid wood in every respect except possibly resistance to splitting. Because of this inherent weakness it is seldom used in small sections, and most joining is of one surface to another. The trick is not to weaken the material further by using the wrong joint. Avoid shouldered tenons and continuous slots. This is particularly important when using furniture-grade particleboard because of the material's hard, dense surface and relatively weak interior. Cutting through the skin exposes the more loosely connected interior particles, which have little resistance to shearing forces. Both particleboard and fiberboard are too weak to be dovetailed, and corners must be joined in other ways. Various methods, including methods for lipping, are illustrated on the next page.

A joining system rapidly gaining popularity in this country is the Lamello. Invented in Europe about 20 years ago, it uses a machine that looks like a small router. It cuts a curved slot in the two surfaces or edges to be joined. Into this slot is glued a lens-shaped beech spline cut on the bias. Each spline is compressed in manufacture so it swells on contact with glue and produces internal pressure on the glueline. This ensures a strong joint. It can join boards edge to edge, edge to surface and also can be used in miters. It works equally well for particleboard, fiberboard (MDF) and solid wood. For further information, write The Wood and Tool Store, 24041 W. Capitol Dr., Pewaukee, Wis. 53072.

Another method for joining particleboard and fiberboard is to use knock-down (KD) fittings. A wide variety is available, as well as hinges and hardware specially designed for use in man-made boards. Generally they involve letting a plate or

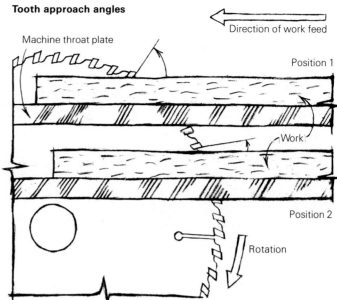

Tooth approach angles

One of the factors determining smoothness of cut, particularly significant in cutting man-made boards, is the height of the blade in the work. Thin stock should be cut with the blade barely projecting above the work (position 1). Although it takes more power to cut this way, the uncut material acts as a backing and minimizes tear-out. Position 2, with the saw raised almost to its arbor, has the smallest approach angle, and blunt tooth forms like the triple chip work best this way because they can exert maximum shear. However, because the tooth makes its exit almost at right angles to the work, it tends to chip out the bottom surface.

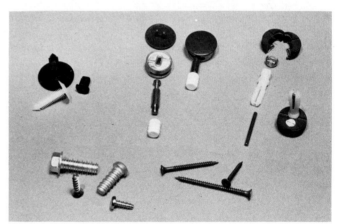

Typical particleboard fasteners, clockwise from top left, include face-joining Christmas-tree fasteners, butt-joining inserts, right-angle-joining inserts, twin-start screws and hi-lo screws.

cylinder into the board to increase the surface area of the attachment. Some of the more useful designs are shown in the photo above, and suppliers include Furntek Corp., PO Box 26792, Charlotte, N.C. 28213, and Fastex, 195 Algonquin Rd., Des Plaines, Ill. 60016.

No hardware is any better than its attachments. Screws and other fastenings used with man-made boards have to be selected with care. When joining panels face to face, all the fastenings used for wood will work for particleboard and fiberboard. Fastening into the edge is the problem because there the material is weak. Smooth nails are useless, and barbed ones not much better. Machine-driven staples coated with epoxy resin are popular. They are driven at such speed that the friction melts the epoxy and creates a glueline. When attaching particleboard face to edge, use 2-in. staples with a 3/8-in. bridge. They hold well with virtually no splitting.

When screwing conventional hinges or other load-bearing hardware to the edge of particleboard, it is good practice first to rout for and then glue in a wood insert. Sheet-metal screws

Joining man-made boards

Figure 1

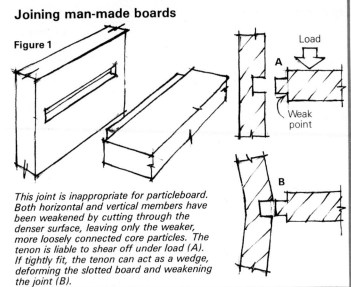

This joint is inappropriate for particleboard. Both horizontal and vertical members have been weakened by cutting through the denser surface, leaving only the weaker, more loosely connected core particles. The tenon is liable to shear off under load (A). If tightly fit, the tenon can act as a wedge, deforming the slotted board and weakening the joint (B).

Figure 2

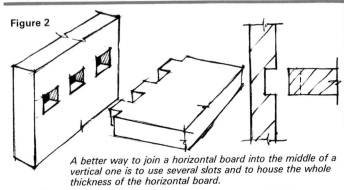

A better way to join a horizontal board into the middle of a vertical one is to use several slots and to house the whole thickness of the horizontal board.

Figure 3

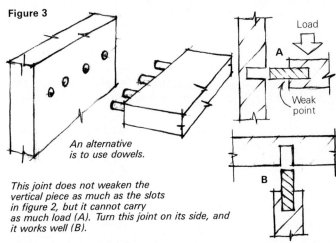

An alternative is to use dowels.

This joint does not weaken the vertical piece as much as the slots in figure 2, but it cannot carry as much load (A). Turn this joint on its side, and it works well (B).

Figure 4

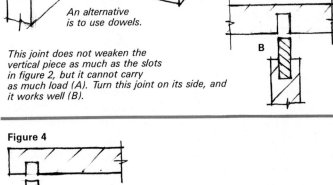

This is an inferior corner joint in man-made boards. The groove weakens the horizontal member at its point of maximum shear. The tongue can break if the carcase is racked. Interrupting the slot and making several short tongues is stronger, but the exposed edge must still be covered.

Figure 5

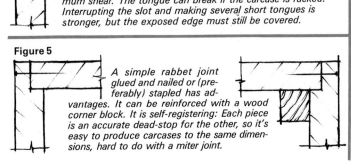

A simple rabbet joint glued and nailed or (preferably) stapled has advantages. It can be reinforced with a wood corner block. It is self-registering: Each piece is an accurate dead-stop for the other, so it's easy to produce carcases to the same dimensions, hard to do with a miter joint.

Figure 6

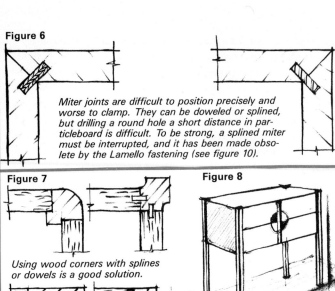

Miter joints are difficult to position precisely and worse to clamp. They can be doweled or splined, but drilling a round hole a short distance in particleboard is difficult. To be strong, a splined miter must be interrupted, and it has been made obsolete by the Lamello fastening (see figure 10).

Figure 7

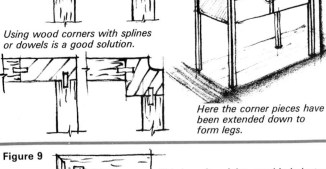

Using wood corners with splines or dowels is a good solution.

Figure 8

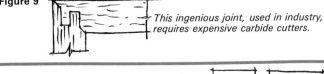

Here the corner pieces have been extended down to form legs.

Figure 9

This ingenious joint, used in industry, requires expensive carbide cutters.

Figure 10

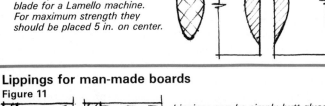

Beech inserts are glued into curved pockets made by the blade for a Lamello machine. For maximum strength they should be placed 5 in. on center.

Lippings for man-made boards

Figure 11

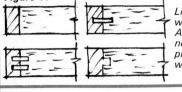

Lippings can be simply butt-glued with yellow (aliphatic-resin) glue. A tongue or plywood spline does not add much strength, but does prevent the lipping from sliding when clamping pressure is applied.

Figure 12

A lipping wider than is needed can be attached and then ripped down after gluing.

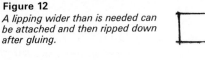

Rip here.

Figure 13

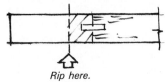

This is an inferior lipping construction because the tongue is weak.

Using flexible films as structural members

Figure 14

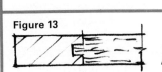

This joint is made by first covering the particleboard with vinyl or Mylar, then V-grooving, folding and gluing the edge. The flexible film acts as a hinge.

Figure 15

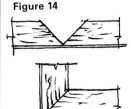
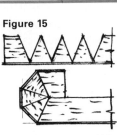

Industry uses carbide cutters to make ingenious folds like this.

have more holding power than regular wood screws, but better still are twin-start, bugle-headed dry-wall screws (available from Equality Screw Co., PO Box 292, El Cajon, Calif. 94022) or the hi-lo screws (available from Shakeproof, St. Charles Rd., Elgin, Ill. 60120). Both these styles have two sets of threads, the hi-lo style with one major and one minor set. This combination severs rather than compresses the stock and increases the holding power of the screw. The twin-start screws were designed for power driving, and are sharp and slender enough to be driven without pilot holes.

Covering man-made boards—Furniture manufacturers often cover particleboard with sheets of printed vinyl, embossed and even "distressed" to give the appearance and texture of actual wood. This only encourages the erroneous notion that these panel products are suitable substitutes for traditional wood. A better approach is to consider them simply as structural vehicles to carry other materials. There is nothing wrong about covering one material with another—leather, gold leaf, mosaic—it's been done at least since Egyptian times. Wood veneers were used in the 18th century to achieve decorative effects that simply could not have been accomplished with solid wood.

The fault lies in the attempt to deceive. When we see a piece of painted furniture, we know very well that it is not made of paint. When we look at the same piece covered in plastic which has the grain and texture of wood, we are confused as to its real nature. Our eyes tell us one thing, our hands another and our noses a third. Slate floors are often only ¼ in. thick. What is underneath them does not matter. The surface of the floor looks like stone, it is cold to the touch and no glass survives a fall. There is a world of difference between this and even the finest imitation.

Both particleboard and MDF make excellent substrates for wood veneers. If you are using furniture-grade particleboard with a well-sanded surface (composed entirely of fine particles) it is not necessary to use an underlayment or base veneer. However, for thin veneers using a base veneer will produce a better final surface, helping to prevent telegraphing through of the particles underneath. The base veneer should be about the same color as the face veneer or it will show at the edges.

A recent development is paper underlayment instead of wood. Yorkite, available from the N.V.F. Co., Box 38, Yorklyn, Del. 19736, is one such product. It is very tough and is made in several thicknesses and colors to match the lippings and face veneers. If underlayment is used on one side it must also be used on the other side, to keep the panel in balance.

The easiest and usually the cheapest finish for man-made boards is paint. Fiberboard, with its smooth, stable surface, can be painted directly. Particleboard should first be filled by priming it thoroughly. Latex paint works well but should be allowed to cure for three or four days and then sanded. If the surface is still not smooth, repeat the process. Once the surface is primed, it can be painted in any of the usual ways—brushed, rolled, sprayed or silk-screened. You can save yourself work by buying the board factory-primed.

For indoor signs and posters, you can seal the raw surface with polyurethane and then stencil or silk-screen directly on it. This is one way the basically bland color of the board can be used as a background.

There are several types of flexible film. The thin, vinyl sheets that industry prints with wood-grain patterns to disguise man-made boards can also function as structural members. The panel can be grooved, folded on itself and glued, using the vinyl as a hinge. Intricate shapes are possible, but the process requires complex machinery carefully adjusted since the particleboard must be cut right through while leaving the vinyl film intact. This technique can be adapted for small shops by using a plastic tape such as Mylar. The tape can be applied either before or after cutting the board. The edges are then glued, the board folded and the tape removed after the glue cures.

Another flexible film is polyvinyl chloride, of which Naugahyde is best known. You can buy it in a variety of colors and textures and get it either unsupported (not reinforced), or with a woven or knitted back. The latter may be glued to the substrate, but the former is only for thermoplastic welding. One common variety of PVC has a thin layer of foam between the film and the cloth back to give it a better feel (known in the trade as "handle"). The PVCs with a backing of cotton cloth glue better than those with synthetic backing. In either case, use white glue, and apply it to the substrate with a roller. Then lay the PVC on and rub over it with a rounded block or rolled-up cloth (not with your hands).

You can also cover man-made board with leather. It too is applied with white glue, which is spread over the board. The leather is then covered with heavy brown wrapping paper, shiny side down, and pressed flat on the board with a warm iron. Don't use the soft kind of paper. It will draw moisture from the leather and stick to it.

There is also cloth. Thicker cloth can be glued on, but there is no need to press it hard like leather. If you do, the glue will be forced into the fibers and spoil the texture. You can often just stretch cloth over the board and staple the edges, using no glue at all.

Semi-rigid materials suitable for small-shop application include Formica and metals such as copper, aluminum and stainless steel. These can be purchased from most building-supply outlets in large sheets and as stamped tiles about 4 in. by 4 in. Visually pleasing, these tiles are easy to apply. They have a lot of technical advantages such as resistance to chemicals and physical abrasion as well as to wet heat, dry heat and pressure. Stainless-steel tile bends easily around corners and comes in a variety of patterns and textures. You can also apply metals in the form of foils. These come backed with adhesive or can be put on with contact cement. Formica is best applied with urea-formaldehyde glue and a veneer press. It can also be put on with contact cement.

Rigid materials include opaque or colored glass, slate, stone and ceramic tile. These are attached to the panel by a special adhesive. There is a large variety of these adhesives available today for gluing almost any material to any other—wood to concrete, for example, or leather to glass. These special adhesives can be ordered through building-supply retailers, if you know what you want. For a listing of the various products made, with a description of their use and working properties, write Gulf Adhesives and Resins Consumer Products, PO Box 10911, Overland Park, Kans. 66210. All-purpose panel adhesives are stocked in most hardware stores, but don't choose these if you can get a formulation specially suited for the materials you're using. □

Simon Watts is contributing editor of this magazine.

Q & A

Drying cherry logs

I just happened on some 16-in. dia. cherry logs, about 6 ft. long. My last experience drying cherry logs was a disaster. Though I sealed the ends, the logs developed deep checks. I think my mistake was to debark them. After painting the ends, could I put my logs in giant plastic bags to slow down drying and to protect them from insects?
— Robert Kinghorn, Excelsior, Minn.

Your disaster is the result of trying to do the impossible. Wood shrinks more in the direction tangential to the growth rings than in the direction perpendicular to the growth rings and radial splits occur to relieve the drying stresses.

Cherry sapwood shrinks more and dries faster than the heartwood. Debarking makes things even worse. To dry big chunks of cherry, leave the bark on and split the logs in half. Lightly coat the split surfaces with wax and paint the ends with glue. Put the logs in a cool place with little temperature fluctuation and keep your fingers crossed for several years.

Your alternative is to decide what you want to do with the wood and cut it into pieces about 30% larger than the finished dimensions. All the problems that arise in drying wood get worse as the cross section of the piece increases.

— Paul Fuge

Pine versus fir

Why is clear white pine preferred over clear fir (which is cheaper and readily available in most areas) in making wooden window and door frames? I'd like to use fir on the job because it's less expensive, but don't want to regret it later. — Jerry Clancy, St. Louis, Mo.

Lumber grade is a prime consideration for sash, trim and millwork. The quality of the finish is affected by knots and other blemishes and by cross grain associated with knots removed by ripping or trimming the lumber.

A second consideration is the evenness of grain with regard to earlywood and latewood. White pines, sugar pine and Ponderosa pine are fairly even-grained, and therefore ideal for millwork. The true firs are uneven-grained, having significantly denser latewood than earlywood. Working them results in more grain-raising and uneven finishing characteristics. Douglas-fir would be most troublesome from this standpoint.

The pines also yield cleaner, sharper detailed surfaces in moldings, with less splintering than firs; pines hold screws and other fasteners better. Grade for grade, pine is the better choice. — R. Bruce Hoadley

Poplar versus red oak

I have a Sperber chainsaw mill and plan to mill the wood for an addition to my home. I would like to use poplar for the framing and red oak for the siding. I'm going to air-dry the oak for a year, tongue-and-groove it and apply it vertically. Is oak suitable for door and window frames as well? Is poplar a good choice for a framing lumber?
— Jim Ryan, Putnam Valley, N.Y.

ED LEVIN REPLIES: As a timber-frame carpenter who works primarily in red oak, I was struck by your choice of oak for siding and poplar for framing, because my intuitive choice would have been the other way around. However, your scheme is workable, with the following qualifications.

Fell and mill the poplar just before use and frame up as soon as possible, letting the wood season in place. If you have to leave the material in the log for any length of time, peeling is recommended. Likewise, if the finished stock cannot be used immediately, sticker it. Choose the material carefully, discarding knotty, shaky or twisted pieces, as well as those having sloped grain.

Poplar is slightly weaker than white pine, putting it toward the lower end of the spectrum of structural timber. Floor and roof framing members should thus be bigger than is usual. Poplar's high initial moisture content (close to 100%) means that the green wood must carry its own weight in water along with any building load. This, coupled with significantly lower strength when green (dry poplar is almost 40% stiffer than green), calls for close attention to the sectional dimensions of floor and roof framing during seasoning. Longer members may need temporary midspan support to prevent permanent sagging. Poplar's strength does not begin to increase substantially until moisture content drops below 25%.

Oak was a common siding material in Colonial times—principally in the form of clapboards. Vertical tongue-and-groove red oak should make a beautiful and durable exterior siding. Narrow boards will minimize cupping. For both siding and window or door frames, drill pilot holes in the dry oak and use non-corroding nails or screws to avoid getting dark streaks on the wood.

Hickory for furniture

I was wondering why I never hear much of hickory being used for building furniture other than chair legs. It has nice grain and is a very tough wood. Is there something I don't know? — Steve London, Dupo, Ill.

I agree that hickory is an admirable wood. It is tough, strong, hard, machines to a silky-smooth surface and takes finish well. It also is a fairly good wood for steam-bending. Historically, it was used more for furniture than it is today and was found especially good for parts that take a lot of stress and are prone to breaking.

I really don't know why hickory is not used more today, but there are two possible reasons. First, hickory has wide sapwood, and darker woods are preferred for furniture, unless they are uniformly light and can be stained. Other species, such as maple, birch and even beech, can be controlled more easily when coloring or staining, and these woods also have strength properties suitable for furniture. Second, high-quality hickory is in short supply. In New England, hickory has been high-graded out over the past 300 years. It has been used as fuel, and was highly sought after for smoking meat. What we have left is generally of poorer quality than other furniture species. The available stumpage is under heavy demand for specialty products, tool handles in particular.

I'm not sure about the supply of hickory in the Midwest, where I understand some of the finest hickory grows. Some of this (especially the pecan hickories) is sliced into face veneers for hardwood plywood, which is popularly used as wall paneling and in large, mass-produced pieces of furniture. In such pieces it is typically defective, but its blemishes are promoted as "character marks." — R. Bruce Hoadley

Catalpa for cabinets

Who has used catalpa as a cabinet wood? I have some—air-dried for seven years. Its color is close to walnut, but with dark streaks, and its grain is similar to butternut. Is this wood suitable for furniture making.
— Don Crandall, Copake, N.Y.

Although catalpa is an attractive wood, it has low surface hardness. For counters, tabletops, chair parts and other pieces that get considerable wear, it dents easily. But for picture frames, cabinet and door panels, catalpa is a satisfactory choice, as it machines well. Flat-grained surfaces are difficult to sand, because the earlywood is much softer than the latewood and sanding can create an uneven surface.

— R. Bruce Hoadley

The State of the Forests
Where our wood comes from and where it's going

by Eugene Wengert

An understanding of the prospects for this country's hardwood use must begin with an inventory of its sawtimber. The United States has approximately 75% as much forest land today as when Columbus landed. This amounts to 737 million acres, or about one-third of the country's land area. Of this, about 255 million acres are used for parks, wilderness and recreation areas, or are unsuitable for growing commercial timber. On these non-commercial areas, equal to the combined land area of California, Oregon, Washington and most of Idaho, timber harvesting and in some cases even timber management is prohibited.

The remaining 482 million acres are our commercial forest land. This does not mean all the wood on it is available for commercial harvest; it means this land is capable of growing wood at the rate of at least 20 cubic feet per acre per year, and that the land hasn't been legally withdrawn from commercial use. The 482 million acres include golf courses, windbreaks around farm houses as well as slopes too steep to log. Only about half of our commercial forests are in production for timber. In all, they contain 2,569 billion board feet of sawtimber—softwood trees 9 in. in diameter or larger at breast height (dbh), and hardwood trees 11 in. dbh or larger. The geographical distribution is shown in figure 1.

Wood use—From our forests comes a wide range of products—paper, lumber, boards, chemicals, fuel etc. In 1977, the total U.S. consumption of wood products, including 10% that was imported, was 13.2 billion cu. ft., several billion cubic feet more than in the 1960s. Most of the growth has been in softwoods, and we're now cutting more softwood sawtimber than is growing to replace it (figure 2). Hardwood consumption has remained fairly constant since the late 1950s.

For convenience, wood use (both softwoods and hardwoods) can be divided into six product classes, as shown in figure 3. The raw material requirements of these products would seem not to be in conflict. Pulp and paper uses logging and mill residues for almost half of its material needs. The remainder can be logs of small diameter or logs otherwise unsuitable for sawmilling. Softwoods are preferred, as they make stronger paper. In the lumber category, profitable sawmilling of hardwoods requires straight logs 10 in. in diameter or larger; many softwood mills can profitably saw smaller logs. Wood fuel is primarily residue-based and does not require the larger logs suitable for sawing. Plywood demand is almost all softwood; logs should be straight and greater than 15 in. in diameter. Particleboard is residue-based, except waferboard, in order to keep the cost competitive with plywood and lumber alternatives. Most miscellaneous uses have special requirements; utility poles, for instance, must be 30 ft. long and at least 6 in. in diameter.

In reality, when figuring the impact of these various demands on the raw material supply, the overriding considera-

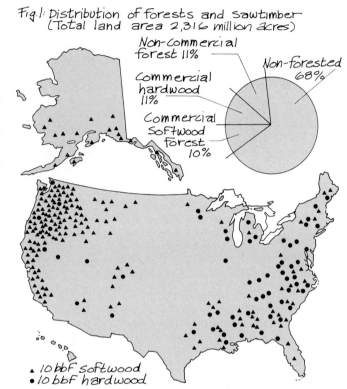

Fig. 1: Distribution of forests and sawtimber (Total land area 2,316 million acres)

Non-commercial forest 11%
Non-forested 68%
Commercial hardwood 11%
Commercial softwood forest 10%

▲ 10 bbf softwood
● 10 bbf hardwood

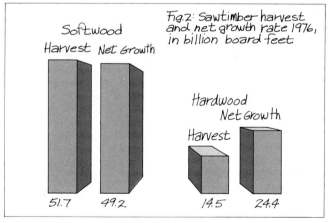

Fig. 2: Sawtimber harvest and net growth rate 1976, in billion board feet

Softwood Harvest 51.7   Net Growth 49.2
Hardwood Harvest 14.5   Net Growth 24.4

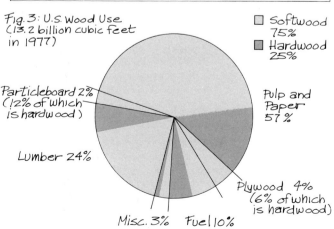

Fig. 3: U.S. Wood Use (13.2 billion cubic feet in 1977)

☐ Softwood 75%
■ Hardwood 25%

Particleboard 2% (12% of which is hardwood)
Lumber 24%
Misc. 3%   Fuel 10%
Plywood 4% (6% of which is hardwood)
Pulp and Paper 57%

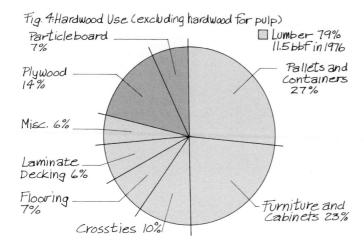

Fig. 4: Hardwood Use (excluding hardwood for pulp)

Particleboard 7%

Plywood 14%

Misc. 6%

Laminate Decking 6%

Flooring 7%

Crossties 10%

Lumber 79% 11.5 bbf in 1976

Pallets and Containers 27%

Furniture and Cabinets 23%

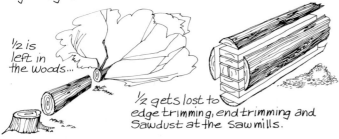

Fig. 5: Only 1/4 of the Wood felled in the forest becomes lumber.

1/2 is left in the woods...

1/2 gets lost to edge trimming, end trimming and Sawdust at the sawmills.

tion is the capital investment in the manufacturing facility. A multi-million dollar pulp, plywood or particleboard plant cannot afford to shut down for lack of raw materials. A small sawmill (and 90% of them are small) cannot compete, so timber that is best suited for lumber may, when supplies are short, get eaten in making other products.

Figure 4 shows how we use our hardwoods. (Exports, about 100 million bd. ft., much of it high-quality veneer logs, are not included). The largest portion goes to pallets and containers—almost 300 million wooden pallets, averaging 25 bd. ft. of lumber each, are made per year. Laminate decking, furniture and face and back veneers for plywood demand the best logs. However, because only about one-fourth of the lumber sawn from a good log is No. 1 Common and better, it is important that economic uses exist for smaller saw logs. Pallets and cross-ties are such products. With these two products potentially using three-fourths of the lumber from a log, it is common that a mill's entire production goes to them, with no sorting for the higher grades of lumber. Even high-yield logs are often sawn for low-value products, because it may be uneconomical for sawmill owners to do otherwise. The furniture and cabinet industries can try to combat this practice by paying more for high-grade lumber, or by learning to use low-grade lumber.

Future wood use—The amount of wood used in the U.S. will continue to increase during the next several decades with a doubling occurring before the year 2030. Much of the increase in supplies will come from hardwoods, as we are now cutting softwoods at a rate greater than their growth rate. U.S. Forest Service projections indicate a doubling of hardwood usage before 2010.

In addition to cutting more trees, improved use of the tree will provide more fiber. Presently, approximately one-half of the tree is left in the woods—some of that material could be sawn, some chipped and some used for fuel. Additionally, of

the one-half of the tree that does go to the sawmill today, only one-half is converted to dry lumber (figure 5). Improved efficiency in milling will increase supplies. The same benefit is possible in the secondary processing plant when lumber is converted to cabinets or furniture.

With the many advantages of wood over other products (low energy to produce, environmentally clean, etc.), the future will bring increased demand for lumber, plywood and particleboard. Wood will be too valuable to burn at locations very far from the production sites, so wood-fuel use will decrease in total percentage. Likewise, the use of wood for pulp will show a slight percentage decrease in overall usage.

The big unknown in the future of wood is the potential for using wood for chemicals. Already, laboratory research has made animal feed, urethane-based chemicals, adhesives, gasoline and much more. When this breakdown of wood can be done economically, a tremendous new market will develop.

Regarding hardwoods specifically, increased mechanization in material handling promises increasing needs for wooden pallets and containers. The growth of this industry is tremendous, having doubled in less than 10 years. The production of furniture, cabinets and millwork will grow as the population matures and disposable income increases. The railroad beds in the U.S. are in need of extensive repair, so the demand for cross-ties is expected to increase. As the preferred species for both pallets and cross-ties is oak, there will be increasing pressure on furniture oak supplies, and it is likely that other species will be used more in furniture.

One unknown in predicting hardwood demand is the use of yellow poplar for construction lumber, which the U.S. Forest Service and others are seeking to develop. To be competitive with the pine 2x4, yellow-poplar construction lumber will be relatively inexpensive compared to furniture stock.

Robert Phelps, a chief economist in the U.S. Forest Service, sees a continuing loss of quality in our hardwood log supplies and, therefore, a decrease in the yield of higher grades of lumber per log. Although supplies of hardwoods seem plentiful, unless the forests are well managed, their quality will not be as high as possible. As improved management now will not benefit lumber production for at least two decades, the furniture and cabinet industries must, in the interim, learn to use a lower average grade of lumber.

Hardwood ownership—Who owns our hardwood timberlands is one of the critical considerations for the lumber producer because the owner determines whether the timber is available for harvest and to some degree the quality and growth of the timber. About three-fourths of the commercial hardwood forest land in the United States is classed as nonindustrial, private forest (NIPF), mainly in the eastern United States. Neither the wood-using industry nor government agencies control enough good hardwood acreage to have a large impact on future timber supplies. Therefore, in considering the present and the future of timber supply, it is necessary to look at the NIPF owners, four million of them.

The primary concern for a large (although unknown) number of NIPF owners is not the production of trees for harvest. They consider wildlife, recreation and other objectives to be more important, even though harvesting can be one of the most useful ways to realize other land-management objectives or benefits. They consider (erroneously, most of the time) that timber harvesting cannot complement these other objectives. In one survey in the East, 41% of the NIPF owners were consistenly against harvest. In addition, the NIPF owner usually does not manage the forest for optimum or even good timber growth, thinning out diseased or poorly formed trees, for example. As a result, much of the NIPF is producing wood volumes and quality below the land's capacity.

Why is this picture so bleak? If there is one common reason, it is that managing land for timber is uneconomical. Thinning and other management is expensive, especially as most NIPFs are in small acreages. Taxes, including capital gains, are high. Hardwood timber returns are often not realized for 75 years. And hardwood stumpage prices are low. To add to the unattractiveness of this situation, the NIPF owner is being underpriced by the federal government: 40% of the timber sold off federal land on the board-foot basis (excluding pulp) has been priced below $80/mbf. More than 21% is sold at below-cost prices. The NIPF owner must pay for forest management, cost of roads, sale preparation, reforestation, and then taxes to support his competitor.

To ensure our future hardwood supplies, we had better be interested in the private-forest landowner and his problems; poor incentives to produce timber for harvest and poor knowledge of the benefits (economic, ecological, scenic and so on) of good management practices should be every hardwood user's concern. (For more, see *Timber Supply—Issues and Options* (Publ. No. P-79-24, Forest Products Research Society, 2801 Marshall Ct., Madison, Wis. 53705.)

Future hardwood ownership—The 1980 ownership pattern of private (75%), public (13%), and industry (12%) will change very little over the next decades. The most significant changes will be as follows:
—Increasing withdrawal of hardwood forests on public lands from commercial timber harvesting into wilderness and other "reserved" lands and resultant increased importance of NIPF.
—Increased incentives and benefits for better forest management on NIPF.
—Increased economic advantages (decreased capital-gains tax) in selling timber on NIPF.
—Increased dependence of the hardwood lumber users on the NIPF for their raw material.

Federal leadership should make reforestation of hardwood sites more attractive, ensuring wood supplies far into the 21st century. Improvements in harvesting will also make the economy of small-tract harvesting more attractive, as necessary to provide the quality and quantity of wood required for our growing needs.

Harvesting—There are many different techniques used to harvest our hardwood forests, from horse logging to helicopter logging, from very selective cutting to clear cutting, and from wasteful cutting to very wise cutting. The basic harvest procedures are determined by economics. Usually, it's more feasible to remove all the mature, salable trees at one time in a small patch than to cut only a few trees every several years. This patch cutting usually aids in reforestation. (In past years we have removed only the good trees in our hardwood forests, leaving the poorer trees to mature and produce seeds for genetically inferior trees in the future.) Also, it is common today that only the merchantable part of a tree (beginning at the decay-free butt and moving upwards in 4-ft. increments until just before a 6-in. diameter is reached) is removed from

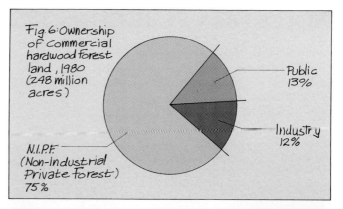

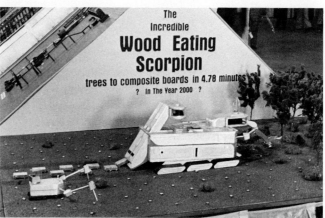

A part of the exhibit that accompanied Wengert's seminar on future hardwood use, this partly science-fiction monster incorporates extant technology in one unit to produce dry, defect-free, dimensioned composite boards from whole trees cut and swallowed at the front end. The smaller unit at left is busily replanting.

the woods and taken to the mill—about one-half of the tree is left in the woods (figure 5).

Present logging practices are, from a material standpoint, wasteful. From an economic standpoint, they are acceptable. A recent Forest Service (Princeton, W.Va.) study of a hardwood logging site found almost 70 tons of residue per acre, of which nearly one-quarter was sawable and three-quarters was chippable. If these residues can be used for fuel, pallets and particleboard (and maybe even furniture parts), this certainly will help the hardwood-supply picture.

Harvesting in the future will be more mechanized with more of the tree (more fiber) removed from the forest. The grapnel skidder will shear the tree close to the ground and carry it to the landing where large branches may be removed and perhaps some of the tops. These residues will be baled (like a hay bale) and then sold for fuel or other residue use. Merchandizing of the long, tree-length logs will take place at the mill. Clear cutting in small patches will continue.   □

Gene Wengert is professor of wood technology at Virginia Tech in Blacksburg, Va. This article is adapted from his contribution to a report, prepared with Mark White and Fred Lamb, that was presented in seminar at the Louisville furniture manufacturer's fair in Sept. 1980. The report, entitled "The Lumber Complex of the Future," goes on to describe present-day sawmilling and lumber-processing techniques as compared with what they will probably be in the year 2000. It was published in summary form in installments through 1981 in the trade magazine, Furniture Design and Manufacturing (400 N. Michigan Ave., Chicago, Ill. 60611).

Notes on Clear Finishes
Why I use Watco, Minwax and Deft

by Oscar MacQuiddy

Oscar MacQuiddy buffs a carved Italian table (c. 1929) he's refinished. The smooth, glossy surface is achieved by rubbing Watco into the wood with fine-grit wet/dry paper. The oil/sawdust slurry fills the grain and protects the wood.

I became interested in wood finishing after I acquired a house full of antique furniture. Most of it needed repair and refinishing, and I enrolled in an evening class where I was assured I would learn all I needed to know to restore my prized antiques. But I was displeased from the start with my instructor's approach. He was meticulous about preparing the surfaces, but then he would brush on a coat of colored plastic, and everyone would stand around admiring this shiny object. And if the next day you dragged your fingernail across the shiny surface, you'd leave a visible gouge. That wasn't what I was after.

I felt that a good finish should go into the wood and then build up a protective layer on the surface. I didn't like this business of applying plastics on top of the wood and then calling it a finish. The way this instructor liked to remove old finishes irritated me as well. Everything went. Good, bad, indifferent—it was all stripped away. I recall my shock one evening when a man brought in several strikingly beautiful pub chairs he had bought in Ireland. After some gluing and minor repairs he asked, "Now what should I do?" The instructor said, "Well, let's get that old finish off." At that point I'd had enough.

I found a day class with an altogether different approach to refinishing. My new teacher, Charles Kishady, was a most remarkable man, thoroughly in command of his subject and able to inspire his students. He came to this country at the end of World War II. Though his parents were Hungarian, he had spent four years in Germany as an apprentice restoring a 13th-century cathedral, and later he graduated from Heidelberg University with a degree in industrial arts. I told Mr. Kishady how I felt about furniture refinishing and what I wanted to do. He said, "Well, go ahead and do it and we'll see how you make out." He left me alone and would simply observe and make occasional comments, such as, "Wouldn't it look better if you did this...?" Or "Wouldn't it look better if you did that...?" I began to understand his suggestions and began also to develop an attitude toward wood that I had never seriously considered before.

As my relationship with this man deepened, together we decided to organize and teach a wood-finishing course at a professional level. But we wanted everything to be done as simply as possible, with all the frills knocked out. Though I'd never thought about teaching before, after a while I found what I had to communicate was extremely well received by my students. Once our program was underway, we tried to teach each student to respect the natural finish that was on

Oscar MacQuiddy, 71, of Southgate, Calif., has been teaching antique restoration and refinishing for 11 years. Before he retired in 1968, he worked for Shell Chemicals. This article is the first of two parts, extracted by Alan Marks from lectures given at The Cutting Edge in Los Angeles.

the article and to restore it when possible. It was really amazing the things we could bring back, and we were committed to saving the patina that develops on wood with time. When we used color, we tried to put it only where it belonged. We removed old finishes only when necessary, cleaned the wood and applied hand-rubbed oil finishes.

It is not necessary to remove old finishes completely, especially those possessing an attractive patina. It is often worth the effort to restore an existing finish, and really it is not that hard to do. Part of the secret is the ability to match the colors. There will be areas where the finish is totally gone, and sometimes these require almost heroic efforts, but they can be restored. Frequently, as when doing kitchen cabinets, all the surfaces will have to be cleaned. Scrub them thoroughly with TSP (tri-sodium-phosphate), which is probably the safest approach, sometimes adding a little Purex to do some bleaching along with the cleaning. In this case you need to wear gloves and avoid splashing the liquid in your eyes.

When the old finish must be removed, methylene chloride remover seems a good choice. No remover is completely safe, but as available products go, it's one of the less toxic members of a highly toxic group called chlorinated hydrocarbons, and it has to be used with adequate ventilation. Ideally, a strong air current should carry the fumes away from the user. Once in the bloodstream, methylene chloride metabolizes to carbon monoxide. Breathing the vapors is harmful to healthy persons, but is especially hazardous to those who suffer from cardiac problems, and they should not use the product.

How do you choose a good brand? When you go to the store, pick up all the cans. The heaviest cans put to one side, because methylene chloride is the heavy ingredient. The can which is the heaviest at the lowest price is the best buy. Standard Brands makes good remover that's as heavy as Jasco. Jasco costs $12; Standard Brands costs $7.

Methylene chloride is an efficient remover. When you apply it, use a brush with a natural wood handle because the remover will take any paint off the handle and stain your work. Working in a shaded area, apply a heavy coat by slopping it on. Don't brush it, just let it sit there. You paid a lot of money for it, so let it do all the work. Let it sit for 15 minutes and slop more on any dry spots that show up during that time. At the end of 15 minutes the finish will soften and lift, and you're ready to remove it. The instructions on the can will tell you to scape it off with a putty knife or to use a rag or steel wool to wipe it off. None of these methods is effective. But if you have access to a supply of planer or jointer shavings, dump a handful in the middle of that table or on that cabinet door and start scrubbing, and you'll clean that surface flawlessly. The wood shavings will get into routed, grooved, relieved and carved areas. They will do a terrific job of cleaning without scratching the wood. With this method you'll be able to strip very rapidly and efficiently, and stripping can turn out to be not such a terrible job after all.

If you find you still have some old finish on the surface, there is an auxiliary method of attack. Get a can with a tight cover and fill it with planer shavings and then saturate the shavings with lacquer thinner or, perferably, acetone. If you can afford it, methyl ethyl ketone would be even better. Take a handful of the wet shavings and continue the scrubbing. The solvent has a paint-remover action and generally by the second application you will have a surface almost clean enough to finish. These chemicals are highly flammable, so use them with great care. Work outdoors if possible or use adequate ventiliation inside.

This method of stripping is very simple, and shavings can be used several times. Even floors can be stripped this way, but you must pay special attention to ventilation. Afterwards, how can you tell if your wood is clean? Sand the surface lightly with 150-grit finishing paper. If it doesn't clog, you know the work is done. If the paper loads up, clean the surface with 1-0 steel wool soaked in either lacquer thinner or a mixture of lacquer thinner and acetone or methyl ethyl ketone. This technique is well suited for cleaning around turnings. Occasionally a little picking will have to be done with a pointed tool, and sometimes a piece of heavy cord can be used to clean the bottoms of grooves. We have used abrasive cords, but they cut so quickly and so deeply that you have to be very careful with them, particularly on old finishes where you don't want to expose bare wood.

When working with paint removers and strong solvents, you must wear gloves to prevent skin irritation as well as possible poisoning from the absorption of toxic chemicals through the skin. Neoprene gloves are best because they hold up longer and are tougher than gloves made from other materials. But when working with oil finishes, it's better to use your bare hands, not only to generate heat necessary for good penetration but also for increased awareness of what is happening on the surface of the wood. During all my years as an instructor, I've seen only one case of dermatitis resulting from contact with an oil finishing product. If you should have an adverse reaction despite the odds against it, consult your doctor about it right away.

Clear finishes are of two basic types—penetrating finishes and surface finishes. It is possible, though, to build up a surface layer by using a penetrating finish that hardens in the wood. As far as penetrating finishes are concerned, you can use an oil that dries or one that doesn't. Non-toxic linseed oil is slow-drying, but it was discovered that by heating it and adding chemicals its polymerization rate could be increased. They used to put lead in it. Today they can't and have to use a cobalt drier, making the oil just as toxic as it was with lead. Originally I worked with linseed oil, but the drying time was slow and unpredictable. Now I use Watco Danish oil, and it

has become standard in my work and teaching. To make Watco they take linseed oil and convert it to a resin. They dissolve this resin in a solvent and add driers to make it penetrate, and this penetrating solution has the property of combining chemically with oxygen to become a polymerized solid. It saturates the wood and solidifies in the cell cavities. Watco oil is quite easy to apply, and the results that it gives are excellent. You just apply it on raw wood until it won't absorb any more and then wipe the surface dry. Repeat this procedure the next day. Watco does alter the color of wood and it does darken somewhat with age, characteristics it shares with linseed oil.

Pure tung oil—not to be confused with heat-treated (polymerizing) tung oil, which is actually a varnish for hand rubbing—is a product I use with reservations. Once applied, its effects are irreversible, though it never completely hardens. But it's a beautiful finish, often producing spectacular results and requiring little preparation, aside from original sanding. On light woods, you get about the same color change as you get with Watco; and on some dark woods, the color change seems to be even less. But heat-treated tung oil will turn other dark woods almost black. I worked once with a man who finished some redwood altars with heat-treated tung oil; they ended up extremely dark, and you couldn't recognize them as redwood. If he had used three or four coats of Minwax Antique Oil, the natural beauty of the wood would have been revealed. When I first began to work with Minwax Antique Oil I was skeptical—it seemed almost too good to be true. It contains such effective driers that it will congeal in the can if half the volume is airspace. You need never worry about it drying hard—it'll dry. You wipe it on the surface, and it acts as a penetrating sealer and sets very hard. I have diluted it slightly on occasion and sanded it in wet as I do with Watco. But you must work quickly because it gets tacky fast, and you wind up with a sticky mess if it's not wiped off in time.

One interesting variation of the penetrating-oil finish is the "salt-pork finish." It is non-toxic, and because the pork fat contains salt, it does not become rancid. I have used it several times to refinish very old raw-wood chests and the paddles bakers use to remove bread from ovens. It can be used to finish all wooden kitchen utensils. Mineral oil has also been used for this purpose; it is definitely a spreading oil. If you take a piece of warm metal and put a drop of mineral oil on it, the oil will disperse and coat the whole surface. Salt pork does the same thing. In the old days people apparently just recoated with it when needed, and it has been claimed that this finish was used by the Shakers.

A friend of mine with broad experience in antique restoration observed that often old kitchen tables were not finished at all; they were just scrubbed at intervals with caustics and water. He speculates that during washing, the oil and tallow spills on the wood surface were observed to resist moisture and to shine with rubbing. So the practice of oiling wood to preserve it was probably a logical development of this observation. The old oil finishes applied by our great-grandparents by way of maintenance perhaps account for the fact that their furniture has survived. The oil was enough to preserve the wood and prevent moisture penetration and moisture-related decay and degradation. I am quite certain that glue joints in old furniture owe their preservation to this application of oil.

In the old days people bought cedar oil, a mineral oil that

was colored red and scented with a cedar extract. Today we use lemon oil—the same oil but colored yellow, and scented with lemon. But we don't use it as generously as our grandparents did. Instructions on the bottle say to use only one or two drops. I suggest that you go to a drug store and buy a pint of light mineral oil and use it as a furniture polish. You'll be getting the same basic ingredient of "lemon oil" but paying a lot less for it. There would be nothing wrong with using this light mineral oil as a non-toxic furniture finish. If the furniture needs cleaning, why not add a small amount of vinegar to it and a small amount of turpentine? Some restorers of antique clocks recommend cleaning and reviving old clock cases with a mixture of turpentine and vinegar and mineral oil.

The first oil/resin mixture used for finishing was varnish. From the Orient came lacquer and shellac which, when mixed with alcohol, yields the formula for the "French polish." The French-polish finish is a beautiful high-gloss, durable finish very slow to create (*FWW* #20, Jan. 80, p. 66). It possesses poor moisture resistance, is very difficult to repair and is quite impractical for commercial use. In order to create a durable, rapid-dry commercial finish, nitro-cellulose lacquer formulations were developed, but because of their fast dry time, spraying was the required method of application. Some years later, Deft Inc. formulated a modified water/white-coconut-oil-base, nitro-cellulose lacquer with special solvents that proved to be an improved brushing lacquer. The product is self-leveling, non-yellowing and easily repaired; it quickly rubs to a beautiful satin sheen and can be applied directly to raw wood. Three coats are recommended, and will produce a bar top finish. Each successive coat melds with the preceding one. When brushing Deft, I prefer satin for a final coat, although gloss is the more durable material. If you are going to rub it out, you might just as well apply two coats of gloss before putting on the final coat of satin. The only mistake you can make is not to use enough finish for the job, but several thin coats are better than thick ones.

The original oil/resin varnish has undergone many formula changes. One of the more recent has been to replace the resin with a polyurethane, a plastic resin. The result is a highly versatile coating. Defthane, a brand of polyurethane varnish, can be applied to raw wood or clean metal, inside or outdoors. Three coats are recommended. Thirty minutes gives a dust-free surface, and you can recoat in six hours. The finish is hard and rubs to an elegant satin sheen. With Defthane, as with Deft lacquer, the best procedure is to start with two coats of gloss followed by a third of satin.

You might wonder, with such a tough, hard finish, how the second and third coats can be made to adhere. Since it will dry in six hours, at the end of four hours it is two-thirds dry. I put on the next coat before the end of six hours. If I rub the surface lightly with 4/0 steel wool and wipe it down thoroughly, the subsequent coat will bond tightly to the first. Buy a large can of gloss and a small can of satin. When the last coat, the satin coat, is thoroughly dry at the end of 12 hours—36 hours is even better—rub the surface with 4/0 steel wool and wax it with Trewax (50% carnauba).

It is at first unsettling to use a water clean-up finish in place of varnish, lacquer and oils. It's hard to believe that anything that can be dissolved initially by water can dry to a durable, non-water-soluble state. But this is true of the new water-wash acrylic finishes. They give excellent results, and I predict that eventually they will enjoy wider use, especially in areas with smog problems. One such product, Wood Armor, is easily applied with a rag, roller, brush or spray gun. It dries quickly, has a pale color, and is non-yellowing. In 30 minutes after application it's dust free, and has a two-hour recoat time. It has no noxious odor, cleans up with water, and it is a beautiful finish for fine paneling where a minimum color change is desired. It comes in gloss and satin, though I prefer satin. I feel that the inside of drawers, the underside of drawers and even the back should have a finish, and Wood Armor works well for this purpose. Cabinet interiors are done to advantage with it. If you want to remove the still-wet finish for any reason, wipe it with a damp cloth before it skins over.

Let us pick up at the point where a piece of furniture has been stripped and prepared for finishing by a light sanding with 150-grit paper. We selected for our purposes a penetrating sealer/oil finish because we're after a traditional look with a soft sheen that doesn't obscure the grain of the wood. Many experts advise rubbing the oil in by hand or with rags or steel wool. We found a method, in the course of instruction, that we believe to be superior to any of these methods.

Working with the grain, start by pouring a small puddle of Watco on the surface. Then wet a pad of 320-grit wet/dry carbide paper and start sanding in figure eights, beginning at a corner and working across the surface. Within a few minutes you will have a slurry of oil and very fine sawdust that is continually being worked into the pores of the wood, which is quickly filled with its own substance due to the sharp cutting action of the carbide grit. After it gets tacky (15 minutes), I wipe off the excess with a rag. The resulting surface possesses an almost glass-like smoothness. Finish sanding across the surface and then sand with long strokes in the direction of the grain to obliterate any cross-grain marks. Actually with 320-grit paper it's almost impossible to leave any such marks except in the hardest of woods. At this point, you have smoothed the surface with a minimum of sanding, prepared and applied a filler, and put on a penetrating sealer.

You really can't simplify it much more. I've done a lot of beautiful work using this method. When I first started using it I applied raw linseed oil, but I didn't like it because the drying time is unpredictable. Watco is relatively fast drying. I know with certainty that in four hours it can be recoated. I felt that it did everything a linseed oil did and did it better. When you consider the amount of sanding saved and drudgery eliminated in achieving this kind of finish, there is no better alternative. A small sandpaper pad will do moldings. It fits anywhere and it will not quickly wear out, because the oil lubricates the cut and keeps the paper from clogging.

Your second coat is applied after the first has dried for at least four hours, or preferably overnight. Rub the second coat in by hand, having again poured oil on the surface. The heat of the hand friction aids in the penetration of the oil. Let it sit for a few minutes, and if you see any dry spots, spread oil from the wet spots over them. Keep the surface wet with oil until there is no more absorption. It is very important with each successive coat to wipe away all excess surface oil. Because this is not a surface treatment, but a penetrating finish, everything on the surface must be wiped away or rubbed into the wood. Excess oil on the surface will become sticky and take a long time to dry. When the second coat has dried, preferably overnight, the third coat is applied similarly to the second, and during the third application, the question of coloring comes into play. And that's another story. □

Coloring With Penetrating Oils

A little dab goes a long way

by Oscar MacQuiddy

In my article on clear finishes (page 212) I said little about the business of coloring wood, except insofar as a clear finish might darken certain woods, as in the case of oils. Color is a quality possessed by tiny particles of a substance. These absorb all wavelengths of light save those in certain portions of the spectrum, which are reflected and which we perceive as color. What makes a thing look green is its ability to absorb red. A stain consists of tiny particles suspended in a liquid or a paste. Because ultimately the test of a color's quality is its degree of permanency and how closely it approaches what you want it to do, I like to use readily obtainable universal colors.

These colors are standardized, and several brands are available. Also, they are inexpensive if you buy them in large quantities; I purchase them in pint containers. For class demonstrations I have pints of all the available colors, and I have never experienced any problems mixing them with any finishing product but lacquer. In my teaching I must use materials that are readily available where artist's supplies are sold, and the colors that are most easily and economically obtained are universal colors. Oil colors are slower drying than universal colors, and they don't burnish as well, probably because the particle size is larger. Universal colors are intended to be mixed with water-based finishes, including Deft Wood Armor. They can be used in varnishes and, most important, in penetrating oil finishes.

In case you think my preference uncraftsmanlike, you might be interested in a conversation I once had. I phoned one of the really fine antique furniture dealers. Saying I was an instructor of furniture finishing, I asked if I could speak with his refinisher. After asking the refinisher a couple of innocent questions to get the conversation going, I said, "Tell me, how do you handle your stains?" He told me that he used universal colors and thinned them with turpentine. Since then I have spoken with other commercial finishers and gotten more or less the same answer. The wide range of color available in universal colors provides professionals with the variety and versatility they need.

The stable earth colors we use are named after geographical areas. You may have heard of raw sienna. Sienna is a part of Italy. The earth there is an intense yellow, and it's used to make pine and maple stains. It has good transluscency although it can be too bright. Since this earth contains a lot of extraneous organic materials, Italians experimented with firing to purify it. It turned red, and became known as burnt sienna. That's the beautiful red we use on mahogany, but used alone it's too red. In another part of Italy called Umbria, the soil is greenish-brown in color, and they'd use it when

they wanted to make a deep, cold walnut. When they wanted to deepen another color they put some raw umber in it. In purifying it they produced "burnt umber," a beautiful brown the natural shade of walnut. Working with these four colors—raw sienna, burnt sienna, raw umber and burnt umber—it is possible, in most instances, to match almost any color you see on wood.

Of course, you do have a wider choice of colors. The Spanish oxides are tremendously stable red colors. Sometimes French ochre, a light, more subtle shade of yellow than raw sienna, matches some of the early pines a little better. Or you can get modern chromium oxides, yellow and green. In my kit I carry the four stable earth colors and three additional yellows—a French ochre, a chromium oxide and a bulletin yellow for the places where I want to add a spot of yellow that's really alive. I carry three reds in addition to burnt sienna—American vermilion, Venetian red, and a tube of French vermilion, for the times I want a red shadow that is warm but not bright. For the greens, I have chromium oxide and permanent green, in its medium version.

In coloring wood, I prefer not to stain. I'm not knocking stains, but I teach students to see the color they want and to set out like an artist to make it. Stains simply don't give the effect I want, but they will give solid color, in particular the 5-Minute Watco stains, which come in nine wood tones and nine colors. I prefer to develop the color gradually with control, which produces subtle nuances and a high degree of transparency. Of course, compatibility with the penetrating oil finish is necessary. In choosing the so-called universal colors, nothing is compromised.

In using universal colors, I like to mix them with natural Watco Danish Oil because the color will penetrate the wood along with the oil and become tightly locked in. But sometimes I use Minwax Antique Oil (a polymerizing tung oil) as the vehicle for the colors, especially where I want a harder, glossier finish that has the appearance of being built up on the surface of the wood. One advantage of using Watco as the vehicle is that if you make a mistake, you've got 30 minutes to rub it off with a clean rag soaked in turpentine or thinner. You can remove close to 90% of it if necessary and you can start again within a few minutes. You have a marvelous leeway in developing color.

Let me emphasize that I'm not talking about dramatic color changes. You don't take ash and make it look like rosewood. This method just isn't practical for that, nor does it produce a uniform color. You use it to create shades of color where they enhance the overall piece. Let's say we have a piece of furniture that has some carving and turnings on it and we want to emphasize the designer's original concept. There will be shadows in the recesses of a carving and at the depths of a turning. Assume we have already done the preliminary finishing. Using a piece of cardboard or plastic as an

Oscar MacQuiddy, 71, lives in Southgate, Calif. This article, the second of two parts, was adapted by Alan Marks from MacQuiddy's lectures at The Cutting Edge in Los Angeles.

artist's palette, we put on it little spots of color (shadows do have color). If it's the shadow on a piece of walnut, burnt umber may approximate it. But perhaps we want a subtler shade. So we add spots of raw umber and a bit of red or yellow on the board. Pour on a tiny bit of Watco and take a ½-in. white bristle brush and capture a little puddle of the oil. Pick up some burnt umber and rub it into the oil. Say we want to go a little toward the red. Wipe off the brush in a rag, pick up a tiny bit of red with the tip and rub it into a little area of the brown spot. Now hold the spot next to the shadow. Say it looks all right, but it's not quite dark enough. Wipe off the brush and pick up a bit of raw umber. Rub it into part of the red-brown area to darken it. Now hold that next to the carving, and it looks mighty close to capturing the tone of the beautiful shadow.

Next, take a shallow catfood can and put in it a tablespoon of Watco, a teaspoon of burnt umber, a tiny bit of red and mix them, watching the tone as it develops. Get it about right and then add a tiny bit of raw umber to darken it. Now we have our shadow color. Using Watco as a vehicle to carry the color, we have produced a rather concentrated stain.

Take a small brush and go over those carvings, covering all the areas, and let it sit until it gets a little tacky. Then get a clean rag and try to remove it. You won't be able to get it all off, and the amount you leave is going to be exactly right. The whole area will accept the tone, and rubbing diligently on the convex highlight areas will expose them to advantage. Now you suddenly discover that you have added depth to this carving, making it appear as the designer once envisioned it, with prominent highlights and deep shadows. When it is thoroughly dry, give it another coat of clear oil rubbed in by hand; then wipe off the excess. This seals in the color. Waxing later will give it a translucency that will make it even more spectacular and will bring even more life to it.

Charles Kishady, my associate (a master antique restorer), suggests that when restoring fine antiques, you should use at least three colors in shadowed areas—a basic color, a lighter color and a darker color. The exciting thing is that you can warm a color with a spot of an analogous color or kill it by adding its complement. If you put on a red and you want to reduce its intensity, green will do it, making it go towards a brown. The tiniest bits of color achieve dramatic changes. You can have one color in the highlight area and introduce a trace of its complement in the shadow. This changes the quality of the shadow emphatically.

I recall refinishing a table with a lot of intricate carvings on the legs and two drawers in front. Because of the old finish, the carving was totally lost. You knew some kind of irregular surface was there, but you didn't have the foggiest notion what it was. I asked the owner, "How would you feel if that carving suddenly came to life and you could see it?" She indicated that perhaps it would be a good thing. So I took the table to my shop, put on a polyurethane varnish and rubbed it out to a durable satin finish. But first I mixed some dark, murky color and smeared it over the carved surfaces. Then I spent an hour trying to get the stuff off. Most of it I removed, but the carving had now dramatically come to life.

I once worked with a student refinishing a lovely little

AUTHOR'S NOTE: The only text I have found that treats the subject of color the way we do in our courses is H.W. Kuhn's *Refinishing Furniture*, Arco Publishers, New York, N.Y. 10003, and I recommend it highly.

cherry coffee table. It had a large white slash of sapwood across the top. A purist might say, "Well, since it is natural you'd expect that white slash in cherry." But all you saw was the white slash. Now I felt it belonged there, but wanted to alter it so your eye didn't stop at it but wandered on around to see the rest of the table. I made some shadow color and put an extremely light coat of the color on the white. It didn't change it much but gave it the general tone of the darker area. Then picking two or three spots along the white slash, I introduced a little more of it, slightly darkening these areas then fading off to a very, very light color. You still noticed the white area, but your eye moved on to look at the whole table. Still, I wasn't satisfied. It had gone a little cold, so I took a tiny bit of American vermilion and burnished it into the top of that table. That changed its entire character. Suddenly the table seemed to move off the ground.

In using this approach to finishing it is important to ask certain questions. If you are considering a chair, for example, do you see merely a chair or do you see a chair with one post that is different? Does it have some quality that makes its back stand out from the rest, or do you see the chair as a whole? Is the ornamentation conspicuous? Do you see shadows? Do you see highlights? Does the carving look like part of the piece or like an unrelated appendage? On an old chair, up for restoration, does it appear as though someone has been sitting in it, has rubbed the back slightly, has rested his arms in certain places?

You can approach furniture finishing as an artist would paint a picture over which he wants your eye to move in certain ways. But you should also be concerned with the effects of use and care. If it is a chair, the places where people habitually put their hands will be a little lighter than the rest. People wonder how to intuit this sort of thing. Let's say the chair you're working on belongs to a wealthy lady. She has a housekeeper who has a lot of work to do, and so cleans well only the places she knows her mistress will notice. She'll notice the overall appearance, but where the posts join the rails her housekeeper will leave a little dirt, and where the spindles join the rungs she won't be able to reach. When you decorate furniture with these things in mind, you discover you're creating authentic-looking antiques.

I had one student who had made many trips to the East Coast and had collected some very beautiful cherry furniture. We restored all of it eventually, but when we first started she said "I don't want any of that stuff [color] on my furniture." But when she saw some finished pieces, she began to do the same with hers; and when she finally completed her work, she was convinced of the merit of shading. Her beautiful cherry tables were all shades of color. When the appraiser came to evaluate them, each was assessed at a top price. The man said he'd never before seen restoration done so well.

As I said in my first article, you don't have to remove old finishes completely when you want to preserve their original patina. After cleaning the surface with TSP, just take a small can of natural Watco, or if the wood has been stained a dark color, pick one of the darker shades of Watco, and a small pad of 4/0 steel wool. Wet the pad with Watco and rub softly with the grain. This will remove any loose finish, and the oil will penetrate into areas where finish is missing. Start by doing a small portion to find out how quickly it is going to dry and how fast you can work; then wipe this area thoroughly with a clean rag. Frequently you will find this surface now almost completely restored. You may have a problem in several spots where color is missing. Since you already know how to recognize what this color consists of, you can match it, and then burnish the color into these spots. And now the piece is thoroughly restored.

In class after my lecture on finishing, I bring in a piece of furniture in sad shape and tell the students, "I am going to restore this piece, and in 20 minutes it will be acceptable to sell." Of course, no one believes me. I pour some Watco into a container, and with some 4/0 steel wool I quickly rub the piece down. I squeeze out some universal color on a palette and show them how to match the color. Then I pick up some more oil, rub the color into spots where it's missing, and presto, the job is 95% done. In two or three places it may be necessary to come back the next day and rub in some more, but it's essentially done at that point. Minwax Antique Oil also works well. Most antique dealers could restore furniture without altering anything, or ruining the original patina. But instead, they usually work their hands to the bone putting on varnish or something else and make a mess of things.

If you need to clean the furniture, rub it down lightly with a mixture of vinegar, turpentine and mineral oil. If the finish is thoroughly dried out, as some old varnish finishes are, you can use linseed oil instead of mineral oil. When working with oil, you must wipe off everything you put on, and you must dispose of the rags properly. To prevent a fire don't throw them in the trash, but spread them out to dry.

I would like to say a word or two here about lacquers. On woods requiring a minimum change in color or texture, water-white lacquers are satisfactory, especially when speed is important. You can put on three or four coats of lacquer in one day. But in working with lacquers, color is sometimes a problem. However, vinyl stains work very well with lacquer, though you don't have the freedom you do when using the penetrating oil finish. But using the vinyl stains and very carefully shading or highlighting before applying the lacquer produces good results.

The 5-Minute Stains made by Watco are aniline dyes dissolved in methanol, and they work very well. Watco is completely compatible with urethanes and acrylic finishes. They will go on over a Watco/universal-color mixture, and the Watco/universal-color mixture can be applied over them. Let this dry, and apply a finish coat of urethane or acrylic to lock it in. You can blend two or three colors to get special tones. Minwax provides aniline dyes in other forms, more subtle in color. In working with stains, stay within the family. If you start with Minwax, work entirely in the Minwax line. If you are using Deft, stay within the Deft family of products. You may avoid some costly errors.

One of my students had built his daughter some walnut cabinets for her kitchen and bathroom. He wanted to finish them so that moisture would be no problem. He'd worked too hard on them to have them spoiled. He said to me, "I want them to look oiled. Can we do it?" I said I could see no reason why not. He brought in some samples of his walnut and we experimented a little. We put on two coats of Watco for the oiled appearance, and we followed that with two coats of satin urethane varnish. When it had thoroughly dried, we rubbed it with steel wool and wax. It resulted in a soft, subtle oil finish, and the wood was completely washable.

I usually finish off with waxing. Of the waxes available, I prefer a hard wax finish that is easily maintained, having to

Oscar MacQuiddy touches some tone into a shadowed area of chair's arm. He mixes earth colors with Watco oil on a cardboard palette to create just the right effect in restoring antiques.

be done perhaps every six months. I call my method the "three-rag approach." Take three clean rags and a can of Trewax, which is comparable to bowling-alley wax or similar to any one of the hard carnauba-wax products. Thoroughly saturate the first rag with wax. Rub that saturated rag on the surface to be treated and attempt to load it with wax, putting on as much wax as you possibly can. Set rag #1 aside and wait about one minute. Then take rag #2 and try to remove every trace of wax. Scrub, rub, get that wax off. Wait five minutes, and take rag #3 and lightly burnish the surface. This procedure may seem unduly complicated, but it works. You put the wax on, thoroughly saturating the surface. You rub it off, and you will have no difficulty burnishing to a soft, shiny, smooth surface.

If you have a problem surface, one not quite as smooth as you would like, particularly when you've applied polyurethane and dust particles have contaminated the finish, another approach is necessary. Take some 4/0 steel wool and after applying the wax, rub the surface with long straight strokes, removing the wax as outlined above. You will smooth the surface and get rid of the excess wax at the same time. Upon wiping the surface down, you will have achieved a beautiful satin finish with a protective wax film. All the dust particles will have disappeared, and you can count on compliments from people who see your work.

The exciting part of teaching these methods of finishing has been being able to communicate my enthusiasm to others, helping them develop an appreciation for fine work, helping them to understand that with simple materials it is possible to work miracles. You don't need to use exotic preparations. You can use things that come off the shelves of discount paint stores. You come to know how it feels to work directly with your hands and to know the effects you are capable of producing. □

Lacquer Finishing
How to spray a mirror finish

by George Morris

High-gloss lacquer finishing is time-consuming and rigorous. It requires meticulous surface preparation, special equipment if you're going to do much of it, and a carefully followed schedule of application with constant inspection and correction along the way. The reward is a stunning, jewel-like surface that offers a high degree of protection. A good lacquer finish has the quality of a mirror, and if improperly prepared, it will unforgivingly reveal every irregularity in the surface. By the time a surface defect manifests itself in the lacquer film, it's usually too late to correct it. Thus it's especially important to learn how to judge the quality of the wood surface before you apply any finish.

Preparing the surface—Looking straight into a surface you can pick out obvious flaws like scratches, nicks and holes, but if that is all you do, you miss most of what will become painfully obvious later. To find less pronounced defects you will need to position a light source and your eye so that shadows are created and observable. Imagine a landscape at the moment the sun is setting. Even the subtlest of features casts a shadow. The surface you are preparing is analogous to the landscape; a light bulb is the sun, and your eye is opposite the bulb. You are now in a position to observe the topography, but what is it you are looking for? The answer is found in recalling what you did to the surface and in anticipating the effects.

If you hand-planed the surface, there may be long, sharply defined ridges recording the path of the edge of the plane iron. A machine planer will yield a scalloped surface, the radius of the cutterhead arc repeated. Sanding and scraping may produce more varied effects, especially as the density of the wood varies. Sanding removes softer areas more quickly than harder areas. If the piece is composed of more than one kind of wood, or if the wood grain is uneven, as in fir or

oak, you can expect the surface to be uneven although you have taken care to work consistently. Relatively dense areas in the wood will stand proud of the surface and, from our sunset perspective, will be revealed as shadows following the figure.

When sanding, back up the abrasive paper with some hard material—wood, hard felt or rubber blocks. For contoured surfaces, back up the paper with posterboard or a bit of flexible plastic, or at least fold the paper in half and glue it to itself with rubber cement. Your paper must not be able to conform to the irregularities you are trying to remove. Take care also to sand in line with the figure, and to release pressure from the paper at the end of each stroke, to avoid swirl marks.

Avoiding the pitfalls of scraping requires more skill. Scrapers work most efficiently on dense wood; softer materials compress under the cutting edge instead of standing up stiffly to be cut down. Thus the scraper's effect on the landscape is opposite that of sandpaper. The softer areas spring back after the scraper has passed, leaving them higher than the denser areas and producing a ribbed surface that on some woods looks like a neatly plowed cornfield at dusk. The fix is a quick follow-up sanding with a hard backup block.

Another effect of poor scraper technique is chatter, analogous in our landscape metaphor to a washboard section in a dirt road. Along a dirt road a car bounces rhythmically in response to some small irregularity in the surface, its tires digging out a little more dirt with each bounce. The next car amplifies the washboard effect. Scraper chatter is produced in the same way, by holding the scraper at a constant skew angle and by passing it a few times over

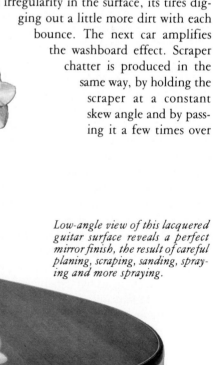

Low-angle view of this lacquered guitar surface reveals a perfect mirror finish, the result of careful planing, scraping, sanding, spraying and more spraying.

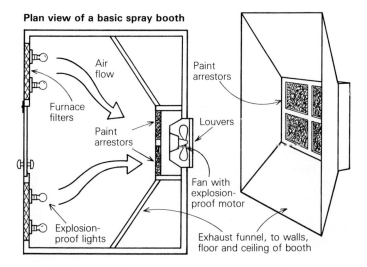

Plan view of a basic spray booth

Air flow

Furnace filters

Paint arrestors

Paint arrestors

Louvers

Fan with explosion-proof motor

Explosion-proof lights

Exhaust funnel, to walls, floor and ceiling of booth

suppliers. In front of the exhaust fan you need a filter wall perhaps 3 ft. square. The filters themselves are called paint arrestors and are also an auto-body-shop supply. For best vapor evacuation, a funnel should be built from the filter wall to the complete height and width of the booth, which should be as small as is comfortable to work in. Clean conditions require that the entry air be filtered, and here furnace-type filters covering an area a few times larger than the exhaust area, directly opposite the fan, will work. The door should provide a tight seal and should open outward, to maximize the usable space inside. The light source should be located behind you, so you can see reflections on the surface of the work as you spray.

Spray outfits are of various types, the simplest being the self-contained "airless" type for which you don't need a compressor. These guns are electromagnetic piston-drive mechanisms that run off standard house current. A small amount of fluid is siphoned up and propelled out the nozzle at 60 cycles a second. Although that might seem pretty quick, it doesn't compare with the force of an air-powered gun. Airless guns also clog easily and have a bad habit of spitting at the work. Nevertheless, they will get the job done faster and more evenly than brushes or pads, and may be all you need.

If time is important, or if you already have a compressor, an air gun is a better choice for its faster rate of application and finer atomization. The size of the gun should match the scale of the work. Most lacquering is done on relatively small objects, so a modest gun with perhaps a pint capacity is sufficient. Whatever the size, don't buy a cheap gun; you will curse that decision from day one.

To power your air gun you need a steady supply of compressed air at between 30 PSI to 40 PSI, the steadier the better. For steady flow and complete control of the pressure, a compressor with a holding tank and an air regulator is superior to cheaper direct-feed, continuous-drive systems.

Application—Lacquering consists of three stages: filling, leveling and polishing. Throughout, you should be inspecting the surface for defects and correcting them, as explained in the box on p.94. There are probably as many ways of getting the job done as there are people doing it, so what follows

Editor's note: You can buy most lacquer-spraying equipment and supplies from auto-body-shop suppliers and from Sears. Major manufacturers of spray units include DeVilbiss Co., Box 913, Toledo, Ohio 43692 and Binks, 9205 West Belmont Ave., Franklin Park, Ill. 60131.

should be seen simply as one good method among many.

The question most frequently asked by the novice is "How many coats of lacquer do I put on?" This question can't be answered as it can for painting; painting is accomplished when the surface is opaquely covered. Lacquering is not simply a covering job, for lacquer is not clear paint. On bad lacquer jobs you can actually see two surfaces, a thick layer of clear plastic and under that the surface of the wood. Done properly, however, you see one surface of polished wood. It is gotten that way not by the mere addition of clear stuff, but by a cyclic process of adding material and sanding it off until the surface being treated is truly flat, at least to the degree that the eye no longer distinguishes any texture. Only enough material must be left on the surface to enable you to polish it without breaking through to the wood. So the answer to the question "How many coats?" must be left at "Enough," that is, however many coats it takes to complete the job of leveling and polishing.

Effective spray technique is largely a matter of speed and consistency, graceful motion and thoroughness. You are trying as quickly as possible to coat a surface evenly and completely, with no unblended areas. In effect, you want to have the entire object wet at once. To do this the gun must be supplying its maximum amount of fluid, and you must move quickly from surface to surface in a preconceived pattern that will ensure thoroughness, with tightly spaced strokes that overlap each other and the object's edges.

The process begins with the application of a sanding sealer diluted with an equal amount of lacquer thinner. Sanding sealer is a kind of lacquer specially formulated to raise the grain of the wood, to provide a base for better adhesion and to be easily sandable. It gives you a preview of the finished surface, allowing you to locate and repair any imperfections.

After perhaps an hour's drying time a wood filler can be used on open-pored woods. Most wood fillers consist of chalk, plus a touch of clay and pigment, carried in a mineral spirit or naphtha vehicle. The pigmented chalk is left in the pores of open-grained woods, where it fills most of the space. Buy neutral filler and color it yourself with dry poster paint, toning it down with lampblack to suit whatever wood you are filling. This will save your having to buy endlessly different colors. Thin the filler about 25% with naphtha and apply it with a rag, working the surface constantly while the filler is drying. It will soon begin to collect on the rag. Now wipe the surface across the grain to clean off all excess filler. For large-pored woods, like oak, a second application may be necessary after three hours' drying time. Eight to twelve hours later, sand the surface clean with 320-grit paper to remove filler residue and raised grain. You will sand through the sealer coat in places, making an awful mess, but the next coat of sealer, applied just like the first, will blend perfectly.

The surface will now appear improved but not yet truly flat, and it will take the remaining sealer coats, applied heavily but sanded almost completely off, along with subsequent lacquer coats, to complete the leveling process. These will be spread out over a period of days, with no more than four coats applied per day. On the first day I stay with the sealer, applying three wet coats one to two hours apart. A wet coat means that the solution is applied so heavily that it floods the surface, leveling itself to a mirror gloss just one taste short of drooling. This welds the material to the previous coat and ensures adequate film thickness. As the lacquer coats build, a

This rosewood surface appeared smooth when viewed head-on, but low-angle light reveals the washboard pattern of scraper chatter. Lacquer will make such flaws painfully obvious, when it's too late to correct them without removing the entire finish. Take a good look at the surface in the correct light before you start to spray.

the same spot. To avoid chatter you must repeatedly change the angle of approach or the skew of the blade, or both.

Other trouble areas surround the designed-in features of a surface: round holes, slots, inside corners and the like. Scrapers and sandpaper tend to fall into slots and holes, producing general depressions around them or, in the case of scrapers, troughs radiating out from them. Only hard sanding blocks can save you. Inside corners require planning and perhaps a specialized tool. If the surfaces adjacent to the corner have their grain running parallel to the crease, it's not hard to sand the corner smooth. But if the grain of one or both surfaces runs perpendicular to the crease, you can clean up using a tool I call a chisel-scraper, simply a chisel sharpened as usual but with a burr added by drawing the edge over a flat steel surface. An ordinary scraper has some thickness, which keeps the cutting edge from reaching into the corner. But a chisel-scraper's edge is thin. An inexpensive ½-in. chisel with its corners removed (for safety) is ideal. However, the best precaution when finishing inside corners is to surface them completely before gluing, and to remove all squeeze-out before it dries. The hidden danger of working around any problem area is that it encourages special attention, resulting in a local surface that's inconsistent with the rest of the object.

Lacquer is a low-wetting finish, which means it does not appreciably penetrate the wood, but lies on it as a film. The surface tension of this film will draw it away from any sharp edge, leaving precious little there and making it easy to sand through later when leveling between coats. Therefore, as part of your pre-finishing surface preparation, soften, if not actually round, all edges of the work to be sure they will remain adequately coated. The slight falling off of a surface as it nears the perimeter has another advantage. It compensates for the tendency in leveling between coats to do extra work near the edges, which makes it more likely you will sand through the film there. This relieving the surface near the edge prevents time-consuming spot repairs later.

Having removed all surface irregularities and prepared all the edges, you can begin final sanding with fine papers backed by hard-felt or rubber sanding blocks. Hardwood blocks with coarse abrasives are good for dimensional leveling, but fine papers on hardwood blocks tend to glaze and will streak the surface with burnish marks. There's little value in finishing beyond 320 grit. You will see some improvement of the surface past this point, but once lacquered the surface will return to what it looked like at 320 grit. Also, grits finer than 320 do little more than burnish the wood, making it more difficult for the lacquer to stick without blistering.

Equipment—Lacquers can be applied by brush, pad or spray, and in most cases the quality of the finished product will be the same. But because some of the exotic hardwoods, rosewood for instance, contain resins that are dissolved by lacquer thinner, the finish can get muddy and can stain adjacent lighter woods when it's dragged around with a brush or pad. Otherwise, small objects such as jewelry boxes can be finished without investing in any more than some good brushes. The steps in the finishing process are the same for brushing or spraying, the only differences being in the speed of application and the time involved in leveling the finish.

The decision to spray may depend upon where you live. All cities and most towns have restrictive codes regulating the design and use of spray facilities, because of the extremely volatile, poisonous and potentially explosive nature of the material. Some codes are stricter than others and require explosion-proof rooms, water curtains, sprinkler systems and asbestos blankets, not to mention outrageously expensive insurance. Spraying is usually illegal in an urban environment, unless you make a substantial investment in equipment. Short of setting up a clandestine operation, you could rent access to a spray booth from a school or body shop. Nitrocellulose lacquer, the type most commonly used for wood finishing, is composed of nitrocellulose (an ingredient in gun powder), various ketones, acetates, toluol, plus other nasty stuff. Codes or no codes, you owe it to yourself and anyone close to you to take adequate precaution against the dangers. You should wear a good-quality chemically filtered respirator, even if you spray outside—an inexpensive alternative to further investment if the environment and weather permit.

If building a booth is possible, the simplest one would need an enclosed space, entry and exit filters, explosion-proof lights, and an exhaust fan with an explosion-proof motor. The fan, mounted in an exterior wall, would necessitate some kind of weather shield—louvers, for instance. Such an assembly can be bought ready to install from most auto-body-shop

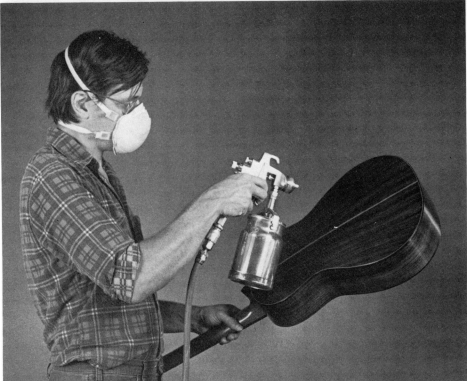

Morris demonstrates the proper relative distance from and angle to the surface being sprayed. Hand-holding the guitar allows more sensitive positioning in relation to the light. He's using a full-size DeVilbiss type JGA gun, siphon-fed from a quart cup, which is suitable for spraying large objects without the need for frequent refills. DeVilbiss type EGA gun, top right, is right for objects the size of a guitar and smaller. Its cup can be replaced with a small mayonnaise jar, permitting quick color changes. The Binks model 18 gun, right, has a pressure-fed hose instead of a cup. The hose supplies lacquer under 10 PSI from a 2-gal. holding tank. Such a system is light, versatile (it can even be used upside down) and good for production work. At top, an edge-grain section of a piece of lacquered rosewood at X28 magnification shows its enormous pores and the filler (white at upper right) under the finish. The lacquer film tapers in thickness toward the corner because the film shrinks as it dries.

thoroughly wet application is necessary or a layered structure will result, which is prone to blistering and ghosting. Also, because of the low solids content of lacquer you need the thick coat just to have anything left after the thinner has evaporated. Straight from the can, the solids content is about 20%, and when mixed with equal amounts of thinner it is 10%. Compared to varnish, which is about 50% solids, this is like mixing one quart of varnish with one gallon of thinner.

Perhaps the most important thing to understand about this low solids content is the fact that while the thinner is evaporating, the lacquer film is shrinking. Only one-tenth of what you spray will remain as a film on the wood. The rate of evaporation and shrinkage is extremely fast at first, so the surface can be touched within minutes of being drenched. But the

evaporation rate decreases rapidly, and enough thinner is trapped within the film so that shrinkage is still perceptible after a week of drying. It is bad practice to apply more than three, at most four, coats of lacquer without allowing an overnight dry to let most of the trapped thinner escape. Otherwise, the thinner will be buried under so much lacquer that it will take weeks to evaporate completely.

After the first three coats of sealer dry overnight, sand the surface thoroughly with 320-grit paper on a block. This dulls the shiny surface, but the low spots will still shine. The goal is a uniformly matte surface with no shiny spots, but you may sand through to the wood in places. When this happens spray more sealer and sand again, until there are no shiny spots anywhere. Now spray one last coat of sealer to coat any wood that's been sanded bare, and begin spraying the first lacquer coats. Lacquer is usually diluted with an equal volume of thinner, and it's sprayed at the same rate as sealer, a coat every hour or two, no more than three coats per day. Let dry overnight and sand with 320-grit paper the next day. Repeat this cycle until you can level-sand the entire surface without sanding through to the wood anywhere. Then apply the final three coats and allow the surface to stabilize and harden for about five days, before final leveling and polishing.

Final sanding can be done with either 500-grit stearated paper dry (available from auto-body-equipment suppliers), or with 600-grit paper wet—there's no difference in the final result. As water can mar the wood if you sand through, I recommend the dry 500-grit paper, used with a felt sanding block behind it and with a reciprocating, in-line motion to prevent build-up of dry lacquer dust on the paper. The surface and paper must be constantly wiped clean, for this white powder clogs the paper and mars the surface.

When free of all telltale shiny spots, wipe the surface clean and continue this abrasive action with the first of two polishing compounds, coarse and fine, which will produce the mirror finish. I use Meguiar's brand compounds, Mirror Glaze I for the coarse and Mirror Glaze III for the fine. (For the name of your local distributor, write to Meguiar's, 17275 Daimler, Irvine, Calif. 92714.) Both can be used on a lamb's-wool pad, rubbed by hand or with a buffer. They are best kept in covered plastic squeeze bottles and should be applied to the pad, not to the surface, to guard against dirt scratching the finish. Use buffing compound sparingly and wet it frequently with water to create a slurry that helps to float the surface clean and keep the abrasive cutting. I usually buff in line with the figure when using the coarse compound, and in a circular pattern when using the fine.

The quality of the finished surface depends completely upon the success of each step, from the preparation of the wood to its final polish. Critical inspection will reveal when a flaw is created. Once you start spraying, it is too late to repair the earlier stages, but if you need to respray once you've begun polishing, first wash the surface with alcohol and water, 50/50, to remove polishing residue. The surface may be rebuffed at any time in the future with the fine compound to restore its original luster. □

George Morris makes guitars in Post Mills, Vt.

Troubleshooting the spray schedule

Drools and sags: The gun is too close to the surface, or you are moving it too slowly, or you have passed over a spot too many times. If caught right away, simply hold the surface horizontal and give no direction for the excess fluid to run, or smear the drool flat with your hand. A flat smear will dry and be sanded out much more quickly than a thick drool. But do not break a drool that has scabbed over.

Overspray: Lacquer not absorbed by the surface because it is dry upon contact. Either the spray gun is being held too far from the surface, or air pressure is too high.

Ghosts: Cloudy, amorphous apparitions, the result of having trapped overspray within the finish. Ghosts are usually discovered while polishing, since the interlayer phenomenon is porous and does not polish. It must be remelted either by some careful work with the polishing wheel, to warm and soften the surface, or by the use of a pulling rubber. Pulling redissolves the surface using a diluted thinner (cut 50% with alcohol). The fluid is applied sparingly to chamois leather wrapped around an egg-sized cotton wad. Stroke the puller quickly and firmly across the surface a few times until the ghost dissolves.

Bubbles: Air trapped by spray turbulence, most common when spraying straight into a corner. To minimize, direct spray in line with the corner.

Blisters: A local adhesion problem encouraged by the surface's being banged. Blisters are more likely if the wooden surface was burnished or coated with something incompatible with the lacquer. Before taking the finish off completely and repreparing the surface, try puncturing the blister with a blade and adding a drop of thinner to act as a glue between film and surface.

Fish-eye: Small circular features, sometimes iridescent, from either oil or silicone on the surface. Remove oil with naphtha, and remove silicone with a lacquer additive designed to eliminate the effect.

Checking: Random fissures in the hardened film caused by uneven shrinkage across the thickness of the film itself. It could be the result of extreme temperature change whereby the film cracks as does glass when quickly passed from boiling to freezing temperatures. Shrinkage can also be uneven if the surface of the film dries before the thinner within the film has a chance to escape. The hardened surface will pull itself apart when the thinner trapped beneath it eventually evaporates, as does a mud pond drying in the sun. The effect is minimized by keeping the film thickness as thin as possible. Trapped thinner is the result of insufficient drying time between coats, or more than a few coats applied in one day.

Crazing: Subtle, small cracks in the film, caused by spraying fresh lacquer over old finish. A close cousin to checking, it is avoided by sanding the old finish very thin before respraying.

Pits: Unfilled pores or gaps in joints. If these are found before spraying begins, it's simply a patching problem to be fixed with wood splints, a sawdust-and-glue mixture or shellac stick melted into the pit and sanded smooth. If pits are found during the spray schedule (they'll appear white when filled with powdered lacquer) lacquer putty will do the trick. Lacquer putty is undiluted lacquer that has been left to evaporate until it's the consistency of thick honey. It must be applied between coats with a small, flat stick, allowed to dry overnight and sanded level the next day before spraying is continued.

Sand-through: If you sand through the lacquer to the wood in the middle of a surface, either respray the entire surface to the edges, masking everything else with newspaper to avoid overspray, or respray through a cardboard mask with a small hole cut in it to minimize overspray. Beware of ghosts. I have had success respraying minor repairs using acrylic lacquer on top of the nitrocellulose finish to prevent these visitations.

Dull spots: If, regardless of how thoroughly a surface is polished, it still does not gloss, you are probably polishing sealer, which will never gloss. The cure is to spray on more lacquer. —*G.M.*

Q & A

Staining walnut

In 30 years of amateur cabinetmaking I have never learned the secret of applying a uniform color of stain to walnut, cherry, birch and other woods. I have used oil stains and water stains, and still get uneven color. Can you help? —R.S. Nelson, Albuquerque, N. Mex.

Applying liquid stain, especially undiluted, to unsealed wood can cause uneven coloring. The reason is that different pieces of wood and even different areas of the same board can absorb colorants to a greater or lesser degree. I know of two ways to solve the problem.

The first is to brush on the stain in several applications, each one thinned down. Skip the darker areas on the following coats, and work on the lighter, less absorbent areas. Blend light and dark sections until you get a uniform color.

The second method is to seal the wood initially with thinned-down coats of finishing product (lacquer or varnish) before applying the stain. Put on the seal coat, let it stand for a few minutes and then wipe the surface with a cloth to get it as dry as possible. Before the seal coat can harden, apply the first coat of stain. No need to thin the stain unless you want to lighten its color. Make sure that the stain and the sealer material are compatible. Water stains won't take to a surface sealed with petroleum-base varnish or oil. —*Don Newell*

A physician friend was visiting me when your question arrived. I asked him how he would answer such a question. He smiled and said, "If the man wants uniform color, he should paint his wood." While his remark might seem a little strong, he was not entirely wrong. A craftsman uses wood because of its endless variety of grain, markings and color. Factories, spawning furniture on the assembly line, are concerned about uniformity. The latest, cheapest, surest and most shameless method is to bleach the wood to a neutral, paper-like uniformity, and on top of such gelded wood they build up a finish with pigmented lacquers and glazes. One may as well use wood-grained contact paper, or a plastic laminate. They are always uniform. —*George Frank*

Auto-finishing tips adapted to wood

My shop is next door to an auto paint-and-body shop. Through the association I have been able to adapt several of their methods and products to wood finishing. It seems that the technology of auto-finish suppliers is steps ahead of their wood-industry counterparts. Certainly their marketing is.

First, I use naphtha (VM&P brand) as a wetting agent for rubbing down intermediate finish coats with wet/dry sandpaper. Naphtha's advantage is that unlike oils or water, it evaporates quickly and cleanly. You can remove the sanding scum with steel wool, wipe with a naphtha-dampened rag, and the surface is clean and dry, ready for the next coat.

Second, two DuPont auto-finish products, the 3679 retarder and the 3602S acrylic lacquer thinner, work very well used with nitrocellulose and acrylic modified wood lacquers. Add the 3679 in small amounts to a cheaper utility thinner to upgrade it for use in finish-coat mixtures. The 3602S is a good damp-weather blush retarder and warm-weather thinner.

Third, I have adapted the auto shop's mist coat to produce a superior finish. After a piece has had its last finish coat and it has "flashed" or surface-dried (5 to 10 minutes) I recoat with a wet coat of one part lacquer to four parts thinner. This procedure seems to eliminate any overspray and overspray dust. It adds greatly to the surface uniformity. Little if any rubbing will be needed to produce a fine finish.
—*Steve Ulrich, Kingsville, Tex.*

Fumed Oak Finish
Old-time process still has advantages

by Sam Allen

If you've ever tried to match the finish on a piece of antique oak furniture, it may have been a frustrating experience. That's because many oak pieces (Mission furniture, for example) were finished by fuming, a process difficult to duplicate using modern stains. The color of fumed oak ranges from a light honey to a medium dark brown. Exposing the wood to ammonia fumes darkens the wood by changing it chemically. Ammonia reacts with tannic acid in oak to produce the color change. Mahogany, chestnut and walnut can also be fumed. As long as the tannic acid content of the wood is the same, the color will be uniform from piece to piece.

Even if you don't restore antiques, you may want to try fuming on your oak projects. Fuming has many advantages. Since it works a chemical change in the wood, it doesn't hide the figure characteristics. No brushing is involved, so irregularities such as streaks, lap marks, stain buildup in corners or on carvings and intricate moldings are completely eliminated. And because the ammonia vapors penetrate the surface of the wood, the color change goes deeper than a thin coating.

The main disadvantage of the process is that ammonia fumes irritate the eyes and nose and cause coughing and choking. For this reason, fuming should be done outside or in a well-ventilated room. The process also requires an airtight container to enclose the piece being finished, which may pose a problem for large furniture.

When you are building a project to be fumed, try to use boards with uniform color. If you can, choose all your lumber from the same tree; it will then fume to the same color. But this is usually impossible. You can sort the boards by numbering them and fuming a small piece of each, keeping track of the results. Then you can select the pieces that most closely match. If you must use dissimilar pieces of oak, the lighter ones can be darkened by sponging on a weak solution of tannic acid before fuming. This will raise the grain, so sand the wood as you would for water stain. Experiment on a sample piece to get the correct amount of tannic acid. About 5% acid to 95% water is usually a good starting solution.

Fuming—Fuming an entire object is not hard to do. Start by finding an airtight container. For a small object, a Tupperware-type box with snap-on lid will work well. For larger pieces, you can construct a plastic tent. Build a framework of 2x4s or 2x2s and cover it with the type of black plastic sheeting used in the garden to keep down weeds. Seal the seams with heating-duct tape. Don't use clear or translucent plastic because sunlight hitting one area of the project and not another will affect the reaction time and make the color uneven.

Next, add ammonia to the container. The best ammonia to use is 26% ammonia, or aromatic spirits of ammonia. Aromatic spirits—the kind used to revive people who have fainted—is available at drugstores in small bottles. If you need only a small amount, this is the easiest to find. If you'll

223

need large quantities, the 26% ammonia sold by chemical supply houses will be cheaper (check the Yellow Pages). Ordinary household ammonia can be used, but the process will be slower. If you use household ammonia, be sure to get the type without detergent, coloring or perfume.

Place the ammonia in several saucers and space them around the inside of the tent. Small objects that need to be fumed on both sides can be propped up on wooden pyramids that come to a sharp point. The small contact area of the pyramid point won't leave a visible mark. Never use metal to support the work. Steel in contact with the wood during the fuming process will sometimes cause a blue-black mark on the wood. Keep this in mind when you are preparing a project—don't install any metal hardware before fuming. Exposed nailheads will create a mark, but nails set below the surface are usually no problem.

The subject of nails brings up another consideration. Ordinary wood putty won't be colored by the fuming process, so don't fill holes until after the fuming is done. Then color the putty to match the finish.

As fuming proceeds, peek occasionally at the wood. Remove the project when the color is slightly lighter than the color you want. After coming out of the tent, the wood will darken slightly since the reaction continues for a while. It usually takes about 24 hours to get a medium dark brown.

When you are restoring an antique, though, you may want to fume only a few small areas, not the entire piece. One way to do this is to glue some cotton in the bottom of a glass jar and add a few drops of ammonia to the cotton. Don't add too much or the ammonia will drip onto the work. Put the mouth of the jar on top of the spot to be refinished. Keep a close watch on the color and stop the ammonia treatment just before the spot reaches the same color as the surrounding finish. Let the wood air out thoroughly and check the color. If it's still too light, put the jar on the spot again for a little while.

Another touch-up technique is not really fuming—the ammonia is applied directly to the wood with a brush. This process will raise the grain if you use water-base ammonia. To avoid raising the grain, use aromatic spirits of ammonia, which is alcohol based. It will behave like a spirit stain. Wet the wood first and sand as you would for a water stain. Let the ammonia stay on the wood until the color is close to the surrounding finish, then wipe it off with a damp cloth. Ammonia evaporates quickly, so you'll have to apply it repeatedly to keep the area wet. Covering the spot with a jar lid or something similar will retard evaporation. Check the color when the wood is thoroughly dry and repeat the application if necessary.

Finishing—You can apply shellac, varnish or lacquer over fumed oak, but if you want to duplicate an original antique finish, the surface coating should be wax. Old-timers frequently made their own wax by shredding beeswax into turpentine. The mixture

Ammonia reacts with tannins to darken oak; old-time finishes bring out the figure. Oak samples, top to bottom, are unfinished, fumed with natural wax, fumed with black wax, and ebonized.

was set aside until the wax was thoroughly dissolved, then turpentine or wax was added until the consistency was like thick cream.

If you don't want to make your own wax, you can use a commercial paste wax such as Trewax. The wax will fill the pores of the wood. The natural tan color of the wax will usually harmonize well with the color of the wood. If you find that the wax is too light or if it goes white after drying, you can add a little burnt umber pigment in the same manner as described below for making black wax.

Black wax on fumed oak used to be a very popular finish. With this finish the pores stand out prominently because they are filled with black wax. This type of finish was generally used on quartersawn oak. To make black wax, liquefy paste wax by warming its container in a pan of hot water. Heat the water first, then remove it from the stove before placing the can of wax in it. When the wax is liquefied, add lampblack or some other color. To be compatible with the wax, tinting colors should be of the universal type (see page 215-217). Let the wax harden again and apply it to the work. The wax will accumulate in the pores as you rub it in, but the coating on the other areas will be so thin that the pigment won't cover the color underneath. You can get the same effect if you are using a finish other than wax by rubbing in Silex wood filler colored with lampblack.

Ebonizing—Ebonizing is another way to finish that uses the tannin content of oak. Ebonized oak is black with white pores. First, put some household vinegar in a glass jar; drop in a handful of steel nails and let the mixture sit about a week. The vinegar is ready when it is grey and cloudy looking. Prepare the wood as you would for a water stain, then brush on the vinegar, which will turn the oak bluish black. Apply several coats of the vinegar, letting it dry between coats.

When the oak is dark enough, brush on some liquid ammonia. This will neutralize the acid left on the wood by the vinegar. At this point the wood should be deep black with a slight purple tinge. Next apply a thin coat of sealer. The purple tinge will disappear and the oak will be a beautiful black. All of the characteristics of the wood will still be visible in the blackened surface. That is why this process is superior to simply painting or staining the wood black.

Now apply white wood filler to make the pores stand out white, and finish as you choose. Because of the contrast of white pores against a black surface, the pores become dominant visually, so select boards that have interesting pore patterns. To emphasize them even more, you may want to brush the boards with a wire brush before applying the vinegar solution. Since oak is so hard, lightly brushing it will not scratch the surface; it will only clear out the pores. □

Sam Allen, 29, designs and builds furniture in Provo, Utah.

Martin Guitar's finish for rosewood

Craftsmen often have difficulty finishing exotic woods like cocobolo, rosewood and other related species. Because these woods are high in natural oils, problems with drying, crazing, clouding, lacquer checking, "peanut shell" adhesion and bleeding often arise. The C. F. Martin Company, whose guitars incorporate exotic woods, has deeloped a solution to these problems. Years of experimentation (and experience) have led to a lacquer finish that is thin, flexible and durable—actually improving the tone of the instrument with age. Although the procedure I'll describe here is used specifically for guitars, it will work as well on other pieces made from highly resinous exotic woods.

We have our finishing materials formulated by Sherwin-Williams Co. to meet our specific production needs. Sherwin-Williams sells equivalent products in its retail stores, and these will give you similar results. So I'll list two stock numbers for each material—the first for the special-formula product, the second for the standard retail item.

The finish room must be dust-free and well ventilated. Martin uses waterfall-type spray booths (made by Eisenmann in West Germany), which trap overspray particles in the air, prevent those particles from settling on the work and reduce the danger of explosion (always a risk with nitrocellulose products). We also use explosion-proof mercury-vapor lights in the finishing area and keep spark-producing devices away. A temperature of 72°F and a relative humidity of 45% are ideal for the wood. During hot, humid months we add a retarder (Sherwin-Williams #R6-K22, #R7-K27) to the lacquer in minute amounts to keep the finish from clouding. During the winter we use humidifiers to reduce static electricity, which causes particles to stick to the work. The irritating and volatile dust produced by sanding between coats must not be allowed to settle back on the work, so we use an efficient dust-collection system to keep the air clean.

To prepare for finishing, sand the surfaces with 180-A paper and then scrape along the grain, removing any scratches left by sanding. Mask any areas not to be finished. Now spray on a coat of vinyl washcoat (Sherwin-Williams #T69-CH6, #T69-F2), making an extra pass over the seams and any inlaid parts. The vinyl washcoat, the key ingredient in the process, seals in the wood's natural oils and serves as a base for the wood filler. After this application cures for at least two hours, abrade the surfaces lightly with a scuff pad (Norton Beartex Pad) or sand lightly with 400-A aluminum-oxide paper. Now the wood is ready for filling.

Martin uses a silica-base filler (Sherwin-Williams #D80-NH46, #D70-T1), which thins with naphtha and mineral spirits. We use it on all porous woods (rosewood, mahogany, cocobolo, zebrawood and others) to provide a uniform base for the lacquer. This filler is syrupy, and you apply it with a brush. It gets leathery after about five minutes, at which point you rub it into the pores of the wood with a cotton rag tied into a bun. Then carefully remove the excess. After filling, fine-sand the spruce top, then wet the top with water to raise the grain, let dry and finish-sand.

Apply another full coat of vinyl washcoat to the top; when it cures, sand it lightly with 400-A paper. Scrape the bindings with a sharp tool to restore their original color, which will have been muddied by the filler. Spray a final coat of vinyl washcoat over the entire body and let it cure for at least two hours. Then spray on a coat of lacquer sealer (Sherwin-Williams #T61-C10, #T60-F10), which must cure for a minimum of 30 minutes (sand the surface if it sits overnight) before the first coat of gloss lacquer is applied. The same day, spray on two or three wet coats of gloss lacquer (Sherwin-

Williams #T71-C10, #T77-F12), allowing 45 minutes drying time between each coat. (The special-formula lacquer is sprayed at 110°F, using heated hoses.) Sand the surfaces lightly the next day with silicon-carbide paper (280-A), taking care not to sand through the lacquer into the sealer coats. Apply another two or three coats of gloss lacquer, depending on the coarseness of the grain, waiting 45 minutes between. Sand again the next day, and apply two more full coats, making six coats in all. Leave the final coat unsanded.

Where inlaid surfaces like the bindings and rosettes have been scraped, you might need to build these back up by applying lacquer with a small brush. We call this process dropping-in, and use lacquer of thicker consistency for this purpose. Let the dropped-in areas dry, and then sand lightly to level them with the surrounding surfaces. Because the spruce top is non-porous, it requires only four coats, with only one light sanding between the second and third coats. A thin film on the top improves the tone of the instrument, and will be less prone to cold checking. The fingerboard, by the way, receives no finish, except for a rubbed-in application of lard oil (animal-fat shortening).

To get a flat finish, the final coat is sprayed on using a 50/50 mix of gloss and flat lacquer (Sherwin-Williams #T71-FC3, #T77-F13) and left unbuffed. Gloss surfaces are buffed with a lamb's-wool bonnet and buffing compound (3-M #A5955) thinned with water. Buffing removes the "orange peel" (minute dimples) and yields a highly polished surface. A final buffing at a high RPM removes all the scratches left by the compound and completes the finish. At this point the guitar can be assembled. The area on the top where the bridge must sit is scribed, scraped and tooth-planed to make a good wood-to-wood glue joint.

Lacquer films are not as hard as polyurethane or other catalyzed finishes, and lacquer-finished surfaces should be protected from abrasion and abusive treatment. When placed in direct contact with plastic and vinyl, the vinyl washcoat can soften and migrate, so plastic or vinyl straps are strongly discouraged. Also the salts and acids contained in human perspiration can erode the finish over an extended period of time, and refinishing may eventually become necessary.

Touch-up aerosol cans of vinyl washcoat, lacquer sealer, gloss lacquer and flat lacquer, as well as walnut-colored filler, buffing compound and polish, are available through Martin's 1833 Shop. For information write C.F. Martin Co., 510 Sycamore St., Nazareth, Pa. 18064. *—Dick Boak*

Follow-up:

...If a lacquer finish, such as the one used by Martin Guitar, is desired, the vinyl-seal step and perhaps even the lacquer-seal step can be avoided by spraying on several light coats of shellac (3 lb. cut or less). Don't brush it on because this can cause blotchy running of the pigment from the pores of the wood, as the denatured alcohol used to thin the shellac also dissolves the pigment. Filler may also be dispensed with as the build-up of shellac and subsequent lacquer coats will eliminate all but the tiniest indication of the pores below the surface.

Two other finishes are possible. One is to apply a wet coat of Waterlox (a tung and linseed mix) and then wipe it off before it begins to set up. Let dry for 24 hours and repeat, after first sanding lightly with 320-grit paper. Wet-sand the final coat (it could take three or more) with mineral oil as a lubricant, and then wipe clean. When dry, apply a coat of wax. Finally, you could use Watco Teak Oil, which is manufactured specifically for finishing rosewood, teak and other resinous woods. *—Joshua Markel, Philadelphia, Pa.*

The Woodcraft Scene

by F. Jack Hurley

LOGGING WITH A HORSE

Big John and Rex Harral.

Skid logs with a horse? Nobody works with a horse anymore. Why would anyone want to? That pretty well sums up the attitude of most of us. Yet there are people who still use draft horses for a variety of chores including hauling timber. Not long ago I ran into an expert on the subject.

Rex Harral is a man of the country, born and raised in the foothills of the Arkansas Ozarks. He is slow of speech and deliberate in his movements. On first impression, he seems a romantic rustic, a figure from the past. Get to know him, however, and these preconceptions break down. In the first place, he is not a romantic at all; the term pragmatist would probably fit him better. In the second place, he is not particularly isolated, for he reads widely and voraciously, especially technical farming publications and craft journals. He is an effective small farmer who supplements his income by making and selling hardwood bowls and traditional furniture. He is also an excellent blacksmith whose woodcarving tools are recognized and sought after throughout the region for their beauty and edge-holding ability.

At sixty, Harral is well past the age when there would be any need to prove his toughness and endurance. His object is to get a job done with a minimum of fuss, so he does use a tractor for certain jobs. On the other hand, if a horse can do a job better, Rex will use a horse. He has always kept a few draft animals. They cost very little to keep, given the fact that pasture is available and that horses burn no gasoline.

Harral insists on using horse power for getting logs out of his woods, 100 acres of mixed pine and hardwood in north-central Arkansas. Harral bought the land nearly 40 years ago and has taken timber off it ever since. Depending on what was ready for the sawmill, and also on his reading of market conditions, Harral has sold from 2,000 to 6,000 bd. ft. of timber every year. This might not sound impressive to a Weyerhaeuser executive, but that timber has played a major role in paying for the land, and has often meant the difference between profit and loss at year's end. In addition, the woodlot has provided all the material for Harral's woodcraft and has heated his home for the past 37 years.

Today the woodlot is in beautiful condition. The trees have grown tall and straight. There is a good variety in size, with roughly 5% of the timber ready for the mill each year. By careful selection and thinning, Harral has made the land far more productive than it was in the early days.

He considers draft horses important in his timber management program. Why use a horse? The photo (far right) of a log being pulled by Harral's best timber snaker, a horse known as Big John, illustrates one reason. Properly hitched together, with the singletree pulling evenly on the tug lines from the horse's shoulders, draft animal and log are hardly more than 2 ft. wide. They move between the young trees, doing them minimal damage. There will be the occasional scuffed bark or bent sapling, but that is all. Contrast this with the tractor or, worse yet, Caterpillar. In either case the woods are likely to be left a tortured mess, carved and crosshatched with temporary roads. Harral's woodlot has only one road and it runs right through the middle. The trees are felled and limbed in place with a chain saw. When all the logs marked for harvest each year are down and ready, Big John drags the timbers out of the woods to gathering points along the road, to be picked up by the log trucks.

A second reason to use draft horses is safety. A good-sized saw log, improperly handled, can kill a man. Using long, cotton lines (roughly analogous to the riding horse's reins) Harral can walk well behind or to the side of the action while still maintaining excellent control of the horse. On a long pull where precise control is not necessary he may even drop the lines and simply control the horse by voice. Harral uses commands that go back to the dawn of western civilization. GiUp! or HiUp! gets the horse moving. Whoa! calls for a stop. Gee! means bear to the right, while Haw! moves the horse to the left. Obviously this sort of response requires training, but that's not as difficult as one might imagine. In fact, many people use large logs when training draft horses to pull. Most draft horses are not as nervous as riding horses, and a few days work with one person leading at the horse's head while another works the lines from behind will generally get things started. From there it is a matter of always accompanying the tug on the lines with the voice commands, until they come to mean the same thing to the horse.

Harral and Big John have worked together for 16 years, since the horse was two years old. Big John is still a strapping, healthy horse with probably a good six to eight years of work left. Man and horse are a well-coordinated team, their movements and interactions honed by practice. "Back up, John," Rex calls, and John immediately takes a couple of steps backward, loosening the tug lines so that the skidding tongs (bottom photo) can be set into a log. "HiUp," comes the command and the big horse moves off at a fast walk, a 10-ft. long, 22-in. log skidding easily behind him. With tugs on the lines accompanied by Gees! and Haws! they reach the logging road. When they get to the gathering point it's "Whoa, John, back up, John." The tongs are released and then man and animal disappear into the woods to repeat the process. No one is overworked. No one appears to be hurrying. Yet at the end of the day there are three or four truckloads of logs at the loading point.

This brings up the final point in defense of horsepower. According to Harral, working in the timber with a well-trained draft horse is actually easier—and more efficient—than working by yourself with a tractor or Caterpillar. "If I used one of those things, I'd be totally wore out with climbing on it to back up a few feet, then off to set the tongs, then back on to skid, then back off to release the tongs. I swear, I don't see how folks do it," he says. As it is, Harral and Big John are tired at the end of the day, but they are not exhausted, and if necessary they can both get up and go at it again tomorrow. □

F. Jack Hurley, woodworker and history professor, lives in Memphis, Tenn. For more about using horses to drag timber, see the quarterly magazine Draft Horse Journal *($10/year) or the* Draft Horse Primer *by Maurice Telleen ($12.95, hardcover). Both are available from* Draft Horse Journal, *Box 670, Waverly, Iowa 50677.*

Above, Harral and Big John ford a stream while maneuvering a pine log away from the drop site. Here, he controls the horse with cotton lines, but sometimes he relies only on verbal commands.

The harness for dragging timber (photo, left) consists mainly of a properly fitted collar and hames. The collar may be leather, as this one is, or cotton cloth, but leather will last much longer. Hames, which ride on top of the collar, are metal or wood, and provide a solid anchor point for the tug lines or the chains. Everything else, back bands, belly bands and rings, simply keep the chains pulling comfortably and the cotton lines from becoming tangled.

Together, horse and log are only 2 ft. wide (photo, right), which makes it easy to drag logs through tight spaces between trees.

Below, proper arrangement of log tongs is important whether you are working with a horse or a tractor. The tongs must be placed far enough forward so that the hinge point of the tongs clears the front of the log and does not ride on top. Otherwise, the tongs will be damaged and the log will dig into the ground and not pull smoothly.

INDEX

INDEX